ACTA UNIVERSITATIS UPSALIENSIS
Uppsala Studies in Faiths and Ideologies
8

ALF TERGEL

Human Rights in Cultural and Religious Traditions

UPPSALA 1998

Tryckt med bidrag från Humanistisk-Samhällsvetenskapliga forskningsrådet

ABSTRACT

Tergel, A. 1998. Human Rights in Cultural and Religious Traditions. Acta Universitatis Upsaliensis. *Uppsala Studies in Faiths and Ideologies* 8. 395 pp. Uppsala. ISBN 91-554-4296-X.

The changes in the ideology of human rights within the denominational communities which have been studied during the half-century from 1945 to 1995, were due principally to the repercussions of radical social transformations upon the churches. A paradigm shift took place in the 1960s with the focus moving away from individual rights to social rights and the right to life. This paradigm change in a most profound sense derived from the fact that the ideology of the welfare state had won general support as well as the conviction that the gap between the developed and underdeveloped parts of the world remained to be bridged. The socio-political processes had an effect on the ideology of human rights.

Alf Tergel, Department of Theology, Uppsala University, Box 1604, S-751 46 Uppsala Sweden

ISSN 1102-7878
ISBN 91-554-4296-X

Typesetting: Editorial Office, Uppsala University
Printed in Sweden by Erlanders Gotab, Stockholm 1998
Distributor: Uppsala University Library, Box 510, SE-751 20 Uppsala, Sweden

Contents

Today more than ever, indeed, the bearing witness to the Gospel in a credible way is only possible by commitment to the rights of man.

Walter Kasper in The theological foundation of human rights, 1988.

Preface

In the preparatory work to the present investigation, I have been in contact with people and institutions involved in research about religion and human rights, and in particular with David Little, senior research analyst in religion, ethics and human rights at USA's Peace Research Institute in Washington DC and with the Jesuits at Woodstock Theological Center and Library, which is attached to Georgetown University. David Little, the Jesuits and representatives of the American society for ecclesiastical history have emphasized the need for analyzing the problem of the church and human rights in the post-war era from the viewpoint of ecclesiastical history. Since no research has been done in this area—one of great contemporary relevance—there is an opportunity for breaking new ground in the search for knowledge.

The American Enterprise Institute for Public Policy Research has a social science library. The Woodstock Theological Center at Georgetown University is a research institute and "think tank" which was established in 1975. It is dedicated to a treatment of human rights which answers to the needs of the various cultural traditions in USA. Washington is also home to the Latin American Documentation Center, an independent foundation which provides information about social rights and publishes LADOC, as well as to the United States Catholic Conference Office of International Justice and Peace which is active on behalf of human rights in America in the fields of training, education, research and publishing.

This latter institution is an offshoot of the Papal Commission Justice and Peace at the Vatican, which produces an extensive literature dealing with human rights issues and which has regional and national associations throughout the world.

In Oslo there is the Institute for Human Rights, which publishes *Nordisk tidskrift om menneskerettigheter*. Research is carried out there on the relationship between human rights norms and various cultural traditions, social contexts and ideologies. Åbo Academy has an institute for human rights[1] and a Danish centre for human rights is to be found in Copenhagen. The latter centre

---

[1] In 1988, the Institute for Human Rights at Åbo Academy issued Hur tackla rasismen, Föreläsningar om mänskliga rättigheter och rasismen.

was responsible for issuing a comprehensive collection of texts on human rights.[2] In Sweden we have the Raoul Wallenberg Institute in Lund.

The Nordic institutes for human rights in Oslo, Åbo, Copenhagen and Lund cooperate with one another and a concrete product of this cooperation is A. Eide, C. Krause and A. Rosas (eds.) *Economic, Social and Cultural Rights A Textbook* 1995. It was published in the wake of the Vienna Congress.

In London, Amnesty International has built up a documentation centre linked to its international secretariat. It also contains a large collection of bibliographical source material and works of reference about international voluntary and government sponsored organizations. The centre also houses UN material. There are author and subject catalogues covering the book collection. London is also home to the British Institute of Human Rights at King's College.

UNESCO runs a documentation centre in Paris which publishes the World Directory of Human Rights Research and Training Institutions.

Valuable material of basic relevance for the present investigation has also been located in the following places: the libraries of the UN, Institute Henri Dunant, the Red Cross and Pax Romana in Geneva, as well as at the archive and library of World Council of Churches in the same city; the ecumenical research institute of the Lutheran World Federation in Strasbourg. Strasbourg contains two important libraries dedicated to human rights, one at the Palais des Droits de l'Homme and the other at the Institut International des Droits de l'Homme. The former is situated at the European Parliament while the latter was founded in 1969 by René Cassin, one of the architects of the 1948 UN Declaration of human rights.

The World Council of Churches contains two bodies dedicated to human rights, namely the Commission of the Churches on International Affairs (CCIA) and the Programme to Combat Racism (PCR) which have specialized in various aspects of human rights issues and which coordinate human rights groups at an international level. Occupying the same premises as the World Council of Churches in Geneva, there is the Lutheran World Federation and World Alliance of Reformed Churches. These church organizations are involved in procedures pertaining to human rights and their activities cover both research into and support for human rights.

The International Institute of Human Rights in Strasbourg is a non- governmental organization. The institution is engaged in education, research and the dissemination of information on human rights. It publishes the *Human Rights Journal*.

Columbia University Center for the Study of Human Rights and the UN Dag Hammarskjöld Library in New York contain material on human rights. In New York there is also the Human Rights Office of the National Council of Churches Division of Overseas Ministries. This ecclesiastical organization is

---

[2] Menneskerettigheder – en tekstsamling, 1–2, 1988.

involved in human rights at international level. Its activities cover research, information and cooperation with human rights groups.

The UN Division of Human Rights at the Palais des Nations in Geneva is interested in the effect of modern scientific and technological development on human rights and publishes documents.

The carrying out of this investigation has led to international and interdisciplinary cooperation. The present monograph should be seen as a Swedish contribution to an area of research which is likely to increase in intensity. Its main focus is not on providing a wide-ranging enquiry over a long period of time but instead on dealing in detail with the question of human rights during a short period of time.

Sweden is a member of the European Union. Concern with human rights has from the very beginning occupied a prominent place on the agenda of the Council of Europe and the United Nations and Sweden has taken part in this work. The non-Christian world religions and the Christian churches have also addressed the question of human rights from their respective standpoints. It must therefore be considered as a central research task to provide a scholarly and historical analysis of the theme of human rights in cultural and religious traditions during the postwar period.

In Sweden, the Council for Research in the Humanities and Social Sciences have contributed to the costs of publishing the work in English.

I am most grateful to Craig McKay for skilfully translating my Swedish manuscript into English.

Uppsala, June 1998

Alf Tergel

PART 1

Origin and Background

CHAPTER 1

Introduction

What more than anything else gave impetus to the process of formulating human rights at international, regional and national levels after the Second World War was the sight of the victims from the Nazi concentration camps in the Spring of 1945. It sent a shock throughout the whole world and it was firmly agreed that such a thing was never to be allowed to happen again. A visible sign of this determination was the establishment of the United Nations.

Following the collapse of the communist dictatorships in Eastern Europe in 1989, the question of human rights has become increasingly important. There is therefore some reason for examining an aspect of this question from a historical perspective.

The defeat of nazism in 1945 marks, for reasons already given, the starting point of the investigation. The collapse of communism in 1989 marks a turning point in the exposition. The human rights movements was one of the forces which paved the way for the collapse of communism. It was directed against totalitarianism in the communist social system.

The clash in ideology and strategic policy between capitalism and communism and the Cold War between East and West ceased after 1989 to provide the main framework within which human rights are defined. Instead it is the world religions which provide the framework for thought and action when it comes to questions of human rights. In 1995, fifty years had passed since the nazi extermination of the Jews and the end of the Second World War. It marks the closing year of the present investigation.

1.1 The Struggle for Human Rights

Every human being is unique. To be a person is to have an intrinsic value—not merely to be important on account of the work one performs. No human being should be used purely as a means by another person. These truths are best expressed by saying that every person has basic human rights. It is a matter of social justice that everyone should respect the basic rights of others.

From the French Revolution to the beginning of this century, certain civil and political rights, in particular the right to vote and the right to have a fair trial, have been accepted. The universal declaration of human rights approved by the UN in 1948 and since then ratified by the majority of countries, concentrates on political rights. It became a controversial issue. Western politicians accused the communist nations of failing to respect the basic human rights of their own citizens. The Eastern Bloc countries replied by accusing the Western democracies of emphasizing political rights while ignoring or playing down the importance of rights such as the right to work.

From the 1960s onwards, the original UN charter on basic civil and political rights has been supplemented by further lists of social, economic and cultural rights. These lists have been steadily augmented. Most recently the UN approved a list of basic rights for children.

Human rights originate with the slogan of the French Revolution, "Liberty, Equality, Fraternity". The concept of liberty embraces personal and civil rights. The concept of equality covers those political rights which guarantee the opportunities of citizens to participate in social decision-making. The concept of fraternity embraces social rights as they have come to be defined in the course of the present century.

Specialized periodicals have been created to illuminate the problems which arise in the formulation and implementation of human rights. Examples of such journals are the *Human Rights Quarterly A Comparative and International Journal of the Social Sciences* and the *Harvard Human Rights Journal.*[1] Another journal is issued as part of the United Nation's work: *Human Rights Teaching Biannual Bulletin UNESCO.*

Human Rights Watch carries out regular systematic investigations into violations of human rights in around seventy countries world-wide. It started up in association with the Helsinki conference and publishes annually the *Human Rights Watch World Report.* It contains five sections covering Africa, the Americas, Asia, the Middle East in addition to the signatories to the Helsinki agreements. It has no government affiliation and is financed by contributions from individuals and foundations.

The struggle for human rights does not simply consist in introducing new legislation so that various rights are recognized. Human attitudes and the economic structure of society also require to be changed. Human attitudes are given expression in differing traditions.

1.2 Human Rights

When we speak of human rights, we mean four groups of basic rights which are important for human beings.

---

[1] See e.g. M. Shurpack, The Churches and Human Rights: Catholic and Protestant Human Rights Views as Reflected in Church Statements Harvard Human Rights Journal, Volume 6, Spring 1993.

1. *The individual human rights* which underpin the Western democracies are internationally formulated in the United Nations general declaration of human rights of 1948. It came into being in the struggle against dictatorship.

2. *The social human rights* formulated in the international conventions on economic, social and cultural rights were drawn up on the recommendation of the socialist states and peoples of the Third World. They came into being during the struggle against economic imperialism.[2]

3. Peoples in the Third World demand *the right to life* and survival, the right to exist. Unless this right is given to all human beings, the struggle for individual or social rights becomes superfluous.[3]

4. *Ecological rights* concern the struggle against the world-wide threats to the life of this and future generations. They are based on the insight that human beings are able to exterminate life on earth and are summed up in the slogan of the World Council of Churches: justice, peace and the integrity of creation. There has been a development from natural rights to the rights of nature.[4]

It is therefore a question of four groups of human rights without which human beings cannot develop their humanity. 1. the person's rights to liberty. 2. the community's social rights 3. the right to existence 4. the right to the continuation of life.

1.3 Human Rights and Other Rights

Can one speak of rights other than human rights? In the three groups of rights considered above—individual rights, social rights and the right to existence, the human being is the subject. Human beings also figure in the case of ecological rights but they have a somewhat different position than in the other three cases. Human beings are part of the ecosystem and a balance in this system is a requirement for their continued existence. But in the case of ecological rights, human beings are not the subject in same unambiguous way that they are in the case of individual rights, social rights and the right to life. Can then one still speak of ecological rights as human rights?

From a theoretical philosophical and theological position, arguments can be adduced against such a categorization. It can appear dubious. But from a historical standpoint, it can be argued that ecological rights are human rights although human beings are not strictly speaking their subject. In the discussions within the UN, UNESCO and international church bodies, ecological rights are looked upon as a category of human rights. It is therefore relevant to use this categorization when, as an historian, one is trying to reconstruct these

---

[2] The relationship between individual and social rights leads one to think of the debate between individualism and communitarism in contemporary political and ethical thought. S. Avineri and A de Shalit (eds.) Communitarism and Individualism, 1992.

[3] K. Tomasevski (ed.) The Right to Food Guide Through Applicable International Law, 1987.

[4] R. F. Nash, The Rights of Nature, A History of Environmental Ethics, 1989, pp. 13–32.

discussions. The way of launching ecological rights as a a type of human rights bore fruit. It was a succesful rhetorical device. For the historian, it is the functional rather than the theoretical point of view which is of paramount importance. Ecological rights function as a category of human rights in the discussion. It is this reality which the historian seeks to describe and not its logical reasonableness. It is therfore relevant in working with human rights from a historical perspective to speak of ecological rights as human rights.[5]

Ethics extends beyond anthropocentrism. It deals not simply with human rights and the ethics of the biosphere. Ultimately it is concerned with an ethic for life.[6]

It follows from A. Eide and J. Helgesen (eds.) *The Future of Human Rights, Protection in a Changing World*, Fifty Years since the Four Freedoms Address, Essays in Honour of Torkel Opsahl, 1991, that the right to an acceptable environment is also included among human rights.

1.4 Different Types of Human Rights

In the present investigation, it is reasonable to begin by spelling out in a more detailed and precise way the different types of human rights we encounter and simultaneously to explain the meaning of different types of human rights. A classical distinction is that between civil and political on the one hand and economic, social and cultural rights on the other. Another distinction is that between individual rights and collective rights. The rights of solidarity are collective rights in contrast to individual rights. To the rights of solidarity belong the right to development, the right to peace, the right to an acceptable environment, the right to social ownership and right to humanitarian support.

The civil rights are devoted to protecting a person's liberty and security as well as their physical and spiritual integrity. Such rights are the right to the life; the right not to be subject to torture or to cruel, inhuman or degrading treatment or punishment; the right not to be held in slavery or be compelled to forced labour; the right to personal liberty and security including the right to fair trial; the right to privacy as regards his family, home and correspondence; the right to freedom of thought, conscience and religion.

Political rights involve the right to freedom of thought, opinion and expression; the right to freedom of assembly and association; the right to take part in the running of general affairs, including the right to vote and to be elected.

The economic, social and cultural rights include the right to work; the right to form a trades union including the right to strike; the right to social security; the right to adequate food, clothing and housing; the right to an adequate living standard; the right to health; the right to education; rights relating to education; rights relating to culture and science.

---

[5] For philsophical questions about human rights, see P. H. Werhane, A. R. Gini, D. T. Ozae, Philosophical Issues in Human Rights, Theories and Applications, 1986.
[6] C. Birch, J. B. Cobb, The Liberation of Life, 1981, pp. 141–175.

The state is now the most important instrument for ensuring civil and political rights as well as social and cultural rights.

The universal declaration of human rights and the American declaration of human rights and obligations deals with civil and political rights as well as with economic, social and cultural rights.[7]

The international convention on civil and political rights, the international convention on economic, social and cultural rights, the European convention on human rights and the European Social Charter distinguish civil and political rights from economic, social and cultural rights.[8]

The difference between civil rights and social rights is not clear-cut but rather a matter of degree.

Certain rights are of an individualistic nature such as the right to private property, liberty of thought and conscience and a person's right to freedom and security; other rights are by nature collective such as the majority of economic and social rights. Some rights have both individual and collective features. This is so in the case of freedom of religion and freedom of expression. Thus it is impossible to divide individual and collective rights into watertight compartments. It is only in society that individuals are able to completely develop their personality.

By a group is meant a collection of persons who share particular distinctive characteristics and/or find themeselves subject to particular situations or conditions. The particular distinctive characteristics can be of a racial, ethnological, linguistic or religious nature. The particular situations or conditions can be determined by political, economic, social or cultural factors.

Collective rights are particularly concerned with the rights of minorities with a view to preserving and developing their specific character and the people's right to self-determination.

While a distinction is drawn between different categories of human rights, the boundaries on the one hand between civil and social rights and on the other hand between individual and collective rights are not sharp.

It is hard to make use of civil freedoms if the individual lacks basic economic and social security. On the other hand, it is difficult to work for improved economic and social security if the individual lacks e.g. freedom of expression and movement.

Collective rights should benefit every individual in the group. On the other hand, individual rights can never be utilized wholly independently of other individuals and society.

1.5 Human Rights and Human Needs

Human rights have been linked,in the general discussion, to human needs. It was primarily the Norwegian Peace Researcher Johan Galtung who was re-

---

[7] G. Melander (ed.) 1990, pp. 13–18, 197–222.
[8] Melander, op. cit., pp. 37–47, 50–68, 119–134, 164–183.

sponsible for this linkage in *Indicators of Social and Economic Change and Their Applications UNESCO 1976* and *Human Needs as Focus of the Social Sciences*, 1977. He put forward a model for basic needs and rights along with the goods and services which answered to these needs and rights. He explained that rights are means while the satisfaction of needs is the goal of human development. Food is a right but in the Third World it becomes an individual and collective physiological need. An unpolluted environment is an individual right but it becomes a collective ecological need. Self-determination and peace are rights which are collective needs for security against destruction and war.

These examples show that the individual and collective aspects of human rights are interconnected when linked to human needs.

1.6 Human Rights and the Intercultural Perspective

A Catholic research project at the University of Frankfurt is reviewed in J. Hoffman Hrsg *Begründung von Menschenrechte aus der Sicht Unverschiedlichen Kulturen Das eine Menschenrecht für alle und die vielen Lebensformen* 1991. Issues about the establishment of human rights from an intercultural standpoint are discussed. Representatives from Latin America, Africa, Asia and Oceania make it clear that the UN Charter on Human Rights which is a product of Western thinking, cannot be universalized. Cultures must be seen as autonomous and cultural differences are not easily bridged.

The book contains particularly interesting sections on human rights in South Africa which is relevant for the problem of apartheid, on human rights in the multireligious context of Asia with particular focus on Buddhism and Hinduism as well as on human rights and Islam.

Since it is my intention in the present investigation to deal more closely with human rights in Latin America, there is some justification in paying particular attention to this continent with the aim of sharply delineating the problems associated with human rights and an intercultural perspective. The peoples of Latin America have lived with oppression for some five hundred years. It began with the European oppression of the Indians and continued with the oppression of the poor by the rich and powerful. This oppression received its contemporary expression in military dictatorships.

The context within which the idea and awareness of human rights was fostered in Europe was completely different from that in Latin America. In Europe, inspiration came from the intellectual inheritance of the Enlightenment which manifested itself in the French Revolution and helped to form the modern liberal democracies. A variant of this development was the history of human rights since the Declaration of Independence which then led to the foundation of the United States. Here a liberal and bourgeois emphasis was laid upon the right of the individual.

Both democracy and the language of human rights was foreign to Latin

America. The church was closely linked to monarchical governments and an oppressive ruling class. Given its experiences of the oppression of Indians and the poor, Latin America can contribute to the discussion about human rights. Spanish theologians developed the doctrine of natural rights and from this there evolved the doctrine of human rights.

According to statistics, some 183 million Latin Americans are classed as poor. This corresponds to 50% of the inhabitants. By "poor" is meant those who lack the very necessities of life. The poor are certainly those who have a right to life but who at the same time lack every means of sustaining it. They not only lack all material things but also the opportunities to develop socially, politically and culturally. This lack of necessities is unjust. It is the product of the abuse of human beings, brought about by unjust situations or socially oppressive structures which prevent individuals from making use of their right to life.

The bishops at Medellin in 1968 and at Puebla in 1979 summarized their analysis of the situation in Latin America by stating that poverty and the increasing gap between rich and poor is utterly scandalous. It is a structural sin in Latin America. Poverty implies institutional injustice and a state of sin. The bishops refer to poverty in Latin America as institutionalized sin. They speak of the rights of the poor in terms of liberation rather in terms of human rights. At Puebla, they referred to a social right whose collective subject was the poor. The rights of the poor are based upon that human solidarity founded upon God's incarnation in Christ. There is no talk of any natural right which the individual enjoys within society. It can be said that at the bishop's conferences at Medellin and Puebla, the prophetic approach introduced by Bartolomé de Las Casas from which so-called liberation theology also derives, becomes apparent.

Assuming a Latin American viewpoint, the following theory of human rights is proposed 1) it is a prophetic activity 2) it integrates human rights with the Christian utopia of the Kingdom of God 3) its starting point is an obligation of solidarity with the poor 4) it presupposes the inherently structural nature of social sin 5) it specifies the necessary steps to be taken in attaining a true humanity 6) in concrete terms it supports actions or movements on behalf of the liberation of the people. Human rights are not to be derived from doctrines such as that of natural rights but should be the product of historical experience. Prophetic action must bridge the gap betweeen the reality of the poor and oppressed and the utopia of a liberated humanity. The prophetic teaching of human rights is directed towards action.

The Argentinian Nobel prize-winner *Adolfo Peres Esquivel* maintained that the 1948 declaration of general human rights could be banished to the category of ideologies which politically underwrite unjust regimes. The foundation of human rights should not be liberal rationalism but the understanding of historical development as process or as constants of the liberation of the people. The general explanation of human rights then becomes a perspective for human community; it should be focused not upon individuals but upon the people and organized peoples. The defence of human rights as the defence of the people's rights, according to Esquivel, gives priority to means for bringing about the process of liberation, thus addressing the problem of historical praxis.[9]

Per Frostin has made the following observation about Latin America. Human rights at Medellin and Puebla are the rights of the poor. In the West, there is a tendency to treat human rights as abstract entities while in Latin America they denote the right to life and human dignity. The perspective of the suffering human being forms the starting point for every discussion of human rights. Frostin lays emphasis on this perspective "from beneath" when human rights are defined. Human rights are often used to justify the status quo. Conceptually there is a yawning gap between abstract formulations of human rights and the concrete situation of the underprivileged.

A prophetic approach which takes into account the real historical opportunities and seeks to exercise influence upon the historical process and to change it, is required. The prophetic contribution consists in showing what actions are required. Emphasis on means for attaining human rights involves underlining the significance of historical practice and the shaping of this practice is a necessary ingredient in the affirmation of these rights. As far as foundations are concerned, this perspective "from beneath" implies that human rights must have a historical and contextual basis. In unfolding such a basis, two aims should be borne in mind. First of all, there is need for a universal basis i.e. one which takes account of all human beings. Secondly there is need for a theological approach which is specifically Christian and which shows how faith and human rights can be integrated.

Human rights can be given a Christological basis in the manner of Bartolomé de Las Casas. "I betrayed Christ in America as our Lord by scourging and crucifying Him not once but millions of times." The liberation theologians following in Las Casas´ footsteps have further developed this theme. They have reflected upon the poorest of humanity from a christological perspective. The scourged Christ is encountered among the Indians and the poor. A clear and well founded doctrine of human rights which determines the relationship between what is universally human and the specifically theological domain in the analysis, is lacking.[10]

1.7 Conflict Between East and West in the UN Declaration of Human Rights, 1948

The liberal tradition of human rights represented by the West and the Marxist tradition of human rights advocated by the East is brought together in the UN Declaration of Human Rights of 1948. Articles 1 to 21 list the rights of the liberal tradition: life, liberty, personal security, property, freedom of association, freedom from arbitrary arrest.[11] Articles 22 to 27 list the social and eco-

[9] J. Aldunate in J. Hoffmann Hrsg 1991, pp. 131–149.
[10] P. Frostin, op. cit., pp. 105–109.

nomic rights emphasized by the socialist nations: rights to social security, work, just wages, education.[12]

The inclusion of both types of rights in the UN Declaration of Human Rights was the result of political compromise. Clear signs of the Cold War between East and West are to be found in the document which regulates attitudes towards human rights at a global level in the aftermath to the Second World War. The underlying conflict between liberal and Marxist views of human rights is abundantly plain for all to see in this document and it is regulated by having both viewpoints brought together side by side in the same document.

1.8 Human Rights and the Third World

The problematic nature of human rights was not simply a matter of the conflict between civil and political rights on the one hand and economic, social and cultural rights on the other. The controversy was also linked to the conflict between North and South, between the industrialized countries and the underdeveloped countries. The difficulties involved are reflected in the discussion about a new strategy for development and in the debate about a new international economic order.

Patterns of development prevented the attainment of human rights. They attacked fundamental values. The human rights issue spilled over into the debate about development.

The international political game was such that it consolidated the hold of the Northern countries over world resources, concentrating them to the industrial countries to the great detriment of the living standards of the underdeveloped countries.

The northern high-consumption life style undermined the liberal dream of expanding prosperity for all and the Marxist utopia of solidarity with the world's proletariat resulting in an egalitarian, classless society. The preservation of this lifestyle embraced access to, and control over, energy and industrial raw materials. This entailed a growing inequality between rich and poor countries, between a small middle class and the great unorganized masses in the latter countries and between the proletariat of the rich countries and the proletariat of the poor countries.

Living standards were of central importance as a basis for attaining human rights.

References

There is an extensive literature dealing with human rights in the Third World. It includes the following works: T. M. Franck, Human Rights in Third World Perspective

---

[11] G. Melander (ed.) 1990, pp. 13–16.
[12] Melander, op. cit., p. 16 f.

I–III, 1982, K. Lederer (ed.) Human Needs, A Contribution to the Current Debate, 1980, M. McDougal, Human Rights and World Public Order, The Basic Policies of An International Law of Human Dignity, 1980, Menschenrechte und Menschenbild in der dritten Welt, 1982 and A. A. Said (ed.) Human Rights and World Order, 1978.

In Human Rights and Development in Africa, 1984, C. E. Welch Jr. and R. I. Meltzer deal with the problems of human rights from a North-South perspective. They discuss the situation in South Africa. Other topics discussed include women's rights, Islamic ideas, the legal and historical background to the African Charter, the role of non-governmental organizations in the preservation and maintenance of human rights and development questions in various North-South contexts. The book also includes a bibliography specially devoted to Africa.

As has been pointed out, South Africa attracts particular interest in the Third World. V. van Dyke has an interesting section on South Africa in Human Rights, Ethnicity and Discrimination, 1985.

In Human Rights: Cultural and Ideological Perspectives, 1979, A. Pollis and P. Schwab hold that the the Third World and socialist perspectives on human rights are often neglected in the West. They argue that more prominence should be given to non-Western perspectives on human rights. They express similar opinions in Toward A Human Rights Framework, 1981.

T. Campbell in The Left and Rights, A Conceptual Analysis of the Idea of Socialist Rights, 1983, puts forward a socialist perspective on human rights. The author asks if the idea of individual rights is closely connected with the individualism of liberal capitalism or whether rights can also have a central place in a socialist Utopia. According to Campbell, what is crucial to the latter is the equal satisfaction of needs.

In Menschenrechte und Dritte Welt, Zur Frage nach den Ursachen von Menschenrechtsverletzungen, 1980, S. H. Heinz holds that weapons training and military education displace human rights. The book throws light on the relationship between development and human rights in the Third World. The development of human rights in Western Europe is linked to Third World development. The two regions, armed conflicts and militarization in the Third World are examined.

R. A. and A. F. Evans, Human Rights, A Dialogue Between the First and Third Worlds, 1983, contains concrete cases along with commentaries.

In This Hemisphere of Liberty: A Philosophy of the America Washington DC American Enterprise Institute, 1990, M. Novak provides a neo-conservative treatment of North-South questions in America which is strongly influenced by Thomist ideas and containing an appeal to the business community to adopt a responsible stand on questions of morality, culture and politics.

1.9 The Church and Human Rights

Simultaneously with the adoption of the document on human rights in the UN and the Council of Europe, these rights were discussed from religious, ecclesiastical and theological points of view. Such a discussion took place within the Orthodox tradition, the Roman Catholic church, the World Council of Churches, The Anglican Union, The Lutheran World Federation, and within the Reformed, Methodist and Baptist World Alliance. An important part of Latin American liberation theology is devoted to human rights.

The aim of this investigation is to trace and categorize material dealing with the churches and human rights at an official level and thereafter on the basis of this material to analyze the arguments which have been advanced and describe the churches´ contribution to the human rights movement. Our task is to answer the question of the nature and extent of the churches´ contribution to the human rights movement. The material to be analyzed relates to ecclesiastical attitudes towards human rights.

Is the church a social force for change when it comes to justifying and campaigning for human rights or does it reflect society's development in the field of human rights, entering only later to legitimize current practice in this area? The problem can also be formulated in the following way. Is the church prophetic in its approach to human rights or does it merely reflect what is going in the human rights movement, providing theological legitimacy?

Does the church exert a prophetic role within the power structures or is it used as an instrument for bestowing ideological legitimacy? Do theological ideas together with social forces and structures, support or hinder the development of human rights in the process of civilization? In what ways do theological interests interact in a variety of contexts around the world?

In other words, the question is to determine what is primary and what is secondary when it comes to the church's role in the human rights movement. Is it a prophetic-religious element or is it a social-contextual element? Or is it impossible to determine what is primary and what is secondary? Is it impossible to say more than that there is some interaction between the prophetic and contextual components in the matter of the church's participation in the movement for human rights?

Is Christian faith used to support, confer authority and legitimize the human rights movement and the values which receive expression in this movement? Or is Christian faith employed to question and criticize the values embodied in the movement, defending itself from acting as a civil religion within this movement?

Or is it the case that the church neither confers legitimacy nor is prophetic in relation to human rights but merely reacts to initiatives within the human rights movement? Does the church adopt what we might call a third position? The church is not silent about issues raised by the human rights movement; but it neither supports nor criticizes ideas, attitudes or actions initiated by this movement.

Consider the following example of the arguments which arise in the discussion of human rights. The right to life is fundamental in the document on human rights. Thus it can be asked what attitude the church takes towards this right and what theological arguments are used to justify it. The right to work is interpreted differently depending on whether one approaches the problem from a socialist or capitalist standpoint. What arguments do the churches and theologians put forward? The right to property is interpreted differently by Marxists and liberals. What arguments does the church put forward? Ideas about justice are intertwined with ideas about ideas about human rights.

Do human rights and liberties presuppose a special view of man and a special notion of human worth? If so, how does this view of man and human worth relate to the anthropology accepted by the church?

Ultimately human rights are a problem of morality. Does the UN declaration of human rights presuppose that those acting in accordance with it, accept the existence of a universal ethical system? Since the moral content of human rights is dependent upon context, does that mean that those actively involved accept some form of ethical particularism? The problem is the relationship between universalism and particularism in ethics.

1.10 Human Rights and the Fall of Communism

Let us consider some concrete issues concerned with human rights activitity. What role did religiously motivated human rights activists play in the fall of communism? Was the movement for human rights one of the forces which paved the way for the collapse of the communist system in Eastern Europe and is the church able to participate in this process of development? Several possible factors have been singled out as playing a part in the fall of the So-viet empire—not least the bankrupt economy—but what part did religion play?

George Weigel in *The Final Revolution, The Resistance Church and the Collapse of Communism*, 1992, and Niels Nielsen in *Revolutions in Eastern Europe, The Religious Roots*, 1991, draw attention to the role of the churches in the collapse of communism. Weigel gives special prominence to the human rights movement inspired by the church as the prime mover in the elimination of the communist social system not simply in the former satellite states or in the states bordering Western Europe but also in the former Soviet Union. He sees the root of the collapse in the changed attitude of mind brought about by John Paul II's Catholic personalism. The Pope created "acting persons" in his old homeland, Poland. He brought about a moral regeneration and a prepare-dess to assume personal responsibility. This change in attitude of mind formed an important precondition for action on human rights issues.

John Paul II's evangelical campaign for human rights was directed against the commmunist social system. His visit to Poland in June 1979 marked the beginning of the end of the empire whose basis had been laid at the Yalta conference in the closing stages of World War II. He released the Poles from the fear which the communist leaders had inspired in them. The repeated en-couragement in his sermons to the Poles was: be not afraid. These were the words which Jesus had spoken to his disciples during the storm on the Sea of Galilee. (Mark 6:50). The task of the church was to defend human rights.

The economic explanation for the fall of communism does not suffice. In Poland, a national moral regeneration took place. The economic crisis was a necessary but not a sufficient cause for the collapse. From the fertile new soil of social solidarity, the Solidarity movement arose. Workers rebelled against the workers' state. This could not have happened without the Catholic church's preaching on behalf of human rights.

In Poland, the Catholic church developed into a counter-society. In East Germany, the liberation movement was rooted in the Lutheran church but, as in Poland, it contained people who took no interest in religion. Fear of state brutality and state oppression was overcome by moral impulses which came from the churches. The human rights movement rapidly grew in strength after the signing of the Helsinki document on human rights in 1975 and this movement was actively sustained by the churches. Lutheranism played an active and socially inspirational role in the struggle against the communist dictatorship in East Germany. This Lutheran activism was in striking contrast to the Lutheran church's reaction to nazism during the 1930s, which apart from the Confessional church was characterized by passivity and a desire to avoid a collision with the state. East German Lutheranism which was reorganized after the war, put its weight behind the demand for human rights and was the driving force in the human rights movement.

In Czechoslovakia, ecclesiastics were behind the Charta 77 movement, in which Václav Havel played a leading role. The non-practising Catholic Havel reminded the communist leader Gustav Husak about the crisis in human identity which a defective awareness of the absolute brought about. Havel's cricism was aimed at the communist social system and its lack of a moral basis founded upon the absolute. In Rumania, the liberation campaign was started by the reform priest Laszlo Tökes' actions in Timisoara. In these countries, however, ecclesiastics did not have a leading role in the human rights movement.

In both Poland and East Germany, the churches were not on the side of establishment authority but spoke up on behalf of the oppressed and persecuted and pressed their demands for the implementation of human rights. Their criticism was aimed at the totalitarian communist social system.

We shall have cause later on to return to the interaction between the projects on human rights initiated by the Vatican, the World Council of Churches and the Lutheran World Federation and the historical march of events particularly in Poland and Germany.

1.11 Christian and Marxists Views of Human Rights

Christians were able to criticize communists for representing a society with an ethic which was not based on the absolute. John Warwick Montgomery, the American lawyer and student of human rights, developed this idea in an article entitled *The Marxist Approach to Human Rights: Analysis & critique* 1983/84. In Marxism, he maintained, there can be no real human rights as long as it teaches that there is no transcendent creator. The Marxist believes that it is the state which is the creator of all rights. Marxist states hold staunchly to the notion of internal sovereignty and a non-interference principle. The protection of human rights is, however, only possible in the case of large and massive breaches of rights. Marxism has an incorrect view of human nature and is unable to offer an unchangeable base for human dignity. According to Montgomery, what is needed, is a transcendent, personal, divine revelation of the dignity of every human being. Only such a revelation can really liberate both society and the individual.[13]

A colleague at the Catholic university in Lublin, Stanislaw Kowalczyk, who had lived in communist Poland, offered another perspective on the relationship between the Christian and Marxist views of human rights. In an article entitled *The Possibilities of Christian-Marxist Dialogue on Human Rights*, 1984, he argued that although Christians and Marxists can never agree completely, they have much to gain from a dialogue. On the positive side of the balance, Marxists speak more about humanism while Christians talk more about practice. Marxists can benefit from the Christians' greater valuation of liberty while the Christians can learn from their partners in the dialogue that rights are not abstract conceptions but are closely linked to the market and workplace. Marxist sociocentrism and Christian personalism can both forget the existence of the other. This dialogue is particularly important in Poland. [14]

Yuri Zamoshkin, a communist at the Institute for USA Studies in Moscow, provided a Marxist perspective on human rights in an article entitled *Individualism and the American Dream: Personality and Society in America from a Soviet Perspective*, 1984. He maintained that the American dream promotes competition and individualism which leads to selfishness. Thus the Soviet perspective is summed up. The American culture's humanistic and democratic ideal is compromised by individualism. Power and affluence are American values and they render human beings hostile to one another. Human rights are despised by American backwoods individualism. American attitudes become more global but the American people in the family of nations is tarnished by continued individualism, which is symbolized by a persistent preoccupation with success and the pursuit of the American Dream.[15]

1.12 Human Rights as a Scientific Problem

Everything indicates that human rights are a function of the social context to which they belong. Different peoples in different parts of the world appeal to different human rights. This tends to show that human rights issues depend upon

---

[13] J. W. Montgomery, The Marxist Approach to Human Rights: Analysis & Critique, Simon Greenleaf Law Review, 1983/84,3, pp. 3–202.
[14] S. Kowalczyck, The Possibilities of Christian-Marxist Dialogue on Human Rights, Soundings, 1984, 67(2), pp. 165–171.
[15] Y. Zamoshkin, Individualism and the American Dream: Personality and Society in America from a Soviet Perspective Soundings, 1984, 67(2), pp. 128–129.

time, place, institutional organization, level of crisis and other circumstances.

A good example of this is to compare the views of human rights in African cultures and Marxist cultures with those in Jewish-Christian and Islamic societies. In the former case, individual rights do not exist outside of the group since a person is only truly a person by virtue of other human beings. In the second case, individual human rights are derived from divine sanction and nature.

The hypothesis of this study is that there is a connection between the definition of human rights and the socio-economic and political character of the society in which they are exercised.

During the period 1945–1989, the world was divided into three parts: the First, Second and Third Worlds. The industrialized democracies of the First World tended to emphasize the civil and political rights which served their individualistic social orders. The Second World's socialist systems sought a closer collectivistic link with human rights which were in agreement with Marxist philosophy. The developing countries of the Third World which displayed a mixture of ideological preferences and stages of economic growth, often demanded greater attention to economic, social and cultural rights with an emphasis on group rights and the rights of the people as a whole.

In the democracies, human rights were primarily a matter of individualistic rights while in the socialist societies collectivist rights were accorded priority. In the former case, human rights embodied the notion of political liberty whereas in the latter case, they embodied the notion of socio-economic equality. The linkage between individual and collective rights and political and economic equality was apparent in the Third World.

There was also a connection between human rights and the issue of environment. An unpolluted environment is a precondition of life. The right to life thus presupposes an acceptable environment. Both aspects of human environment—the natural one and that brought about by human beings—are important for the enjoyment of fundamental human rights.

My main hypothesis is this: religious, cultural and socio-economic systems play an important role in the formulation of ideas of human rights. The hypothesis can also be put in the following way. There is reason to assume that religious, cultural and socio-economic systems form important background factors in the fomulation of ideas about human rights.[16]

The question which interests me concerns the extent to which the four aspects of human rights described above, recur in the church's attitudes to human rights and the extent to which these four aspects are reflected in ecclesiastical, theological and religious arguments. Are theological arguments employed to

---

[16] The third part of J. Berting et alii, Human Rights in a Pluralist World: Individuals and Collectivities, 1990, examines how different attitudes to human rights as individual and collective rights are linked to religious, cultural and socio-economic systems. Human rights are interpreted differently within differing cultural, religious and socio-economic systems. The book is based on two international conferences on human rights at Maastricht 1987 and Middelburg, 1988.

justify and give authority to one or several of the four standpoints and what is the connection between these arguments and the social, economic and political environment in which they are asserted?

1.13 Theology and Human Rights

Have the churches sought to base their defence of human rights during the postwar period by looking for justification in the Bible and theology, or have human rights been presented as an outgrowth of Biblical texts and theological tradition? What is primary and what is secondary? What is presented as cause and what is presented as effect? Is it theology or human rights?

What role does faith play in the potential conflict between different types of human rights? For what purpose are appeals made to faith? Has a development taken place which has meant a switch of emphasis from a Western liberal view of human rights to an acceptance of the socialist criticism, the Third World's interest in standard of living and the ecologically justified demand for the continued existence of life?

Theologians maintain that Christian anthropology forms a basis for the Christian view of human rights. Thus questions inevitably arise about the form this anthropology takes, how it is justified and how it is constructed.

Catholics, Lutherans and the Reformed churches go their different ways on this matter, or devise different types of anthropologies on which human rights are based. This is the reason why these three traditions are particularly examined in the present study.

Human rights received particular attention during the 1970s from the Roman Catholic church, the World Council of Churches, the Lutheran World Federation and the World Alliance of Reformed Churches. In every case, the problem came to the fore at a major assembly and was subsequently discussed at conferences and by theologians. This resulted in the drawing up of ecclastical documents about human rights.

In the Roman Catholic church, the Synod of Bishops in Rome delivered its view of human rights in 1974, the Papal Commission Justitia et Pax published the document *The Church and Human Rights* in 1975 and a special issue of Concilium devoted to human rights was published in 1979.

At the World Council of Churches, theological work on human rights was initiated in 1974 at St. Pölten and the whole issue of human rights was discussed at the world church conference at Nairobi in 1975.

A consultation about human rights was held within the Lutheran World Federation at Geneva in 1976. Theologians took up the discussion and there was an interdenominational exchange of views at Geneva in 1980.

In the World Alliance of Reformed Churches, the study of the theological basis of human rights took place at the meeting in Nairobi, Kenya in 1970 and Jürgen Moltmann played a leading role in the formulation of human rights theology.

References

J. Schwartländer directed a research project on human rights at the University of Tübingen and published Menschenrechte- eine Herausforderung der Kirche, 1979. He speaks of human rights as a new world ethos[17] and raises the question of whether human rights are a secularized world order.[18] J. Schwartländer also published Menschenrechte Aspekted ihrer Begründung und Vervirklichung 1978 and Menschenrechte und Demokratie, 1981.

Nine theological educational establishments in Boston, USA participated in the Boston Theological Institute, which published A. J. Dyck, Human Rights and the Global Mission of the Church, 1985. Part I of this book deals with the biblical and theological roots of the rights, while part II discusses rights from the viewpoint of the church in the world. The position of the family in racist South Africa and the contributions of the Christian institute directed by Beyers Naudé are examined.[19]

J. Baur has published Zum Thema Menschenrechte Theologische Versuche und Entwürfe, 1977. The book is intended as a contribution by theologians—as opposed to lawyers—to the ecumenical debate about human rights. It discusses human rights from the following perspective: Old Testament, ecclesiastical history and systematic theology. The problem of human rights is assigned to the domain of systematic theology. Reference is also made to the ongoing discussion of human rights within the confessional traditions.[20]

Theology and human rights were a recurring theme in theological literature e.g. R. Coste, L'Église et les droits de l'homme, 1988, W. Harrelson, The Ten Commandments and Human Rights, 1980, and R. Traer, Faith in Human Rights: Support in Religious Tradition for A Global Struggle, 1991.

J. F. Collange, Théologie des droits de l'homme, 1989, is an interesting example of this type of literature. First of all, general material on human rights is presented from a historical and contemporary perspective. The author then turns to a discussion of theological views. He begins with the story of the Creation. Thereafter he passes to the Incarnation. Human rights are thus given a theological basis. The book also contains a chapter dealing with cultures, religions and human rights.[21]

J. M. Aubert in Droits de l'homme et liberation évangélique, 1987, is concerned with the division of human rights into individual and social rights and deals with them from a theological standpoint after presenting a historical introduction.[22] Emphasis is laid upon considerations relating to social rights in contrast to the usual approach which places individual rights first.

Aubert has acted as Catholic Professor of Theology in Strasbourg just as Collange has has a similar role in Protestantism. It seems that the place is a source of inspiration for attempts to link human rights to the Christian Gospels. A Protestant ecclesiastical historian in Strasbourg, Marc Lienhard was interested in Luther and human rights and wrote on this theme under the auspices of UNESCO.[23]

---

[17] J. Schwartländer (hrsg), 1979, pp. 53–55.
[18] Schwartländer, op. cit., pp. 55–57.
[19] A. J. Dyck (ed.), 1985, pp. 53–63.
[20] J. Baur (hrsg), 1977, p. 98 ff.
[21] J.F.Collange, 1989, pp. 338–343.
[22] J.M.Aubert, 1987, pp. 13–87, 91–134, 137–270.
[23] Human Rights Teaching Biannual Bulletin, Vol. II, No. 1, 1981, pp. 24–37.

1.14 Human Rights—From Classical to Ecumenical Theology

Historically it is customary to distinguish three types of human rights theology— the Roman Catholic, the Lutheran and the Calvinist variants.

1. According to *the scholastic theological tradition* and Roman Catholicism the crucial aspect of human rights is to be found in the conflict between Nature and Grace. The sphere of Grace lies above and beyond that of Nature. The sphere of Nature, the general sector of life, is good but the sphere of Grace is still better. Grace does not renew nature but complements it. Every domain has its God-given task. Faith belongs to the life of the church and reason rules in society.

Human rights issues are assigned to the order of reality. They essentially belong to natural theology but also to the church, by Grace. The church is to serve as the conscience of society. For this reason, it can speak out on human rights issues when these rights are violated.

Critics of Catholic scholastic theology have maintained that the nature-grace dichotomy underestimates the effects of the fall of man. Moreover the criticism has been put forward that this dichotomy distracts attention from the worldly sphere of human rights and focuses instead on the spiritual sphere of grace and the church. The emphasis is on liturgical holiness and divorce from the world. In official pronouncements, man's inhumanity to man is condemned.

2. *Luthers theology* is centred on formal and material principles: the Scriptures alone, as the sole authority to the revelation, and salvation through faith alone. Moreover, Law and Gospel correspond to the two kingdoms in Luther's theology. He illuminates the connection between law and Gospel and the two kingdoms by means of the image of the two hands of God.

Luther set forth his teaching on the two hands. God's left hand means that he operates in human life through structures and principles at work in political economic and cultural institutions. They affect the life of everyone. The struggle for human rights belongs to this domain of divine activity. However the Gospel provide the one thing that is necessary. Salvation through Jesus Christ is the work of God's right hand. This salvation is a gift of grace given by God for Christ's sake and received by faith alone.

The Lutheran doctrine of the two kingdoms and the underlying law-Gospel distinction has been criticized as quietist by Ernst Troeltsch—that is to say, improductive in the matter of social justice—and as dualistic by Calvinists because it restricts the dominion of Christ to personal salvation rather than to a recognition of his Lordship over all domains of life and over the world. Against this criticism, it has been argued that Luther does not deny God's intervention in the earthly sphere. The world is the kingdom of the left hand.

The worldly kingdom is not, however, under the dominion of Christ in the same sense as the kingdom of God. The spiritual and earthly kingdoms are both manifestions of Christ's kingdom as opposed to the Kindom of the Devil. The dominion of Christ is only fully operative in individual persons through their faith. It is through human beings that Christ influences the social order.

Christians are thus the link between the two kingdoms. Through the faith at work in love, they are Christs for their neighbours and oppose social injustice. The Lutheran standpoint rejects a Utopian society. Even if God works through human beings in society, it is impossible to create a perfect society. As long as sinful human beings act, it is impossible to build a society without sin. The world can never be the kingdom of God. Luther means, however, that Christians place the rights of others before their own. Christians do not live their lives for themselves but for others.

3. *Classical Calvinist theology* proceeds from the glory of God. The whole creation stands in relation to the Creator. Created in the image of God, human beings have a threefold existence: they are the servants of God, they have been entrusted with the stewardship of the creation and they are the guardians of the human rights of their fellow men. God is responsible for divine rights and human beings are responsible for human rights. In the covenant entered into in the creation, human beings have rights relating to God and God has rights with regard to human beings. We have rights with respect to others and they have just demands on us.

Thus in classical Calvinist theology, human beings are the servants of God, the keepers of their fellow human beings and the stewards of creation. Human life in this theology emerges as a unity while simultaneously it is multi-dimensional. In Calvinist thought, it is of crucial importance that human beings by virtue of the order of Creation discover the meaning of life within the framework of different spheres of interest such as marriage, family, work, divine service, politics, art, science and journalism. Guaranteeing human rights means ensuring that other human beings also have the opportunities to indulge in these activities.

Calvinist classical theology emphasizes God's covenant with human beings as the source of human rights. Since human beings are created in the image of God, they have been given the right to life. The Creator guarantees this right as He does other rights. Human rights are part of being a human being.

Scholastic theology with its foundation in natural law is increasingly giving way within Roman Catholicism to a Biblical and Christologically oriented theology advanced by the exegetic movement and the development after the Second Vatican Council. The Lutheran doctrine of justification and the doctrine of the two Kingdoms have become objects for renewed interpretations in the light of the Lutheran church's liberation struggle in East Germany. Calvinist covenant theology with its starting point in the Kingship of God has developed against the background of apartheid in South Africa and Martin Luther King's civil rights activities in the USA. All this has obviously consequences for theological arguments about human rights. At the same time, the different emphasis accorded by the East, West and Third World to the concept of human rights is also reflected in this process of theological development.

The idea of human rights was developed in the Catholic church through the Second Vatican Council, Pacem in Terris, the CELAM meeting in Medellin in 1968 and the Synod of Bishops in Rome in 1971. Between the CELAM meetings in Medellin in 1968 and in Puebla in 1979, the Catholic church in Latin America made human rights demands on a growing number of military juntas. The inherent force in the church's action against the state rested on its solidarity with the people. The Catholic periodical *Concilium* welcomed contributions on current problems of interest and invited theologians to reflect about human rights.

The same idea of human rights evolved through various meetings within the World Council of Churches, the Lutheran World Federation and the World Alliance of Reformed Churches. In the Protestant tradition, the discussion is reflected in such publications as The Ecumenical Review, International Review of Mission, Lutheran World and Reformed World. There are also echoes of the liberation struggle in South America in the Protestant theology of human rights. The Gospel supply the crucial incentive in the struggle for human rights and the rights of the people. Ultimately human rights are moral demands. In ecumenical theology, they are given a theological basis.

An important explanation of the variety and creativity in theological speculation in Catholic circles is the increased freedom given to theology following the Second Vatican Council. At the same time, Catholic theologians still work from the premiss that human rights derive from natural law or Biblical anthropology based upon the incarnation.

Together Catholics, Lutherans and the Reform thinkers create an ecumenical theology of human rights. It finds expression e.g. in Journal of Ecumenical Studies. In this ecumenical theology there is some common ground but also a clear diversity of opinion.

An interesting example of the ecumenical approach to human rights theology is the work of the American theologian,Kathryn Tanner, *The Politics of God, Christian Theologies and Social Justice*, 1992. She holds that human beings' views of God and the world affect their understanding of rights and duties with respect to their fellows. Tanner is keen to assign a socio-cultural perspective to values and beliefs. They are interwoven with social relationships. This implies that the meaning attached to human rights is determined by the socio-cultural situation of their advocates. Tanner develops a human rights theology which forms part of her theology of social justice. Human beings are co-workers in the divine plans of Providence and Salvation for the world. The rights which Tanner specifies, have primarily a social dimension. Oppressive social structures conflict with the rights of all human beings as creatures made in God's image. Social structures which exploit and dominate are incompatible with human rights. Tanner's social vision reflects the situation of the homeless, the poor and of coloured people in USA.

Another American, Stephen Charles Mott, formulates the problem in a similar way in *A Christian Perspective on Political Thought*, 1993. Human beings are agreed that justice requires us to do what is good and that means what is good for our fellows human beings. Justice is a social norm which regulates how human beings act in relation to one another. Lack of agreement among students of justice centres upon the good which justice requires us to do. Justice acquires its meaning from the social context in which human beings act.

The Catholic theologian Edward Schillebeeckx, who puts forward a theology aimed at social problems, formulates the issue in *God is New Each Moment*, 1983 in the following way. The Kingdom of God is to be found wherever justice is done to those who have been deprived of their rights.

A noteworthy feature of ecumenical human rights theology is that alongside individual rights, social rights and the right to life there is to be found a fourth category of rights, namely the ecological. This latter type of right is stressed in the slogan of the World Council of Churches-Justice, Peace and the Integrity of Creation. The major question for the future is how one can resolve the conflict between human needs and nature's finitude. Human and natural history are linked to one another: they are interdependent. Nature is as important a partner as capital and labour. Future generations have a right to live in an ecosystem which is suited to them.

The challenges for the movement for human rights have come first from the Cold War, then from the socialist bloc, the Third World and finally from the ecological crisis. These challenges have required theologians within differing ecclesiastical traditions to construct theologies about human rights which answer to the various demands of the historical situation. The historical context,in the form of the political situation, denominational allegiance and ecumenical goals, is the determining factor in this process of development.

The human rights theologies which emerged during the postwar period naturally have links with classical theology but they also display new approaches mainly because they were developed in a time very different from the denominational and political conflicts of the sixteenth century. The Second Vatican Council was a milestone marking the subsequent integration into the Catholic church of central components of Protestant theology. Through active Catholic participation in the ecumenical movement, Protestants have absorbed into their theology various ideas which previously had been considered as purely Roman Catholic. The polarization between Catholic and Protestant views declined and an era of cooperation began.

1.15 Human Rights, Civil Religion and Political Theology

Human rights are linked to legislation and the values embodied in current laws. Via legislation, there is a link between human rights and values in society and the state. The latter are usually summed up in the term *civil religion*.

Religion in the strict sense is in turn linked to social values. It serves to innoculate the body of society with values. Religion is often the most important contributor to the building of society's basic value structure. Politics is a function of culture and religion is to be found at the very heart of culture.

In other words, the question is therefore to decide the role played by religion in modern society and in the life of the state. Is religion relevant to political life and is it exploited by politicians?

In addition, there is the question of the relationship between civil religion and political theology. In political theology, theological principles for various political programmes are presented. It is not entirely clear what meaning is attached to the concepts of civil religion and political theology nor is it plain where the demarcation line passes between civil religion and political theology.

Neo-conservatives such as Michael Novak and Peter Berger have advocated a political theology aimed at supporting a capitalist political economy. Critics of these neo-conservative theologians have maintained that both capitalist and socialist views of political economy have their strengths and weaknesses. It has been stressed that human avarice in capitalism corresponds to the Christian notion of sin. In addition, it has been pointed out that in socialism selfcentredness is viewed as a product of social structures. Sin, according to this way of looking at things, is the result of social evil, not its cause.

The problematic aspects of the concepts of civil religion and political theology are discussed in L. S. Rouner (ed.) *Civil Religion and political theology*, 1986. This discussion is of interest for an analysis of the formulation and development of human rights in cultural and religious contexts, since social values and beliefs constitute the roots and fertile soil from which human rights spring.

1.16 Religion and Morality

Do the churches hold that religion has really promoted the humane and human rights or has it had the opposite effect? From a historical point of view, religions display the same ambivalence as other types of human activity. They have contributed to moral progress and at the same time they have opposed and have been an obstacle to moral advance.

Do the churches mean that religion provides the morality upon which human rights are based, its absolute character whereas the lack of religion leads to a relativization of that morality? In Kant's view, belief in God supplied morality with a secure and certain foundation. Theologians stressed that religion gives morals a universal and unconditional validity. They held that religion gives morality an absolute authority.

Moral life is naturally possible without religion. This was a truth underlined by both churches and theologians. History supplied a number of good examples. Many of the pioneers on behalf of human rights in Enlightenment England and France did not believe in God whereas several opponents of human rights were practising Christians.

The theological issue was how to find a criterion to distinguish between acceptable and unacceptable interests underlying human action. How was one to motivate unselfish action towards our fellow human beings and at the same time reject brutality and unreliability?

It is asserted that the criterion for right conduct accepted by the great world religions is that we do to others what we would wish done to ourselves. The criterion for a good religion and an acceptable morality is according to this way of arguing that they promote what is humane and foster human rights.

Hans Küng clarifies the issue of religion and morality in *Global Responsibility, In Search of a New World Ethic*, 1991. Democracy's dilemma is that it does not prescribe moral values while at the same time presupposing that certain of these values are operative. Democracy is neutral with respect to differing religions and views of life but in order to function it presupposes the existence of a certain minimal ethical core and thus a consensus about certain values, norms and attitudes.

Non-religious people can defend with the help of a humane system of ethics human dignity and human rights. Arrayed behind the first paragraph of the UN Declaration of human rights are to be found believers—Jews, Christians, Moslems, Hindus, Sikhs, Buddhists, Confucians, Taoists—and non-believers—humanists and Marxists. "All human beings are born free and equal in dignity and rights. They are endowed with reason and conscience and should act towards one another in a spirit of brotherhood."[24]

1.17 Religion and Politics

After the Second World War, Christianity and the church because of pluralism and secularization, chiefly in Western Europe, were threatened with ending up politicized or marginalized.

The marginalization of religion resulted in Christianity and the church being expelled to a cultic and moral ghetto in society and ceasing to be relevant for the shaping of social life.

The politicization of religion meant that Christianity and the church assigned power a transcendent and mystical foundation and provided justification for the status quo. They functioned as the servants of those in power.

The marginalization and politicization of Christianity and the church had an effect on the attitudes of the church to human rights. They acted as effective barriers to the active involvement of the churches in the human rights movement.

---

[24] G Melander 1990, p. 13. The most complete collection of documents on human rights is to be found in A. P. Blaustein, R. S. Clark, J. A. Sigler (eds.), 1987.

The best example of how Christianity and the church were not driven to marginalization and politicization is the development in England in the Twenties, Thirties and Forties. Christians such as the economic historian *R. H. Tawney* and Archbishop *William Temple* made important contributions to the building of the British welfare state. The Christian values in the foundation of the British welfare model which they infused, have been later questioned. J.H. Oldham introduced this English-style social Christianity into the ecumenical Life and Work movement. It exerted a major influence upon the American Reinhold Niebuhr and he in turn, to an even greater extent, influenced social Christianity within the ecumenical movement. In England, it has been further developed by social theologians such as *Ronald H. Preston* and *Duncan B. Forrester.*

The English social theologians worked with so-called middle axioms which mediated between Christian principles and concrete political decisions. They presented a Christian social vision but left it to the politicians to implement this vision in practice.

The struggle for human rights in general and opposition to racism in particular was to be found in the extension of these middle axioms. The World Council of Churches drafted a programme aimed at combatting racism.

The critics of these middle axioms have held that they were produced by theologians but applied by laymen; moreover, they led to a division between theory and practice. In Latin American liberation theology, on the other hand, ordinary people participate in the theological and ethical discussion. Laymen and theologians fight side by side for the implementation of human rights.

The Lutheran doctrine of the two Kingdoms on the other hand, could be carried to the point that religion and politics were completely divorced from one another. Christian principles cannot be applied to social life. Love and justice are assigned to different domains of life. In the ecumenical movement, they were brought together and justice was presented as a practical application of love. The existence of the doctrine of two Kingdoms would seem to be the most important explanation why Lutherans have not played a prominent role in the development of social Christianity within the ecumenical movement. Its formulation was mainly due to Calvinist influenced theologians from the English-speaking world.

References

Duncan B. Forrester throws light on the issue of religon and politics with material from England in The Future of Welfare, 1985 and in Beliefs, Values and Policies, Politics in a Secular Age, 1989 while Ronald H. Preston investigates the same problem complex in The Future of Christian Ethics, 1987. Alan M. Suggate provides a portrait of the social theologian Temple in William Temple and Christian Social Ethics Today, 1987.

1.18 Religion and Racism

Racism constitutes the most flagrant breach of human rights. Racism in the form of apartheid in South Africa, is in this connection one of the most illuminating examples. Elements of racism are also to be found in antisemitism. In racism, one's own particular race is defined as something apart from other races. The deviant race group is subject to negative discrimination and barred from participating in the life of society. Racism is an expression of ethnocentrism.

The breaches of human rights which constitute racism are classified by the World Council of Churches as sin. Racism is identified as a moral problem. It is considered similar to slavery as a social manifestation of human sin. It could be eliminated. The World Council of Churches devised a programme with the aim of inspiring the churches to active participation in combatting racism. This was done first after the meeting of the World Council of Churches in Uppsala in 1968. The World Council of Churches saw it as its task to take a moral lead in liberating the non-white peoples from white racism. It created a special fund for assisting the victims of white racist oppression.

For Jürgen Moltmann, white racism found itself on a collision course with the universal declaration of human rights. It functioned as an instrument for oppression thus ensuring political, economic and cultural privileges for the white population while making the non-white population into second class citizens. The solution of the race question requires a change in racist power structures so that those without power are given some of the power. This demands an abandonment of the race mentality. The abolition of slavery in the USA did not lead to an automatic elimination of the racist frame of mind of many whites.

The blacks in South Africa were denied fundamental human rights as these are defined in the UN universal declaration of human rights. According to paragraph 21:1, it is laid down that each person has the right to take part in the government of their country either directly or via a representative.[25] The blacks in South Africa were denied this right. They were not allowed to vote in the election of their own representatives to parliament and could not themselves be elected to serve in it. In paragraph 21.3, it is laid down that the will of the people shall constitute the basis for the authority of government.[26] Governmental power in South Africa, however, was exercised without the consent of the disenfranchised majority. The govermental decision to place the blacks in the so-called homeland was also taken without their consent. South Africa was not a signatory to the UN declaration of human rights.

The crucial problem in South Africa from the church's viewpoint was that God became a pawn in the political struggle, being presented as white or black to suit the interests of the protagonists.

---

[25] G. Melander (ed.), 1990, p. 16.
[26] Melander, op. cit., p. 16.

The World Council of Churches, the Lutheran World Federation and the World Alliance of Reformed Churches all declared apartheid to be a sin. The apartheid system is an expression of heresy and is incompatible with Christianity. This is shown by J. de Gruchy and C. Villa-Vicencio in *Apartheid is a Heresy*, 1983 and in C. Villa-Vicencio, *A Theology of Reconstruction, Nation-building and Human Rights*, 1992. The latter work otherwise points out that South-African liberation theology must be reconstituted in order to participate constructively in the building of South Africa after apartheid.

This orientation and exemplification of the problem religion and racism is given here because it is spotlighted by the situation in South Africa. The clashes are also reflected in the American civil rights movement under the leadership of Martin Luther King. However there is no counterpart to the officially supported South African apartheid in the USA. The black South African Anglican priest Zolile Mbali deals with the fundamental problem of religion and racism in his work *The Churches and Racism, A Black South African Perspective*, 1987.

1.19 The Basic Functions of Religion

Religions appeal not simply to the intellect of human beings but also to their feelings. They relate to the totality of human existence. They are aimed not at an intellectual élite but chiefly at the broad ranks of the people. The great world religions share the characteristic that they are religions with wide popular support. They permeate peoples and cultures and the beliefs they embody have been tested by human experience over a long period of time.

The importance of secular ideologies has declined while that of the old religions has grown. The polarization between communism and capitalism is exaggerated.

A religion is a living system of religious convictions, liturgical rites, spiritual experiences and institutions of various kinds which are subject to development and possessed of its own special character. A religion is thus not a static entity but incorporates a tradition with links to its roots. At the same time, it is also a living reality involved in continuous change. A religion is primarily a dynamic living reality and not a set of doctrines, a symbolic system or an organizational structure.

Religion provides a kind of deeper dimension to existence. It gives life meaning, even in face of suffering, injustice and meaninglessness. In fact it gives life meaning even in the face of death.

Religion provides a motivation for values and norms; it bases them on the absolute. It gives morality a wholly different type of authority from what is possible when ethics are humanly grounded.

By means of symbols, rituals and experiences, religion is able to create a kind of feeling of being at home, a feeling of comfort, identity, faith, security, self-reliance and hope.

Religion can provide motivation for protest and struggle against unjust conditions. It can motivate and inspire work for social change.

Religion,however, has a dual aspect. It can contribute to human oppression but also to human liberation both at the individual and the political and social level. It can be used to suppress human rights but also to maintain and defend them.

Religions can be authoritarian and in this way give rise to intolerance, injustice and social isolation. They can legitimize immorality and war.

Theological support for Hitler's Third Reich contributed to the extermination of six million Jews. A theology in South Africa has been used to support apartheid. Columbus colonized America while bearing both the Cross and the sword. The conquistadores, with the church's blessing, slaughtered the original native peoples. In the American South, Biblical teaching was used to support slavery.

However, religions can also have liberating effects and act for the benefit of humanity. They can create generosity, tolerance, solidarity, creativity and social commitment.

The basic functions of religion in history and at the present time have been both reactionary and progressive. Religion both hinders and promotes progress. The main focus of interest in the present investigation is to capture the progressive functions of religion within the domain of human rights.

1.20 Human Rights as a Research Problem in Ecclesiastical History

The Cold War conflict between East and West presented itself in the domain of human rights as a polarization between individual and social rights. In the Third World, this conflict has been questioned. It is considered to be irrelevant. In that world, the problem is to satisfy the basic necessities of life and to survive. For this reason, the right to life is considered the primary human right.

Within the churches, the polarization between individual and social rights was dominant as long as the development was determined by the Cold War conflict between East and West. But when this conflict loses ground to the North-South distinction, the Third World emphasis on the right to life becomes of central importance. This shift from the Cold War conflict between individual and social rights to emphasis on the right to life brought about by the North-South conflict, was especially apparent in church activities during the 1970s.

When the churches in the West during the Cold War fought on behalf of individual human rights, they risked justifying the economic structures of national and international capitalism with all the injustices which that system embodies.

In the 1980s, the ecological problem as well the situation of animals came to the fore and left its mark in the churches in the form of demands on behalf of the rights of nature and animals.

The feminist movement has also demanded equal rights for women and the Green movement has pressed for the rights of plant and animal species at risk.

Human rights involve underlying beliefs and values and the task is to identify these and make them explicit.

Different aspects of the social question cropped up in the churches because the historical context was subject to continuous change. During the 1960s, the main social issue was social justice and action for social justice. This trend culminated around 1968. From the 1970s, new dimensions of the social problem were discussed. There was increasing consciousness of the ecological problem. Peace and the economy were two other items which became of central importance for the churches during the 70s and 80s.

Human rights have figured on the agenda of the churches throughout the whole post-war period but the historical situation during the 70s and 80s gave them a high priority and a new direction. The central element in human rights as a problem in ecclesiastical history is the interaction between changing historical environments and the varying meanings and implementations of human rights.

1.21 Religion and Human Rights

There is material not only about the theme of the church and human rights but also about the theme of religion and human rights. As a matter of principle, it is interesting to consider the wider perspective. However, much has been already written about the world religions and human rights, whereas little research has been done on the question of the churches and human rights. There is therefore some justification for concentrating in this investigation upon the problem of the churches and human rights while at the same time devoting a section to the world religions and to relating human rights to what is central in their systems of belief.

References

Good examples of the research carried out on the theme of religion and human rights are A. S. Rosenbaum (ed.) The Philosophy of Human Rights, International Perspectives, 1980; Leroy S. Rouner (ed.) Human Rights and the World Religions, 1988; Abdullahi Ahmed An-Nai'm and Francis M. Deng (eds.) Human Rights in Africa, Cross-Cultural Perspectives, 1991; and Abdullahi Ahmed An-Na'im, Human Rights in Cross-Cultural Perspectives, A Quest for Consensus, 1992.

1.22 From Churches and Human Rights to Religions and Human Rights

There is a connection between the problem of the church and human rights and that of religion and human rights. Whereas within the churches, attention is first paid to what they can do in the domain of human rights, in theory and practice and by word and deed, later on they become interested in what the world religions can do collectively to promote human rights. The first phase of this trend reached its peak during the 1970s while the latter phase was pursued on a broad front from the beginning of the 1980s. This means that Christians are not simply concerned with Christian faith and human rights but also with the issue of non-Christian world religions and human rights. Naturally exponents of Judaism, Islam, Hinduism, Buddhism and Confucianism are also preoccupied with this. But they were concerned with the issue of their religion and human rights long before the representatives of the Christian churches began to extend the discussion of human rights to cover all world religions— not simply Christianity.

We can thus discern an evolution from the theme of the churches and human rights to one of the religions and human rights. The relevant question therefore becomes not simply what we can do on the basis of our Christian faith and tradition to promote human rights but also what the adherents of all world religions can do collectively within the human rights movement.

A concrete outcome of the above development is Studia Missionalia, 1990 which is published by the Gregorian University in Rome and has its general theme *Human Rights and Religions*. In addition to expositions dealing with human rights in Christianity, the mission journal contains essays by Christians on human rights in an Islamic context, in Hinduism, Buddhism and in African culture.

Human rights involve a universal view of what is human and what is right. They presuppose a universal ethics which means that they ought to be believed and observed universally. What articles of faith and what sort of cultural and social patterns form the basis of belief in human rights and for action on their behalf? This question is central to the Concilium 1990/2 which bears the title *The Ethics of World Religions and Human Rights* and was published by the theologians Hans Küng and Jürgen Moltmann.

It may be asked what is the point of Christians first concentrating on what their own tradition has to give the human rights movement and then turning to the contribution of the world religions to this issue. The focus on Christian faith and human rights reached its zenith during the 1970s while the shift of focus to world religions' contribution to the global movement of human rights begins in the 1980s. I hope that my study will provide an answer to this question.

1.23 Human Rights and the Dialogue Between World Religions

The cooperation between the world religions within the human rights movement forms the endpoint of a development which started with the dialogue between representatives of the various world religions. This process accelerated during the 1980s and found expression in conferences and publications which analyze the relation between the various world religions and advocates a dialogue between them. In the harvest of books generated by this trend there may be noted an issue of the Catholic periodical Concilium for 1986 edited by Hans Küng and Jürgen Moltmann, with the title *Christianity among World Religions* and *Toward a Universal Theology of Religion*, 1986, edited by Leonard Swidler. This latter publication originated with a symposium at Temple University, Philadelphia in 1984. It was sponsored by the Journal of Ecumenical Studies and the Department of Religion, which were both founded some twenty years before. Another work belonging to the same type of literature is *World Religions and Global Ethics*, 1989, edited by S. Cromwell Crawford.

Hans Küng in Tübingen played a leading role in the dialogue of religions and his later publications, among them *Christianity and the World Religions*, 1987, are specifically concerned with presentations of the great world religions. He reflects over the relationship between Christianity and the other world religions by providing a highly knowledgeable and easily understood introduction to them, presented with accustomed elegance, with the explicit purpose of doing them justice as a Christian and Catholic ecumenical theologian. He traces various lines of development, with the aim of providing a fresh definition of the relationship between Christianity and the world religions.

Küng is also the person who more than anyone else has helped to link the dialogue about religion to cooperation between the representatives of the various world religions in the movement for human rights. The religious dialogue is given a concrete cooperative project in striving on basis of the world's various religious traditions to work for the formulation and implementation of human rights. The United Nations and UNESCO are natural platforms for these activities.

1.24 Human Rights in Cultural and Religious Traditions

One result of the foregoing reflections is the conclusion that the issue does not really consist in choosing between the title religion and human rights or the title the church and human rights. The difference between them is obviously more apparent than real. Instead it is a matter of tracing the treatment of the human rights issue within cultural, religious and denominational traditions. This way of specifying the task, indicates that the present study does not primarily deal with the development of human rights in the social, political, economic and legal spheres but rather its development in the cultural and religious sphere.

The ecclesiastical traditions are important components of Western civilization and culture as these find expression above all in Europe and North America. In a corresponding way, the non-Christian world religions constitute important components in the different local cultures of the Third World.

There is a latent conflict between human rights as universal ideals and human rights as they are expressed in local society. The UN represents the universal ideals while its member states represent local societies and cultures. Religion and ideology are important constituents of the latter.

There is a conflict between universal human rights and their local interpretation and implementation. The interpretation and implementation of human rights depends on different cultural contexts: Hindus and Moslems in Pakistan, Jews and Moslems in the Middle East, Catholics and Protestants in Northern Ireland—all of them emphasize the significance of human rights but they are not agreed about how these rights should be interpreted and implemented in the local communities.[27]

In a global context, human rights cannot succeed in opposition to these religions but only with their support. At UNESCO, stress has been laid on the importance of the world religions in helping to implement UNESCO's programme *Education in human rights.*

References

In International Human Rights: Universalism versus Relativism, 1990, A. D. Renteln proposes that social scientists should use local data for identifying within different cultures moral norms which function as benchmarks for human instruments of justice. The hope is to surmount the problems raised by cultural relativists, by empirically identifying shared values.

In Universal Rights in Theory and Practice, 1989, J. Donnelly presents a theory of international human rights which provides a critical answer to demands about cultural relativism and rejects the view that economic development must be secondary to human rights.

In Die Universalität der Menschenrechte, Studie zur ideengeschichtlichen Bestimmung eines politischen Schlüsselbegriffs, 1987, L. Kühnhardt points to a central item in the legimization of the new epoch: the universality of human rights as a key concept in political ethics.

1.25 The Organization of the Present Study

Work on the human rights issue went on at the same time in different churches and ecclesiastical and religious bodies. It is therefore relevant to arrange the present enquiry under the following headings:

---

[27] D. Hollenbach, Human Rights and Religious Faith in the Middle East: Reflections of a Christian Theologian,in Human Rights Quarterly Vol. 4, No. 1, 1982, pp. 94–109.

Given this disposition of material, the most apt title for this enquiry is *Human Rights in Cultural and Religious Traditions*.

In nearly all religious and denominational traditions one is preoccupied with the human rights issue. However, this does not mean that that there are necessarily new insights and fresh ways of treating the theme to be found everywhere. As a result, there is no reason to study treatments of the human rights issue which do not reflect the new orientation. This applies in the case of the Orthodox tradition, the Anglican Communion and the Methodist and Baptist World Alliances. [28] For the above reason, these are not the subject of special comment in the present study. Most of what is said in this connection is covered in dealing with the World Council of Churches.

In a study of *Eastern orthodoxy and Human Rights*, the human rights scholar A. Pollis draws the conclusion that civil and political rights cannot be based on orthodox Christianity since orthodox thinking is not relevant to current realities. No guidance is forthcoming from Orthodox Christianity with respect to social and political issues. It speaks only to those for whom the life of the spirit is the essential thing in life.[29]

Stanley S. Harakas at Holy Cross School of Theology, Brookline, Massachusetts, puts forward a different view in the article *Human Rights: An Eastern Orthodox Perspective*. In Eastern Orthodoxy, rights arise from the ontological reality of a created humankind. Human rights reflect the Trinity's symbolic community. Orthodox Christian ethics defines human rights not in terms of themselves but as a mutual assumption of moral responsibility. The language of human rights has in our own days received greater expression and emphasis within the Orthodox church. Human rights constitute one of the most promising domains for ecumenical cooperation.[30]

---

[28] Anglican Consultative Council Report of the 4th meeting 1979, 8th May–18th May 1979, A Theological Basis of Human Rights 1979, Board of Church and Society of the Methodist Church (ed.) The Quest for Human Rights in Engage/Social Action, March 1979, H. Brackney (ed.) Faith, Life and Witness, The Papers of the Study and Research Division of the Baptist World Alliance, 1986–1990, 1990, The YMCA and Human Rights: a Study on the Christian basis of Human Rights, 1980.

[29] Human Rights Quarterly, Vol. 15, 1993, pp. 339–356.

Anastasion Yannoulatos of the University of Athens, like Harakas, perceives a connection between Eastern Orthodoxy and human rights, in an article with that title. He maintains that Orthodox believers respect other human beings as they freely are, without wishing to compel them to accept Christian views. Orthodox history displays a mature respect for human rights and in the course of the last six centuries has been responsible for keeping alive in the minds of the oppressed a belief in the rights of equality, human dignity and liberty. The idea of personality as a fundamental principle in the creation of political institutions and in social manifestations of the life of the individual, has become a basic part of popular consciousness.[31]

In the Roman Catholic church, the Lutheran World Federation and the World Alliance of Reformed Churches, theologically original discussions of the human rights issue have taken place. John Paul II proposed a theology of human rights based upon Catholic personalism.[32] In my own view, the Reform theologian Jürgen Moltmann is the most original and significant human rights theologian. In Latin America, the human rights issue is an important aspect of liberation theology.

The Czech Josef L. Hromadka was a protagonist of social rights. He was the leader of the Christian peace conference. Like Reinhold Niebuhr, he had a Lutheran background and began life as a priest in the Lutheran church. Like Reinhold Niebuhr, he later joined a church with something of a Reform character. In both cases, this Lutheran and Reform combination led to an active social Christianity. The Church of the Bohemian Brothers reckoned Hus as one of their spiritual fathers.[33]

Both John Paul II and the World Council of Churches viewed action on behalf of human rights as part of the church's evangelical task. Human rights became a central Christian project supported by both the Vatican and the World Council of Churches.

Three particular groupings merit special study in grasping the interaction between what happens on the human rights front within the central ecclesiastical organs and in various historical circumstances and contexts.

1) Within *the Catholic Church*, it is a question of determining the interaction between the human rights projects initiated by the Vatican and the development of the human rights movement in Latin America and Poland.

2) In *the Lutheran Church*, the object is to see the relationship between ideas about human rights within the Lutheran World Federation and events, particularly in East Germany.

3) In *Reformed Christianity*, the issue is the relationship between the activi-

---

[30] S. S. Harakas, Human Rights: An Eastern Orthodox Perspective, Journal of Ecumenical Studies, 1982, 19(3), pp. 13–24.

[31] A. Yannoulatos, Eastern Orthodoxy and Human Rights, International Review of Mission, 1984, 73 (292), pp. 454–466.

[32] Jean Paul II, Les Droits de l'homme (Octobre 1978–Décembre 1979), 1980.

[33] Christian existence in Dialogue: Doing theology in all seasons. In memory and appreciation of Josef L. Hromadka, WCC CCPD, 1990.

ties in the World Alliance of Reformed Churches and apartheid in South Africa, the civil rights movement in USA and the Carter administration's human rights campaign. Liberal-Puritan Christianity and the movement for human rights are closely linked in the USA.

What happens on the human rights front within the World Council of Churches is related not least to the struggle for liberty in East Germany, South Africa and the USA. Its activities are directed against the totalitarianism of communism and the discrimination in apartheid and racism.

1.26 Relationship to the Author's Previous Research

My research on human rights in cultural and religious traditions is linked to my previous study *Church and Society in the Modern Age* which was published as a monograph in English in 1995. It contains an account of the church's official position with respect to the dominant social models—socialist, capitalist or some intermediate form—during the last hundred years. The present investigation, on the other hand, deals with the church's attitudes to human rights since the Second World War. The formulation of the problem and the temporal perspective differ from the earlier work and the material on which my analysis is based derives from other sources. The link between the two studies is that both analyze the role and function of the church in modern society albeit from quite different standpoints. The previous study was concerned with the church's contribution to the question of what constitutes the good society and what form it should take. The present work deals with what the Church has to offer when it comes to defending the integrity of the individual human being.

In the previous investigation, it was a matter of determining the church's contribution to the concrete meaning of social justice. In the present study, it is a question of discovering what the church has to say about the issue of personal value and liberty and of establishing how respect for human value is based and maintained. The earlier study sought to identify the church's view of society in the period 1885–1985 whereas the present investigation aims at studying the church's view of man as this is expressed in work concerned with the human rights issue in the postwar period.

As I indicated in my earlier research, there is a clear connection between the church's sociology (i.e. view of society) and its anthropology (view of man) but in order to specify this relationship an analysis of the view of man is required. In my view, this can be accomplished by investigating the issue of the church and human rights.[34]

Work on the question of how the church understands the good society has

---

[34] W. Pannenberg, Anthropolgy in Theological Perspective (1985), H. D. McDonald, The Christian View of man, 1981.

revealed the need for trying to explain what human beings are. My hope is that the project human rights in cultural and religious traditions will contribute to answering this question.

1.27 Research Carried out on Human Rights in Cultural and Religious Traditions

As mentioned in the preface, no real research has been carried out on human rights in cultural and religious traditions in the postwar period. The American society for ecclesiastical history has called for such research and the present investigation is intended, at least to a limited extent, to answer this need.

On the hand, the issue of religion and human rights in a wider and longer perspective has been the subject of scholarly study and the best known from the standpoint of ecclesiastical history are surely those due to the sociologically influenced ecclesiastical historian from the turn of the century, namely Ernst Troeltsch who published his analyses in *Die Bedeutung des Protestantismus für die Enstehung der modernen Welt*, 1911. This appeared in English as *Protestantism and Progress, The Significance of Protestantism for the Rise of the Modern World,* 1912. He held that the advocacy of human rights did not begin during the Enlightenment when they were advanced by the wellknown writers of this period on purely worldly grounds and for secular reasons. They had already been put forward during the Reformation by radical Protestants in their attack, not least, on the Lutheran Reformation. The Enlightenment concept of freedom was unknown for Luther but not for the Baptists. The radical reformers insisted on human rights and gave this demand a religious justification. Oliver Cromwell provided a religious motivation for this demand in the social turbulence which characterized England in the middle of the seventeenth century. The theory that the integrity of inner life should not be subject to interference by the State is a purely religious idea held by the Puritans which was subsequently secularized and transmuted into the modern rationalistic notion of tolerance. What happened during the Enlightenment was that the demand for human rights was adopted by prominent Enlightenment authors who then gave it a purely secular foundation. According to Troeltsch, the link between religion and human rights was dissolved.

The ideas of human rights and freedom of conscience have for Troeltsch a religious basis. They have entered constitutional law. They are part of the American constitution. From there they passed to France and other constitutions. They originated with the radical reformation. It was not the Enlightenment but the radical wing of the Reformation which was the spiritual father of human rights. They were manifested in the English Revolution and implemented in Cromwell's state.

Modern society with its demands concerning human rights, which place the individual at the centre and assert the integrity of the person, is in Ernst

Troeltsch's view a product of the religious individualism of the radical reformation movements. It is however difficult to free oneself from the impression that the so-called cultural Protestantism to which Troeltsch belonged, is projecting its own, turn of the century ideal into its reading of history and sees it implemented by the radical reformers.

Ernst Troeltsch described the relation between the modern secular political world and its religious roots and origin in his exposition in *Die Bedeutung des Protestantismus für Enstehung der modernen Welt*, 1911.

Troeltsch's discussion of religion and human rights lacks immediate relevance for the present study. At the same time, it serves to remind us that the problem as it relates to the period from the Reformation to the Enligtenment has been a subject for study and research.

A work with nearly the same wide historical perspective of Troeltsch is *Creeds, Society and Human Rights, A Study in Three Cultures*, 1984 by the American Max L. Stackhouse. It focuses on the function of the human rights concept in various societies such as modern America, Marxist East Germany and Hindu India. The temporal perspective goes far beyond developments after 1945. Since the book was written in the early 1980s, the author fails to note the role which the Lutheran church played as a driving force within the human rights movement in East Germany. The revolution of 1989 refutes Troeltsch's thesis about the social passivity of Lutheranism. Luther may have opposed the Peasants' Revolt of 1525 but his latterday followers inspired the revolution of 1989.

For Stackhouse the problem is the relation between the universalism of the concept of human rights and particularism in three different cultural and religious contexts. Human rights presuppose universality. But what is truly human is defined in different ways in differing civilizations.[35]

There are reasons for supposing that the human rights issue in the postwar period is linked to the old discussion about natural rights. In the Catholic tradition, the concept of natural right plays a key role and ethics are given a natural law foundation. In the Protestant tradition, on the other hand, there is in addition to a morality founded on natural rights an ethics which is Christologically based. Karl Barth is an exponent of the latter approach. While human rights are based on natural rights in the Catholic tradition, there is a split in the Protestant tradition. There has been no real research into this from a historical point of view but the present study is intended to assist in remedying this deficiency.

John Warwick Montgomery, the American lawyer attached to the international institute for human rights in Strasbourg, has reviewed in *Human Rights and Human Dignity*, 1986, an extensive amount of material—both source material as well as expositions and analyses—emanating from both law and theology. He writes, however, from a conservative theological point of view

---

[35] M. L. Stackhouse, Some Intellectual and Social Roots of Modern Human Rights Ideas, Journal for the Scientific Study of Religion, 1981, 20(4), pp. 301–309, and Theology, History and Human Rights Soundings, 1984, 67(2), pp. 191–208 by the same author.

openly displaying his sympathies and antipathies, and argues for a Christian solution of the human rights issue. To argue for a denominational Christian solution of the human rights issue along evangelical lines in a multicultural and multireligious world, however, does not seem particularly far-sighted. If people with different cultural and religious backgrounds are to cooperate on this issue, solutions must be sought along lines where all the participants can work together. Montgomery is a representative of the strong evangelical Christian tradition in the USA.

Montgomery's exposition of human rights is a good illustration of the hypothesis of the present study: the way in which he attacks the problem of human rights and provides a foundation for them, reflects his own evangelical background.

A completely different approach to the theology of human rights is that of the South African anti-apartheid theologian, Charles Villa-Vicencio in his work *A Theology of Reconstruction, Nation building and human rights*, 1992. The book has been written at Georgetown University where there are a number of Jesuits specializing in human rights problems in the Third World, particularly in Latin America.

Villa-Vicencio emphasizes that in the ecumenical theology of human rights there is the idea that all human beings are made in the image of God and that without human rights, God's purpose with the world cannot be realized. The ecumenical theology of human rights has its starting point in what it means to be human and the consequences this has for all areas of society, including ecology. The ecumenical theology of human rights begins with anthropology. Its contribution to the human rights movement is a theological interpretation of humanity. The rights are needed to protect what is human.

Starting from a basically theological position, Villa-Vicencio provides an interpretation of the human rights discussion in the Catholic, Lutheran and the Reformed traditions as well as in the ecumenical tradition during the postwar period and later I shall have reason to return to this from a historical genetic perspective.

He holds, however, that the differing theological traditions tend to proceed in the same direction as regards their exposition of the theological meaning of human rights. They are moving towards what one might call unity in multiplicity.

Catholic human rights theology begins with the Thomist view of nature and grace while Lutheran and Calvinist human rights theology starts from the doctrine of sin and grace. Villa-Vicencio holds that despite the diffference of theological emphasis, there is suffcent common ground to create an ecumenical position on the issue of human rights.

The research carried out on human rights at Woodstock Theological Center, which is attached to Georgetown University, can be traced in a number of monographs: *D. Hollenbach, Claims in Conflict, Retrieving and Renewing the Catholic Human Rights Tradition, 1979, A. Henelly and J. Langan (eds.) Hu-*

man Rights in the Americas, The Struggle for Consensus, 1982 and *M. E. Crahan (ed.) Human Rights and Basic Needs in the Americas, 1982.*[36]

In *Human Rights, Justification and Christian Ethics,* 1996, the Swedish ethicist Per Sundman analyzes four main models of human rights to be found in various important authors, among them, the aforementioned Stackhouse, Montgomery, Villa-Vicencio and Hollenbach, on the basis of the views they hold with respect to the function of human rights, their meaning and justification. Terminologically he speaks of an evangelical model, a natural law model, a liberation model and a constructivist model. These models do not coincide with human rights as they are to be found in the great world religions and the Christian confessions. But there are elements of them in several religious traditions and communities. Sundman's models are clearly defined and conceptually precise. They help to depict contemporary thinking about human rights.

Sundman does not link the ideology of human rights to social changes: his purpose is not to specify the interaction between human rights and social events. In other words, he does not provide human rights with a historical perspective. He himself argues for the constructivist model. In his view, human rights are not universal but contextual.

---

[36] The centre for the study of human rights at Columbia University in New York has published with J. P. Martin as editor, a bibliography, 1983. T. P. Fenton and M. J. Heffron (eds.) 1989 contains information on material dealing with human rights and is extremely comprehensive. It is more up to date than the bibliography from Columbia University but it does not contain a special section on religion and human rights. It provides a list of titles of books dealing with human rights and a short summary of their contents. Among other bibliographies of human rights, there is J. B. Friedman and M. I. Sherman (eds.), 1985 which presents a legal perspective and W. Miller, 1976. Literature with a focus mainly on human rights in Latin America is presented in Human Rights in Latin America, 1964–1980: A Selective Annotated Bibliography. Compiled and Edited by the Hispanic Division, 1983.

CHAPTER 2

Human Rights—a Historical Perspective

2.1 The Emergence Ideas About Human Rights

Human rights are usually defined as the legal basis for human community. Human community aims at an ideal association of human beings which exists for the individual and collective welfare of its members.

The idea of human rights can be traced to the natural law doctrines of the Stoics. The Stoics viewed nature as a universal system of rules. The laws of nature are elements of a universal order.

In medieval times, the doctrine of natural law was incorporated in a theological tradition. Thomas Aquinas interprets the natural law as one which is in accordance with the divine will. Natural law is accessible to reason.

In its view of natural rights, Catholic scholastic theology brings together the ancient and medieval doctrines. A social consciousness of human rights and duties grows from a life based on reason and love. Human beings are created in the image of God. They are intelligent and capable of unselfish love and by virtue of this capacity, are called "persons". The rights of human beings are based upon human nature. These rights have priority before society and the state. The doctrine of human rights is thus deduced from nature, not from the Bible.

The crucial difference separating Catholics and Protestants in their attitude to human rights ever since the Reformation is that while Catholics emphasize the philosophical basis of their rights, Protestants give them a Biblical foundation. However the distinction in attitude is not watertight—orthodox Protestants carry on the Scholastic tradition. At the same time, it indicates the main line of demarcation. Following the Second Vatican Council, the gap has narrowed and arguments for human rights based on the Bible have become increasingly common in Catholicism.

Hugo Grotius helped to bring about the secularization of the theory of natural law. Natural law is valid independently of the existence of God.

Natural law is based upon natural religion. The source of natural law is God who bestows it on human beings. Their task is to strive for what is good for all. Natural law is exemplified by each human being contributing to the good of all. Natural rights are deduced from natural law. They are correlated with natural duties.

The tradition of natural law is linked to Locke's Second Treatise of Civil Government[1] but it is much wider than so during the 17th and 18th centuries. Natural law, natural rights and duties are of central importance for this period.

The great natural law theories of the 17th century are steps in an attempt to provide a moral formulation of political theories within Protestantism. At the same time, there are many links between Scholastic and Protestant natural law.

The Scholastic natural law would appear to presuppose a measure of knowledge about God, the world and human nature, which is readily vulnerable to sceptical criticism. It proceeds from an idea about God and the relation between God and human beings which can hardly be thought natural if it is apparently unable to convince non-Christians. One of modern scepticism's points is that this cannot be done. Because religion and moral ideas vary so much with respect to time and place, they cannot be given any theoretical support.

Protestant theology maintained that Scholastic natural law seems to presuppose a moral agreement between God and human beings. The starting point for Protestant thinkers was the complete lack of agreement between God and human beings. This discrepancy made it impossible to give rational reasons for human morality by reference to God and His eternal law. Only faith can bridge the gap between human beings and their Creator. This led to an abiding ambivalence within Protestantism towards natural law as a rational basis for morality. On the one hand, only faith can provide a basis for morality. On the other hand, there is a pressure on thinkers to put forward what is possible in purely human terms. If human rationality cannot create the link between human conduct and divine reward or punishment, human beings are forced to live by faith alone or to find a purely human basis for reward and punishment.

Hugo Grotius and Thomas Hobbes devised theories of natural rights.[2] Human beings have no fundamental rights. For both these thinkers, rights are elements of human nature. They are something which human beings possess. If they did not have them, human life would be impossible. A right is seen as a moral force which does not come into conflict with other moral forces.

The most important modern exponent of the theory of natural law is the English 17th century philosopher, John Locke. A number of scholars assign him to the Calvinistic tradition which culminated in Puritanism. The 18th century philosophers Montesquieu, Voltaire and Jean-Jacques Rousseau also had a central role in fashioning ideas about human rights. Locke's arguments were put forward in writings linked to the Glorious Revolution of 1688. Certain rights, above all the rights to life, liberty and property were assigned to individuals as human beings. The revolution resulted in the English Bill of Rights of 1689.

---

[1] J. Locke, The Second Treatise of Civil Government, 1976. See also Locke's Two Treatises of Government, 1988, 267–428.

[2] T. Hobbes, Leviathan, 1969.

John Locke employed the theory of natural law as a basis for a theory of natural rights. The individual has by nature the right to life, liberty and property. Locke held that a social contract justifies society's role as a defender of the individual's natural rights. The government is the executive charged with implementing such rights in society.

The "bourgeois" revolution in England and the arguments which supported it form an important background to the revolutions in North America and France. Thomas Jefferson who had read Locke and Montesquieu, looked upon human rights as a product of the laws of nature. It was he who penned the Declaration of Independence of the thirteen American colonies of 4 July 1776. All human beings are created equal and the creator has bestowed upon them rights such as life and liberty. The formulations behind the English and American revolutions recur in the Declaration of the Rights of Man and the Citizen of 26 August 1789. Men are born free and equal. The aim of political activity is to preserve the natural rights of human beings. Among these rights, liberty and property are especially singled out. Liberty is defined principally as the right of free association and freedom of religion.

Locke employed his individualistic theory of rights to justify the sovereignty of Parliament, an Englishman's rights against the Crown and the Glorious Revolution of 1688. Locke influenced Jefferson. The latter's phrase about life, liberty and the fullfilment of happiness in the Declaration of 1776 is a modification of Locke's natural rights to life, liberty and property. Immanuel Kant carried through the secularization of natural rights which had begun a century earlier.[3] Rousseau based human rights on society's General Will.[4] Edmund Burke viewed the idea of human equality as a fiction while Jeremy Bentham treated natural rights as nonsense. David Hume considered natural law and natural rights as unreal metaphysical phenomena.[5]

References

The social contract theory in Hobbes, Locke, Rousseau and Hegel has been studied by P. Riley in Will and Political Legitimacy, A Critical Exposition of Social Contract Theory in Hobbes, Locke, Rousseau, Kant and Hegel, 1982.

J. Finnis takes up the problem of natural law and natural rights in Natural Law and Natural Rights, 1980. Natural law and human rights are also discussed in L. L.Weinreb, Natural Law and Justice, 1987 and R. P. George (ed.) Natural Law Theory, 1992.

R. Tuck presents a history of theories of natural rights in which figure names such as Hugo Grotius and Thomas Hobbes, in Natural Rights Theories, Their Origin and Development, 1979. J. Hampton gives an analysis of Hobbes in Hobbes and the Social Contract Tradition, 1986.

A valuable historical perespective on the evolution from natural law to human rights is to be found in M. J. Lacey and K. Haakonssen (eds.) A Culture of Rights, The Bill of Rights in Philosophy, Politics and Law—1791 and 1991, 1991.

---

[3] Gau-Jeng Ju, Kants Lehre vom Menschenrecht und von den staatsbürgerlichen Grundrechten, 1990.

[4] J. J. Rousseau, On the Social Contract, 1978 and A Discourse Upon the Origin and Foundation of the Inequality of Mankind, 1949.

[5] E. Baker (ed.) Social Contract: Locke, Hume, Rousseau, 1971.

N. S. S. Iwe covers the whole history in The History and Contents of Human Rights, A Study of the History of Human Rights, 1986. This contains, among other things, an analysis of the American Bill of Rights, the French Declaration of the Rights of Man and the Citizen.

L. Kühnhardt describes human rights as an important ingredient in the history of political ideas in Die Universalität der Menschenrechte. Studie zur ideengeschichtlichen Bestimmung eines politischen Schlüsselbegriffs, 1987. In his view, historical origin, cultural roots, and philosophic and theological foundations are important constituents of human rights from an analytical standpoint.

E. Fuchs and P. A. Stucki provide a historical account of human rights along with a theological and philosophical perspective in their work, Au Nom de l'autre, Essai sur le fondement des droits de l'homme, 1985.

J. Punt present a historical survey in Die Idee der Menschenrechte Ihre geschichtliche Entwicklung und ihre Rezeption durch die moderne katholische Sozialverkündigung, 1987. Despite the book's survey character, it is well-written.

M. Palumbo provides a popular history of the movement for human rights in Human Rights: Meaning and History, 1982. The choice of texts in the book is highly illuminating.

E. W. Bockenförde and R. Spaemann have published Menschenrechte und Menschenwürde Historische Voraussetzungen-säkuläre Gestalt-christliches Verständnis, 1987. In this book, it is pointed out that the church is interested in the relationship between Christian and secular views of human rights. Originally they were based upon the relation of human beings to God. Theologians raise the question of whether human rights can survive the metaphysical-religious idea of human value. Trutz Rendtorff deals with the problem dealt with by Georg Jellinek, Max Weber and Ernst Troeltsch, namely that the idea of human rights has its roots in the Reformation rather than the Revolution and that these roots are religious rather than political.[6]

The theme of Christianity and human rights is taken up by S. H. Evans in a series of lectures inspired by the aims of the international institute for human rights, founded in Strasbourg in 1969.[7]

2.2 John Locke's Theory of Rights

Because John Locke is the most important modern exponent of the theory of natural law, there is some reason for pausing to consider his theory of human rights. It recurs both in the English, American and French Revolutions. A. John Simmons has published an informative modern work on the subject, *The Lockean Theory of Rights*, 1992.

Locke's starting point is the idea that a right is a kind of moral check or sovereignty over some special area of our lives, defining a moral sphere within which we are free to act. The core of this doctrine of natural law is that there are universally binding moral rules which we can learn to recognize by using our natural capacity. This forms a frame of reference to which we can appeal in assessing and criticizing human institutions and actions. The theory of natural law in this sense presupposes some form of value objectivism. Locke's theory

---

[6] E. W. Böckenförde und R. Spaemann, Hrsg, 1987, 95–101.
[7] S. H. Evans, Christianity and Human Rights, An Introduction to the Study of Human Rights (ed.) Sir Francis Vallat, 1971, 15.

of natural law is based upon a commitment to God's role as legislator and creator. However the theory of natural law can be defended independently of such a commitment.

The basic principle in natural law is that God wishes the continued existence of human beings. God gave the world to humankind as a whole. Taking into account human needs and God's intentions, it can be seen that there must be a way to make what was common property, private. According to Locke, God wishes us to have private property. Property is necessary for our survival. From this, it follows that we have a right to acquire property. This is the right to property. Every human being has this right as part of his birthright. Thus in Locke's view, the right of private ownership is necessary for our survival. What is reckoned as justice in political society depends very much on what kind of ownership rights persons in that society have. For Locke, justice is the ownership of those things to which a human being has a right. Locke's theory of justice is a theory of just ownership. Property is the fundamental idea in terms of which justice is defined. Justice obtains when every person owns that to which he has a moral right or when the person does only what he has a moral right to do. Locke's theory of justice is an expression of moderate individualism.[8]

2.3 The Birth of the Ideology of Human Rights

The turning point with respect to human rights came about with the rise and fall of Nazi Germany. The laws which authorized the extermination of the Jews cannot be based upon any utilitarian, idealistic or other doctrine. Certain actions are intrinsically wrong. Human beings have a right to be respected.

Today the majority of lawyers, philosophers and ethical thinkers irrespective of culture and civilization are agreed that every human being possesses certain fundamental rights. The ideology of human rights is generally accepted. The second half of the present century marks the birth of the recognition of human rights. It is present in the founding document of the United Nations.

The UN Charter was adopted at San Francisco on 26 June 1945 in the wake of the experiences of the Second World War.

The Universal Declaration of Human Rights, 1948,[9] the International Covenant on Civil and Political Rights, 1966[10] together with its Optional Protocol to the International Covenant on Civil and Political Rights,1966[11] along with the International Covenant on Economic, Social and Cultural Rights 1966[12] make

---

[8] The importance of John Locke in the History of Ideas is treated in I. Harris, The Mind of John Locke, A Study of Political Theory in Its Intellectual Setting, 1994.

[9] G. Melander, (ed.) 1990, 11–18.

[10] Melander, op. cit., 49–68.

[11] Melander, op. cit., 69–73.

[12] Melander, op. cit, 35–47

up what is usually called the International Bill of Human Rights. The covenants and optional protocol began to be implemented from 1976. The Eastern bloc emphasized the Covenant on Economic, Social and Cultural Rights while the Western Powers laid particular emphasis on civil and political rights. The socialist countries also underlined the role of the state in securing human rights.

The UN document on human rights applies at the international level. Corresponding documents were also drawn up on a regional basis by the Council of Europe, the Organization of American States and the Organization for African Unity. In 1950, the Council of Europe issued the European Convention for the Protection of Human Rights and Fundamental Freedoms.[13] In 1969, the American Convention on Human Rights was adopted and took effect from 1978[14] as did the Council of Europe's Convention from 1953.[15] 1981 saw the adoption of the Organization for African Unity Charter on Human and Peoples' Rights which took effect from 1986.[16]

In Helsinki on 1 August 1975, the states in Eastern and Western Europe together with USA and Canada announced their commitment to respecting human rights and basic freedoms. However the UN was not permitted to intervene in the affairs of individual states.[17]

A number of organizations with no governmental affiliations work to promote human rights. Among these are Amnesty International with its headquarters in Geneva, the International Commission of Jurists, the Martin Luther King Jr. Foundation and the World Council of Churches. These organizations are transnational and their influence depends on the extent to which they can influence public opinion.

The voluntary organizations also include trades unions and political organizations along with various non-Christian religious groups. The latter include Buddhist, Moslem and Hindu associations.

Human rights deal partly with attitudes and questions of justice and partly with actions to promote human rights. Both these aspects are to be found in organizations dealing with human rights after the war, whether they are governmental or voluntary.

The voluntary human rights organizations have a consultative status within the United Nations. They have direct access to the UN Commission on human rights, the International Labor Organization and the United Nations Educational, Scientific and Cultural Organization (UNESCO).

While international society tended to be increasingly heterogeneous culturally and ideologically, the upholding of human rights ideas required agreement about fundamental values. For the ideology of human rights to function some

---

[13] Melander, op. cit., 117–134.
[14] Melander, op. cit., 195–223
[15] Melander, op. cit., 117.
[16] Melander, op. cit., 225–242.
[17] Melander, op. cit, 109–115.

minimum of ideological consensus was required. Ideas about human rights belonged somewhere between the conflicting approaches of particularism and universalism.

References

The starting point for human rights is the Nazi treatment of Jews before and during the Second World War. H. Fein addresses this problem in Accounting for Genocide, National Responses and Jewish Victimization during the Holocaust, 1979.

Human Rights Comments and Interpretations, A Symposium edited by UNESCO with an Introduction by Jacques Maritain, contains a number of different contributions written from varying perspectives. The work is based on a UNESCO symposium in 1949 where the question of the philosophical basis of human rights was put to various internationally famous experts. The proceedings of the symposium were published in the following year. Maritain wrote an introduction as well as an essay on the philosophy of human rights. He maintains that no declaration of human rights can be final. It is always linked to the state of moral consciousness and civilization at a given moment in history.[18]

In his work Mänskliga rättigheter, 1984, H. Danelius examines the UN and human rights as well as human rights in Europe. The subject is tackled from a legal point of view and deals with the application of rights in specific cases by courts of law. Major international documents on human rights are printed at the end of the book. A shift in focus takes place between 1948 and 1966. Initially the main focus is on individual rights contra the state but latterly it also embraces the responsibility of the state and society for human beings and the human community. Human rights are both about the individual's relation to society and society's relation to the individual.

In the Roots and Growth of the Universal Declaration of Human Rights 1948–1963, 1964, E. Scwelb identifies the historical roots of the declaration and describes the development of the human rights issue up to the 1960s.

P. Sieghart brings together a large amount of material dealing with human rights in his fundamental work The International Law of Human Rights, 1983 and shows that these ideas first and foremost yield individual rights against the state.

The same author returns to the human rights issue in The Lawful Rights of Mankind, An Introduction to the International Legal Code of Human Rights, 1985.

There is an extensive literature on the birth of the ideology of human rights at a global and regional level. R. F. Drinan, Cry of the Oppressed, The History and Hope of the Human Rights Revolution, 1987 offers a history of the human rights movement's legal, moral, spiritual and religious roots. In this movement, independent non-governmental organizations play an important part. J. A. Joyce, The New Politics of Human Rights, 1978, provides a history of the human rights movement from 1948, covering theory and practice, principles and applications. H. Kanger, Human Rights in the UN Declaration, 1984 offers a dissertation in analytic philosophy. L. J. Macfarlane, The Theory and Practice of Human Rights, 1985, provides a survey of the subject. Also to be noted are J. P. Riga, Human Rights as Human and Christian Realities, 1982, D. C. Kramer, Comparative Civil Rights and Liberties, 1982 and F. G. Jacobs, The European Convention on Human Rights, 1975.

The voluntary organizations receive their due quota of attention. J. Lissner analyzes their human rights activities in The Politics of Altruism, A Study of the Political Behaviour of Voluntary Development Agencies, 1977. There is the book of E. Larsen, A Flame in Barbed Wire, The Story of Amnesty International, 1978. J. A. Joyce deals with the ILO system in World Labour Rights and Their Protection, 1980.

---

[18] Human Rights, Comments and Interpretations, 1950, 74.

Finally A. G. Mowen in Regional Human Rights, 1991, presents an analytical survey of the African, European and inter-American institutions and procedures for implementing human rights.

2.4 Individual and Collective Rights

There is a lack of unanimity about the genetic roots of human rights. In the Marxist-Leninist social doctrine, human rights are based upon the laws promulgated by the government and reflecting each society's underlying economic relationships. In capitalist society, human rights reflect the interests of the capitalist class while in a socialist society they reflect the interests of the proletariat.

Given the division into exploiters and exploited, it is difficult within the Marxist-Leninist theory to find a place for human rights until the exploiters have been expropriated and all are free in a socialist society. If the idea of human rights is to survive the transition from a capitalist to a socialist society, it must take the form of a theory of needs.

Because rights in Marxist-Leninist doctrine emanate from the basic underlying economic structure and from the place of the indivual in a system of production, it is not surprising that economic and social rights take precedence over civil and political rights. The primary freedom in socialist societies is economic, namely freedom from exploitation. This is brought about by concentrating power in the hands of the working class.

The question of individual and human rights was brought to the fore during the 1970s in connection with the rights of the Soviet dissidents. From the viewpoint of the Soviet leaders, the dissidents sought to overthrow the Soviet regime and thus constituted a threat to order, security and the progress made under the socialist system. In the eyes of the West, human rights meant the right of individuals to express themselves freely, including the right to defend those things which conflicted with the interest of the state. For the Soviet leaders, human rights meant the right of the individual to express themselves in a responsible manner but also the right of society as a whole to protect itself against irresponsible opinions which try to undermine democratic government or promote racism, sexism, pornography or anything else which is damaging to the public good.

Society must protect itself against persons who threaten to overthrow the social system. It is therefore important to emphasize the rights of society as a whole as well as the rights of the individual. From a socialist point of view, collective rights were more important than individual rights. The dissidents were interpreted as activists aiming to destroy so-called socialist democracy.

It is usually said that the roots of the Russian people's preference for social rights is to be found in Russian history with its invasions and occupations by foreign armies. These experiences have made national security a matter of

66

absolutely central importance. USA has never experienced invasion by a foreign military power.

The individualist attitude towards human rights is dominant in the UN declaration of human rights of 1948. In the first article, emphasis is laid upon the individual's dignity and value. No stress is laid on the dignity and worth of society. The ensuing twenty seven articles set out the rights of the individual in relation to society. It is first in article 29 that the rights of society are mentioned. The individual is imperfect when cut off from the community. The individual has "duties to the community in which alone the free and full development of his personality is possible".[19] The individualist perspective on human rights is given more weight than its social counterpart even if the latter is not wholly absent. The universal declaration of human rights is basically a statement about the rights of individuals with respect to their governments.

The declaration contains thirty articles. The first twenty deal with civil and political freedoms. Article 22 guarantees the right to economic, social and cultural rights.[20] This is subject to the qualification that it is to be implemented in accordance with the organization and resources of each state. Such qualifications do not occur when it is a question of civil and political rights. This diminishes the importance of what articles 23 to 27 say concerning social, economic and cultural rights.[21]

If the UN had been equally concerned about social, economic and cultural rights as it was about civil and political rights, the declaration would have been formulated differently. Only six articles deal with social, economic and cultural rights while three times as many are devoted to civil and political rights. In addition, the UN would have attached conditions to both types of rights if they had been accorded equal importance, and not simply to social rights.

The declaration would also have created a better balance between the right to private property and the right to fundamental economic necessities. The right to own property in article 17 is presented as an absolute right.[22] By contrast, other economic rights are made conditional in article 22.[23] The right of capitalists to ownership and enterprise is given more weight than the rights of the workers with respect to wages and guaranteed employment. The economic rights to prosperity are stressed more than the rights of the workers and the poor which figure only in articles 23 to 27.

The universal declaration of human rights essentially bears the imprint of the values of the Western democracies with a certain attention being paid to social, economic and cultural rights thus taking into account the communist and Moslem worlds as well as the Third World. The dominant element is the Western view of political freedom and democracy as opposed to economic rights.

---

[19] G. Melander (ed.), 1990, 17.
[20] Melander, op. cit., 16.
[21] Melander, op. cit., 16–17.
[22] Melander, op. cit., 15
[23] Melander, op. cit., 16

The conception of human rights which evolves within European culture is an instrument against despotic powers. It is concerned with a universalistic and ethical conception of the individual. The idea of human rights contains fundamental protection and guarantees which apply to every individual irrespective of context, social position, ethnic background and race. Human rights are related to individualism but within the European tradition it is a matter of two types of individualism: possessive individualism related to the theory of contract and universal ethical individualism which is linked to a view of human rights. These two forms of individualism are promoted by two trends in Western societies: capitalism and the market economy and a purified, rationalized view of monotheistic religion, natural religion.

As to the relationship between individual rights and collective rights, the former are more fundamental. According to some, collective rights should not be called human rights at all.

In the socialist system, the legitimization of the idea of human rights differs from the legitimization of this idea in market economies. A necessary condition for human rights is the reconstruction of the existing social structure on a basis of equality.

In the eighteenth century European tradition of human rights, the idea of human rights is intended to protect the independence of the individual against the incursions of the state. In the socialist view of human rights derived from Marx, the state is the only organ by means of which human rights can be given and made effective. Human rights do not chiefly apply to independent individuals as is the case in the Western view.

References

There are a number of works which shed light on the issue of individual and collective rights, among them J. Berting et alii (ed.) Human Rights in a Pluralist World: Individuals and Collectivities, 1990 and W. L. Holleman, The Human Rights Movement: Western Values and Theological Perspectives, 1987. Holleman in his informative work, looks at the positions adopted by theologians with respect to individual and social rights and examines their arguments.

2.5 Human Rights and Communism in Eastern Europe

Marxism has both a humanistic human rights tradition and an authoritarian one. Marx and Lenin were opposed to the rights which were typical of capitalism and favoured the bourgeoisie. However this does not mean that they were opposed to rights as such. Political rights are a necessary complement to other social and economic rights. It is incorrect to treat Marxism as a philosophy which is indifferent to human rights.

As has been maintained, there is a difference between individualistic and collectivist types of human rights. The situation in the Soviet Union, according to certain scholars, did not depend on Marxist political theory but on an authoritarian state permeated by orthodoxy. Both the structure before 1917 and the traditions of the Orthodox church did not allow individual political rights to play a part. Individualism was a belief linked to the Renaissance and the Reformation which had little influence on Tsarist Russia.

There was however a potential conflict between individual and collective rights in the socialist countries. The Russian Revolution served to catalyze the development of social and economic rights. The right to work and the rights to social security and education were recognized. Emphasis was laid on freedom from economic exploitation and the right to employment.

The development of men and women's human rights was regarded as dependent on the interests of the proletariat. In the Soviet Union, human rights were linked to the state's ability to liberate the proletariat. Needs were to be met by economic planning and social development and not through the articulation of individual demands within a free-market economy.

Russia in contrast from the rest of Europe never experienced a period of liberal democracy. Individual liberties were never attained.

The state in the Soviet Union (Party and government) played a dominant role in the definition and implementation of rights. Planning secured the right to full employment but the lack of a market and the absence of private ownership eliminated the rights to individual production and trade. The European thinkers of the 18th and 19th century emphasized the rights of the individual as individual.

Aspects of Marxist theory which were alien to bourgeois society and which were regarded as characteristic bourgeois class rights, were compounded with traditional values and led to the introduction of a political system which gave scant emphasis to individual human rights.

In Poland, Solidarity campaigned for human rights. Solidarity was a mass movement drawing support from workers, intellectuals and peasants. It contained communists, non-communists and anti-communists.

In the Soviet Union, a number of human rights movements emerged agitating for the rights contained in the UN declaration of human rights. However they did not enjoy the same success as Solidarity in Poland.

Nationalism and the church were two traditional powerful forces in Poland whereas the church had little popular support in the Soviet Union. In those parts of the Soviet Union where the church was in a stronger position, there was a corresponding greater support for Western ideas about human rights. In Poland, the church and the intelligentsia have a long history as independent forces in asserting the traditions of the Polish nation. Russia has had no tradition of pluralism and has always been more isolated geographically and intellectually from the West.

Solidarity in Poland, the political reform movement under the leadership of Dubček in Czechoslovakia, paved the way for increasing demands for civil rights in state socialism. This is true even although the reform movement in

Czechoslovakia led to a Russian invasion, Solidarity was crushed and the dissident movement witnessed many violations of rights.

References

The literature on human rights with particular emphasis on the East-West dimension is extensive. See for example A. D. Sakharov, Progress, Coexistence and Intellectual Freedom, 1968, V. Chalidge, To Defend These Rights, Human Rights and the Soviet Union, 1975, which deals with developments up to 1973 and M. Bordeaux, H. Henly, F. Voss eds. Religious Libery in the Soviet Union, WCC and USSR, a Post-Nairobi Documentation.

2.6 The Helsinki Meeting 1975 as a Turning in the Movement for Human Rights

In putting his name to the Helsinki document's basket 3, which concerned human rights, Leonid Brezhnev signed the official death certificate of Stalin's empire. This event and those which followed it paved the way for the fall of communism in Eastern Europe.

Helsinki groups were formed throughout the communist world. Among the Soviet human rights activists, there were such people as Jelena Bonner, Juri Orlov, Alexander Ginsburg, Anatoly Sharansky, Pjotr Grigorenko. In Central Europe, the Helsinki document was crucial for the building of Charta 77 with Václav Havel as the leading intellectual spokesman in Czechoslovakia. In Poland the Solidarity leaders cited the document in defence of their organization.

The Helsinki process led to a number of concrete results. In Czechoslovakia, intellectuals and concerned citizens with varying ideological backgrounds signed Charta 77 in 1977. Its manifesto was based on Czechoslovakia's ratification of the final Helsinki document and of the two UN Conventions on human rights. It held that in Czechoslovakia human rights only existed on paper. Examples were given of how rights were violated in Czechoslovakia. Measures were taken against the signatories of Charta 77. The communist signatories held that the reactions of the government served to discredit socialism not simply in Czechoslovakia but throughout Europe.

The normalization under Husak did not go according to communist plans. Behind Charta 77, there were both leading cultural figures and the church. The charter was an initiative to provide an intellectual and moral foundation for a broadly based defence of human dignity and human rights. The Catholic cardinal Tomasek derived human rights from the Gospel and its demand that we should attend to the persecuted.

In Yugoslavia, Milovan Djilas, a former leader of the communist party, appealed to Western European communist parties to support Charta and the movement for human rights not only in Czechoslovakia but also in his own country where there were as many political prisoners as in the Soviet Union.

70

In the Soviet Union, a committee was set up under Juri Orlov to monitor the implementation of the Helsinki agreement. Andrej Sakharov formed the Soviet committteee for human rights. In 1978, Juri Orlov was sentenced to seven years in a labour camp and banishment for five years following a trial from which all Western observers and Andreij Sakharov were excluded. The Helsinki document showed that in communist countries human rights were no more than scraps of paper.

The Helsinki groups were persecuted. Communist authorities accused them of being agents of Western propaganda. The activists held the governments responsible for the maintenance of those human rights which they had endorsed in the Helsinki document.

Western human rights organizations worked on behalf of the Helsinki groups in the communist countries. Among such Western groups was Scientists for Sakharov, Orlov and Sharansky. They gave material and moral support to human rights activists behind the Iron Curtain and helped the Carter and Reagan administrations to spotlight Soviet and Warsaw Pact violations of human rights at follow-up conferences to Helsinki, which were held at Belgrade (1977–78), Madrid (1980–83) and Vienna (1986–89).

The policy of *glasnost* brought about the return of the Sakharovs from Gorki to Moscow at the end of 1986 as well as the release of 200 dissidents and permission for well known Jews to emigrate from the Soviet Union.

The brutal nature of Soviet totalitarianism was displayed in the Soviet authorities' inhumane treatment of prominent figures such as Alexander Solzhenitsyn and Andrej Sakharov and the show trials against Anatoly Sharansky, Juri Orlov and Vladimir Bukovsky.

There were many contacts between Western journalists and Soviet dissidents at the beginning of the 1970s. Andrej Sakharov's interviews with the Western press in his Moscow apartment, are the best illustration of how information about the activities of the dissidents was easily spread. In 1980, such contacts were almost completely broken by the KGB's arrest of dissident leaders. This break in contacts was best symbolized by the inner exile in 1980 of Sakharov and his wife, Jelena Bonner, to Gorki, a city which was closed to Western visitors.

In Russian political and social thought, individual rights have always been subsidiary to collective ones. For this reason, the dissidents were accused of injuring the Soviet state and the interests of its people. The Soviet leaders could not comprehend the Western support for the dissidents' cause.

References

A. Bloed (ed.) From Helsinki to Vienna: Basic Documents of the Helsinki Process. 1990, A. Bloed and P. van Dijk (eds.) The Human Dimension of the Helsinki Process, the Vienna Follow-up Meeting and its Aftermath, 1991.

Dokumente der Moskauer Helsinki-Gruppe, Texte der Förderungsgruppe zur Erfüllung der Beschlüsse von Helsinki in der UDSSR,1977, deals with human rights in the Soviet Union in the aftermath to the Helsinki meeting.

A. Sakharov, Memoirs 1990, and Alarm and Hope, 1978. L. Alexeyeva, Soviet Dissident, Contemporary Movements for National, Religious and Human Rights, 1987.

Dramatic events led to revolution and a change of system in Czechoslovakia, backed up with civil support. A firsthand view of this upheaval is presented in B. Wheaton and K. Zdenek, The Velvet Revolution: Czechoslovakia 1988–1990, 1991. See also H. Gordon Skilling, Charter 77 and Human Rights in Czechoslovakia, 1981.

In I. G. Stokes (ed.) From Stalinism to Pluralism: A Documentary History of Eastern Europe since 1945, 1991, the historical developments are sketched by several authors from the Yalta negotiations of 1945 to Vaclav Havel's New Year Message of 1990, "People, your political power has been restored".

2.7 Human Rights as an Instrument of Foreign Policy

At Helsinki 1975, it was agreed that the maintenance of human rights is important for the foundation of a lasting peace and for security and cooperation. Human rights groups were set up in the Soviet Union but were persecuted until the Vienna conference on security and cooperation in 1986. The new "openness" in the Soviet Union had an effect on human rights. In 1989 at the end of the conference, an agreement for the protection of human rights was signed with the Soviet Union as one of the signatories. At Helsinki, the signatories bound themselves in the declaration on principles guiding relations between the participating states, to respect human rights and basic liberties including freedom of thought, conscience, religion and belief.[24]

The movement for human rights launched by President Jimmy Carter was preceded by the civil rights movement in the USA led by Martin Luther King Jr. and by the Helsinki process. From 1977, Jimmy Carter concentrated his campaign for individual human rights exclusively on political rights and this produced reactions in the Third World and the communist countries. When he became president, he sent a letter to the Soviet dissident Andrej Sakharov, promising continued commitment to the promotion of human rights. At the UN in 1977, Carter maintained that those who had signed the UN charter had also bound themselves to respect human rights. No member state of the UN can insist that the violation of the rights of its own citizens is purely an internal matter for that state.

In opposition to Jimmy Carter's advocacy of the Western view of human rights, the Third World and Communist leaders insisted that human rights were more a matter of economic, social and cultural guarantees than political and civil rights.

In 1981, Konstantin U. Chernenko. later the General Secretary of the Soviet communist party, published a book entitled *Human Rights in the Soviet Union*. He held that human rights in the West often exclude social and economic rights. In Western countries, there was no guaranteed right to employment, to

---

[24] The Helsinki Final Act from 1 August 1975 in P. Sieghart, The International Law of Human Rights, 1983, p. 31.

free higher education or to free medical care. In the Soviet Union, according to Chernenko, socio-economic rights and liberties provide the foundation for the enjoyment of political and personal rights.[25]

Among Christian thinkers, there was divergence of opinion about states making possible use of human rights as an instrument in regulating their relations to one another. Jacques Maritain adopted a more or less idealist standpoint while Reinhold Niebuhr was more of a realist. This is clear from their written works: J. Maritain, *Integral Humanism, Temporal and Spiritual Problems of a New Christendom*, 1968 and *The Rights of Man and Natural Law*, 1943, R. Niebuhr, *The Structure of Nations and Empires: A Study of the Recurring Patterns and Problems of the Political Order in Relation to the Unique Problems of the Nuclear Age*, 1959. Niebuhr reckoned that national self-interest and sin would constitute the crucial factor in attempts to implement human rights. Niebuhr's realism was based on the assumption that nations must act in their own interests. At the same time, this realism also embodies a belief in the value of the person as one created by God. It appeals to nations to seek domains where the advancement of human rights coincides with national interest.

The USA used human rights issues to hide interventions dictated by its own national interest. The rhetoric of human rights was employed to undermine ideologically and economically the Allende government as part of the Cold War policy against the Soviet Union and to justify the covert war against Nicaragua. At the same time, the human rights situation in El Salvador was defended when it was in fact worse than in Nicaragua.

President Carter's human rights initiative was followed by passivity when Ronald Reagan was elected to the presidency in 1980. International security and arms agreements moved to the centre of political attention.

The Soviet invasion of Afghanistan, the collapse of the Polish Solidarity movement, the shooting down of a Korean commercial aircraft and the discussion of President Reagan's Star Wars meant that less attention was paid to human rights issues.

During the 1970s, due to relatively good US-Soviet relations, Western support was more successful in protecting dissidents in the Soviet Union and preventing them from being imprisoned than was the case during the 1980s. As a result of the Soviet Union reducing contacts with the West in response to the deterioration in East-West political relations, Western influence had little effect in preventing the Soviet persecution of dissidents.

Human rights were also used as an instrument in the fight against racism in South Africa. South Africa was the only country in the world to have a system of legalized racism. Only the whites who formed 16% of the population enjoyed full civil rights. The apartheid system rested on inequality. Blacks were not allowed to vote; they had no freedom of movement and were unable to live and work where they pleased. The freedom to express one's opinion, the free-

---

[25] K. U. Chernenko, 1981, p. 4, 142. See also, L. I. Brezhnev, Socialism, Democracy and Human Rights, 1980.

dom of the press and the right of free association—all these were denied them. A number of countries, notably Norway, Canada, Sweden, Denmark, France, Japan and the USA, actively opposed the racist social system in South Africa by trade and investment embargoes. Their actions demonstrated a worldwide opposition to support for the apartheid regime in South Africa.

References

Human rights have functioned as a tool of foreign policy. There is an extensive literature on this subject. N. H. Kaufman, The Dynamics of Human Rights in US Foreign Policy, 1981; J. Muravchik, The Uncertain Crusade: Jimmy Carter and the Dilemmas of Human Rights Policy, 1986; N. C. Nielsen, The Crisis of Human Rights, An American Christian Perspective, 1978, with main emphasis on human rights during Jimmy Carter's presidency; M. Novak and R. Schifter (eds.) Rethinking Human Rights, Speeches by United States Delegation to the 37th Session of the United Nations Commission on Human Rights, Geneva, Switzerland, February 2–March 14, 1981; The Foundation for Democratic Education, INC 1981; B. M. Rubin and E. P. Spiro (eds.), Human Rights and US Foreign Policy, 1979, a product of the Carter administration's focus on human rights issues; C. Stern, Strategien für die Menschenrechte, 1980, provides a panoramic view of human rights in the Jimmy Carter era.

In Human Rights and World Politics, 1991, J. Donelly introduces human rights as a postwar global issue with a comparative discussion of human rights and the part they play in the foreign policy of many Western countries.

J. Wronka analyzes the interaction between the UN and the USA on human rights in Human Rights and Social Policy in the 21st Century, A History of the Idea of Human Rights and Comparison of the United Nations Universal Declaration of Human Rights with United States Federal and State Constitutions, 1992.

2.8 Three Generations of Human Rights

Individuals have played a central role in the struggle against injustices in the sphere of human rights. Andrej Sakharov founded the movement for human rights in the Soviet Union in 1970; similarly Martin Luther King Jr. displayed heroic courage in the field of human rights in the USA. They took personal risks in the fight for human rights.

A tested division of human rights according to different generations, beginning with the French Revolution's slogan " Liberté, Égalité, Fraternité" supports the truth of the contention that human rights depend on the social context in which they arise. This division was put forward by the French lawyer Karel Vasak in The International Dimensions of Human Rights, 1–2. 1982. For part of the 1970s, Karel Vasak was head of UNESCO's section for human rights and peace.

The first generation of civil and political rights arose among the 17th and 18th century reformist thinkers associated with the English, American and French revolutions. These rights emerge from the political philosophy of liberal individualism and the economic and social doctrine of laissez-faire.

The second generation of economic, social and cultural rights can be traced to the socialist tradition beginning with the followers of Saint-Simon in early 19th century France and extending to subsequent movements dedicated to the revolutionary struggle. These rights are a response to capitalism's use and abuse of the concept of individual liberty which tolerated and legitimized the exploitation of the working class and the colonial peoples.

In the first generation, the notion of freedom was central whereas in the second generation social equality was assigned the greatest importance.

The third generation of rights is a product of the rise and fall of the national state in the second half of the twentieth century. They presuppose *a social and international order* for their implementation. A basic underlying factor is the growth of Third World nationalism and its demand for a global distribution of power, affluence/welfare and other important goods. This generation of human rights has both an individual and collective dimension. It is the collective right of all peoples to ensure *a new international economic order* which will remove obstacles to their economic and social development. It is also the individual right of all human beings to enjoy a development policy which is based upon the satisfaction of material and non-material needs.

The three generations of rights are associated with different stages of modern history. The first generation of rights came into being with the "bourgeois" revolutions of the 17th and 18th centuries; the second generation of rights was brought about by the social, political and Marxist revolutions of the twentieth century; and the third generation of rights enters the scene with the anti-colonialist revolutions which began after the Second World War.

The three generations of human rights are codified in the UN general declaration of human rights: the first generation in articles 2–21,[26] the second generation in articles 22–27[27] and the third generation in article 28 which proclaims that "everyone is entitled to a social and international order in which the rights and freedoms set forth in this Declaration can be fully realized."[28]

References

Martin Luther King Jr. was one of the most significant human rights activists in the postwar period. There is an extensive literature both by and about him. His speeches have been published in J. M. Washington (ed.), A Testament of Hope, The Essential Writings and Speeches of Martin Luther King, Jr., 1986. For an illuminating intellectual biography, see J. J. Ansbro, Martin Luther King Jr., The Making of a Mind. It identifies and discusses the sources which influenced King's intellectual views, among them Anders Nygren and Gandhi as well as personalism. King's views were made up from many differing components which the book uncovers. An inspiring portrait of King is given by S. B. Oates in Let the Triumph Sound, The Life of Martin Luther King Jr., 1982. A. D. Morris, The Origins of the Civil Rights Movement, Black Communities Organizing for Change, 1984, is illuminating about the Civil Rights movement.

---

[26] G. Melander (ed.), 1990, 13–16.
[27] Melander, op. cit., 16 f.
[28] Melander, op. cit., 17.

2.9 The UN Documents on Human Rights

The UN documents on human rights have been formulated in the light of grave anomalies since 1945. They are aimed primarily against racism and sex discrimination. At the Nuremberg trial in 1945, the Nazi leaders were found guilty of crimes against humanity.

Adolf Hitler, Josef Stalin, Idi Amin och Pol Pot have all been responsible for colossal acts of barbarism.Idi Amin in Uganda, Pol Pot in Cambodia and Alfred Stroessner in Paraguy are guilty of mass murder.

During the 1970s and 1980s, people have vanished in Argentina, Brazil, Chile, Guatemala, the Philippines, Afghanistan, Cambodia and Ethiopia. They have been arrested, tortured and killed.

Racism was displayed in the treatment of Jews in Nazi Germany and of blacks in South Africa. Apartheid means race segregation and limits the lives of non-whites socially, politically and economically. The blacks were denied political rights; they had no freedom of movement, freedom of residence, freedom of employment or freedom to marry. Strikes in the mines where 90% of the workers were black, were brutally suppressed. Their wages lay under an existence minimum and they had to work in conditions which were inhuman from a health and safety standpoint.

Discrimination against women is widespread. They represent half of the world's population and a third of its labour force but receive only a tenth of the world's income and own less than one per cent of the world's property. Women form the majority of the world's illiterate, unemployed and poor. Women and children make up most of those starving. The majority of refugees are women and children. Girls are more often the subject of sexual assault. Women have less hours for themselves: apart from their paid employment, they look after the home.

In addition to its general documents on human rights, the UN has found it necessary to issue special documents directed against race discrimination, the discrimination of women and children and against all forms of religious intolerance. Racial, sexual and religious discrimination are rejected in the political and economic convention (1966,1976). The international convention for the elimination of all forms of racial discrimination was adopted in 1965 and took effect from 1969.[29] The convention on the elimination of all forms of discrimination against women was adopted in 1979 and took effect from 1981.[30] The convention on the elimination of all forms of religious intolerance was adopted in 1981.

References

In The Social and Legal Status of Women: A Global Perspective, 1990, W. Hagon compares the status of women in five countries, taking into account cultural back-

---

[29] Melander, op. cit., 19–33.
[30] Melander, op. cit., 79–92.

ground, legal traditions and social status. K. Tomasevski is the author of the volume Women and Human Rights, 1993. For more about women's rights, see A. Yotopoulos-Marangopoulos (ed.) Women's Rights Human Rights 1994 and The Human Rights Watch Global Report on Women's Human Rights, 1995.

An illuminating treatment of children's rights is to be found in M. Freeman and P. Veerman (eds.) The Ideologies of Children's Rights, 1992. See also S. MacPherson, Five Hundred Million Children, Poverty and Child Welfare in the Third World, 1987.

T. J. M. Zuijdwijk studies complaints to the UN about national governments' violations of human rights in Petitioning The United Nations, A Study in Human Rights, 1982.

In The United Nations and A Just World Order, 1991, R. A. Falk, S. S. Kim and S. H. Mendlovitz (eds.) provide a theoretical foundation for evaluating UN promises in the post Cold War world.

In The Age of Rights, 1990, L. Henkin present a learned exposition of the global growth of human rights in the postwar period, which emphasizes the comparison between the significance of rights in international law and in the constitutional context of the USA.

2.10 John Rawls and Agnes Heller on Human Rights

Amnesty International is perhaps the voluntary organization which is best known among activists for its work on behalf of people who have been victims of human rights violations. It is an organization which is geared to action in concrete cases. This does not mean, however, that Amnesty is not interested in the presentation of the human rights issue from a more theoretical perspective. Proof of this is to be found in the publication S. Shute and S. Hurley (eds.) *On Human Rights, The Oxford Amnesty Lectures 1993* (1993) with contributions from several internationally famous philosophers including John Rawls and Agnes Heller.

John Rawls is professor of philosophy at Harvard University and is one of the foremost political philosophers in the English-speaking world. In *A Theory of Justice,* 1971, he attacked utilitarianism. In contrast to the utilitarians, Rawls distinguished between a theory of rights and a theory of goodness. The former he based upon principles of universal rationality but this was not the case with the latter. Rawls' ethical theory combined universalism with agnosticism.

Later Rawls no longer insists on this contrast. The theory of rights is not based on principles of universal rationality. It is, however, more general in application than the theory of goodness which is relative to particular people. The generality of rights is now confined to the limits of liberal societies. Universalism in liberal politics seems to have been given up and with it the idea of a universal human rights perspective.[31]

The Hungarian born thinker, Agnes Heller, belongs to a group of scholars

---

[31] A detailed examination of John Rawls' philosophy of human rights is given in R. Martin, Rawls and Rights, 1985.

forced for political reasons to leave their positions at Budapest University in 1973. After a decade in Australia, she took up her present position as Hanna Arendt professor of philosophy at the New School for Social Research in New York. Her writings include the monograph Beyond Justice, 1987 where she criticizes the tendency of treating ethics and politics as being in harmony with one another. This assumption, she holds, underlies Rawls' work. Rawls is not necessarily condemned when he distinguishes between the right and the good. What is required is a recognition of the independence of rightness and goodness, politics and ethics. Liberty must be seen as the very centre of moral value and not simply as a political necessity. In the project *A Theory of Morals*, 1988, Heller develops a theory of moral value in accordance with this view.

Heller takes up crimes committed in the name of totalitarian regimes, whether to the left or right, nazi or communist. She asks if those guilty of these crimes should be punished. Her answer leads to a discussion of evil. She considers several arguments which can be used to support the view that even perpetrators of such evil are not to be prosecuted.

She examines a third—paradoxical—standpoint that although perpetrators of such detestable crimes are to be punished, they also should not be punished. The contradiction inherent in this view arises from a contextualized moral conflict. What is crucial is the break-down in consensus about how the perpetrators of such horrendous crimes are to be punished. This loss of consensus can destroy moral intuition and thereby the law of nature. Since new generations forget old crimes, there can be no consensus with respect to responsibility and the trials of war criminals. We have therefore a responsibility to tell and retell in our own times the history of what happened so that it is never forgotten and justice can be done.[32]

2.11 Scholarly Research on Human Rights

In this section, three basic books on human rights are presented. With a decade between their appearance, they constitute our present knowledge of human rights.

The *first* work by the French legal thinker, Karel Vasak, was originally published in French. An English edition appeared in 1982 with the title *The International Dimensions of Human Rights, I–II*. It is a fundamental classic exposition, perhaps the most extensive treatment which has been published. In addition to giving a historical perspective, both parts of this work describe current regulations and institutions relating to human rights.

The *second* work was published in 1992 and arose from a human rights conference in Canada held in 1989. It was entitled *Human Rights in Cross-Cultural Perspectives, A Quest for Consensus* and its author was the Moslem

---

[32] For an insight into the Heller's formative experiences, see A. Heller and F. Féher, From Yalta to Glasnost, The Dismantling of Stalin's Empire, 1991.

legal thinker Addullahi Ahmed An-Na'im. An-Na'im is an expert on human rights and Islam and on human rights from a bicultural perspective. In 1990, he published *Toward an Islamic Reformation: Civil Liberties, Human Rights and International Law.*

The *third* work, based on a German symposium, *Menschenrechte und kulturelle Identität, Ein Symposion*, appeared in 1991. The Jesuit, Walter Kerber, was responsible for publishing the book and the Protestant theologian Wolfhart Pannenberg is one of the contributors.

The above three works lay the foundation for a modern scholarly study of human rights. There is a gap of ten years between the publication of the first work and the other two. This reflects the shifts in focus and changes which have taken place in the field of human rights. All three are essentially written by lawyers although this legal approach is less dominant in the later works.

The three works are fundamental because they define a framework for research on human rights which cannot be ignored by later researchers in the field. Two possibilities exist. Either new research is linked to the framework laid down by these three works or else it adopts a quite independent approach and can justify this decision.

One of the weaknesses of the above works in my view is that they are so obviously the work of lawyers. The legal approach is entirely dominant. This means that technical views steer Vasak´s book. However a shift in emphasis is under way and this is reflected in the monographs of Ahmed An-Na'im and Kerber. In these latter works—at least in An-Na'im—there is an attempt to place the human rights issue in a historical context. This leads to a much broader perspective than is found in Vasak's work. The material in An-Na'im is mainly empirical whereas Kerber is more concerned with theoretical aspects.

The books of An-Na'im and Kerber illustrate a desire to make human rights an intercultural, interreligious and interdenominational matter but in both books it is admitted that they in fact derive from a Christian Western tradition. Closely linked to the cross-cultural aspects of human rights is the question of their universality and relativity. By insisting on their specifically Western character, one thereby also declares that they are relative.

Pannenberg and An-Na'im point out that the maintenance of human dignity requires that it is based upon the absolute. German secular society and the German secular state are neutral with respect to views of life or religion but they are also practically involved in the sphere of human rights. They face, however, a future problem with a concept of human dignity which is not grounded on the absolute. Pannenberg takes a pessimistic view of secular society's possibilities in the future.

The books of An-Na'im and Kerber are contemporaneous. One has emerged in the English-speaking world and the other in the German-speaking world but both tackle the problem from a bicultural perspective. Both also allow non-lawyers to express opinions. Pannenberg is one of the leading contemporary Protestant theologians and his participation is interesting. Both Pannenberg and

Küng treat human rights as an object for theological reflection. Pannenberg provides a deep and detailed theological discussion of the human rights issue.

There is a dramatic parallelism between Christians and Moslems when it comes to arguing theologically on behalf of human rights. This is apparent when one compares the books of Kerber and An-Na'im. The theological instruments and terms vary when Moslems and Christians motivate or justify human rights. Christianity and Islam after all represent different cultural and religious traditions. But the parallelism is apparent in their view about the relationship between what is universal and what is relative in human rights. Because Moslems and Christians base human rights on the absolute, universalism is conspicuous in their theological argumentation. On the other hand, Christians and Muslims are at pains to stress the relativity of human rights depending on the social and cultural context in which they are applied. Human rights are universal in theory but relative in practice. This way of arguing occurs among Catholics from Jacques Maritain to Hans Küng. Proceeding from natural law, they look upon human rights as an outgrowth of *lex naturae*. In Islam, human rights are an outgrowth of *sharia*.

Karel Vasak

Philip Alston is a prominent human rights expert. He is an Australian lawyer who has served at the UN centre for human rights. In 1992, he published a broad assessment of how the various UN organs had dealt with human rights issues in the book *The United Nations and Human Rights, A Critical Appraisal*. Almost 800 pages long, it provides a critical analysis of UN action on behalf of human rights between 1945 and 1991. The first part of the book deals with the work of the human rights organs within the UN. The second part deals with those organs charged with monitoring the implementation of agreements. The last part of the book deals among other things with the coordination of human rights activities within the UN system.

Alston is an eminent expert in regard to the human rights issue. He was responsible for revising Karel Vasak's 1978 almost 800 page long treatise in French on human rights and publishing it in 1982 in English translation in two volumes in cooperation with UNESCO.

A revised French edition of the original 1978 work appeared in 1990—A. Lapeyre, F. de Tinguy, K.Vasak, *Les Dimensions Universelles des Droits de l'Homme, I–III*. The first part deals with the spiritual and intellectual aspects of human rights. The second part discusses the legal aspects of the subject while the third part analyzes the economic and political dimensions.

As is apparent, the new French edition of Vasak's classic work reflects a shift in view regarding human rights so that they are no longer treated as an exclusively legal subject. The political, economic, cultural and religious aspects are now included in the discussion although it is the legal viewpoint which is dominant. The three editors are jurists.

The stronger position of religion in 1990 is emphasized by the fact that in the introductory volume of the new French edition, there is a discussion of the great cultures, world religions and human rights. Jewish, Christian, Moslem, Buddhist and Hindu views of human rights are presented alongside Asiatic, African, Chinese and socialist views of the issue. The relationship of the American and French revolutions to human rights receives special attention as does the relationship between the Anglican church and human rights. The precursor to the modern declaration of human rights, Magna Carta, was proclaimed in medieval England. Karel Vasak concludes the first part of his work with a categorization of human rights.

This shift from the dominant influence of capitalist and socialist ideologies in the first edition to that of the world religions and great cultures in the new edition of *Les Dimensions Universelles des droits de l'homme* reflects the changes which have taken place in the world with the collapse of Soviet communism and the end of the Cold War. Instead, the world's great cultures and religions enter as dominant and formative factors in the civilization process and world development. It is also evident in the significance of the world religions for human rights. This is reflected in the new French edition of Karel Vasak's fundamental work on human rights.

It is mainly jurists who contribute to Vasak's 1982 edition in English and the views that they hold of the human rights issue reflect that fact. However, they have different national and cultural backgrounds and these various traditions are expressed in their presentations. At the same time the work as a whole illustrates an early appreciation that human rights constitute an intercultural, interreligious and interdenominational matter.

Vasak sees it as his task to provide a scholarly formulation of human rights. In 1965, at the initiative of UNESCO, a critical examination took place at Oxford of the philosophy of the declaration of human rights and its meaning in different religious traditions, ideological and cultural contexts and against a background of differing dominant sets of values. In the second half of the present century, these rights are a fitting object for scholarly investigation. The contemporary phenomenon of human rights demands the development of a genuine knowledge of human rights where they are studied independently of a particular school of thought or of a particular interpretation of reality.

At a colloquium at Nice in 1971, René Cassin, the principal architect of the universal declaration of human rights and the head of the international institute of human rights in Strasbourg, provided, at the request of UNESCO, a rigorous definition of the study of human rights. According to Cassin, it is a specialism within the social sciences, devoted to studying human relations in the light of human dignity with the aim of determining those rights and duties which are necessary for the development of every human being's personality.[33]

In the UN, UNESCO's special task is the development of an independent

---

[33] K. Vasak 1, 1982, XV f.

science of human rights. A systematic study within the auspices of UNESCO has been initiated by the international institute for human rights in Strasbourg.[34]

It is necessary to create a legal system for the protection of human rights. For this, the cooperation of those exercising political power is required.[35]

Abdullahi An-Na'im

In the introduction to *Human Rights in Cross-Cultural Perspectives, A Quest for Consensus*, 1992, An-Na'im gives a definition of the term culture. It is used to denote the totality of values, institutions and patterns of behaviour which are passed on in a society and this broad cultural perspective covers views of the world, ideologies and known behaviour. In this sense, liberalism and Marxism are part of, or are ideological manifestations of, the culture of certain societies.[36]

An-Na'im makes some general observations about the implementation of human rights in a chapter entitled *Toward a Cross Cultural Approach to Defining International Standards of Human Rights.* An intelligent way of protecting and promoting human rights is to focus on the underlying causes of violations of these rights. These violations are the result of widely varying factors and forces including economic conditions, structural social factors and political action. Most often violations of human rights depend on human action or lack of it:they arise because individuals act or refrain from acting in a certain way. People are driven by selfish motives, by an avid desire for wealth or power or by a mistaken view of what is in the best interest of all. Even when they are motivated by selfish ends, human rights thinkers try to rationalize their behaviour by claiming that it is in accord with a morally justifiable goal.[37]

An-Na'im raises the problem of cultural relativity and universal validity as it arises in the issue of the formulation and implementation of human rights. The concepts he uses are cultural relativity and cultural universality with respect to human rights.[38]

In a chapter entitled, *Postliberal Strands in Western Human Rights Theory, Personalist-Communitarian Perspectives*, it is asserted that Jacques Maritain bases his conception of natural law upon the idea that there exists a human nature which is common to all human beings. Maritain then combines this with cultural relativity.[39]

The Norwegian, Tore Lindholm, has written on research programmes in the field of human rights in a chapter entitled *Prospects for Reseach on the Cultural Legitimacy of Human Rights, The Cases of Liberalism and Marxism.* In order to understand the worldwide discrepancy between theory and practice in the matter of human rights, we must understand the fundamental factors and

---

[34] Vasak, op. cit., XXI.
[35] Vasak, op. cit., 7.
[36] A.A. An-Na'im (ed.), 1992, 2.
[37] An-Na'im, op. cit., 19.
[38] An-Na'im, op. cit., 22–29
[39] An-Na'im, op. cit., 121 f.

forces which contribute to the maintenance of such discrepancies. On this point, Lindholm is in agreement with An-Na'im.[40]

1. We can study a particular empirically given culture and ask what difference this culture makes as regards the recognition and promotion of human rights

2. Alternatively we can choose some doctrinal component or manifestation of culture, e.g. an articulated system of belief or a political theory, and determine its role and potential as a positive factor or obstacle to the implementation of human rights.[41]

The first type of studies are to be carried out by social scientists and the latter by philosophers and historians of ideas. There is no sharp line of demarcation. Interdisciplinary cooperation is desirable.[42]

Lindholm approaches human rights from the perspective of analytical philosophy. A thorough study of the relation between ethics and human rights in modern philosophy is to be found in C.S. Nino, *The Ethics of Human Rights,* 1991. Nino presents a treatise in moral philosophy which sketches how the problem is tackled in modern philosophy.

An-Na'im sums up by saying that human rights are based upon particular cultural and philosophical assumptions. In the beginning, they were based on Western cultural and philosophical assumptions. Western hegemony (in economic, technological, intellectual and other fields) exerts a profound influence upon the ruling élites and upon research workers, scholars and activists in the Third World. In that world, people react to such philosophical ideas rather than attempting to articulate their own ideas and assumptions. This applies also to international discussions where questions of human rights are being negotiated and applied. Discussions of human rights tend to depend on certain underlying assumptions.[43] An-Na'im adopts a position somewhere between the universalists and cultural relativists, as regards human rights: "the reality of relativity does not mean, in my view, that an acceptable degree of genuine universality cannot be achieved."[44] Human rights must emanate from the world views and values of human beings: they cannot be forced upon them from the outside. If the present conception is not universally acceptable, we must work to make it so.[45]

Walter Kerber

In his editorial introduction to *Menschenrechte und kulturelle Identität*, 1991, Walter Kerber remarks that it is tempting to see human rights as a bridging concept which can form the basis of a nascent world culture.[46] There is a conflict between the universal claim of human rights, which is evident in the universal declaration of human rights of 1948 and the fact that this claim is

---

[40] An-Na'm, op. cit., 388.
[41] An-Na'im, op. cit., 390.
[42] An-Na'im, op. cit., 390.
[43] An-Na'im, op. cit., 427f.
[44] An-Na'im, op. cit., 430.
[45] An-Na'im, op. cit., 431.
[46] W. Kerber, Hrsg 1991, 10.

essentially rooted in the Western European moral and religious tradition and Western law.[47] This characterization of the problem is in agreement with that put forward by A. A. An-Na'im in his earlier analyzed work on human rights in a bicultural perspective.

In an article entitled *Transzendentale Intressen: Zur Antropologie der Menschenrechte,* O. Höffe maintains that there is a widespread view that the idea of human rights is linked to a determinate view of humanity. There is a Jewish view of humanity, a Moslem view and an atheist one. The view of humanity which has emerged in recent times, is individualistic. The concept of a view of humanity involves some degree of cultural relativization.[48] If we wish to provide legitimacy for human rights, we must free ourselves from views of humanity which are specifically Western and instead develop a doctrine of humanity which is independent of specific histories and cultures.[49]

Wolfhart Pannenberg spoke about *Christliche Wurzeln des Gedankens der Menschenwürde,* maintaining that according to the Christian conception, human beings derive their value from the fact that they are created in the image of God.[50] His contribution gave rise to a lively discussion at the symposium. The state and society are secular in Germany but what constitutes their rights requires some ultimate legitimacy. Without such a legitimacy, Pannenberg asserts, there is a vacuum. Religion can fill this vacuum although it does not need to do so. The secular institutions of society are faced with a crisis of legitimacy. A future without religion can be tricky for the state and society but not for the church.[51] In the USA, Pannenberg found civil religion which was composed of elements from the churches. The American nation had a religious foundation. There was no parallel to this in Germany.[52] Pannenberg, however, had no wish to recreate a denominationally monolithic society. Its history was too frightening.[53] At the same time, historically there has never been a society without legitimacy.[54]

In *Menschenrechte als Fundament einer Weltverfassung,* W. Schild emphasized that the classical theory of human rights presupposes the liberty, equality and independence of a person. The real situation in the world, however, is quite otherwise. The North-South conflict attests empirically to wide differences when it comes to opportunities for freedom. Many people in the Third World have no chance of becoming independent. Already as children, they are merely chattel, labour power and sexual objects which must be sold if they are to survive. Nor is it even the case in the Northern countries, that liberty, equality and independence can be taken for granted.[55]

---

[47] Kerber, op. cit., 11.
[48] Kerber, op. cit., 17.
[49] Kerber, op. cit., 18.
[50] Kerber, op. cit., 61–76
[51] Kerber, op. cit., 105 f.
[52] Kerber, op. cit., 103 ff.
[53] Kerber, op. cit., 115.
[54] Kerber, op. cit., 116.
[55] Kerber, op. cit., 177 f.

CHAPTER 3

Human Rights and the World Religions

3.1 Introduction

The close ties between the world religions and human rights is evident from
the fact that human rights are usually based upon a particular religious or
cultural framework. This conviction was in evidence at two meetings in 1949
and 1965 and again at two later occasions round about 1980. In the case of the
first three events, UNESCO acted as organizer. In 1949, it organized a symposium in London and in 1965 it arranged a round table meeting in Oxford. In
1979, a meeting of experts was held in Bangkok and dealt with the place of
human rights in cultural and religious traditions. The contributions to the discussion were published by UNESCO in *Human Rights Teaching Biannual
Bulletin, Vol II, No 1, 1981*[1] and Vol IV, 1985.[2]

On three occasions, UNESCO arranged for the subject of human rights to be
addressed and analyzed. The first two meetings are separated by sixteen years
and the later two by fourteen years. Thus in the course of a thirty year period,
these analyses have taken place at fairly regular intervals. In each case they took
place in the shadow of the Cold War and in the case of the two later meetings
against a background where there was increased emphasis on the conflict between North and South. The pairs capitalism and communism, industrialized
and underdeveloped countries, form the poles in world development.

The question posed already at the very first UNESCO meeting in 1949 was
whether there is a common normative basis for the idea of human rights. It is
striking that the participants presuppose the existence of human rights in their
own cultural spheres.[3]

---

[1] Meeting of experts in Bangkok, 1979: R.J.Zwi Werblosky, Judaism and Human Rights, T.
Ishida, The place of human rights in Japanese religious and cultural traditions, I. H. Al-Mafregy,
Islam and Human Rights, S. Chamarik, Buddhism and Human Rights Human Rights Teaching,
UNESCO 2:2, 1981.

[2] The London symposium, 1949: Chung-Shu Lo, Human Rights in the Chinese traditions, S. V.
Puntambekar, The Hindu concept of human rights. The round table meeting at Oxford, 1965:
Masami Ito, The problem of human rights in other Asian traditions, R. Thapar, The problem of
human rights in the Hindu and Buddhist traditions, A.A.W. Wafi, The problem of human rights in
the Islamic tradition, Human Rights Teaching, UNESCO IV, 1985.

[3] UNESCO (Hrsg) Human Rights. Comments and interpretations. A symposium edited by
UNESCO with an introduction by Jacques Maritain, 1949.

In 1986, UNESCO in cooperation with the international institute for philosophy in Paris published *Philosophical foundations of human rights*. The introduction to the publication was written by Paul Ricoeur. The essays in the book were written in the belief that human rights have a philosophical basis in different societies. Special sections were devoted to the cultural and religious context of human rights. In addition to the Western points of view with their distinction between individual and collective rights, a good deal of space was given to non-Western and post-colonial perpectives.[4]

The Journal of Ecumenical Studies at Temple University, Philadelphia was responsible for the fourth event by arranging, in the summer of 1982, for the publication of a series of articles on the attitude of various religious traditions to human rights.[5] *These contributions* were published in book form by Arlene Swidler with the title *Human Rights in Religious Traditions,* 1982. Her particular interest was otherwise in the role of women in religion and she was one of the founders and regular contributors to the Journal of Ecumenical Studies.

The first part of Karel Vasak's previously mentioned revised edition of *Les Dimensiones Universelles des Droits de l'Homme I–III* is devoted to an analysis of human rights within cultural and religious traditions. In 1978, however, the theme of human rights and world religions was only a marginal topic. The centre of stage was occupied by the relationship between human rights and ideologies such as capitalism and socialism. After the end of the Cold War and the collapse of Soviet communism in 1989, the question of human rights and the world religions became a dominant theme. The change in the world political situation was reflected in views about the role of the world religions in relation to human rights. Light was shed on the function of human rights in the great world religions.[6]

In the previously mentioned work, *Die Universitalität der Menschenrechte. Studie zur ideengeschichtlichen Bestimmung eines politischen Sclüsselbegriffs*, 1987, L. Kühnhardt provides an analysis of the relationship between the world religions and human rights from the standpoint of constitutional law. He is interested in the way in which the world religions have influenced ideas of human rights in the concept of the state and political society.

There is an extensive scholarly discussion of the historical roots of human

---

[4] Philosophipcal foundations of human rights, 1986: A.E.S. Tay and E. Kamenka, Human rights: perspectives from Australia; R. Inagaki, Some aspects of human rights in Japan; M.A. Sinacoeur, Islamic tradition and human rights; F. Zakaria, Human rights in the Arab world: the Islamic context; A.A. Mazrui, Human rights and the moving frontier of world culture; R. C. Pandeya, Human rights: an Indian perspective; F.M. Quesada, Human Rights in Latin America; P. J. Hountondji, The master's voice- remarks on the problem of human rights in Africa.

[5] A. Swidler (ed), Human Rights in Religious Traditions, R. Hassan, On Human Rights and the Quaranic Perspective; K.K.Inada, The Buddhist Perspective on Human Rights; K. Mitra, Human Rights in Hinduism; F. Polish, Judaism and Human Rights, Journal of Ecumenical Studies, 19:3 (Summer, 1982).

[6] A. Lapeyre, F. de Tingny, K. Vasak I, 1990: Judaism and human rights pp 81-112, Christianity and human rights pp 113-139, Islam and human rights pp 149-173, Buddhism and human rights pp 175-188. The section on Christianity and human rights was written by the Strasbourg theologian J.F.Collange who also published a monograph on Christianity and human rights.

rights. We touched upon this in the previous chapter. These roots are not simply secular but also include metaphysical, that is to say, philosophical and theological ideas. A. S. Rosenbaum gives an introduction to these issues in *The Philosophy of Human Rights, International Perspectives*, 1980.[7] According to some scholars, the American Bill of Rights of 1776 has religious roots and Max Weber and Ernst Troeltsch have asked what will happen with human rights when religion no longer has the same influence in the contemporary world. If religion provides a legitimacy for human rights, what is likely to happen when society loses its religious foundation?

It is an incontrovertible historical fact that the development of modern democracy has to some extent been influenced by the Judaeo-Christian view of the equality of human beings. All human beings are conceived as being equal before God. He has created and redeemed them. For that reason, they are all brothers and sisters.

The foundation of equality and liberty is to be found outside human nature. It is not present in humankind. In the Judaeo-Christian tradition, human rights are based upon God as creator while in the secular tradition such a foundation for human rights is lacking. The notion of human rights for all human beings, developed without reference to religious belief is a modern idea from the end of the eighteenth century.[8]

The attribution of a secular source to human rights is a phenomenon of modern times. In the American Declaration of Independence, the secular basis of human rights is emphasized. Human rights are ensured through a government which derives its legal power from the people and not from some supernatural source. For this reason, the American conception of liberty is secular just as American humanism is secular in character.

The concept of liberty as a political idea is, however, both theological and secular. Its theological character was influenced by Augustine and the philosophy of Thomas Aquinas. They put forward a theocratic view of liberty which dominated Europe for centuries. The modern conception of liberty is secular in contrast to the theocratic view. It recognizes the right of human beings to be free and their right to judge over their own political fate without any external intervention.

Secular humanism wishes to eliminate God and religion from its conception of human beings. In seeking to do this, it ends up, in the eyes of certain critics, sliding from the anthropomorphism of religion to anthropocentrism in the manner of Auguste Comte and Karl Marx.

Human rights are always a product of a given social structure and visibly incorporate to a greater or lesser extent certain religious components. Religions can facilitate or hinder the implementation of human rights. The

---

[7] A. Pollis, The Philosophy of Human Rights by A.S. Rosenbaum ed. Review in Human Rights Quarterly, vol. 4, no. 4, Autumn 1981, pp 150-152.

[8] J.V.Schall, Human Rights: The So-Called Judaeo-Christian Tradition, Communio:International Catholic Review 1981, 8(1), pp 51-61.

UNESCO problem was concerned with how religious traditions can contribute to respect for human rights in a world where there are examples of just the opposite.

References

Broad comparative approaches from the viewpoint of religious studies which are also relevant for the human rights issue, are to be found in R. M. Green, Religion and Moral Reason: A New Method for Comparative Study, 1988 and J. Hick, An Interpretation of Religion, 1989. For the understanding of cultural traditions, the following work is illuminating: R. C. Ulin, Understanding Cultures: Perspectives in Anthropology and Social Theory, 1988. Anthropology and human rights are discussed in T. E. Downing and G. Kushner (eds.) Human Rights and Anthropology, 1988.

3.2 Judaism

There are two notions in Judaism which are linked to the idea of human rights, namely the idea that human beings are created in the image of God and that Israel is God's chosen people. The Biblical myth in the form of a pictorial account of how human beings were created in the image of God and how we are all children to Adam and Eve, provides a framework for a religious philosophy of human dignity and human rights.

The idea of human rights is linked ultimately to the story of creation. According to it, human beings were made in the image of God. For this reason, all human beings must be treated with dignity. Implicit to the idea of the divine creation of human beings is the belief that all human beings are equal. Man and woman are equal because they were created in God's image. Human life is a divine gift. God giveth and taketh. Life and its fulfilment is the ultimate aim of the divine law. God also gives us property and land for ownership. It is dependent upon the will of God whether human beings are to have property and enjoy it. God also confers upon human beings the duty of work. They shall work for six days and rest on the seventh.

Human value thus derives from its divine origin and nature. Human beings are made in the image of God. They embody a divine image. In Jewish tradition, human rights are derived from Jewish belief. They were seen as being incorporated in Judaism. Although the concept or phrase itself is lacking in the biblical and rabbinical literature and in Philo, according to the Jewish view it is nonetheless there. Because the Hebrew bible or the Old Testament is common to both Judaism and Christianity, their contents furnish the source from which human rights can be traced.

The Jewish people looked upon itself as an instrument for God's purpose with the history of mankind. In this respect, it was a chosen people. Its struggle for survival as a persecuted minority reinforced the particularistic tendencies in group attitudes. The same experience also fired enthusiasm for, and devotion to, the cause of universal human rights. The fact that God has chosen

Israel for a special task does not conflict with the idea that all human beings are equal.

The expression "human rights" is based upon two assumptions. First of all, it assumes that there is a universal humanity and secondly, it assumes that each one of us belongs to this humanity. In Judaism, it is taught that human rights belong to the path which God has chosen for the world. To deny these rights is to stray from the divine path. There is an objective moral law which promotes norms for a just social order but human beings break the law in society and in private matters. The foundation of human rights in Judaism is to be found in the divine order of things. Human beings, like the rest of nature, have been created by God. Corresponding to this order, there are our human capacities, our conscience and reason. If the laws which steer relations between human beings are in accordance with divine law, they answer to the requirements of reason and satisfy our natural feeling for justice.

God is the originator both of human rights and of humankind's capacity to discover and defend them. With this discovery, we encounter the divine. We learn to know God by practising justice. When this knowledge leads to action, we serve God. Above all, economic needs must be satisfied. Human rights, like other moral ideals, are sometimes vacuous and hypocritical, consisting merely of words. Actions, therefore, play a fundamental role in Jewish teaching. It is better to define Judaism with reference to certain characteristic actions rather than in terms of a set of articles of belief. Judaism is a belief which can only be expressed in action.

The lack of human rights for Jews was an important factor in the growth of Zionism at the end of the nineteenth century. Theodor Herzl organized the political Zionist movement. The aim of Zionism was to bring about human rights for Jews by the creation of a Jewish state and a national consciousness for the Jewish population. The foundation of this state would guarantee universal human rights for Jews. Herzl's Zionism laid particular emphasis on the idea that the Jewish state would mark the end of antisemitism. The aim was a Jewish state in Palestine.

Judaism emphasizes individual rights and individual duties. The vision of social justice as preached by the Prophets is probably the most important contribution which Judaism has made to Western culture.

References

In Human Rights in Jewish Law, 1984, H. H. Cohen has traced counterparts to what we call human rights within the Jewish tradition. An older treatment of the same issue is to be found in M. R. Konvitz (ed.) Judaism and Human Rights, 1972. In D. Sidorsky (ed.) Essays on Human Rights: Contemporary Issues and Jewish Perspectives, 1979 emphasis is laid on the fact that human rights are rooted in the Nazi extermination of the Jews. In a chapter of this book, entitled Jewish Issues on the Human Rights Agenda in the First Half of the Twentieth Century, L. C. Green sketches the relationship between the movement for human rights and Zionism in the twentieth century.

3.3 Islam

A Moslem on Human Rights in Islam

There are a number of Moslems who have written interesting presentations of Islam for the Western reader Among these, we find A. A. Mawdudi, a conservative Sunni Moslem who criticized Western society and culture for its decadence and looked upon Islamic culture as greatly superior to its Western counterpart. He was a Moslem thinker with a not inconsiderable authorship which included such writings as *The Economic Problem of Man and its Islamic Solution, 1978*; *Islamic way of Life*, 1979; *Towards Understanding Islam, 1980*; *Unity of the Muslim World 1982*; *Rights of Non-Muslims in the Islamic State, 1982*; and *First Principles of the Islamic State, 1983.* In spite of his condemnation of both capitalism and socialism, he believed in a capitalist economy based upon free enterprise. As long as wealth can be earned lawfully, the state has no right to deny the individual the right of private ownership. In analyzing this problem, he provided an exposition of Islam on the basis of the Koran which reminded one of the papal social encyclicals from Rerum Novarum, 1891 to Centesimus Annus, 1991.[9] *The Islamic economic system* allows private ownership of the means of production, reasonable profit achieved as the result of investment as well as a recognition of the laws of supply and demand. Mawdudi is sceptical about certain aspects of capitalism but he condemns socialism. Socialism conflicts with human nature and the teachings of Islam. The command economy upsets the balance of economic life. For Mawdudi both capitalism and socialism are rooted in a materialistic view of life. This emerges as secularism in Western democracies and as atheism in communist countries.

In 1975, Mawdudi gave a lecture in Pakistan which was published the following year as *Human Rights in Islam* which more or less presents a programme aimed at disseminating widely in Western circles information about Islam's view of human rights. It echoes with familiar formulations and generally accepted value judgements from the Western discussion of human value. This would indicate that it is aimed more at groups outside Islam than within.[10]

Mawdudi begins by maintaining that the Islamic political system is based upon three principles: The Oneness of God, The Prophet and the kalifat. God is the creator of the universe. The principle of God's Oneness denies the idea of humankind's legal and political sovereignty. No individual, family, class or race is above God. Only God is the ruler and His word is Islam's law. According to Mawdudi, the medium by which we receive the law is known as the Prophet. We have recieved two things from this source 1) the Koran, the book in which God has set forth His law and 2) the authoritative interpretation and exemplification of this book of God by the Prophet Mahomet, by means of word and deed, in his capacity as God's representative. The principles upon

---

[9] A. Tergel, Church and Society in the Modern Age, 1995.
[10] C. Hedin, Alla är födda muslimer, 1988, p. 159.

which human life is to be based, are to be found in God's book. The Prophet has presented a model for life in Islam by setting forth the law and providing the necessary details. The combination of these two elements is called *shari'a*. *Kalifat*, Mawdudi stresses, means representation. Whatever represents God, can exercise divine authority. The state which is set up in accordance with the political theory of Islam, becomes a kalifat under God's dominion. Its task is to carry out God's purpose and will by acting on God's earth within the limits He sets and in accordance with His instructions.[11]

The kalifat consists of the whole society which is willing to fulfil the conditions for representation by accepting the principles of God's Oneness and the Prophet. Every person in a Moslem society enjoys the rights of God's kalifat and in this respect, all individuals are equal. No one has priority over another nor can one deprive another person of their rights. Their will is crucial for the formation of the government which acts in accordance with their wishes.[12] According to Mawdudi, the aim of the Islamic state is to encourage the qualities of purity, beauty, goodness, duty and welfare and to suppress and hinder all kinds of exploitation, injustice and disorder which are, in the eyes of God, ruination for the world.[13]

Islam has laid down universal, fundamental rights for humanity as a whole, which must be observed and respected unconditionally. Human blood is sacred and cannot be shed wantonly. It is not permitted to oppress women, children, the old, the sick and the wounded. Women's virtue must be respected unconditionally. The hungry must be fed, the naked must be clothed and the wounded must receive medical treatment whether they belong to Moslem society or are its enemies.[14] Islam has laid down, Mawdudi emphasizes, certain laws for non-Moslems who live within the boundaries of the Islamic state and their rights must form a part of the Moslem constitution. The Islamic state guarantees their protection. A non-Moslem's life, property and honour must be respected and protected in exactly the same way as that of a Moslem citizen. Non-Moslems shall be granted freedom of conscience and belief as well freedom to perform their religious rites and ceremonies in their own way. They are not merely allowed to propagandize on behalf of their own religion but are also allowed to criticize Islam. These rights are unconditional.[15]

When one speaks in Islam of human rights, what is meant according to Mawdudi, is that they are guaranteed by God. No authority has the right to take them away. Human rights are part of Moslem belief. Every Moslem who claims to be a Moslem, must accept and recognize them, as well as seeing that they are implemented. The rights which are sanctioned by God, are enduring and eternal.[16] The first and fundamental right is the right to live and respect for

---

[11] A.A. Mawdudi, 1976, p.7.
[12] A.A. Mawdudi, op.cit., p. 8.
[13] A.A. Mawdudi, op.cit., p.9.
[14] A.A. Mawdudi, op.cit., p. 10.
[15] A.A. Mawdudi, op.cit., p. 10 f.
[16] A.A. Mawdudi, op.cit., p. 14 f.

human life.[17] The second right is to make life secure.[18] Respect for woman's virtue is the third right.[19]The right to a basic standard of life is the fourth right.[20] The individual's right to liberty is the fifth right.[21] The right to justice comes in sixth place.[22] The equality of human beings comes in the seventh place.[23]

In summary,according to Mawdudi's exposition it can be said that if an ideal Moslem society existed, then the human rights which form an integral part of this society, would be recognized and implemented by law. A. A. Mawdudi analyzes the question of Islam and human rights from both Moslem and Western intellectual positions. His presentation of the problem provides a good example of how an ordinary reflective Moslem regards the issue.

Islam and Human Rights

Islam is a monotheistic religion which only recognizes two others, namely Judaism and Christianity. They are also monotheistic. The idea of human rights does not have its roots in Islam but in Europe. Human rights have been formulated in Islamic terms as is shown in the Islamic declaration of human rights of 1981. Once human rights have become an integral part of the Moslem tradition, they can be given a theological basis. For Moslems, human rights are based upon God. Divine right is present in every individual and collective right. An individual's rights are no more than their interests in this world and the next. All rights are divine rights. Human beings have certain rights which are guaranteed by God.[24]

The myth of human beings being created in the image of God which is found in Judaism and Christianity, is also to be found in Islam. As a result, human beings are God's representatives on earth. They are entrusted by God with ruling themselves. God has created human beings who seek perfection by seeking to imitate what is perfect. From the Moslem point of view, God is both freedom and necessity and human beings, since they are made in God's image, partake in both of these. Personal freedom is to be found in submission to the will of God and in inner purity so that human beings are released from all external conditions which set limits to freedom. Human rights are a consequence of human obligations to God, nature and other human beings. If we accept these obligations then we receive certain rights which are determined by divine law. Those who fail to meet these obligations, have no legitimate rights.

---

[17] A.A. Mawdudi, op.cit., p 17.
[18] A.A. Mawdudi, op.cit., p.18
[19] A.A. Mawdudi, op.cit., p.19.
[20] A.A. Mawdudi, op.cit., p 19.
[21] A.A. Mawdudi, op.cit., p. 20.
[22] A.A. Mawdudi, op.cit., p. 22.
[23] A.A. Mawdudi, op.cit., p. 23.
[24] For rights which can be derived from the Koran, see I M Malik, The Concept of Human Rights in Islamic Jurisprudence in Human Rights Quarterly, Vol 3, nr 3, Summer 1981, pp 61-63.

When Moslem writers discuss human rights and Islam, they distinguish between the function of human rights in Moslem societies and their function in Western societies. They accept the secularized view of human rights in the West but defend the religiously based Islamic view of human rights in Moslem countries. The secularized view does not belong to the Moslem world and they do not attempt to carry over the Islamic conception of human rights to the West.[25]

When Moslem writers put forward their view of human rights and Islam, they tend to polemicize on two fronts. First of all, from their Third World perspective, they emphasize a synthesis between individual and social rights in contrast to the clash of views between West and East during the Cold War. Secondly, they lay stress upon a religious view of human rights in contrast to the secularized view adopted by the Western world. The Cold War between the First and Second World produced a conflict between individual and social rights with the First World favouring individual rights and the Second World favouring social rights. Islam belonged essentially to the Third World and sought from its position to work for a balance between social and individual rights.[26]

The individual is not a sovereign entity in Islamic law, shari'a, as is presupposed in the liberal view of human rights. Only God is sovereign. According to shari'a, the individual has no right to private property. Everything belongs to God. Shari'a provides a basis for a right to the use of property. This view of ownership is contrary to the liberal understanding of the rights to ownership as these are reflected in Article 17 of the Declaration of Human Rights.[27] Islam advocates not a liberal state, but an Islamic theocracy. The duty of the state is to create conditions whereby Moslems can exercise the only fundamental human right, the right to serve God. From a Moslem perspective, the Western state is based upon a false dichotomy between the individual and society. It assumes that the interest of society can never coincide with that of individuals and that the common good never coincides with individual good.[28]

Another conflict also arises between the Western secularized view of human rights and the Moslem religiously based view. The Islamic criticism is that human rights are anthropocentric and not theocentric. They are based upon a human contract and not upon divine law. There is a gulf between the Western view of human rights with its roots in the Enlightenment and the Moslem theocentric view.

---

[25] See e.g. J. Berting et al. (ed) 1990, pp 133-143, 145-148 and A. A. Abdullahi- F.M.Deng,(eds), 1991, pp 104-132.

[26] R. A. Jullundhri, Human Rights and Islam in A.D.Falconer (ed) Understanding Human Rights, An Interdisciplinary and Interfaith Study, 1980, p 42.

[27] O. Melander,(ed), 1990, p. 15.

[28] A.A.Said deals with this theme in two essays in 1979: Human Rights in Islamic Perspectives in A. Pollis and P. Schwab (eds) Human Rights: Cultural and Ideological Perspectives, 1979, pp 86-100 and Precept and Practice of Human Rights in Islam in Human Rights Quarterly, Vol 1, nr 1, Jan-March 1979, pp 63-73.

References

There are several illuminating books and articles dealing with human rights and Islam, written by Moslems familar with the Western way of thinking. Among these are B. Tibi in The Crisis of Modern Islam. A Preindustrial Culture in the Scientific-Technological Age, 1988. He presents Islam as an ideology and indeed a political ideology. Islam is also presented as an Arabic ideology and culture. Tibi makes use of a typology which is reminiscent of Max Weber. He is quite correct in characterizing religions as traditional structures which form important elements in different cultures. This is most certainly true in the case of Islam. W. Brugger examines the theme of Max Weber and human rights in Menschenrechtsethos und Verantwortungspolitik, Max Webers Beitrag zur Analyse und Begründung der Menschenrechte, 1980. B. Tibi has also authored the book Islam and the Cultural Accommodation of Social Change, 1990. Among other works dealing with similar themes, there are S. M. Haider (ed.) Islamic Concept of Human Rights, 1978, M. Z. Kahn, Islam and Human Rights, 1970 and S. Kotb, Social Justice in Islam, 1953.

Although Islam extends far beyond the confines of the Arab world, the thought and acts of this world are closely bound up with Islam. Political and social thought in the Middle East is presented in K. H. Karpat (ed.) Political and Social Thought in the Contemporary Middle east, 1982. For women's rights see L. Beck and N. Keddie, Women in the Muslim World, 1978 and J. J. Nasir, The Status of Women Under Islamic Law, 1990.

The Idea of Islamic Reform

Islam is not a homogeneous entity but a multiplicity of interpretations and practices which vary in space and time. However, there does exist a unitary Islam represented by the scribes. There are also divergences to be found among them but they embrace a collection of traditions which contain many elements common to all of the Moslem world.

There is much in the Moslem tradition which is incompatible with human rights. In his work *Towards an Islamic Reformation. Civil Liberties, Human Rights and International Law*, 1990, Abdullahi Ahmed An-Na'im shows which areas of Islam are incompatible with human rights. In Islamic law, there is no such thing as equality before the law. Non-Moslems and women are subject to systematic discrimination. Freedom of religion and freedom of speech are lacking and apostasy from Islam is punishable by death. Punishments such as whipping, stoning, amputation and crucifixion are contrary to the human rights demand for humanity.

An-Na'im holds that this conflict can only be resolved through a new interpretation of Islam. He proposes Islam's fundamentally humane spirit as a suitable basis. There is a humane Islam which was revealed to Mahomet in Mecca. It is concerned with individual responsibility, divine omnipotence and love.

The later Islam is tied to a particular historical situation while the earlier Islam is norm-giving. This way of looking at the Koran implies that not everything in it is valid but must be judged in relation to both content and historical context. This means that An-Na'im rejects major parts of the Moslem revelation as irrelevant for today's situation. An-Na'im lives in voluntary exile in the West.

An-Na'im combines scholarship with activism. Every form of Moslem fundamentalism is alien to him. His starting point was the reformist Moslem movement, the Republican Brotherhood in Sudan. Conservative and fundamentalist Moslem leaders reject An-Na'im. His thinking is rooted in his own experiences as a jurist in Sudan.

The book *Islamic Law Reform and Human Rights, Nordic Human Rights Publications*, 1993 published by T. Lindholm and K. Vogt is based upon a seminar which took place in Oslo in 1992. The majority of contributors are positive to the idea of Islamic reform but are sceptical about whether An-Na'im's project can succeed.

Bassam Tibi adopts a secular standpoint and argues that the best way of bringing about a genuine respect for human rights is through an intensification of the secularization process in the Moslem world. Tibi maintains that human rights are part of the modernization process. He is disappointed with attempts to formulate Moslem accounts of human rights. They fail to meet international standards. This is evident in the limitation imposed on the individual in Moslem accounts. He speaks of a difference between cultural modernism and premodern doctrines. He stresses that Islam imposes cultural limits when it comes to the process of establishing respect for human rights.

Tibi develops his thoughts on Islamic reform in more detail in *Islamic Law Reform and Human Rights*, 1993 and in the journal article *Islamic Law/ Shari'a, Human Rights, Univeral Morality and International Relations.*[29]

Ahmed Abdullah An-Na'im and Bassam Tibi have been strongly influenced by West European and American universities. Bassam Tibi explicitly advocates a partial secularization of Islam. However they have little influence in the Moslem world. Developments in the political sphere tend to go in the opposite direction. The foregoing thinkers find themselves outside this process. The trend is instead towards Islamic fundamentalism and not towards Islamic liberalism.

Islam is much more of a religion of the book than other religions. In Christianity, the book points towards a person. The Bible is a witness to Jesus Christ. It does not cover the whole revelation but is a symbol for the revelation. The Koran does not refer to Mahomet. It is a verbally inspired formulation of the divine revelation.

The Islamic declaration of human rights of 1981 shows nonetheless that human rights can be pressed into a framework for shari'a and turned into a religious instrument. The Islamic declaration of human rights is a theological work which deserves to be defended by Islam. Human rights are made to serve religion. It is designed for a Moslem society. Its global implementation presupposes an Islamic world order.

References

K. Dwyer in Arab Voices: The Human Rights Debate in the Middle East, 1991 explains why Moslems argue that human rights are of central importance for Islam and what

---

[29] Human Rights Quarterly, Vol 16 Nr. 2, May 1994, pp 277-299.

these rights mean for men and women in the Middle East. For an illuminating work about the human rights issue in Islam, see A. E. Mayer, Islam and Human Rights: Tradition and Politics 1991.

There is an extensive literature about the role of Islam in the historical development of the Middle East. See M. Gilsenan, Recognizing Islam Religion and Society in the Modern Middle East, 1990; E. Mortimer, Faith and Power, The Politics of Islam, 1982 and E. Burke III and I. M. Lapidus (eds.) Islam, Politics and Social Movements, 1988.

B. Lewis's Islam and the West, 1993, is instructive about the issue of Islam and the West. Fundamentalism is a prominent feature in all world religions, not least in Islam. This issue is the subject of the American fundamentalist project J. Piscatori (ed.) Islamic Fundamentalisms and the Gulf Crisis, 1991 and M. E. Marty and R. Scott Appleby (eds.) Fundamentalisms Observed, 1991. Further information about Moslem fundamentalism is to be found in Y. M. Choueiri, Islamic Fundamentalism, 1990. A. Al-Azmek holds that fundamentalism is not a mainstream development in Islam in Islams and Modernities, 1993. The project religion and human rights which was set up in 1993 aims at increasing understanding of the relationship between religion and human rights. In its publication Religion and Human Rights, 1994, by J. Kelsay and S. B. Twiss, it discusses both fundamentalism and the relationship between universality and relativism in human rights.

3.4 Hinduism

Hinduism in general exhibits great variety and this is also true with respect to the history of human rights. It attaches greater weight to human duties than to human rights. Duties and rights are dependent on one another.

Hinduism could function both in support of human rights and in opposition to their implementation. Hinduism is a good illustration of the ambivalence of religion as regards the question of human rights. Orthodox traditionalists viewed Hinduism and the caste system as indissoluble. If the caste system is abandoned, Hinduism will vanish. This gave anti-Hindus an argument for asserting that Hinduism must be eliminated because only a non-Hindu system can ensure human rights. Modernist Hindus such as Gandhi and Radhakrishnan, however, argued that the removal of the caste system can be justified on the basis of a superior and more adequate understanding of Hinduism and its sacred writings. Human rights are promoted by progressive Hinduism. Mahatma Gandhi speaks for the movement for human rights within this type of Hinduism. He fought for an improvement in the conditions of the untouchables. Thus one and the same religion, in this case Hinduism, can be used for diametrically opposite purposes in arguments and actions relating to human rights.

In Gandhi's eyes, neither theistic nor non-theistic Hindu theology justified inequality between human beings. For theological Hinduism, human equality is based upon the fact that all human beings are created by God. Non-theistic Hinduism emphasizes the identity of being of all humans. Within non-theistic Hinduism, it was maintained,in analogy to Western secular humanism, that the freedom of the self is the very essence of human nature and that the protection of this freedom is a protection of human rights.

Nearly all wars have been fought on the grounds that they would secure rights and liberties. Medieval Europe was the scene of brutal wars, massacres and crusades to secure religious rights. During the twentieth century, world wars have been fought to preserve equality, liberty, justice and peace. Both the Allied and Axis powers during the Second World war declared that they fought on behalf of human rights. Human beings have murdered in God's name. In the historical situations which have been mentioned, there were important reasons for scepticism towards theistic religion.

The following points are adduced in polemicizing against theism. A cause of the conflict between religion and science is that despite the recognition of God as the supreme,omnipotent, omniscient and omnipresent being, traditional theology has always laid too great a stress on the view of God as a transcendental being and as an external authority who intervenes in human affairs and whose wrath entails punishment for those who break His commandments. Morality is therefore introduced from above. It is not an inner development. The following arguments are used to support non-theism. If God—the creative power from whom human beings derive as the highest product or crown of creation—is the supreme source of everything which lives, exists and has its being, then those elements within human beings which manifest their creative power, must be the very essence of their personality. Creative, not destructive, power in human beings is supreme: it is most expressive of their innermost self. When a human being's thoughts are creative and positive, when their feelings are harmonious and suffused with love and their actions are inspired by goodness and benevolence, their personality becomes integrated and their self from which intelligence, love and benevolence arise, is manifested. The recognition of this self as the origin of ethical, political and social judgements is a precondition for what is called many-sided humanism.

Non-theistic Hindu theology lacked a traditional transcendental concept of God. God is understood as the innermost core of human beings and human rights are then defined using this as a starting point. This way of arguing reminds one of the Western theologian Paul Tillich and secular humanism. Human beings' mental welfare, their happiness, peace of mind and refinement of personality depend upon their mutual relation to society and the state. They can choose a selfish attitude, laying aside obligations and merely claiming rights or a liberal attitude which entails the discharge of obligations and thereby the acquisition of human rights as a natural consequence. For non-theistic Hinduism, as for secular humanism, human rights are based upon the self.

As an illustration of non-theistic Hinduism, the argument could be formulated as follows. It was an unambiguous action on behalf of individual rights which enlisted Hindu tradition for this purpose. But these individual rights can be placed in a social context. There is a clear connection between individual and social rights. They depend upon one another. There is in human beings a spiritual presence which makes them dissatisfied with more superfical earthly matters. Human beings have within them a deeper self, which may be called the soul or spirit. In every human being, there is a light or inspiration which no power can crush. This is the true or real person. Our task is to discover that essential being, protect it and ensure that it can be used for its own good and for the good of humanity. It is the nature of man's real and deeper self to seek the true, the good and the beautiful in life, to venerate them and to fight on their behalf.

There is also a unpredicatble element in the human will and human nature is infinite in its composition. No system, order or law can satisfy the deep potential demands, whether in the domain of religion, politics, society or education, of a deep and complex personality. Human beings are often equipped with great potential energy and creative power which cannot be accommodated within the limitations of old formulations and doctrines. No system can satisfy a dynamic personality's growing demands. There is always something unanticipated or unfulfilled in the system. It is for this reason that we demand freedom for human beings. There is always a tendency towards new values and new ideals which arise within human life. No final formulations and systems can satisfy great thinkers and the needs and visions of all peoples and periods. Freedom is necessary because authority is not creative. Freedom gives scope for developing personality and creates conditions for its growth. No uniformity or conformity can help. It is first of all necessary to be a human being, to respect humanity and personality, to tolerate our dissimilarities and other paths for inner and external group behaviour.

Although it is necessary to speak of human rights in India, it is hardly possible in the light of the prevailing socio-cultural and religious-political situation. There are no human beings in the world, only people belonging to particular religions, races, castes or groups. We are involved in a state of war in the destruction of opposing groups. Our classes and societies think in terms of conquest and submission, not in terms of community and citizenship. A war is going on between groups and societies, rules and ruled, in the social community where all understanding of humanity and tolerance, humility and respect, has vanished. What matters in the world is destruction and despotism, world conquest and world order. The enormous hatred generated against human life and human progress has not left any room for humanity or human love in world politics. We desire freedom from want and war, from fear and frustration in life. We desire freedom from an all-consuming belief about the state, society and the church so that the individual can live an ordered life. We must have freedom to develop the idea of the good human life.

We must refrain from those things which make human beings too preoccupied with what is temporal and introduce higher spiritual goals and values. This is the foundation on which social life is to be built. We do not simply wish for the material conditions for a happy life but also the spiritual advantages of a good life. Human freedom has been debased by economic technocracy, political bureaucracy and religious intransigence. Five freedoms and five individual

98

duties are necessary for the good life. The five social freedoms are 1) freedom from violence 2) freedom from want 3) freedom from exploitation 4) freedom from disgrace 5) freedom from an early death and illness. The five individual duties are 1) the absence of intolerance 2) sympathy 3) knowledge 4) freedom of thought and conscience 5) freedom from fear and hopelessness.

References

M. Gandhi in None High, None Low, 1961 and in Autobiography: The Story of My Experiments with Truth, 1983 and S. P. Radhakrishnan in The Hindu View of Life, 1961 discusses the above issues. R. C. Zaehner, Hinduism, 1962 and M. Biardeau, Hinduism: The Anthropology of a Civilisation, 1992 are also illuminating.

3.5 Buddhism

Some people hold that Buddhism can hardly be presented as a religion: it is more of a philosophy of life. Buddha had a dynamic view of reality. Life, both in individual and social aspects, is a stream of changes. Fundamentally, however, life is essentially suffering. Human rights in Buddhism are linked to the question of human nature. Human nature is the source of human rights. Human relations have their basis in human nature. Individuals are responsible for bringing about an external concern with everything which lies within their experience. Human rights are expressions of human qualities such as security, freedom and life.

Dhamma is the name for the truth of existence, the true nature in which experiences take place. It is life's path of enlightenment. There is a link between the Buddhist norm and human rights. When human beings act morally, their true selves are revealed. Buddhism makes five moral requirements 1) to abstain from killing any living being 2) to abstain from stealing 3) to abstain from illicit sexual intercourse 4) to abstain from lying and 5) to abstain from using means of intoxication. Other traditions have similar requirements. In the Buddhist tradition, morality has precedence over politics. All living things have a right to live. To destroy life irrespective of its form, is a crime. Non-violence is therefore a consequence of this attitude.

Buddhism preaches non-attachment to worldly possessions. Property is considered as something evil. In practice, however, the acquisition of property is treated as something normal. The individualist tradition in Buddhism supports the kind of social and moral attitudes involved in human rights. Stress is laid on the rights of the individual. The Buddhist treats the notion of human rights as a legitimate extension of human nature, a formalization of mutual respect and concern for all human beings who derive from this nature. Buddha saw the norm for existence as a relation-dependent origin, in which every being is involved with every other being in the dynamic process of experience. To be a self means to go outside one's own self.

References

The Dalai Lama in A Human Approach to World Peace, 1984, provides a good insight into Buddhist thought. More about Buddhism and human rights can be found in C. Humphreys (ed.) The Wisdom of Buddhism, 1979 and W. Rahula, What the Buddha Taught, 1974.

3.6 Chinese Religion

Chinese philosophy has its roots in Buddhism, Taoism and Confucianism. The theory of individualism which forms the basis of human rights in the West, has no counterpart in Chinese thought. Chinese ethical theories hold that human life is primarily social. The family or community is the foundation which underpins and supports human relations. The human rights issue is seen from the perspective that relations between human being are only a step towards achieving harmony between all beings. The aim is to balance the rights of the individual with the interest of the community as a whole. From a Chinese standpoint, a person exists for others and is dependent upon others. It is impossible to deal with a person without at the same time taking account of the feelings of others. A person exists as a necessary part of the whole.

The idea of human rights involves the demand that every human being in their striving after self-fulfilment should be a moral person so that the ideals of universal harmony and peace are attained. A bridge is constructed between the ideal of universal harmony and the ideal of individual independence and freedom. The idea of human rights lacks Chinese roots: it comes from the West. The term "human rights" is translated by two words meaning "power" and "interest". The idea of human rights, however, as far as factual content is concerned, developed early in China. The right of people to revolt against their oppressors was introduced at an early stage. The will of the people is interpreted as the will of heaven. A ruler has a heavenly obligation to look after the interests of his people. When a ruler no longer governs to the advantage and welfare of the people, the latter have a right to revolt against him and unseat him. In Confucianism, there is the idea that a government should work according to the will of the people.

The idea of mutual obligations is considered as the basic teaching of Confucianism. The five fundamental social relationships which are described by Confucius and his followers, are the relations 1) between ruler and ruled 2) between parents and children 3) between man and wife 4) between older and younger brothers and 5) between friends. Instead of emphasizing rights, Chinese ethical thought laid stress upon the sympathetic attitude of treating fellow human beings as having the same desires and therefore, enjoying the same rights as oneself. By fulfilling these mutual obligations, one prevents violation of the rights of the individual. When it comes to the relations between the individual and the state, it is held that the people is the root of the country. In

100

earlier times, the broad masses of the people did not demand their rights. The welfare of the people depended on the good-will of the ruling class which neglected its obligations and exploited its subjects.

Emphasis is laid upon the right to live. The world is big enough for everyone. The earth's natural resources are sufficient for all people to live comfortably. Every individual has his due place in society and is likewise expected to contribute to society. No individual should be permitted to have more than his due or to live more extravagantly at others' expense. Arguments about human rights since the Communist revolution in China in 1949, are based upon the socialist view that collective rights are more important than individual ones and that the latter rights can only be satisfied if the people's rights are attended to. The Confucian tradition is used wherever it can be employed to bolster the interests of the commmunist state.

References

An interesting treatment of Confucianism can be found in S. Cromwell Crawford, World Religions and Global Ethics, 1989. H. Küng and J. Ching, Christianity and Chinese Religions, 1994 is also illuminating. The human rights situation in China is analyzed in R. Edwards, L. Henkin and A. Nathan (eds.) Human Rights in Contemporary China, 1986.

3.7 Japanese Religion

The Japanese religious situation is syncretist. Shintoism can mean different things. Sometimes it means a folk religion in Japan and on other occasions it refers to Shinto sects which have been influenced by Buddhism and Confucianism. Both Shintoism and Buddhism lack belief in a single absolute God. In both religions, there are many Gods or divinities, each with different functions. The Japanese religious tradition emphasizes the group rather than the individual. Both Shintoism and Buddhism have been closely linked to nationalism and the family. State Shinto, however, lacked a theoretical creed and it cannot be called a religion in the strict sense.

The role of religion in Japanese society is different from that in other societies in the sense that it is less influential than elsewhere. More important is the lack of a transcendent and universal religious creed which is operative in society. This creates various problems. One major problem is the lack of a transcendent or universal system of values which can support the idea of equal rights for all human beings. Since the boundaries of religion are unclear, it is difficult to identify what in the religion is inimical to human rights. Often threats arise from social pressures which are not necessarily dependent upon religion but in which religious elements are discernible.

The French concept of civil law became in Japanese the rights of the subject. It was an absurd idea that the subject could enjoy rights. Ideas from Western countries, however, made inroads. The theory of natural rights was expressed in Japan as a system of rights conferred on people by heaven. Heaven is considered the ultimate being in Confucianism. The ideology of human rights due to Western influences gradually gained ground in Japan from the end of the 19th century. However the traditional idea of absolutism lived on and imposed limits on its spread. An illuminating example is the position of women in Japanese society. Women were placed on an equal footing with men in the legal sense before the Second World War but the Confucian idea that a woman should obey her father before marriage, her husband during marriage and her son in old age forced women to accept a subordinate role throughout the whole of her life. The rights of woman did not work in practice. The situation in Japan, however, changed after the Second World War and an awareness of human rights developed in Japanese society.

References

An instructive guide to the above issues is given in J. Hsiung, Human Rights in East Asia: A Cultural Perspective, 1985.

3.8 Conclusions

The link between the world religions and ideas of human rights developed after the Second World War and was conditioned by attitudes in Europe and North America, with their strong Jewish and Christian influences. The idea of human rights originated in these geographical areas and was intimately associated with Judaism and Christianity and the various institutional expressions of these religions. In the period 1945 to 1995, the world religions were often used to justify and present the ideas of human rights outside North America and Europe. This was done by indicating points of contact between the ideas of human rights and the teachings of the great world religions. In this way, an essentially Western human rights ideology can be linked to central value-systems in the non-Jewish and non-Christian world religions. This has come about, however, after pressures from the West and under the influence of the old Jewish-Christian Western civilization. During the first decades of the UN and UNESCO's existence, the old Western powers dominated the world scene but from the middle of the 1960s, the so-called non-Christian countries of the Third World began increasingly to play an ever more central role in world politics and within the UN. Marxism was a crucial contributing factor in shifting the discussion from individual to collective rights. The ideology of human rights is not simply a subject where world religions come together: it is also a domain for ideologies competing with one another in an attempt to influence and determine world development. Ethics in Judaism and Christianity and the other world religions exhibit clear points of contact and their common ethical values such as respect for human life and human dignity can be linked with what is fundamentally a Western ideology of human rights. Thus this ideology can be made accessible outside those geographical regions which have been strongly influenced by Western enlightenment culture. They serve different interests in new parts of the world with elements taken from the dominant religions in these areas. The ideology of human rights is transformed from being essentially Western to being global in character. This process of development took place during a period between the fall of the Nazi dictatorship and the collapse of Soviet communism. It was also a period when the world religions contributed to the transformation of the ideology of human rights from something that is mainly concerned with Europe and North America to something that involves the whole world.

PART 2

Roman Catholic Christianity

CHAPTER 4

Human Rights and the Church in Latin America

4.1 From the Human Rights Movement to the Democracy Movement

The human rights movement arose mainly during the 1970s, as a reaction to the violence of the dictatorships in Latin America. From the start, the movement had strict ethical and humanitarian ideals and in several countries was led by organizations linked to the church. Often these were organizations which had been formed by the victims' relatives who were looking for people who had disappeared. The human rights movement subsequently developed on a wider front in terms of movements which questioned the legitimacy of the dictatorships and were working towards a return to democracy. In Chile, Argentina and Uruguay, the human rights movement formed the core of the democratic resistance movements.

Initially, the human rights movement was a defensive reaction to violence. It gradually evolved to become part of a movement for democracy. Human rights became the starting point for a new social doctrine where attention was fixed not only upon physical and civil rights but also upon social and economic rights, the right to a clean and sound environment and society's right to development. The human rights movement developed from protesting against the violence of the dictatorships to demanding the democratization of the whole social structure.

4.2 The Interpretation of Latin American Development

The nations of Latin America share a common language (Spanish, or in the Brasilian case, Portugese), a common religion (Catholicism), a common history which goes back to the discovery of America in 1492 and many common political, economic, cultural and sociological features. They also differ from one another. Paraguay differs from Argentina; Venezuela is different from Colombia; Costa Rica is unlike other Central American countries and so on. In short Latin America exemplifies diversity within unity.

A number of different models are used to interpret Latin American development.

1. *Marxism.* The Marxist intellectual framework can be useful for helping us to understand Latin America's development since the nineteenth century. Feudalism has been replaced by more capitalistic structures. In certain countries, there has been a transition from capitalist to more social democratic and socialist forms.

The engine behind these changes has been economic development. This development helped to undermine the old landowning class and stimulate the rise of the new business and entrepreneurial élite. It paved the way for the emergence of the middle class and gave rise to the trades union movement.

The Marxist paradigm offers an explanatory model for understanding the broad currents of development in Latin American history. It also,however, has its limitations. The majority of Latin American priests and officers come from the ranks of the middle class. The Marxist class theory does not explain why one group of officers or priests are drawn to the Left while others are drawn to the Right nor does it account for the various subdivisions within the respective groups.

2. *The development model.* This model has its origins in the social, economic and political developments of the 1960s. It was presented as an alternative to Marxism. It was based on experiences of development in USA and Western Europe and assumed that these experiences were universal and repeatable. The developing countries of Latin America were to be placed on a firm footing by means of development aid and technological know-how.

Aid was given to sponsor economic development in Latin America in the hope that it would lead to a higher standard of living. Economic growth was supposed to create a stable middle class and an enduring democratic and socially just political system similar to those of the USA and Western Europe. However, despite economic growth, the middle class did not become a bastion of stability. Lasting stability and democracy was not guaranteed.

The development categories had limited relevance in the case of Latin America. The developmental model was based on insufficient knowledge of Latin America and of its middle class,armed forces, trades unions and so on. Like the Marxist model, the developmental model was based on a vast global theory which is only in part applicable to Latin America.

3. *The power élite model.* The political system consists of a number of rival power élites—church, army, oligarchy. These groups seek influence and political power in accordance with special rules.

New groups can join the system subject to two conditions 1) they must demonstrate that their power could threaten the system 2) they must be prepared to moderate their demands in order to allow the older power élite to retain their influence.

This explanatory model was applicable where the Marxist and developmental models were not. It led to greater understanding of the dynamics of political change in Latin America. The model envisaged the Latin American political system as flexible and capable of modification but it did not explain the reversion to more authoritarian structures. It did not allow for international or external forces.

4. *The corporativist model.* The starting point of this model was dissatisfaction with the inability of the three previous models—the Marxist model, the developmental model and the power élite model—to explain the development which had taken place. It tried to understand Latin America on its own terms, by taking account of its often Catholic, authoritarian, hierarchical, corporativist underlying assumptions rather than in terms of some ethnocentric North American list of political preferences.

The corporativist model sought to throw light on phenomena which remain unexplained on the basis of other models. It tried to clarify the corporative organization of Latin American social and political life, contrasting it with the pluralistic system of the USA with its many different interest groups. It was also useful in improving understanding of the structure of Latin American labour-employer relations, the dominant and paternalistic role of the state, the nature of group interaction the quasi-mercantilist nature of the economy, the special position of the church and army, the social security system and the functions of the bureaucracy.

The corporativist model caused disquiet because it seemed to presuppose the identification of corporativism with fascism. But fascism is only one form of corporativism. Corporativism in Latin America usually took more catholic and non-totalitarian forms. Corporativism could occur in democratic or open forms as well as in authoritarian ones.

5. *The bureaucratic-authoritarian model.* The bureaucratic-authoritarian and corporativist models were put forward for the same reason. They both tried to explain why development in Latin America had failed to correspond to the development patterns of the already industrialized nations and why the most advanced of the Latin American nations—Argentina, Brazil and Chile—during the 1960s and early 1970s reverted to authoritarian rule, albeit of a modernized type which differed from the one-man dictatorships of the past.

The bureaucratic-authoritarian model arose from the failure in Latin American developmental strategy to produce locally what had previously been imported. This resulted in unemployment, economic stagnation, a growing balance of payments problem and increasing mass unrest. The military (the bureaucratic authoritarian establishment) intervened to prevent outbreaks of revolution and to pave the way for a more conservative development strategy.

The model was useful but problematic. It did not apply to all countries equally well. The political trends towards democracy at the end of the 1970s meant that the bureaucratic-authoritarian explanation needed to be seriously reassessed.

6. *The dependence theory.* The dependence model held that the basic problem as regards the underdevelopment of the region, derives from Latin Amer-

ica's dependence on the outside world i.e. on the USA. It assumed that development in the USA had taken place by allowing Latin America to remain underdeveloped. Latin America is dependent upon the external world. USA is sometimes too involved in the internal politics of Latin America. Large US multinational companies become involved in practical matters there. The international banks dictate the rhythm of Latin American development.

Dependence is, however, not the only cause of Latin American underdevelopment. The dependence model is often used by Latin Americans to blame their problems on the USA instead of examining their own societies for the causes. The dependence model has been used as a Marxist-Leninist argument against US imperialism and as an argument for justifying guerilla warfare. However a model which like the dependence model is able to clarify certain phenomena, should not be treated as the only viable one.

7. *The democratic struggle model.* This model maintains that the USA can still serve as relevant example for other nations and that the USA can and should support democratic development in Latin America. It is thus a updated version of the developmental model. The democratic struggle model begins by assuming that Latin America is continually locked in a struggle between democracy and dictatorship. It holds that US institutions can be exported to Latin America and that US capital, technology and know-how can provide Latin America with democracy.

There is some doubt whether US institutions can be transplanted to nations with a completely different culture and history. The choice in Latin America is not always between dictatorship and democracy. The dictatorship-democracy dichotomy has its limitations.

8 *Summary.* In order to explain developments in Latin America, most scholars find that they make use of a combination of models rather than simply depending on one or two of them. They select insights from different models and combine them in a useful and panoramic whole.

References

J. H. Warda discusses US policy in Latin America in the period 1981–1986 in Finding our way? Toward maturity in US-Latin American Relations, 1987 in terms of the foregoing interpretative models. Michael Novak provides a critical examination of the role which dependence theory plays in Latin American liberation theology in Will It Liberate? Questions about Liberation Theology, 1986.[1] Contributions to the interpretation of Latin American development are also presented in R. H. Chileote (ed.) Revolution and Structural Change in Latin America, 1–2, 1970; T. J. Farer, The Grand Strategy of the United States in Latin America, 1988; A. G. Frank, Latin America: Underdevelopment or Revolution, 1969; J. Lang, Inside Development in Latin America, A Report from the Dominican Republic, Colombia and Brazil, 1988; D. Lehmann, Democracy and Development in latin America, Economics,Politics and Religion in the postwar Period, 1990; G. O'Donell, P. C. Scmitter and L. Whitehead (eds.), Transitions from Authoritarian Rule, 1987 and 1988 and finally J. Petras, Politics and Social Structure in Latin America, 1970.

---

[1] M. Novak, 1986, pp 126-153.

4.3 The Explanation of Violations of Human Rights

In his works *Political Repression and the Defence of Human Rights*, 1987 and *Political Culture and Gross Human Rights Violations in Latinamerica* in A.A. An-Na'im (ed.) Human Rights in Cross-Cultural Perspectives 1992, H. Fruhling presents an explanation of human rights violations in Latin America.

Fruhling argues that they arise because of a lack of consensus among the political actors. Major human rights violations are the result of the state's inability to maintain its social authority by other means. The systematic violations of human rights are the product of an alliance between existing repressive institutions. They demand an ideological justification which is capable of overruling every moral scruple about the use of violent methods. Once violence has been institutionalized as a permanent instrument of power, it is exceedingly probable that more violence will occur.

This explanation of human rights violations in Latin America seems reasonable and helps to throw light on events in this continent.

Hugo Fruhling puts forward four hypotheses

1.The modernization of Latin American societies increased social divisions. Society lacked institutional instruments to deal with the new demands imposed on the state.

2.The process led to a radicalization of those in power and to opposition from intellectual élites in Chile, Argentina, Uruguay, Brazil and Colombia during various stages of the 1960s,1970s and 1980s. The rise of radical politics was nourished by external ideological influences. The Cuban and Nicaraguan revolutions influenced the views of the Left.

3.The process of political polarization led in certain cases to the installation of highly repressive military regimes (Brazil 1964, Uruguay and Chile 1973, Argentina 1976) and in other cases to the maintenance of the civil government of the state while guerilla groups (Colombia and Peru) operated in the country.

4.On the one hand, major and systematic violations of human rights showed a determination to resist socialist change and to reintroduce the old hierarchical order which had been disturbed by the mobilization of the people. On the other hand, particularly in the South, these violations became instruments for disciplining the masses and for introducing new values which emphasized the private accumulation of capital rather than the distribution of income and social reforms.

The process which has been described led to a polarization of forces. Political compromise and negotiation were abandoned as methods of resolving conflicts and were replaced by war. In the struggle against the state, respect for human rights became a weapon in the hands of the opposition. New social movements sprang up which defended human rights. They were supported in their struggle by North American governments, political parties and churches.

According to this explanation, the violent outlook common in Latin America is rooted in that continent's traditions of resolving conflicts, not by discussion, but by force of arms. However, the movement for human rights caused social scientists and the political élites on the continent to discover the values which form part of the democratic system.

When the colonial system collapsed, its centralism and authoritarian tradition were inherited by the new republics. The institutional custom of compromising between alternative political centres of power never became part of the Latin American tradition. Political centralism was reintroduced through the lack of a religious opposition. The religious authority of the Catholic church was never challenged from the inside. The Catholic church was hierarchically, not democratically, organized. Political and religious centralism was accompanied by economic centralism.

In Latin America, apart from the political system, the authoritarian Catholic church constituted one of the most powerful forces and its failure to look critically at the political scene and its actors was of crucial importance for the continuation of the authoritarian and centralist political system.

The fact that Catholicism continued to be the official religion of Latin America, gave rise once more to a powerful tendency towards political centralism. However, the influence of the Catholic church was not particularly great in Mexico or Uruguay. Moreover, as a result of the Second Vatican Council, the church redefined its relationship to political ideologies. The new definition inspired a growing commitment to social change, popular participation and human rights. These changes did not affect the positions adopted by the church in Colombia and Argentina. Opposition to the army and to human rights violations was vigorously supported by the church in Chile, Brazil and El Salvador. While Catholicism remained the most influential religion in the region, its weight and political importance varied from country to country. It is difficult to maintain that major human rights violations are consequences of a Catholic inspired authoritarian tradition.

According to this way of interpreting the situation in Latin America, we must distinguish between the Catholic church before and after the Second Vatican Council and also carefully observe that it did not play the same role in all the Latin American countries; its profile varied geographically. In other words, the Catholic church in Latin America was not some monolithic entity but rather a complex and differentiated body with many different aspects. Reality was complex and intricate and cannot be summed up in a simple formula.

The Latin American republics inherited an authoritarian tradition from the old colonial powers Spain and Portugal. However, this tradition was not the only one which influenced the social actors and intellectuals. Liberalism and Marxism also had an important influence during various historical periods.

Major systematic human rights violations took place in Brazil, Chile, Argentina, Uruguay, Peru and Colombia from the 1960s to the 1980s. This occurred in southern Latin America after military regimes had been come to power. In Peru and Colombia, human rights violations took place despite the existence of democratic political systems.

The countries of Latin America went through a process of industrialization and modernization. The economy in this modernization process did not contribute to political and social stability.

Revolution was the central theme of the political intellectual discussion in Latin America during the 1960s. The introduction of authoritarian systems was preceded by attacks on the state by the opposition. Conservative and revolutionary forces found themselves involved in a power struggle over the replacement of the socio-economic system. The conservatives were also influenced by ideological factors. They came to the conclusion that the only way of establishing order was through the introduction of military rule.

Military rule with its subsequent acts of suppression and human rights violations was justified by an appeal to the doctrine of national security which puts national security before individual security and the needs of the state before individual rights. This doctrine of national security was used to justify the removal of dissident thinkers and the dissolution of political parties and trades unions. The reasons for the extensive violations of human rights are to be found, according to this explanation, in the social crisis and the process of political polarization.

Human rights violations were committed not only by military regimes but also by democratic governments. This supports the view that these violations were a product of social instability.

The rise of repressive regimes in Latin America led to a reaction in the shape of a network made up of human rights organizations, church institutions and private research centres. Their aim was to fight against human rights violations, to promote social services for the poor and to carry out research to improve social and economic conditions.

The development of this network of independent non-governmental organizations was made possible by drawing on international support. The Catholic church was active on behalf of human rights in Chile, Brazil and to a lesser extent in Peru. These organizations received economic and political support from North Atlantic governments. The emergence and development of the non-governmental groups was an encouraging phenomenon from the viewpoint of human rights. They were chiefly responsible for monitoring governmental violence.

They paved the way for democracy in Latin America. They were at the forefront of the movement which placed the integrity and dignity of the individual human being at the centre and which ended by demanding the democratization of the political system in Latin America.

After the collapse of the Soviet Union, it became difficult for the military in Latin America to justify their repression by reference to a foreign communist threat to the Christian civilization of the continent. This argument was central to the actions of the military dictatorships and often won support within the Catholic hierarchy. It could no longer be convincingly employed after the collapse of the Soviet empire.

4.4 Human Rights and the Carter Administration

Human rights formed a central element in American foreign policy during Jimmy Carters period in the White House 1977–1981. However, Carter's human rights campaign produced mixed results. A number of people escaped torture. Others were released from prison. Military repression was inhibited.

A number of human rights organizations worked counterproductively. By condemning whole nations, whole regimes and the whole military establishment as violators of human rights, as in the case of Brazil and Argentina, they forced general opinion to fall into line behind repressive regimes. They challenged national sensitivity. Such condemnations failed to take account of the differences between repressive elements within the Latin American military establishment and more democratic elements, thus forcing the latter to defend the military establishment as a whole.

Jimmy Carter's human rights campaign was to a high degree inspired by the civil rights movement in the USA and by human rights activities within the Reformed and Baptist World Alliances. The World Alliance of Reformed Churches (WARC) met in 1970 in Nairobi and began a theological study of human rights. Andrew Young—a young pastor who was a disciple of Martin Luther King Jr—became involved in this study. He then lent his support to Jimmy Carter's candidature for the US presidency. The language of human rights thus became part of a lively political rhetoric. Impulses from the human rights debate—due not least to the exertions of the former civil rights activist and Martin Luther King co-worker, Andrew Young—were passed on to the Carter administration. Young was the US ambassador at the UN in the period 1977–79. Church and theological activities on the human rights front had political consequences and influenced Jimmy Carter's foreign policy. It was a product of the American Puritan tradition in the domain of human rights.

Carter's human rights campaign, however, alienated important countries such as Argentina, Brazil and Chile and brought about few changes in their behaviour. Right wing dictatorships were condemned; left wing dictatorships did not receive the same attention. The human rights campaign in Latin America is often seen as an extension of the civil rights struggle in the US Southern states during the 1960s.

References

The Carter administration's role in the human rights movement has attracted the interest of scholars. Several illuminating monographs have been published. Among them is to be found D. Keogh (ed.) Central America, Human Rights and US Foreign Policy, 1985; J. Muravchik, The Uncertain Crusade: Jimmy Carter and the Dilemmas of Human Rights Policy, 1986; L. Schoultz, Human Rights and United States Policy towards Latin America, 1981; and H. J.Warda (ed.) Human Rights and US Human Rights Policy: Theoretical Approaches and Some Perspectives on Latin America, 1982.

4.5 A North American Reaction to Jimmy Carter's Human Rights Policy

In Christian Century, a well known publication in the USA, J Patrick Dobel reacted critically to Jimmy Carter's human rights policy with an 1977 article entitled *Bearing Witness and Human Rights*. It was directed against the emphasis on individual rights abroad at the expense of social rights in the USA. President Carter's approach to human rights, contrary to fears of the realists, the hopes of the idealists and the shortcomings of the cynics, can best be grasped for what it is in style and substance, namely an example of bearing witness to America's well known belief in the importance of human rights. As an ethical and political strategy, bearing witness has only gone half of the way. To bear witness also requires action, albeit of a special kind. The actions must be non-violent and usually within the framework of the limitations of daily life. When Carter speaks and acts on behalf of a national commitment to human rights, he must be prepared to seriously confront America's own obvious deficiencies, particularly in regard to rights to basic subsistence, housing and health care.[2]

4.6 The Organisation of Human Rights Work

From the 1970s, human rights organizations in Chile and Brazil were linked to the Catholic church. In Chile, the ecumenical Comité Pro Paz was set up after the military coup in 1973 and replaced in 1975 by the Catholic Vicaria de la Solidad, headed by Cardinal Raul Silva. Human rights work took up the cause of victims of General Pinochet's repression after the military coup against the Allende regime in 1973. The base communities were closely involved in this work. During the first years, the work was dominated by documentation and protests against imprisonment, torture and disappearance and the defence of political prisoners. The work was concerned with political problems. Later the focus turned to economic questions. The church provided canteens for the people and children and productive workshops for the unemployed.

In Brazil, in his diocese of Sao Paulo, Archbishop Paulo Everisto Arns and the group associated with the journal Clamor within Justicia Y Paz, worked on behalf of the persecuted. Cardinal Arns was a source of inspiration for the human rights organizations in his diocese. In the forefront of the Justice and Peace Commission, he was responsible for introducing a number of programmes which sought to deal with violations of civil, social and economic

---

[2] P. J. Dobel, Bearing Witness and Human Rights, Christian Century, 1977, 94(27) pp 751-753. For US strategy in Latin America, see T.J.Farer, The Grand Strategy of the United States in Latin America, 1988.

rights.[3] In the early 1960s, Dom Helder Camara and his associates in Brazil paved the way for Cardinal Arns' activities without the majority support of the bishops. However, we shall deal with Camara as a pioneer of the human rights movement later on.

In Uruguay and Argentina, the Catholic church hierarchy adopted a concili-atory attitude to the military. We shall have reason to return to the development in Argentina under the military dictatorship during the period 1976–1983. Co-lombia had the most conservative Catholic hierarchy in Latin America. In Peru the bishops were split into progressive and conservative wings. In Bolivia, the Catholic church sometimes adopted a radical attitude to repressive rightwing regimes. In Paraguay, the Catholic church's demand for democracy became a turning point for Stroessner's long dictatorship.

During the 1970s, various regular organizations emerged in defence of hu-man rights. The 1980s witnessed a growing awareness of the relevance of such rights for democracy and social development. The trend was towards national human rights organizations drawing support from popular movements. In all countries there emerged what can be called a human rights movement.

Four types of human rights institutions/organizations were formed:

1. Social organizations linked to the base communities, base committees, trades unions and/or relatives of the victims of repression. The latter had,in general, national coordinating bodies and participated in some way or other in regional organs. The strongest and most clearly defined of these groups were those in Peru and Chile.

2. Organizations/institutions which documented crimes against human rights, provided legal defence for political prisoners, influenced public opinion and arranged education and occasionally carried out research dealing with hu-man rights issues. These might be linked to different churches such as Vicaria de la Solidad in Chile or might be run by private individuals within the human rights area with a national, autonomous structure.

3. Organizations which specialized in providing rehabilitation and individ-ual help to victims of repression. These organizations often coordinated their activities and took part in international exchanges of experience. In Chile and Peru, they also administered substantial economic resources canalized via in-ternational aid.

4. Organizations/ institutions which were to be found in several countries, which were regionally represented and/or were attached to international hu-man rights bodies. One example is Amnesty International. These organizations also normally disposed over funds made available through international aid.

---

[3] John B. Breslin in A Voice for the Voiceless America, 1981 144 (24) pp 504-505 gives a survey of the cardinal's actions on behalf of human rights and his criticism of American policy on this issue. Clara Pope shows how the Brazilian Catholic church led the human rights campaign and discusses the relationship between this campaign and the movement for redemocratization. It focuses upon S'o Paulo diocese. See C. Pope, Human Rights and the Catholic Church in Brazil, 1970-1983: The Pontifical Justice and Peace Commission of the S'o Paulo Archdiocese, Journal of Church and State, 1985, 27 (3), pp 429-452.

Peru and Chile were the two countries where work at local level had progressed furthest. In Peru, there were both regional and local human rights committees which in turn coordinated their work with the national so-called Coordinadoran. In Chile, the human rights commission Vicaria de la Solidaridad and the committees of relatives of victims were engaged in work throughout the country. In other countries, the work was assigned primarily through a central organization with subsections or autonomous groups in the various regions.

One issue encountered difficulties and gave rise to conflicts within the human rights movement in Latin America. In all countries, the transition from dictatorship to democracy and the level of political violence occasioned crises of identity. The dividing line was the defence of individual and political freedoms as opposed to the promotion of social and economic rights. The concept of human rights could be used to cover all work which aimed at achieving social justice.

References

A. K. Gauding provides a good survey of the organization of human rights work in Latin America in Hellre tända ett ljus än förbanna mörkret. Om Diakonias arbete för mänskliga rättigheter i Latinamerika, 1991. A. Henelly and J. Langan (eds.) deal with efforts to achieve consensus on strategies among secular and religious organizations concerned with the defence of human rights. M. E. Crahan in Human Rights and the Liberation of Man in the Americas, 1982, considers strategies and results in the work of independent, non-governmental organizations dedicated to promoting human rights. In L. M. Colonnese (ed.) Human Rights and the Liberation of Man in the Americas, 1970, a multiform picture of human rights in Latin America is presented and reflects how the situation was assessed in 1969. The attainment of human rights is seen as a stage in the struggle for human liberation in Latin America. The indigenous Indian population plays a central role in the human rights movement in Latin America. U. Wiesemann writes about this subject in Mission und Menschenrechte, 1979.

4.7 Inidvidual and Collective Rights in Latin America

The majority of Latin America's population were poor. Human rights on this continent had therefore to be seen from their horizon. For them, issues such as freedom of thought, freedom of opinion, freedom of expression, freedom of the press and freedom of association were of secondary importance. Their fundamental rights were concerned with survival: work for all, land for those cultivating the soil, just wages, housing, free education, health care and protection against economic exploitation. Civil and political rights meant little for the poor as long as their fundamental needs remained unsatisfied. Respect for the right to life was another name for justice. From a Latin American perspective, human rights were thus primarily a matter of the right to life. The individualistic view of human rights is founded on the Anglo-Saxon tradition. On the basis of the Spanish tradition, one preferred in Latin America to speak of the rights of the people. The emphasis was thus laid not upon individual but on collective rights.[4]

Group rights are more important in Latin American culture than in the North American one. This is hardly a matter of Marxist influence. J. J. Rousseau emphasized the general will in *The Social Contract or Principles of Political Right.* This does not mean that there is necessarily a causal connection between Rousseau's general will and the Latin American social aspect of human rights. But it would be wrong to associate these rights purely with Marxism. Social rights also have their roots in the Enlightenment.[5] In Latin America, human rights primarily meant collective rights. In North America, the situation was reversed. Collective rights could be traced not simply to Marxism but were also rooted in the writings of an Enlightenment thinker such as Jean Jacques Rousseau. Thus priorities as regards human rights differ between North and South America and both types of rights have their historical roots in the Enlightenment. E. Weingärtner in *Behind the Mask, Human Rights in Asia and Latin America, An Inter-regional Encounter,* 1988 emphasizes the priority of collective rights.

4.8 Human Rights and the Church

The backcloth to Medellin 1968 was the revolution in Cuba. Medellin was the church's response to the causes which produced profound social changes in Latin America. The Cuba model was popular and reached its high point at the Medellin conference. Medellin and the student movements coincided in time. Medellin rejected violence as a method for bringing about social change.

Military dictatorship was another response to the forces pressing for revolutionary changes. The doctrine of national security was counterposed to that of communist subversion. Neo-liberalism, not socialism, was promoted as an economic model with the USA as the paradigm. In the local Latin American churches, there were those who were opposed to the terrorism of the military regimes. These protestors took a stance in defence of human rights.

The Medellin church demanded the liberation of the poor and this demand assumed concrete form in the struggle for human rights. It was the base communities which nurtured this struggle.

The USA put forward its doctrine of national security as an element of its foreign policy during the Cold War. It was developed within military circles. The ideological war between the USA and the Soviet Union was to take place in the Third World. American officers passed on the doctrine of national security and the war of ideology to Latin American officers. If necessary, the military must seize power in Latin America. The doctrine of national security in-

---

[4] W.L. Holleman, 1987, p. 22.
[5] Holleman, op.cit., p.24.

cluded the view that Latin American democracies were too weak to fight the war waged by Communist ideology. The military who seized power in Latin America were exponents of the doctrine of national security. The Vatican sided with those who supported the military. CELAM never condemned the doctrine of national security. Throughout the whole period of the military dictatorships, CELAM failed to defend unequivocally those human rights which had been violated in so many countries.

Those bishops who campaigned on behalf of human rights in their respective countries, were sidestepped by Rome. Helder Camara was not supported by the Roman Curia. When Cardinal Raul Silva in Chile took a stand against General Pinochet, it was in oppostion to the will of Rome. Neither Rome nor CELAM were prepared to support Cardinal Paulo Evaristo Arns in Brazil in his fight for human rights.

At the national conferences of bishops, the military coups were warmly welcomed. The military were regarded as saviours of the nation from the on-slaught of communism. However, when repression went too far, there was a split in the bishops' attitudes towards the military. Some were positive and some were negative. The proportions varied from country to country. One bishop who went against the general pro-military stance adopted at the national conferences of bishops, was Oscar Romero in San Salvador. There, military repression was extreme and Romero became a victim of it in his defence of human rights. Priests too were murdered when they actively opposed violations of human rights.

The doctrine of national security bound Latin America to the USA. The so-called theory of dependence was an important element in Gustavo Gutiérrez' liberation theology. One goal was to free Latin America from Yankee imperialism.

The base communities made their breakthrough in Brazil. They were legitimized and supported by the conferences of bishops held at Medellin in 1968 and at Puebla in 1979. They spread throughout Latin America. Leonardo and Clodvis Boff assigned the base communities a central role in their liberation theology.

Those bishops who at a national level condemned the abuse of power, also pointed to the deeper underlying causes of the violations of human rights: an unjust economic framework, an improper distribution of land and wealth, lack of an effective social participation on the part of the poor and the ideology of national security. The bishops pointed out that there was a connection between violations of classical civil rights and the desire on the part of affluent élites to retain economic power. What was needed, was to bring about far-reaching changes in the economic and social system as a necessary step in guaranteeing the maintenance of human rights.[6]

E. Cleary (ed.) Path from Puebla, Significant Documents of the Latin American Bishops since 1979, 1989, is an extensive collection of documents from the Latin American bishops with a focus on social and economic rights throughout the continent. The attainment of social justice is a prerequisite for maintaining human dignity.

References

The journalist P. Lernoux has published two lively and moving accounts of the human rights situation in Latin America and the role played by the church in this historical process of development. In Cry of the People: The Struggle for Human Rights in Latin America, the Catholic Church in conflict with US Policy, 1982, he describes the Catholic church's opposition to the military regimes' oppression in Latin America. He analyzes the involvement of the US Defense Department, the CIA and the business corporations in the genesis of these regimes. In Notes on a Revolutionary Church: Human Rights in Latin America, 1978, he explains and illustrates how priests, monks and nuns have been victims of oppressive measures in South America. Their treatment points to grave violations of human rights. Special attention is paid to Brazil, Paraguay, Uruguay and Argentina. The military dictatorships found it difficult to tolerate priests, monks and nuns who were actively involved in pressing for social justice.

The literature about human rights and the church in Latin America is otherwise vast. It deals with the church programme for human rights in various Latin American countries. There is also an analysis of how and why the churches are involved in human rights, the extent of their work and the effect of new structures both upon society and the churches themselves. We shall content ourselves here with noting the most important works dealing with human rights and the church. J. Comblin, The Church and Defence of Human Rights in E. Dussel (ed.) The Church in Latin America 1492–1992, 1992; J. Comblin, The Church and the National Security State, 1979; M. Dodson, The Christian Left in Latin American Politics. Journal of Inter-American Studies and World Affairs, vol. 21 February 1979:45–68; D. Keogh (ed.) Church and Politics in Latin America, 1990; M. Lange–R. Iblackes (eds.) Witness of Hope, The Persecution of Christians in Latin America, 1980; H. D. Levine (ed.) Churches and Politics in Latin America, 1979; H. D. Levine, Religion and Political Conflict in Latin America, 1986; J. E. Mulligan, The Nicaraguan Church and the Revolution, 1991; P. Richard, Death of Christendom, Birth of the Church, Historical Analysis and Theological Interpretation of the Church in Latin America, 1987; B. H. Smith, Churches and Human Rights in Latin America; Recent Trends in the Subcontinent, Journal of Inter American Studies and World Affairs, vol. 21, February 1979: 89–127.

Illuminating documents which reflect different aspects of the church and human rights are to be found in Between Honesty and Hope Issues by the Peruvian Bishops' Commission for Social Action. Documents from and about the Church in Latin America where the crisis deepens and violence threatens, 1970 in IDOC International The Church at Crossroads, Christians in Latin America: from Medellin to Puebla 1968–1978 (1978) and in J. Eagleson and P. Scharper (eds.) Puebla and Beyond, Documentation and Commentary (1979).

The question of human rights was closely linked to liberation theology and the base communities. Texts from liberation theologians such as Segundo, Dussel, Alves, Boff, Gutiérrez, Assman, Bonino are to be found in R. Gibellini (ed.) Frontiers of Theology in Latin America, 1983 and S. Torres and J. Eagleson (eds.) The Challenge of Basic

---

[6] Latin American Bishops discuss Human Rights. Papers collected and reprinted from LADOC, presumably published 1977. The pastoral letters deal with violations of human rights in Argentina 15 May 1976, The Common Good and the Present Situation, Brazil 16 September 1976, Pastoral Message to the People of God, Chile 25 March 1977, Our Life as nation, El Salvador 5 March 1977, The Situation Today, Nicaragua 8 January 1977 Renewing Christian Hope, Paraguay 12 June 1976, Amidst Persecutions and Consolations as well as Bolivia, Chile, Colombia, Ecuador, Peru and Venezuala 4 May 1976, The Church and Andean Integration.

Christian Communities, 1981. J. L. Secundo, The Liberation of Theology, 1975 provides a typical presentation of liberation theology. There is an illuminating discussion of the connection between liberation theology and social development by C. Smith in The Emergence of Liberation Theology, radical Religion and Social Movement Theory, 1991. Michael Novak of the US is one of liberation theology's critics. In M. Novak (ed.) Liberation Theology and the Liberal Society, 1987, Latin American liberation theology is brought face to face with North American liberal society. Michael Novak and those who share his position give a critical analysis of the Marxist and socialist elements in liberation theology from a standpoint he calls democratic capitalism.

4.9 Camillo Torres in Colombia

Camillo Torres (1929–1966) was a pioneer of individual and collective human rights in Latin America. He held that a priest's task was not limited to preaching the Gospel and giving the sacrament : he must also be involved in trying to bring about social justice.

Camillo Torres was said to come from a family which was not a practising Catholic one. It also included freethinkers. He discovered Christianity as a way of dedicating his life to his fellow human beings as an expression of love among equals. He decided to dedicate himself to brotherly love and therefore became a priest. However, love must be effective. He therefore combined his priestly duties with scholarship and became a sociologist. He came to see that society must be organized along different lines. He saw that the laity neither wanted, nor were capable of this. He therefore appealed directly to the people.

Camillo Torres had to choose between being a priest and practising that love which is total commitment to the people. He chose to serve men without renouncing his Christian witness. The church failed to convince him to stay clear of politics and the political power with which it had been linked for years.

On 24 June 1965, Camillo made a public statement. He had chosen Christianity since it embodied the clearest way of serving one's neighbour. He had become a priest as a commitment to loving his fellow human beings. As a sociologist, he had wanted to make that love effective through technology and science. His analysis of Colombian society had led him to the conclusion that revolution was necessary in order to give food to the hungry and water to the thirsty, to clothe the naked and to ensure the welfare of the majority. He looked upon the revolutionary struggle as a Christian and priestly one. Only through it, could those conditions be brought about which would allow human beings to love one another and to realize the love which human beings owe to their fellows.

Such work is incompatible with the church's demands on its priests. Torres neither wished to go against the church nor against his own conscience. He therefore left the priesthood. As he saw it, his commitment to living a life of real and practical love towards his fellow human beings demanded this sacrifice. Love must be the fundamental criterion underpinning human decisions. The Christian community cannot be true to its mission unless it shows in practice its love towards our fellow human beings.

The Bishops in Colombia delivered their pronouncement on 7 July 1965: a priest in his role in the community must sacrifice all personal political interests so that he can—guided by the church—faithfully interpret God´s word as it applies in the life of the community.

Camillo Torres drew up a a programme for the Colombian people's united front which was published on 26 August 1965. Those who had power in Colombia formed an economic minority which never made a decision contrary to its own interest. However, decisions which favoured the majority were needed in the socio-economic sphere. The political power structure had to be changed so that the majority were responsible for making the decisions.

The land should belong to those who cultivate it. Whatever is deemed to be for the general benefit of the people, is to be expropriated without compensation. All who live in houses in the towns, are to become owners of the houses in which they live. All public or private investment has to follow the national investment plan. A progressive tax is to be imposed on all those who live above a certain minimum. Banks, hospitals, the transport system, radio, television and companies exploiting the natural wealth of the country are to belong to the state. The state is to be responsible for the free education of all Colombians. Women are to participate on equal terms with men in the economic, political and social activities of the country.

As regards Camillo Torres' attitude to communism within the united front, he himself looked upon the front as essentially revolutionary. At the same time, communism contained revolutionary elements. For that reason, he found it impossible to be anti-communist. Communists defend both what is just and what is unjust. To condemn indiscriminately what is just and unjust, is un-Christian. Camillo was not himself a communist. But he was prepared to fight alongside communists for common goals: against the oligarchy and US dominance and for the people's right to exercise power.

On the question of implementing human rights, Camillo Torres' message to women issued on 14 October 1965, is illuminating. Colombian women, like all women in underdeveloped countries, have always been assigned an inferior position to men. Among the common people, women often have a great number of physical duties but more or less no intellectual rights. The working class woman does not enjoy any social or legal protection. When the man leaves the family, the wife is left to carry the whole burden. The middle class woman is also exploited by men. It is possible that in this class, relations with men are more on an equal footing. But families cannot survive if the woman does not work. We know that the working woman, the office girl suffers from all types of exploitation and pressure from her boss. The upper class woman devotes herself to doing nothing apart from playing cards and taking part in the social round because of the lack of intellectual and professional opportunities in the community. The Colombian woman is a human being and not simply an instrument. She is aware that she is exploited not merely by society but also by her man. After the revolution, she knows that equality of rights and obligations will not simply remain an empty phrase but a reality which she herself will be in a position to guarantee.

On 15 February 1966, Camillo Torres died in battle.

References

J. Gerassi (ed.) Revolutionary Priest, The Complete Writings and Messages of Camillo Torres, 1971, contains primary material from Camillo Torres' own hand. G. Guzman, Camillo Torres, 1969 and W. J. Broderick, Camillo Torres, A Biography of the Priest-Guerillo, 1975 are traditional biographies.

4.10 Brazil

The relationship between church and state in colonial and post colonial Brazil was one of subordination and patronage. The national conference of the Brazilian bishops, CNBB which was founded in 1952, supported the military coup of 1964 but towards the end of the decade became the sole effective opponent of the military regime. The Brazilian church worked actively for reform throughout the 1970s and 1980s.

The base organizations were protected by the Brazilian church which in 1968 began to take a more committed position on human rights and latterly on social issues. In Brazil the church was the first to encourage the rural poor to organize themselves. Helder Camara (born 1909) and Paulo Freire (born 1921) paved the way in the early 1960s for a human rights movement in Brazil. Their activities formed part of the struggle for human rights. Paulo Freire with his *Pedagogy of the Oppressed* introduced a method of increasing awareness of the issues involved. The term *conscientization* was one employed by Brazilian radical Catholics. Dom Helder became the voice of one crying in the wilderness.

The Brazilian Church

In *The Catholic Church and Politics in Brazil 1916–1985* (1986), Scott Mainwaring puts the Brazilian Catholic church into its historical and political perspective. Mainwaring makes a general pronouncement about the study of the church as an institution. The church proceeds from its beliefs but like all institutions, it develops interests and tries to defend them. The aim of every church is to disseminate its religious message but depending on its understanding of this message, it is interested in defending its unity, its position relative to other religions, its influence in society at large, its number of members and its financial situation. Nearly all institutions are concerned about their own survival and many are keen to expand. These concerns easily lead to the adoption of methods which are incompatible with fundamental goals.[7]

Since the mid 1960s, lay and grassroots movements have played an important role in the transformation of the Brazilian church. They introduced the notion of belief linked to radical politics. Several Latin American liberation theologians like the Brazilian Leonardo Boff and the Peruvian Gustavo Gutiér-rez have admitted that these grassroots and lay movements formed the starting point for their theological ideas. The grassroots movements were not solely responsible for the transformation of the church. Without the support of the hierarchy, they would have been unable to transform it. The transformation process was dialectical. It was only on the basis of institutional acquiescence that the radical lay movements were able to emerge and it was only when the hierarchy actively supported change that the church strongly defended human rights.[8]

Popular Catholicism composed of traditional articles of belief and practices, developed in Latin America in general and in Brazil in particular outside the institutional church. The gulf between the institutional church and popular practice was considerable. Among ordinary people, the institutional church was weak but the religious articles of belief formed the world view of the popular majority. The Brazilian church was an important institution. Its symbols and interpretations helped to give different social classes and institutions an identity and to define social and political patterns of action. The people viewed not simply politics and social position but also family, success and failure, health and sickness in terms of religious symbols and acts.[9]

Between 1955 and 1964, CNBB was the most important force within the Brazilian church. It was created in 1952 on the initiative of Dom Helder Camara, at that time assisting Bishop in Rio de Janeiro. It was one of the first national conferences of bishops anywhere in the world and the first in Latin America. It has played a highly important role in the development of the Brazilian church. One of the basic axioms of the reformists was that the church is part of the world and must participate in it. The church cannot be completely above the world but should act as a symbol which helps to transform the world. For the reformists, the Christian message involved creating a just social order.[10]

Paulo Freires' method and movement for grassroots education worked with the poor. Education became a means of bringing about social change. The movement encouraged people to see their problems as part of a larger social evil. The main idea was that human beings must be agents of their own history.[11]

---

[7] S. Mainwaring, The Catholic Church and Politics in Brazil 1916-1985 (1986), 1f.
[8] Mainwaring, op. cit., 14 f.
[9] Mainwaring, op. cit., 16 f.
[10] Mainwaring, op. cit., 48 f.
[11] Mainwaring, op. cit., 66 f.

Changes in the church during the period 1964–1973 depended on a combination of transformations in Brazilian politics and society and upon changes in the international church. The young popular church was encouraged by Rome and by the Medellin conference of 1968. *Populorum progressio*, published in 1967, was a source of inspiration for progressive Catholics throughout the whole of Latin America. In Rome, the episcopal synod on justice confirmed the church's need to support justice. Medellin was a turning point for the popular church in Latin America. The conference represented a triumph for the popular church. Salvation was understood as a process which begins on earth; faith was linked to justice; it was recognized that structural changes were needed in Latin America;and the base communities were encouraged. Medellin provided progressive elements in the Brazilian church with legitimacy. The conference stimulated what subsequently became known as liberation theology with several of the pioneer figures in Brazil such as Leonardo Boff and Hugo Assman.

A combination of a new institutional identity and new social political and economic conditions thus explains the change in the church. It was a question of an interaction between these factors.[12]

Between 1974 and 1982, the Brazilian church became the most progressive church in the world. It was then that the popular church emerged. The Brazilian church went further than any other Catholic church in the world in combining belief with commitment to social justice and the poor. The base communities multiplied rapidly.[13]

Helder Camara

Archbishop Helder Camara of Recife in North East Brazil had worked ever since the Second Vatican Council and his own elevation as archbishop in 1964, for social and political change in Latin America. This assumed that those in power would display a minimum of respect for human rights. Like Gandhi in India and Martin Luther King Jr in the USA, he was a convinced advocate of non-violent methods in bringing about social change and achieving justice and development in the Third World.

Helder Camara was ideologically close to Gandhi and Martin Luther King. In *The Spiral of Violence* he referred to Gandhi and emphasized that the success of his method of non–violence required that the regime in power showed at least a minimum of respect for human rights.[14] *The Spiral of Violence* deals with social injustice and advocates measures to improve the inhuman conditions of life in the Third World. Confronted with the underdeveloped countries' hopes of an inner development, the socialist countries whether of the Soviet or Chinese model, remain as coldhearted and insensitive as their capi-

[12] Mainwaring, op. cit., 113 ff.
[13] Mainwaring, op. cit., 145.
[14] H. Camara, Våldets spiral (The Spiral of Violence),1971,p 25.

talist counterparts. The latter with their defence of private ownership, their support for the established order and their stand against socially subversive elements and chaos, defend their political prestige and the interests associated with it. They are servants of those who hold economic power and the international trusts. The socialist countries are hard and unyielding. They do not allow any form of pluralism; they thrust dialectical materialism down the people's throat; they demand blind obedience to the party; they establish a totalitarian regime and introduce continuous uncertainty and fear in the same way as external right wing fascist dictatorships.[15]

In the capitalist world, religions run a real and serious risk of being completely absorbed into the system. They can certainly display boldness when it comes to putting forward beautiful principles but they lack the courage to carry them into action, perhaps unconsciously fearing that they themselves might suffer as a consequence. In the socialist world on the other hand, religions have been reduced to the status of alienated and alienating forces. They are absolutely forbidden to display any commitment in the social economic domain or to become involved in the real process of development.[16] According to Camara, time is working in Gandhi's favour. In the atomic age, war on an international scale is equivalent to suicide. The only adequate answer to violence is to have the courage to deal with the injustices from which violence springs.[17]

Camara points out that Catholic Latin America at Medellin Colombia in 1968 as well as the Protestant churches at Uppsala, Sweden, came to very serious conclusions about existing injustices. In the same year, in Beirut, Catholics and Protestants together signed an important document dealing with justice at the the international level.[18] Camara raised the question of who can succeed in persuading universities to contribute to constructing new models of development which are independent of both the capitalist and socialist states. It is possible, he concluded, that one path to solution is via a socialization which really guarantees the development of each and every human being.[19]

In 1969 Helder Camara gave a lecture *The inhuman conditions* which was later published with the title *Race with time*. It is easy to see that our own rights should be respected but it is difficult to respect the rights of others. How can one say, Camara asks, that all human beings are born free and equal in dignity and rights when not even the member states of the UN are equal in dignity and rights. As long as there are strong and weak states in the UN and as long as certain members control the decision–making process, three propositions are valid. 1) Expositions of human rights are no more than eloquent and high sounding phrases which create illusions. 2) Such expositions will be unable to

---

[15] Camara, op.cit., p 28.
[16] Camara, op.cit., p 30.
[17] Camara, op.cit., p 30f.
[18] Camara, op.cit., p 44.
[19] Camara, op.cit., p 45.

lead to any contribution which really does bring about a development effectively serving the whole of mankind or which can establish a solidarity extending to all mankind. 3) Any such exposition will not be of any use to the great powers. They will continue to give priority to the arms race, research in outer space for strategic purposes, increasingly inhuman forms of warfare, economic blockades, aid contributions which are more apparent than real and an effective global proletarization.[20]

As long as human rights depend on the power to gain respect—and in spite of the enormous waste of money, time and effort—the international bodies will only be able to achieve superficially admirable successes which in reality are only a drop in the ocean. As long as human rights depend on the power to gain respect, the international bodies will fail at the crucial moment whenever there is a collision with the interests of the great powers. It is utopian, according to Camara, to believe that one could equip the United Nations so that it disposed over superior power to that of an individual superpower. The military power at the disposal of the UN will always be dependent on the superpowers.[21]

If the moral forces in the world could combine on human rights and were united in a common action to exercise, in a politically realistic way, a voluntary moral pressure on their respective countries with a view to achieving a synthesis, the impossible might be brought about. An effective implementation of human rights demands that clearsighted and brave minorities within the different world religions form common cause with universities in all countries and with the mass media, workers and employers, technologists, politicians and the military.[22]

We want, Camara concludes, to eliminate poverty from the world, a poverty which is an affront to the Creator. We want all human beings to be able to fulfil themselves in such a way that no-one is reduced to the status of a mere object; we want all human beings to truly experience that they are created in God's image and likeness; we want all human beings to be able to fulfil their deepest vocation as co-participants in the creation, called by God to reign over nature and to bring the work of creation to fulfilment. We wish for human rights to be more than mere empty words.[23] For Camara, the ideal is a Christianity which, instead of being alienated and alienating, is an incarnation of the divine just as Christ is.[24]

Camara draws attention to the discrepancy between what he holds to be the true meaning of human rights and the actual situation in which people live in Latin America. It is the social aspect of human rights which is at the forefront of his concern. He wants people to escape from living in poverty and to be given tolerable living conditions.

---

[20] Camara, Kapplöpning med tiden (Race with time) 1970, p 23 f.
[21] Camara, op.cit., p 24.
[22] Camara, op.cit., p 25.
[23] Camara, op.cit., p 31f.
[24] Camara, op.cit., p 57.

References

There is an instructive monograph on Helder Camara written by J. de Broucker with the title Dom Helder Camara, The Violence of A Peacemaker, 1969. In addition there is a short biography of a non-violent human rights activist who was nominated by British and American Quakers to the Nobel Prize of 1973 in B. R. Nute, Hélder Camara's Latin America. London, Friends Peace and International Relations Committee, 1974.

CNBB

At the beginning of 1973, the general council of the national conference of Brazilian bishops (CNBB) issued a statement on human rights. Such rights are based on the Gospel.[25] The church must help the humiliated people to be given their rights and to inform people, support them and encourage them to build trades unions, cooperatives and similar organizations.[26] The church must mobilize the laity in a campaign to illuminate and defend human rights and to protest whenever they are violated.[27] The church ought to teach the faithful about a person's rights and about their theological justification. It should emphasize the close connection between promoting human rights and God's presence in history.[28]

Human rights directed the church's attention towards the underprivileged classes and supported their just demands with practical action.[29] Priests must as a part of their evangelical mission persuade the faithful to fulfil their individual obligations by thinking of the need of their fellow human beings and forming teams at every level to develop personality.[30] The church ought to be conscious of its responsibility for defending human rights, not simply in the abstract, but by standing up for them, as a symbol and witness of these rights, and by forming groups to ensure that they are observed.[31] The priests should give the liturgy a social dimension in order to make people notice the living conditions around them and to get them to pray for the oppressed.[32]

The human rights which are least respected in practice, are the right to proper sustenance, the right to a just wage, the right to work and the right to humane working conditions, the right to own land for those who cultivate it and the right to life.[33] The bishops emphasized that it is the natural right of human beings to fulfil themselves as persons and to have socio-economic structures which allow for their personal development.[34]

---

[25] Brazilian National Bishops Conference. A Universal Declaration of Human Rights. LADOC 4 (October 1973): 1-7. Proposal 1:5 p. 1.
[26] Op. Cit., Proposal 1:6 p. 1.
[27] Op. Cit, Proposal 1:7 p. 1.
[28] Op. Cit, Proposal 1:11p. 1.
[29] Op Cit, Proposal 1:12 p. 2.
[30] Op Cit, Proposal 1:13 p. 2.
[31] Op Cit, Proposal 1:15 p. 2.
[32] Op.Cit., Proposal 1:16,p. 2.
[33] Op Cit, Proposal 2:1,2,3,4,7,17 p. 2f..
[34] Op Cit, Proposal 7:1,2 p. 4

The bishops wished to eliminate the differences between peasant families and large landowners in holding land,[35] between employers and workers,[36] between rich and poor in access to higher education,[37] between rich and poor with respect to income[38] and finally between white and black.[39] The Indians who were threatened with extermination should be given every conceivable support.[40]

It is the social and collective rights which form the focus of the Brasilian bishops' attention. It is meaningless to speak about the implementation of individual human rights as long as the poor and oppressed lack the basic necessities of life.

Leonardo Boff and the Base Communities

The base communities first sprang up in Brazil at the begin of the 1960s. There were several factors underlying their emergence. The activities of lay groups were encouraged within the Church during the 1950s by Catholic action. This was accelerated by the Second Vatican Council and the meeting of the bishops in Medellin in 1968. The military coup in Brazil in 1964 made the church draw closer to the most disadvantaged classes in Brazilian society. Through the support of the base communities, the church sought to provide the poor and oppressed with a sanctuary where they could express their dissatisfaction with the regime.

The majority of base communities were to be found among the lower classes either in city environments or in semi-urban zones. The base communities consisted of manual workers. They brought together people sharing the same belief, belonging to the same church and living in the same area. They were church groups because they gathered within the church. The base communities can be characterized as small associations of Catholics, meeting regularly to enrich their insights about the Christian Gospel, to reflect about social needs and to seek adequate solutions to these needs. They celebrated mass together and spread God´s word. They had sociopolitical goals. They were instruments of social change.

The Brothers Clodvis and Leonardo Boff define them as a liberating force which works for a new social order in which justice and equality prevail.[41] Leonardo Boff writes that they pave the way for a society of solidarity instead of bourgeois society. The method of changing society is presented as a three-fold task: see-judge-act. The concrete social issues concerned such things as running water, street lighting, bus transport and the cost of living. Those things of immediate interest led to concrete actions.

---

[35] Op Cit, Proposal 9:1 p. 4.
[36] Op Cit, Proposal 9:2 p. 4.
[37] Op Cit, Proposal 9:7 p. 5.
[38] Op Cit, Proposal 9:9 p. 5.
[39] Op Cit, Proposal 9:10 p. 5.
[40] Op Cit, Proposal 10 p. 5.
[41] C. Boff Feet-on-the Ground-Theology A Brazilian Journey, 1987.

For Leonardo Boff, the base communities were a miniature of a new society where there is respect for our fellow human beings, a spirit of cooperation, a feeling of solidarity, a recognition of the value of the lower classes and support for the poorest of the poor. The tasks of God´s people in their organization of base communities is, among other things, the defence of human rights. Leonardo Boff developed the idea of base communities in his liberation theology. One of his most famous work is *Church, Charism and Power. Liberation Theology and the Institutional Church, 1981.* In it, he maintains that the church which is based upon priestly power and upon the sacred authority of the hierarchy, represents Roman centralism. This church does not question the legitimacy of authoritarian regimes, only their abuse of power. A prophetic spirit was lacking in any diocese in Latin America which adhered to this model.The struggle for human rights was not waged openly but via secret contacts between the hierarchy and the military leaders. In this type of church, the role of the church was confined to the sacramental. The church was not meant to intervene in the domain of politics.[42]

In the base communities, Boff continues, people assumed responsibility for their fate. In the beginning, they read the Bible. Such a community gave the faith of its members a new depth. They came to see that the problems they encountered, were of a structural kind. Their marginalization was perceived as a consequence of the capitalist system's socio-economic character. The desire for liberation was placed in a concrete, historical context. The community looked upon it not simply as liberation from sin but also as a liberation which has economic, political and cultural dimensions.[43] The Christian community from Boff's perspective, must defend human dignity. Human beings are seen as the image of God. This anthropology forms the basis of human rights and obligations.[44]

A network of centres for the defence of human rights was created in Brazil. These centres would come to form a network giving access to sources of information and legal advice for peasants and worker organisations.

References

There are several illuminating works dealing with the base communities as the foundation of social change and their role in fostering the growth of human rights in Brazil. Among them there are D. Berbe, Grace and Power, Base Communities and Nonviolence in Brazil, 1987.; W. E. Hewitt, Base Communities and Social Change in Brazil, 1991; W. E. Hewitt, Strategies for Social Change employed by Communideded Eclesiais de Base (CEBs) in the Archdiocese of Sao Paolo; and L. Lebrvre, Economic Human Rights: Satisfaction of Basic Needs and D. H. Pollack, Debt Development and Democracy: Recent Trends in Latin America in P. Blanchard and P. Landstreeht (eds.) Human Rights in Latin America and the Caribean, 1989.

---

[42] L.Boff, 1981, p. 5.
[43] Boff, op.cit., p. 8.
[44] Boff, op.cit., p.32.

The Brazilian Church from a North American Perspective

In 1975, Brady Tyson at the American University in Washington DC wrote an article on *The Mission of the Church in Contemporary Brazil: The Case of a Church in a Land of Poverty and Repression*. It gives a good picture of how the task of the local church in Brazil was understood in the USA. It maintains that violation of human rights along with poverty constitute major challenges for the church. However God works by gathering together the poor in their own church, by forcing the Roman Catholic church out into the wilderness, by forming a prophetic minority, by fostering dedicated opposition to permanent poverty and by the movement for pastoral renewal within the Roman Catholic church. The church is open to temptations not to care about the world, to run away from its responsibility and to combine forces with the forces of repression and the prosperous classes of society.[45]

Summary

The local church in Brazil underwent a transformation from supporting the status quo to active participation in the defence of civil and human rights. The Brazilian church came to be seen as one of the most politically progressive churches within Catholicism because of its stand on behalf the poor and oppressed. The base communities aim at achieving social change or transforming existing social structures. Through the national conference of the Brazilian bishops which was founded in 1952, the church has worked to create national programmes for the defence of human rights. CNBB encouraged the creation of human rights groups at all levels within the church and inspired the creation of the base communities. The base communities in Brazil consist of lay people with a similar social situation and with the same commitment to the poor. The base communities embody a religiously motivated commitment to temporal justice. They work for a more just social order.

4.11 Gustavo Gutiérrez in Peru

The central figure of liberation theology, Gustavo Gutiérrez worked in Peru. In his classical work *A Theology of Liberation: History, Politics and Salvation*, 1973 he describes Catholic, political and social activism and its philosophical presuppositions. Among the issues mentioned is the church's commitment to human rights.[46]

He returns to the same theme in *The Power of the Poor in History*, 1983. The issue of human rights was given a new emphasis in Gustavo Gutiérrez' thought. There are two reasons for this. 1) the swelling list of martyrs in all the countries 2) the greater attention paid to the issue by the outside world. The Carter administration focused attention on human rights and withdrew assistance from countries which were guilty of flagrant violations.

---

[45] Brady Tyson, Missiology 1975 3(3) pp 287-306.
[46] J. Klaiber sketches the modern history of the Catholic church in Peru in The Catholic Church in Peru 1821-1985. A Social History, 1992.

Gutiérrez placed social rights at the centre—people's right to food, clothing, education, housing, health care and employment. Wherever children grow up in a society where their parents are unable to find work with the result that the children grow up undernourished and people are deprived of housing, education and health care for their children, human rights are being violated. Such rights must be at the very centre of humanitarian efforts in Latin America.[47] The ruling classes regarded their interests as being threatened by Christians who worked on behalf of the poor. In Brazil, the torture and murder of Christians involved in the popular movement culminated in 1968–69. This type of persecution of the church spread from Brazil to Argentina, Chile, Honduras, El Salvador and Mexico.[48] Workers and students also suffered the same fate. They are history's anonymous witnesses. They too were persecuted for a righteous cause. They appeared dangerous to those wielding power.[49]

Liberation theology expresses the right of the poor to think. By this is meant the right to express the other right which an oppressive system denies them, namely the right to a humane life.[50] Theology is created by people who are part and parcel of particular social processes. All theology is in part a reflection of the concrete social process. Theology is not something revealed and timeless. It is an attempt to express the Word of the Lord today in the language of today. No meaningful theology can be decoupled from concrete history and presented as a set of abstract ideas. For Gutiérrez, reflections about belief are an attempt on behalf of the individual believer to think about their belief in definite social conditions in order to work out interpretations and lines of action which will influence these conditions and which will play a role in the events and struggles of a given society. Theologians do not work in a historical vacuum. Their thought has its own particular starting point. It is the product of the fundamental material conditions of society.[51]

The eighteenth century bourgeois revolutions in Europe produced a code of modern liberties. Contemporary theology in Europe and North America is based upon them. They are the creation of the bourgeois middle class.[52]

The starting point of liberation theology is not the issues of the modern bourgeoisie but the issues facing the poor. The oppressed and marginalized, Gutiérrez emphasizes, are oppressed and marginalized by the bourgeois class. It is a question of a cleavage between the perspective of modern bourgeois theology and liberation theology or the perspective of the oppressed. This cleavage is to be found at the historical, political and social levels.[53]

Liberation theology pays attention to the historical and concrete situation of the poor and exploited. It refuses to gloss over the conflict-filled nature of

---

[47] G. Gutiérrez 1983, p 87 f.
[48] Gutiérrez, op.cit., p 88f.
[49] Gutiérrez, op.cit., p 89f.
[50] Gutiérrez, op.cit., p 90.
[51] Gutiérrez, op.cit., p 90f.
[52] Gutiérrez, op.cit., p 91f.
[53] Gutiérrez, op.cit., p 92.

society. The issues of the oppressed concern the economic, social, political and ideological roots of the society which oppresses them.[54] Gutiérrez sums up by saying that the main issue for liberation theology is not the lack of faith on the part of the bourgeois middle class. Liberation theology expresses the dialectical opposite of bourgeois ideology. Its starting point is the lower depths of history, society's exploited and marginalized people. The dividing line in liberation theology is between oppressor and oppressed sharing the same belief. This dividing line is not religious but economic, social and political.[55]

4.12 Oscar Romero and the Jesuit Murders in El Salvador

In 1980, archbishop Oscar Romero was murdered. In 1989, six prominent Jesuit intellectuals, together with their domestic help and daughter, were murdered. The crucial problem in El Salvador—that which overshadowed all others—was the poverty of the majority. 66% of the population lived beneath an existence minimum where their fundamental needs remained unsatisfied while 80% of the national income went to 20% of the population.

In a country where, practically speaking, all the media were in the hands of the military regime, Oscar Romero decided that the Sunday mass which was transmitted by the archdiocese's own radio station, would be an occasion when the people of El Salvador could learn what was really happening in their country. In addition, help was arranged for families who were victims of human rights violations. In addition, reports about the human rights situation were regularly published. Romero's activities were a threat to powerful interests. The USA put pressure on the Vatican to silence him after his criticism of American military help to El Salvador. But Romero could not be silenced.

Archbishop Oscar Romero published a pastoral letter on 6 August 1977. As the Body of Christ in history, the Church must do what Jesus did in His life, namely proclaim the Kingdom of God. The Kingdom which Jesus proclaimed was one in which human beings would live together as brothers and sisters and as the children of God. He called all classes but preferred the known sinners, the prostitutes, the tax gatherers, the lepers, the Samaritans and all those rejected through the ages. The church must give priority to those rejected today—the homeless, the slumdwellers, the exploited workers, those in prison, those abused and maltreated by the powerful. Like Jesus, the church must condemn sin. He condemned the commercialization of the temple, the keeping of the letter of the law rather than its spirit of justice and mercy, the rich who refused to share their worldly goods, the narrowminded who despised sinners and Samaritans, the leaders who laid unbearable burdens on the shoulders of

---

[54] Gutiérrez, op.cit., p 92f.
[55] Gutiérrez, op.cit., p 93.

the people. Sin stands in the way of the Kingdom of God and a life of justice and love. The church must reject that selfishness which lurks in each and every heart, that sin which dehumanizes and uses money, property, profit and power for a purpose other than that of life. The church must also condemn the social, economic, cultural and political structures which oppress people and impoverish them.

In El Salvador, Romero reminded the people that the law recognized the church but that priests and catechists were attacked when they tried to carry out their mission of proclaiming and bringing about the Kingdom of God. The people of El Salvador were the subject of aggression and their rights were trampled on. Their rights were a part of the responsibility of the church. The church is persecuted because it really wishes to be a church of Christ. As long as the church is content to preach eternal salvation without involving itself in the real problems of the world, it will be respected and praised and receive privileges. But if it is faithful to its mission of condemning that sin which reduces many to a state of wretchedness and if it proclaims the hope of a more just and humane world, it will be persecuted and libelled and called subversive and communist.

On 17 February 1980, Oscar Romero wrote to President Jimmy Carter and requested him not to send military help if he truly wished to defend human rights. Instead of promoting greater justice and peace, it merely increased injustice and the oppression of the people whose struggle was often about the most fundamental rights. The present regime had produced more dead and wounded than its predecessor which had been condemned by the Inter American Human Rights Commission. After the security forces had received US equipment and training, they had oppressed the people with increased violence through the use of deadly weapons. It would be unjust for foreign powers to intervene in the affairs of the people of El Salvador, oppressing them and denying them the right to vote independently on the political and economic policy which the nation was to follow. It would violate a right which the Latin American bishops meeting at Puebla, had openly acknowledged when they spoke of popular self-determination which allows peoples to organize themselves according to their own wishes and in accordance with their historical tradition and to cooperate in a new international order.

Oscar Romero was murdered on 24 March 1980. He was under threat because of his forthright sermons. He opposed the war waged by the military regime against its opponents. He appealed to the military and police to refuse to kill civilians. Oscar Romero found himself caught between political extremist groups. He occupied the political middle ground and tried to act as a mediator in the prevailing political turbulence. This led to his elimination.[56]

In the morning of 16 November 1989, six Jesuits, among them some of El

---

[56] Robert F Drinan expresses disquiet about the situation in El Salvador as well as dissatisfaction with the Reagan administration's US policy in Human Rights in El Salvador America 1982 146(7) pp 130-132.

Salvador's best known intellectuals at the campus of the Central American university were murdered—Ignacia Ellacuria, 59, the vice-chancellor of the the university; Ignacio Martin-Baro, 47, Ellacuria's deputy; Segundo Montes, 56, director of the human rights institute; Juan Ramon Moreno, 56; Amondo Lopez Quintona, 53; Joaquin Lopez, 71. The soldiers also killed the domestic help, Julia Elba Ramos, 42, and her daughter Celina Mariceth Ramos, 15. The leader of the Jesuits in Central America, Father J. M. Tojeira, made the following statement concerning the death of the six university teachers: "One of the basic questions concerns Christian life which embodies love for the poor, respect for human rights and brotherly love. These are values which are underwritten by that absolute value which is God Himself." The murderers were sentenced for crimes against human rights.

The murder of Archbishop Romero in 1980 and the massacre of the six prominent Jesuit intellectuals in 1989 along with their domestic help and her daughter are milestones in a violent decade in the history of El Salvador.

References

R. Armstrong and J. Schenk give the historical framework of developments in El Salvador in El Salvador The Face of Revolution 1982.

There is an extensive literature about Oscar Romero and the Jesuit martyrs in El Salvador. There are Oscar Romero's own expositions as well as analyses of his contributions. Among the former, there are O. Romero, Voice of the Voiceless—the Four Pastoral Letters of Oscar Romero and Other Statements, 1985 and Romero, Martyr for Liberation, 1982 which contains his two final sermons. The analytical works include J. R. Brockman, The Word Remains: A Life of Oscar Romero, 1982; P. Erdozain, Archbishop Romero, Martyr of El Salvador, 1981; J. Sobrino, Archbishop Romero Memories and Reflections, 1990 and Report of Human Rights compiled by American Watch Committee and the American Civil Liberties Union, 1982. The murdered Jesuits have also left a legacy of writings and there are a number of books about the consequences of their murder: The Jesuit Assassinations The Writings of Ellucuria, Martin-Bado and Segundo Montes, with a Chronology of the Investigation (Novemeber 11, 1989–October 22, 1990) 1990, El Salvador's Decade of Terror Human Rights since the Assassination of Archbishop Romero 1991 and M. Lindholm, Moderna martyrer. Om Ignacio Ellacuria och andra jesuiters kamp för fred och rättvisa i El Salvador, 1992.

4.13 The Church and the Dictatorship in Argentina 1976–1983

The examples of the struggle for human rights in Latin America which have hitherto been presented are concerned with actions dedicated to bringing about these rights in the face of various forms of oppression. We shall conclude our account with an example of the church working together with an oppressive regime to oppose the implementation of human rights. This is illustrated by the case of Argentina under a military dictatorship in the period 1976–1983.

Catholicism in Argentina emphasized the Catholic identity of the people. It supported Peronism and the authoritarian right. Peron maintained that his social policy was inspired by the social doctrine of the church. The Christian democratic party which was founded in 1955, was unable to win a footing in the masses and was divided in its attitude to Peronism after the fall of the leader. The hierarchy continued to support Peronism as an expression of national identity and popular culture but was at the same time suspicious of its working class background.

During the military dictatorship in Argentina in the period 1976–1983, great numbers of people disappeared and the bishops and priests within the armed forces justified torture, murder and other violations carried out by the armed forces. The Argentinian bishops were divided into three groups 1) a small group which unambiguously acted in favour of human rights 2) other bishops who were aware of the crimes which had been committed but confined their activities to the church 3) the majority of bishops who supported the military regime, with many of them adopting an aggressive attitude to human rights organizations and the victims of state terrorism. Among them were some who justified torture and murder.

The Argentinian episcopate comprised more than eighty members. Only four of them opposed violations of human rights committed by the terrorist regime: Eurique Angelli from La Rioja, who was murdered by the armed forces in what was meant to look like a traffic accident on 4 August 1976; Jaime de Nevares from Neuquén; Miguel Hesayne from Viedma who supported the meeting for human rights; and Jorge Novak from Quilmes who became bishop on 19 September and joined the ecumenical movement for human rights. The families of those who were under arrest, who had vanished or who had been murdered or tortured were able to call on the support of the three latter bishops.

There was an agreement between the leaders of the coup and the majority of bishops. The regime would be given free hands to take repressive measures and could reckon with the support of the bishops. In return, the military would defend Western Christian civilization and simultaneously maintain and consolidate the privileges of the Church. At the time of the military coup on 24 March 1976, the Catholic episcopate was in a position to exercise decisive influence. The military regime claimed to defend Christian values and base its actions upon them. It could not survive open criticism from the bishops. The Argentinian episcopate made a political choice. It allied itself with temporal political power. The episcopate knew the truth but chose to hide it in exchange for the goodwill of the military. The Papal nuncio, Pio Laghi, acquiesced in the ideology of the military dictatorship although he was aware of its crimes. He gave communion to representatives of the dictatorship while, at the same time, he was aware that they were guilty of grave crimes.

The bishops failed those members of their communities who had gone missing. They did not dare to report those who were responsible despite knowing their identity; and they failed to do anything about the serious crimes which had been committed. A person who had disappeared, was totally abandoned. The armed forces kidnapped people, isolated them and kept them from knowing where they were. People were tortured to the limit of their endurance. They were humiliated and after a period of days, months, years, they were then coldly and brutally murdered. Finally the body was hidden. There is evidence of cases where bishops can be seen to have been servile and flattering to those wielding power while displaying insensitivity to the persecuted and other victims. They refused to do anything to help the families of the missing but instead supported the government, with a view to gaining material advantages. The bishops knew the truth but they hid it in order to help the military regime. Those who were active in human rights organizations were accused by the bishops of being communists. The military regime tried to base its actions on a pretended defence of Christian values and would not have survived open criticism from the bishops.

Paul VI held that the disappearances and murders required an adequate explanation. The Argentinian church should not try to retain its privileges. It must be content to serve the faithful and society with an eye to the security of all people. On three occasions, John Paul II made reference to the problem posed by the disappearances in Argentina. The Pope, however, did not understand the nature of military oppression in Argentina and the brutality and cynicism of the methods employed in the disappearances carried out in God's name. At Puebla, John Paul II maintained that human dignity is an evangelical value which cannot be despised without simultaneously attacking the Creator. The defence of human rights can be derived from the Gospel.

A reason for the stance taken by the Argentinian episcopate is to be found in the tradition of dependence on the state which has characterized the history of the Catholic church—and particularly the episcopate—in Argentina since colonial times. The Spanish monarchy had power over the church for example in the appointment of bishops. Thus in the Argentinian church, there was a historical tradition of patronage. After independence, ensuing national governments considered that they had inherited this patronage. The present constitution guarantees the Catholic church the right to exercise, freely and fully, its spiritual power and to conduct freely public acts of worship; it grants it its own jurisdiction. The approval of the Argentinian government is still required, however, for the nomination of bishops. Patronage no longer exists but there is still governmental involvement in the appointment of bishops. It cannot be ruled out that the military regimes refused to endorse the candidature of bishops who adopted a critical position on the human rights issue. During the military dictatorship in the period 1976–1983, no priest who had defended human dignity, stood a chance of becoming bishop.

Another reason for the bishops' attitude to the military dictatorship was the need to win economic support for the church in general and for the bishops in particular. During the period of patronage, the state had paid the bishops' salaries. According to an ordinance of President Videla, bishops were to receive for the duration of their lives a salary which was 70% of that awarded to a federal judge. State economic support was given to Catholic worship, to church activities such as private Catholic schools, to priests attached to state institutions and to church bodies carrying out useful social or cultural activities. It was thus a question of support for various pastoral activities. In addition to the salaries of the bishops, the Church was also in other ways economically dependent upon the state.

A third reason for the attitude of the bishops was their intellectual training. An important constituent was the basic doctrine of integralism and the ideology of national Catholicism. Both these figured in pastoral letters, sermons and official pronouncements. Together they formed an attitude. Integralism treats the church as a complete and perfect society. The church was seen more as a juridical entity than as a mystery of faith or as a sacrament of salvation. The most desirable situation for the church is the Catholic state. This led to an idealization of certain historical epochs, particularly the medieval age in Europe when the power of the church permeated the whole fabric of society and had influence over the power of the state. The integralists blamed the destruction of this ideal society on philosophical nominalism, the Reformation, Cartesian philosophy and the French Revolution with its slogans of freedom, equality and brotherhood. The French Revolution gave rise to liberalism which in turn gave rise to all the other modern heresies: socialism, anarchism, communism and indifferentism. Integralism had no understanding of the salvation account put forward at the Second Vatican Council, that human history progresses through sin's opposition to the Kingdom of God. The solutions to political and social problems are similar to mathematical theorems, namely unchangeable principles which human beings must accept. In integralism, all authority comes from above. It did not view the church as a body which partakes in temporal sin, a church which does not yet embrace that kingdom of God proclaimed by Jesus and to which men and women are called through conversion.

The ideology of national Catholicism became a kind of national religion. Religion and the motherland were intertwined. It was a matter of a symbiosis between religion and extreme patriotism which reduced Christianity to the status of an ideology. In Spain, Catholicism had functioned as a national ideology for many centuries. In Argentina, an attempt was made to preserve this national ideology based upon Catholicism. An underlying combination of ideas determined the bishops' reactions to the military dictatorship. How were they to behave towards a regime which, in their eyes, appeared as an integral part of the Catholic State and which protected the church and was ready to expel heretics and the enemies of the faith? The armed forces treated Catholicism as an element which bound the nation together and acted as an instrument for exerting social control. The military regime fostered the illusion among the bishops that they lived in a Catholic land and permitted them to exercise their influence. Integralism and national Catholicism were diametrically opposed to pluralism and democracy.

In 1980, Adolfo Perez Esquivel won the Nobel peace prize. He was an Argentinian whom the dictorship had persecuted. It had cast him in prison for a year and a half without cause. Adolfo Perez Esquivel was a committed Christian and Catholic. The bishops—apart from those involved in human rights—did not congratulate him.

In addition to the official church, the persecuted church was also a reality in Argentina during the dictatorship. Several priests, monks and nuns suffered a martyr's death besides a number of bishops. This fact reflects the gap between the higher orders of the priesthood who conspired with the regime and the lower orders who lived in close touch to the people. This gap was characteristic of the Spanish church and its spiritual descendants in Argentina.[57]

References

The lawyer E. F. Mignone provides an initiated account of the church and the dictatorship in Argentia 1976–1983 in The Catholic Church, Human Rights and the Dirty War in Argentina in D. Keogh (ed.) Church and Politics in Latin America 1990 and in Witness to the Truth, The Complicity of Church and Dictatorship in Argentina 1976–1983. The latter work is basic for the understanding of the relationship between the church and the movement for human rights in Argentina during the dictatorship 1976–1983. It is a study based on a thorough knowledge of material reflecting the standpoint adopted by the bishops. Also informative is P. Rice, The Disappeared: A New Challenge to Christian Faith in Latin America in the previously mentioned work of D. Keogh. A legal evaluation is to be found in M. L. Bartolomei, Gross and Massive Violations of Human Rights in Argentina:1976–1983. An Analysis of the Procedure Under ECOSOC Resolution 1503, 1994.

4.14 Summary

A succession of authoritarian regimes came to power in Latin America in the decade from the mid 1960s to mid 1970s: in Brazil (1964), Argentina (1966 and again in 1976), Peru (1968), Ecuador (1972), Chile (1973) and Uruguay (1973). These were right–wing regimes; those in Peru and Ecuador were military populist experiments. All were opposed to the democratic process. All closed down opposition political parties, trades unions and mass media. For a decade, Latin America was plunged into one of its darkest periods since the beginning of this century as far as violations of human rights and democratization were concerned. The military dictatorships promulgated the doctrine of national security and were supported in Rome. The archbishops Helder Camara in Brazil and Oscar Romero in San Salvador took a stance against violations of human rights. The local churches resisted the terrorism of the military regimes and assumed the leadership of the struggle for human rights. From the

---

[57] Robert F Drinan provides a historical sketch of human rights since 1976 during the administrations of President Videla and President Viola. He notes the disappearance of thousands of people and the reaction of the Catholic hierarchy. Human Rights in Argentina America 1981 145(10) pp 198-200.

Medellin meeting of 1968, liberation was reduced to the struggle for human rights. The USA adopted the doctrine of national security as a foundation stone of its general security policy during the Cold War. The first national paramilitary coup took place in Brazil in 1964 and then again in 1968. The coup in Chile was carried out by military who had been trained in the North American doctrine. In 1976, it was the turn of Argentina.

CELAM never condemned the doctrine of national security nor did it defend the military dictatorships' violation of human rights. The Latin American bishops who led the struggle for human rights were spurned by Rome. Helder Camara was persecuted by the Roman Curia during his period as archbishop in the years 1964–1984. Some of the conferences of bishops supported the military: Argentina, Uruguay, Colombia, Ecuador, El Salvador (with the exception of Oscar Romero and his successor) and Guatemala. The Puebla meeting of 1979 condemned the doctrine of national security but the hidden hand of Rome altered the final text. The military were protected by Rome.

The believing Church was usually deeply involved in human rights and was prepared to set aside institutional cares and risk church interests in opposing the authorities on human rights issues. This was the case in Chile where the archbishop in Santiago, Cardinal Silva Henriques, decided in 1973 to critically distance himself from the Pinochet regime. In Central America and Brazil, the church adopted a very clear attitude towards human rights. This is exemplified by the witness of the martyred Bishop of El Salvador, Oscar Romero, of Archbishop Helder Camara of Brazil and of Cardinal Arns among others. The Peruvian conference of bishops set up a special human rights office to which people could come with their problems and expect to be defended. The believing church was a victim of human rights violations including forced disappearances. In Argentina, priests and persons belonging to religious orders disappeared and were never heard of again. Christians in Latin America suffered in their defence of human rights. However, it is important to distinguish between the official church which often conspired with the violators and forces of oppression and the church of believers which was affected by human rights violations.

CHAPTER 5

Human Rights and the Roman Catholic Church

5.1 Jacques Maritain and Human Rights

The neo-Thomist, Jacques Maritain, played a key role within the movement for human rights in the development leading up to the Second Vatican Council. He was a central figure in bringing about the UN declaration of human rights and contributed to dicussions on this issue with arguments from a Scholastic natural law standpoint. He wrote the introduction, as well as the section on the philosophy underlying human rights, in *Human Rights Comments and Interpretations*, 1950, the publication which arose from the first UNESCO symposium on the human rights issue.[1]

Jacques Maritain published a number of works in which he touched upon the issue of human rights. Among them were *The Person and the Common Good* 1947, *Man and the State* 1951 and *The Rights of Man and Natural Law* 1971. Certain formulations in the latter work suggest that it was written during the Second World War.[2] On the fortieth anniversary of *The Person and the Common Good* in 1989, M. Novak published *Free Persons and the Common Good*. For Maritain, human rights form part of his personalistic philosophy.

A short doctoral dissertation by Hans Brugger entitled *Les Droits de l'homme dans la pensé de Jacques Maritain* was presented in Rome in 1986 and the previous year saw the publication of John. W. Cooper's monograph *The Theology of Freedom, The Legacy of Jacques Maritain and Reinhold Niebuhr*. A useful guide to Maritain's moral theory, on which his doctrine of human rights rests, is J. E. Hug's *Moral Judgement: the Theory and Practice in the Thought and Practice of Jacques Maritain*, 1980.

No special attention is paid to human rights in *The Person and the Common Good*. It is devoted to Thomist social philosophy with themes such as individuality and personality, person and society. In *Man and the State*, Maritain presents his view of human beings and the state and is thus involved in a discussion of human rights. These are based not upon positive, but upon natu-

---

[1] Human Rights Comments and Interpretations 1950, pp. 9–17, 72–77.
[2] J. Maritain The Rights of Man and Natural Law 1971, p. 23. The book was first published in 1943. Its French title was Les Droits de l'homme et la loi naturelle 1975.

ral law. In advancing this natural law position, Maritain aligns himself with Thomas Aquinas.[3]

We shall, first of all, consider certain ideas about human rights which are presented in *The Rights of Man and Natural Law*. Every human being embodies a mystery, namely the human personality. Respect for the value of this personality is the hallmark of every civilization worth the name. We must be prepared to give our lives in the defence of human rights.[4] A human being is an animal and an individual which controls itself by means of its intelligence and will. It does not simply exist on a physical plane. Through knowledge and love, it partakes in a spiritual existence. Personality arises out of the soul. The spirit is the basis of personality.[5] Religious thought alludes to the religious side of our nature when it asserts that human beings are created in the image of God. Human value is based upon this fact. Human beings have an absolute value by virtue of their relationship to God.[6]

Human beings are part of society.[7] Society's goal is the general or common good.[8] There is always a latent conflict between the individual person and society.[9] Maritain's view of society is personalistic because it treats society as totality composed of individual persons whose dignity takes precedence over society. The person is part of society and the community. The general good takes precedence over that of individuals.[10] Maritain's conception of society is theistic, in the sense that God is seen as the principle and goal of human beings and as the source of natural law and society.[11] Those who do not believe in God can cooperate with Christians in bringing about justice, liberty, love and the general good. Religion provides civil society with its values.[12] Maritain distinguishes between three views of society: (1) the bourgeois-individualistic viewpoint according to which the task of the state is to ensure the material welfare of the individual; (2) the communist-totalitarian viewpoint which holds that the task of the state is industrial dominion over nature; and (3) the totalitarian-racist viewpoint according to which the task of the state is political dominion over other human beings. Maritain holds that personality is sacrificed in all three types of society.[13]

For Maritain, the task of political society is to promote the general good of the broad ranks of society so that every person can achieve an independence secured by work, property, political rights etc.[14] The idea of natural law or

---

[3] J. Maritain, Man and the State, 1951, pp. 76–107.
[4] J. Maritain, The Rights of Man and Natural Law, 1971, p. 2.
[5] Maritain, op. cit., p. 3.
[6] Maritain, op. cit., p. 4.
[7] Maritain, op. cit., p. 6.
[8] Maritain, op. cit., p. 8.
[9] Maritain, op. cit., p. 18.
[10] Maritain, op. cit., p. 20.
[11] Maritain, op. cit., p. 21.
[12] Maritain, op. cit., p. 22.
[13] Maritain, op. cit., p. 42 f.
[14] Maritain, op. cit., p. 44.

natural right has its roots in the Stoics of classical antiquity and was further developed by Thomas Aquinas during the Middle Ages.[15] Natural law is an unwritten law of human nature according to which human beings must act.[16] Natural law is thus an unwritten law and our awareness of it has increased in step with the development of human moral consciousness.[17] Natural law and the light of moral consciousness recognize rights linked to human nature. Human beings have rights because they are persons. They are not means towards an end but are ends in themselves. Human beings have the right to be respected; they are the subject of rights; and they possess rights.[18] The philosophy of human rights is based upon the idea of natural law. Since we are subject to cosmic laws, we have rights with respect to other people.[19] There is a connection between natural and positive law—the laws of a given society. A nation's laws are an extension of natural law. The unwritten law makes human law ever more perfect and just. It is the foundation of human rights.[20] Human beings' right to exist and their right to personal liberty belong to natural law.[21] Human beings transcend political society by virtue of the absolute values to which they relate.[22]

Maritain distinguishes between three types of rights: (1) the rights of human beings:to these belong the right to exist and the right to personal liberty.[23] (2) The rights of a citizen in a society: these include the right to participate in political life.[24] (3) The rights of the social individual: to these belong the right to choose freely our work.[25] Jacques Maritain's mode of argument reflects not only his affinity with the natural law tradition with its roots in classical antiquity and scholastic philosophy but also his affinity with the liberal human rights tradition. In his view, human rights are based upon human dignity which is threatened by totalitarian ideologies and states, and preeminently by nazism. Human rights are principally concerned with calling attention to, and protecting human integrity and freedom.

Further observations about the personalist philosophy which Jacques Maritain develops in his work *Man and the State,* are in order. Personalism allowed for a balance between individual and social rights. The roots of this philosophy could be traced to Thomas Aquinas. However, it was reformulated anew by Jacques Maritain in the course of his discussion of human rights. The personalist view of human rights emphasizes both the social and personal aspects of being human in the world. In personalism, human dignity has both individual

---

[15] Maritain, op. cit., p. 59 f.
[16] Maritain, op. cit., p. 61.
[17] Maritain, op. cit., p. 63f.
[18] Maritain, op. cit., p. 65.
[19] Maritain, op. cit., p. 66.
[20] Maritain, op. cit., p. 70 f.
[21] Maritain, op. cit., p. 71.
[22] Maritain, op. cit., p. 73.
[23] Maritain, op. cit., p. 111.
[24] Maritain, op. cit., p. 112.
[25] Maritain, op. cit., p. 113

and social dimensions. According to the personalist conception, people both have a unity as selves and are at the same time open to the greater unity constituted by the community of persons.[26]

Personalism aims to resolve the conflict between individual and social rights and believed that it had clearly succeeded in accomplishing this. The idea of human rights is based upon the vision of humanity as a global community in which human beings respect their fellow human beings' dignity. Human rights presuppose that the state serves human beings and that its power is limited. Jacques Maritain was one of this century's most significant human rights thinkers. He exerted a major influence on the formulation of the UN universal declaration of human rights. For Maritain, human rights involve a view of humans as both individual and social beings possessing a character which transcends political society. By combining human rights with natural law, it is clear that Jacques Maritain follows in the footsteps of Thomas Aquinas. For him, natural law is the foundation of human rights.

5.2 John XXIII and Human Rights

It was John XXIII who began in earnest the preoccupation with human rights within the Catholic church when in 1963 he issued the encyclical *Pacem in terris*. It deals in detail with the issue of human rights. *Pacem in terris* is the central document concerning human rights within the Roman Catholic tradition. It was issued during the Second Vatican Council and appeared at a time when the Catholic church was careful to maintain that human rights have social as well as individual aspects. In the Cold War between East and West, the communist states emphasized social rights whereas the Western countries laid stress on individual rights. The Catholic church advocated peaceful coexistence between East and West and John XXIII was a warm supporter of the idea of peaceful coexistence. The thesis of *Pacem in terris* is that the protection of human rights forms the foundation of world peace. John XXIII aimed at doing justice to the requirement of both individual and social rights in the encyclical.

Pacem in terris was published on 11 April 1963 but it had been first conceived during the Cuba crisis of October 1962, when the Cold War between East and West threatened to turn hot. The Cuba crisis was the culmination of a period of great international tension, illustrated by East-West confrontation over Berlin, the Congo and South East Asia. The encyclical contained a four-part appeal. *First of all*, it appealed for respect for the individual. A dialogue between human beings presupposes the recognition of the dignity and rights of the individual. *Secondly*, it appeals for cooperation between nations. Individuals are not alone. They are part of a political society. *Thirdly*, the encyclical calls for the creation of a supranational authority. Cooperation between nations requires a coordinating body dedicated to the universal common good. *Lastly*,

---

[26] J. Maritain, Man and the State, 1951, p. 107.

it appeals for cooperation between human beings in economic, social and political fields despite their opposing ideologies.

The first part of the encyclical is devoted to the analysis of human rights. John XXIII presents a bill of rights which are universally valid and inviolable. On the basis of *Pacem in terris,* the main constituents of these rights can be given as follows (1) The right to life (physical and personal security) (2) the right of free association (fundamental social rights) (3) the right to develop and realize our own personality (moral and cultural rights) (4) the right to a free choice of occupation (labour or professional rights) (5) the right to make use of created things (economic rights) (6) the right to the protection of, and participation in a political party (political rights).

Every human being is a person with rights and duties. The conception of human rights adopted is a personalistic one. The subject of these rights are persons themselves because they have intelligence and free will and are both capable of, and responsible for, the fulfilment. of their moral destinies. The source of human beings' rights is to be found in their personal existence. They are bearers of these rights.[27] Human beings have the right to live and to live a life which is worthy of a human being. Life is a gift and human beings have a right to it and must respect it. Human beings have the right to everything which is necessary for the maintenance and development of life.[28] There are rights relating to moral and cultural values. Their realization presupposes correct information and an adequate education. There are numerous reasons for this. A political democracy requires enlightened citizens who are able to understand the issues.[29] Human beings have the right to worship God in accordance with an enlightened conscience. The principle of religious freedom is developed. Human beings must follow their conscience: this is a human right.[30] They have the right to choose freely their own stance in life.[31] There are certain rights relating to economic life. Human beings have both the right and duty to work, thus contributing to society. Private property is a right. However, it is subsidiary to the fundamental right of all people to make use of the material things of the world.[32]

Pacem in Terris defends the right to meet and associate freely and the rights of emigration and immigration. Human beings are social beings. Everyone requires to live a social life. This social disposition is the origin of the rights to hold meetings and form associations.[33] The encyclical sets forth its views on political rights. Personal rights are superior to all demands made by the state.[34]

---

[27] PT 8–10. The Latin text is to be found in AAS 55 (1963) 257–304. The numbers refer to the paragraphs in the English and Swedish translations. The English version of the document is to be found in M. Walsh and B. Davies eds. Proclaiming Justice and Peace 1991.

[28] PT 11.

[29] PT 12–13.

[30] PT 14.

[31] PT 54–17.

[32] PT 18–22.

[33] PT 23–25.

[34] PT 26–27.

Finally the encyclical points out in the section specifically devoted to human rights that rights and duties are necessarily combined in the same person. Relations between persons are governed by mutual rights and obligations. There is mutual cooperation and an attitude of responsibility.[35]

In the first part of the encyclical, John XXIII develops his doctrine of human rights. His approach is personalistic. The value of the individual lies at the very core. Human rights are examined in the light of natural law, personality and human dignity. These are the key factors in the view of human rights put forward in *Pacem in Terris*. Human beings' basic rights and duties are seen as deriving from human nature according to their innate law of order. Human dignity is a crucial factor in the view of human beings' rights and duties.[36] Human dignity is the same for all human beings. By virtue of it, they are all equal. The encyclical makes human dignity the foundation of human rights. The latter are an outgrowth of personal dignity. They are therefore universal, indestructible and unchangeable.[37] The structure of society is directed to protecting and promoting human dignity, as it is expressed in human rights and duties.[38] Rights and duties are an expression of human dignity.

The common good is based upon the protection of rights and duties. It is served by protecting human rights and duties. "Today there is agreement that the common good consists above all in the protection and maintenance of personal rights and obligations."[39] Human rights are seen as one side of the common good, the key concept in Catholic social philosophy. "Thereby it is strongly emphasized that the most important task for the authorities is to recognize, respect, coordinate, protect and promote the citizens' rights and duties"[40] It is the task of the state to monitor, protect and promote the common welfare of all its citizens. This task is aimed at the common good of the whole society. John XXIII laid down that authority must be exercised in the interests of the common good. This is the principal reason for its existence.[41] The State is to intervene when associations and trades unions in the exercise of their rights threaten the common good. The State must frame laws which effectively protect associations and trades unions. "A well ordered society presupposes that both individual citizens and all kinds of corporations are effectively protected when they enjoy their rights and fulfil their obligations, whether it is a question of relations between citizens themselves or between citizens and the authorities."[42]

Women demand, both in the home and in everyday life, the rights and duties which they are due as human beings.[43] The working class's consciousness of

---

[35] PT 28–34.
[36] PT 44–48.
[37] PT 145.
[38] PT 44.
[39] PT 60.
[40] PT 77.
[41] PT 84.
[42] PT 69.
[43] PT 41.

its personal value as a collection of human beings, has rightly led it to refuse under any circumstances to submit to arbitrary treatment, as though it were devoid of intelligence and liberty. It wishes to be treated as a human community.[44] All classes are conscious of their natural dignity. The old idea of human beings' natural inequality has been discredited.[45]

In *Pacem in terris*, the social issue is tackled from what is essentially a human rights perpective. The encyclical exemplifies the transition from emphasizing that human rights are primarily individual rights to stressing that human rights have also social consequences. In other words, human rights are also social rights. There are a number of reasons for this change of emphasis but one of them is the insight that lack of human rights is rooted in social structures. In order to establish human rights and make them work, changes in social structure are required where there are obstacles to the maintenance of fundamental human rights. The Roman Catholic church subordinated the individual to the community. After the Second Vatican Council, one sought for a balance between the rights of society and the rights of the individual. This balance is reflected in *Pacem in terris* which is taken to be the central document concerning human rights within the Roman Catholic tradition. The balance between the individual and the community is achieved by the link with personalism. In contrast to Western liberalism, Catholic personalism maintains that human dignity is based both on duties and rights. The starting point of personalism is that men and women are social beings.[46]

In *the second part of the encyclical*, which deals with the relationship between citizens and their government, emphasis is laid on the harmony between the individual and social domains. Individual good must be ensured by means of the common good. *Pacem in terris* represents a synthesis after a long period of conflict and raises additional questions. The official teaching of the church presents two key ideas which harmonize with one another: human beings' personal character as manifested in intelligence and freedom on the one hand and nature as the source of rights and duties on the other. The doctrine aims to be universal and is not particularistic either as regard to its basis or in its application.

References

The best interpretation of Pacem in terris as a human rights document is P. Riga, Peace on earth A Commentary on Pope John's Encyclical 1964. It is a basic commentary, albeit uncritically Catholic and American. The primary emphasis is on what Pope John has to say about individual rights although his conception of social rights is also discussed. J. Y. Calvez also offers a commentary on the encyclical in Johannes XXIII und die Menschenrechte 1966.

In several works, D. Hollenbach has examined the question of the Catholic church and human rights. This brings him to the question of human rights in Pacem in terris.

---

[44] PT 40.
[45] PT 43.
[46] PT 28.

He was active at the Woodstock Theological Center which was founded by the Jesuits in 1974 as a forum for theological reflection about contemporary human problems and participated in the project Human Rights, Needs and Power in an Independent World. As part of this project Hollenbach wrote two books. Claims in Conflict: Retrieving and Renewing the Catholic Human Rights Tradition, 1979 and Justice, Peace and Human Rights, American Catholic Social Ethics in a Pluralistic Context, 1988. The author's American background tends to make him mainly discover the liberal tradition of human rights in the Pontifical document and the teaching of the Catholic church. The value and dignity of personality is given central importance. Claims in Conflict was reviewed by J. E. Will in Human Rights Quarterly, Vol 3, no 1, February 1981.

Another American, G. Weigel, president of the Ethics and Public Policy Center in Washington DC, examines the treatment of the human rights issue, particularly in Pacem in terris, in G. Weigel and R. Royal eds Building the Free Society Democracy, Capitalism and Catholic Social Teaching, 1993. It is written from a neo-conservative standpoint.

In Katholische Kirche und moderner Pluralismus Der neue Zugang zur Politik bei den Päpsten Johannes XXIII und Paul VI und dem Zweiten Vatikanischen Konzil 1978, G. Lindgens discusses the relationship of Johannes XXIII and Paul VI to the Second Vatican Council. The church is defined as the new people of God in the constitution Lumen gentium. The relationship between the church and the world is given a new definition in the pastoral constitution Gaudium et spes. The approach is anthropological. Socialization and personalization are basic concepts. Human beings and their value are given a central role. The general or common good plays a central role in the political theory. Peter Hebblethwaite draws a portrait of the Pope behind Pacem in terris in John XXIII, Pope of the Council, 1984.

5.3 Paul VI and Human Rights

The term human rights was used by Popes before John XXIII but it first made its real breakthrough with the latter, becoming an integral part of the social doctrine of the church. This was brought about by the encyclical *Pacem in terris*. The human rights issue was pursued more energetically in this encyclical than it had been in earlier Pontifical documents.

John XXIII's predecessors viewed human rights exclusively in terms of the neo-scholastic theory of natural law while he defined them also with reference to the conflicts of actual society. Human rights were linked to actual concrete law and to natural law. In John XXIII's approach, individual right was balanced by the general interest. The general good could only be attained by attending to the right of the individual. The state was responsible for achieving a balance in society between different groups of interests.

In his teachings about human rights, Paul VI built both upon the ideas of John XXIII and the Second Vatican Council. He absorbed influences from both. Taking these as his starting point, he further developed them. Like John XXIII, Paul VI linked human rights to the issue of peace. This can be seen in the encyclical *Populorum progressio* of 1967. Paul VI took up the question of human rights in various connections. He issued statements on the twentieth and twenty-fifth anniversary of the declaration of human rights in 1968 and

1973 respectively. He returned to the issue *in Octogesima adveniens*, 1971 which was addressed to Cardinal Maurice Roy, the chairman of *Justitia et Pax*. The latter body had been set up during the pontificate of Paul VI as a follow-up to the new social signals which had been given in *Gaudium et spes* during the Second Vatican Council.

Paul VI and the UN Declaration of Human Rights

Two documents were issued by the Vatican in connection with the twentieth anniversary of the UN declaration of human rights: the first appeared on 15 April 1968 and the second on 4 December 1968.

Like John XXIII, Paul VI takes human dignity as both the starting point and goal of human rights. Human rights signify an important step in the establishment of an adequate legal and political framework for global society. Racial discrimination causes many problems—social injustice, extreme poverty and ideological oppression. It is also the cause of revolutions because there is considerable temptation to respond to such violations of human dignity with violence. To speak of human rights is to assert the general good of all human beings and to strive to build a society based on brotherhood.[47]

Human rights form a basis for cooperation between human beings and without them, genuine peace can never be achieved. Contemporary events show that fraternal cooperation in an atmosphere of respect and understanding are cruelly contradicted in many parts of the world by racial, ideological and religious discrimination through the oppression of weak nations, through regimes which deny their citizens a just liberty and through threats and violence instead of negotiations to resolve conflicts. By its promotion of human rights, the church seeks to follow the example of Christ who gave us the commandment to love from which are derived the norms that govern moral life and which approves and underlines the respect due to every human being.[48]

The Vatican issued a statement on the twenty-fifth anniversary of the UN declaration of human rights on 10 December 1973. As in the corresponding document issued in connection with the twentieth anniversary, peace and rights are linked to one another as cause and effect. There can be no peace unless we respect, defend and promote human rights.

We cannot be indifferent to the need to create a state of coexistence which guarantees for individuals, societies and minority groups the right to life, to personal and social dignity, to development within a secure and improved environment and to a just distribution of the resources of nature and the fruits of civilization. Human rights are based upon the recognition of the dignity of all human beings and of their equality and brotherhood. The duty to respect these

---

[47] Paths to Peace: A Contribution, Documents of the Holy See to International Community, Permanent Observer Mission of the Holy See to the United Nations, 1987, p 76 f.
[48] Op. cit., 78.

rights is a universal one.[49] Paul VI points out violations of human rights such as racial discrimination, ethnic discrimination, the inhumane treatment of prisoners and the violent and systematic elimination of political opponents. The causes of these violations must be identified and eliminated.[50]

Octogesima Adveniens and Human Rights

In the introduction to *Octogesima adveniens* of 14 May 1971, Paul VI says that he wants to draw attention to a variety of contemporary social problems. It is not his intention to provide a universal panacea or patent solutions. Because circumstances vary from country to country, there are no general solutions. It is a matter of finding solutions which are appropriate for each respective country.[51] Paul VI points to urbanization. By this term, he means the conditions arising in underdeveloped countries when people move from the countryside into the cities with overpopulation as a result. If they are unable to make a living in the countryside, they will be no better off in the cities. For countries in Asia and Latin America, this is one of the fundamental social problems.[52] In his analysis, Paul VI shows that people in the Third World are often denied the right to life. He puts forward ideas which were developed in detail in the 1967 encyclical, *Populorum progressio*, devoted to the development issue in the Third World.

Paul VI draws attention to the position of women in society. The issue is about equal wages for equal work carried out by men and women.[53] This problem is clearly linked to the issue of human rights. It is a question of discrimination on the basis of sex. Paul VI also deals with discrimination on the basis of race or colour. This is linked both to the question of the position of blacks in the USA and to apartheid in South Africa.[54] The race problem, together with the issue of women and the problem of underdeveloped countries, form different aspects of human rights. The failure to solve these problems shows that human rights in these areas have not been achieved. The problem of labour emerges in a new form. One aspect of it concerns foreign workers or *gastarbeiter*.[55] The treatment of these workers reveals a lack of human rights.

Two primary global problems are the population explosion and the pollution of the environment. The first of these problems is discussed by Paul VI in detail in *Populorum progressio* and also in the the encyclical *Humanae vitae*. A new feature is the environmental issue i.e. pollution and the disturbance of

---

[49] Op. cit., 79.
[50] Op. cit., 80.
[51] Octogesima adveniens is to be found both in the original Latin and in German translation in Paul VI Apostolisches Schreiben Octogesima adveniens Lateinisch-deutsch Eingeleitet von Oswald von Nell-Breuning SJ (Nachkonziliare Dokumentation Band 35), 1971, 1–7. The following references are to the paragraphs in this edition.
[52] Op. cit., 8–12.
[53] Op. cit., 13.
[54] Op. cit., 16.
[55] Op. cit., 14–15, 17.

150

the ecological balance. Paul VI emphasizes the seriousness of the problem.[56] Environmental pollution belongs to the domain of human rights since it involves ecological rights. The first part of *Octogesima adveniens* as regards the foregoing points is therefore clearly linked to the human rights issue. The apostolic letter shows that in the case of individual, social and ecological rights and the right to life, human rights have not been attained.[57]

In the second part of *Octogesima adveniens*, Paul VI continues his social analysis which is clearly linked to the issue of human rights. He considers the claims for equality and participation in the decision-making process. The Pope looks upon them both, as an expression of human dignity and freedom. In his opinion, they are justified claims. He begins by touching on how equality and participation in the decision-making process can be achieved, not simply at work and in economic life, but in all areas of life. In the Pope´s view, legislation is insufficient by itself and not even the norms of international law suffice. If the right attitude is lacking—if our approach to our fellow human beings does not correspond to the spirit of the Gospel—then human law is to no avail. On the other hand, according to Paul VI, this does mean the need for a reform in attitude instead of the need for institutional reform: what it means, is that one should press for institutional reforms on the basis of a Christian attitude.[58]

The institutional reform entails that democracy is introduced, not only at the level of the state, but that it is also brought into the social sphere, including the economy. The Pope holds that instead of introducing political democracy from the top downwards, one should aim at basic democracy, starting from the bottom. Economic democracy is part of basic democracy. This democracy forms the foundation and determines the structure of the society and economy. Political democracy emerges from and is, so to speak, the final crown of basic democracy. Only a democratic state can protect the democratic structure in society and the economy. Thus Catholics should not content themselves with activities in the social and economic sphere but should also take part in political democracy. Basic democracy is a precondition for the realization of human rights in all their aspects. It is for this reason that Paul VI advocates it in *Octogesima adveniens*.

Democracy presupposes a definite view of man. Christians have such a view by virtue of their Christian faith. Yet it is not only the Christians who have such a definite view of man. The socialist, Marxist and liberal movements have failed to grasp the transcendental dimension in their view of man and have reduced it to something immanent. In addition, the socialist and Marxist movements have made their view of man entirely collectivist, whereas the liberal movement have made it entirely individualist. A corollary of this analysis of our view of man is that when it comes to human rights, the emphasis is placed

---

[56] Op. cit., 18–19, 21.
[57] Op. cit., 18–19, 21.
[58] Op. cit., 22–23.

differently in differing political traditions. Marxists and socialists are primarily interested in social rights, whereas liberals emphasize individual rights. These consequences are not explicitly drawn in the Pontifical text but are present in the very conception of human beings.

Paul VI does not look upon politics as ideology but views it as a practical matter. In politics one grapples with the problems which life itself raises. Since politics is not an ideology, the state is unable to force some ideology on people. This would be tyranny. The confessional state is thereby excluded. Political parties must not try to impose some view of the world on citizens. Questions about our view of the world should be left to free cultural and religious associations. Political parties can scarcely be seen as parties projecting a world view. A party, however, can admit its adherence to certain values but leave it to its members to give a motivation and foundation for these values.

Politicians must base their value norms on a world view. However the same party can contain people with different world views, Christians of different denominations, Christians and non-Christians and believers and non-believers. The ultimate basis of their world view leads to practical decisions which are in agreement or compatible with it.[59] In the case of the issue under discussion, this means that although human rights can be justified or motivated in different ways, the important thing is that we are agreed about these principles and strive to make use of the state as an instrument in bringing them about.

In *the third part* of *Octogesima adveniens*, it is stressed that the church should participate in bringing about greater justice in the distribution of worldly goods both at the national and international levels. The strong must not oppress the weak. Paul VI wrote extensively about this in *Populorum progressio.*. He now returns to this theme. The programme is to be carried out at the international level, in the global economy and in world trade.[60] The right to life for people in the underdeveloped Third World hinges on the implementation of these ideas.

Octogesima adveniens gives no support to the idea that Paul VI is only or primarily interested in propagating for individual human rights. He lays just as much emphasis upon social human rights when he advocates standing up on behalf of the rights of the poor and oppressed. These rights can only be brought about by profound structural changes, not simply inside nations, but also in respect to the relations between nations, particularly in the economic relations between the underdeveloped countries and the industrialized ones. In *Octogesima adveniens*, Paul VI further pursues the themes that he had already mentioned in *Populorum progressio*.

References

The Popes from Leo XIII to Paul VI are presented from the standpoint of their contribution to human rights, by P. E. Bolté in Les droits de l'homme et la papauté contem-

---

[59] Op. cit., 22–41.
[60] Op. cit., 42–47.

poraine: synthese et textes 1975. The declaration of human rights is discussed article by article with reference to what the different Popes have had to say on the subject. This is followed by the author's analysis. Bolté presents his work in an anachronistic and unhistorical way. He allows documents from Leo XIII to Paul VI and the Second Vatican Council to illuminate the main themes in the declaration of human rights from 1948. Even if these texts deal with the same subjects as the declaration of human rights, they belong to historical contexts which are quite different from that of the declaration. It is therefore anachronistic to use these texts to show that the Popes have pursued lines of thought which are in keeping with those to be found in the declaration of human rights. The author's approach may be possible from a systematic point of view but it is impossible from a historical-genetic standpoint. In the author's defence, it should be said that he only relates the contents of the declaration of human rights to material from the church's pronouncements after the Second World War, while, in his analyses, he even makes reference to pronouncements from the period before the Second World War. Proceeding in this way, he shows that the teachings of the church are in accordance with the contents of the declaration of human rights and illustrates how the Popes and the Catholic church have dealt with the issues raised by the declaration.

At Rome, a doctoral dissertation was submitted in 1984 entitled Menschenwürde und Recht. Die Menscherechte in der neueren theologischen Diskussion. Another dissertation on human rights based on church material was submitted to the Law faculty, namely F. Hafner, Kirchen im Kontext der Grund- und Menscherechte, 1992. It contains extensive material but the analytical results are meagre. P. Hebblethwaite provides a detailed portrait of Paul VI in Paul VI, The First Modern Pope 1993.

5.4 The Synod of Bishops and Human Rights

The Synod of Bishops presented their views regarding the human rights issue in *Justice in the World*, 1971 and in a joint declaration with Paul VI in 1974. In October 1974, the Synod issued a call for human rights and their implementaion in the world.

The following exposition falls naturally into *four* parts. *First*, selected parts of *Justice in the World* are presented with reference to the theme of the present investigation. *Next*, those who were responsible for formulating the commentaries and views in *Justice in the World* are presented. *This is followed by* a discussion of the most important exposition of *Justice in the World*, namely that of the Jesuit General, Pedro Arrupe. This forms part of the follow-up to the Synod. *Finally* the Synod of Bishops' declaration of human rights, 1974, is presented.

Justice in the World

One of the results of the Second Vatican Council was the establishment of the Synod of Bishops. It meets in Rome and represents the conferences of bishops throughout the world, along with certain members appointed by the Pope. The third conference of bishops took place from 30 September to 6 November 1971 and discussed among other things *Justice in the World*.

The bishops' document interprets the signs of the times. The influence on the meeting of the Latin American bishops at Medellin in 1968 is plain to see with the result that the theme of liberation is given a central place in the discussion. The bishops regard action on behalf of justice and participation in the transformation of the world as part of the proclamation of the Gospel. Such action is part of the Church's mission to redeem mankind and liberate it from every form of oppression.[61]

Economic injustice and the lack of social participation prevents people from obtaining their fundamental human and civil rights.[62] The right to development is seen as an outcome of the fundamental human rights on which nations are based.[63] The right to development is discussed in *Populorum Progressio*.[64] Justice is violated by forms of oppression which derive from the curtailment of the rights of the individual.[65]

People's relationship to their fellow human beings is linked to their relationship to God. Their response to God's love is to be seen actively operating in their love and concern for their fellow human beings. Christian love towards our neighbour and Christian love of justice cannot be distinguished. This is because love involves an absolute demand for justice, namely a recognition of the dignity and rights of our neighbour.[66] The mission of preaching the Gospel requires that we work for the liberation of mankind even in this world. *If the Christian message of love and justice fails to be active by working for justice in this world, it will experience difficulty in enjoying credibility among our contemporaries.*[67] The church cannot offer concrete solutions to social, economic and political problems. Its mission embraces the defence and promotion of the dignity and fundamental rights of human beings.[68]

Human rights must be upheld within the church for those people who are in various ways involved in it.[69] It is important that women participate both in the life of society and in the life of the church.[70] There should be freedom of thought and expression within the church.[71] Church members should have some part in the decision process within the church.[72] The church must adopt an attitude to material possessions in such a way as to proclaim the gospel for the poor. If the church chooses to live among the rich and powerful, its credibility will be diminished.[73]

---

[61] JM 6. The Latin text to Justice in the world. De justitia in mundo is to be found in AAS 63 (1971) 923–942. Our references relate to the paragraphs in the English translation to be found in M. Walsh and B. Davies eds. Proclaiming Justice and Peace, 1991.
[62] Op. cit., 9.
[63] Op. cit.,15.
[64] Op. cit., 56.
[65] Op. cit., 24.
[66] Op. cit., 34.
[67] Op. cit., 35.
[68] Op. cit., 37.
[69] Op. cit., 41.
[70] Op. cit., 42.
[71] Op. cit., 44.
[72] Op. cit., 46.
[73] Op. cit., 47.

The bishops invite cooperation with other churchs in the work of securing the dignity and fundamental rights of mankind.[74] The international world order is based upon the inviolable rights and dignity of human beings.[75] The bishops place particular emphasis on the satisfaction of human beings' right to life in the developing countries of the Third World.[76] Ecological rights are also part of the picture. It is impossible to see what right the richer nations have to demand an increase in their own material needs if it leads either to others remaining in poverty or to a deterioration of the physical environment. Environment forms the basis of life on earth.[77]

In the document of the Synod of Bishops, human rights are seen as part of justice in the world and this in turn is regarded as an outcome of the Christian message of love.

The Architects of Justice in the World and Commentaries Thereon

When the Synod of Bishops issued its document *Justice in the World* in 1971, it was the subject of commentary in a number of pamphlets published by the Pontifical Commission, Justitia et Pax. They were numbered from 1 to 5 and were written by persons who were known for their involvement in the movement for social justice within the Catholic church. Among the authors were three Jesuits and two women.: 1) P. Land, *An Overview*, 1972;[78] 2) P. Arrupe, *Witnessing to Justice*, 1972;3) J. Alfaro, *Theology of Justice in the World*, 1973; 4) M. Linscott, Education and Justice, 1972; 5) B. Ward, *A New Creation ? Reflection on the Environmental Issue*, 1973.

The President of Justitia et Pax, Cardinal Maurice Roy, wrote a foreword to *Land's* book. Justice is a dimension of the Gospel. Land worked in the secretariat, Justitia et Pax, and simultaneously lectured on economics and social doctrine at the Gregorian University. Land's commentary deals with human rights in the bishops' document and discusses if bringing about justice is seen as a step in the work for human rights in the social dimension.

Barbara Ward is a well known English economist and a member of the Pontifical Commission, Justitia et Pax. She acted as Professor in International Economic Development at Columbia University in New York. She served as an expert at the Synod of Bishops which led to the publication of *Justice in the World*. In her book, taking the documentaion of the Synod as her point of departure, she raises the issue of environment and propagates for ecological rights.

---

[74] Op. cit., 61.
[75] Op. cit., 64.
[76] Op. cit., 66.
[77] Op. cit., 70.
[78] This document has also appeared in French.: P. Land, Vue d'ensemble La justice dans le monde Synode des eveques Commission Pontifical Justice et Paix, 1972.

Juan Alfaro, Mary Linscott and Barbara Ward helped to formulate the theme of justice in the world which was the subject of the bishops' pronouncement in 1971. They are also among the architects of the bishops' document. There is therefore good reason to suppose that there is a close connection between the contents of the bishops' document and the content of their pamphlets. In the pamphlets, they are able to further develop ideas which are merely embryonic in the bishops' document. All three belonged to the think-tank behind *De Justitia in Mundo.*

Of the five pamphlets commentating *Justice in the World*, that of *Pedro Arrupe* is the most interesting because of his position as General of the Jesuit order. It shows that the leader of this highly important body within the Catholic church took a strong stand on behalf of social and international justice. He gave the Jesuit order a radical social profile and as a consequence, he supported efforts to bring about human rights.

Pedro Arrupe and Justice in the World

The Jesuit order,the largest religious order of the Church, was led by Pedro Arrupe. Among its members was the leading theologian Karl Rahner and it influenced the document which was prepared and subsequently accepted during the Second Vatican Council. The Jesuits also played a key role in Latin America as liberation theologians and activists working to bring about justice for the poor.

Pedro Arrupe served as the General of the Jesuit order between 1965 and 1980. He was regarded by many as the most significant General in the history of the order since Ignatius Loyola himself and was credited with a broad vision of the role of the Jesuit order within the Catholic church. Pedro Arrupe turned the attention and concerns of the Jesuit order towards questions of social justice. He wrote *Witnessing for Justice in the World* for Justitia et Pax. It is a commentary to the Synod of Bishops' *Justice in the World,* 1971.The pamphlet was published separately. The book is also included as an essay in P. Arrupe, *Justice with Faith Today, Selected Letters and Addresses*, 1980 in which, addressing the Jesuits in the USA in November 1967, he also develops his ideas about racism. As a participant at the Puebla meeting in 1979, he was the subject of an interview in *Justice with Faith Today* which was published with the title *The Jesuits in Latin America.*

One of those sharing Arrupe's opinions within the Order, was Jean Yves Calvez. The latter was an advocate of the social dimension of evangelization in his broadly based works dealing with the issue of social justice. In *Foi et justice La dimension sociale de l'evangélisation* 1985, Calvez takes the same line on questions of social justice as that adopted by the Jesuit order under its General, Pedro Arrupe. The general meeting of the Jesuit order in 1975 issued a decree which was concerned with promoting justice. Calvez dealt with the human rights issue in *Droits de l'homme, justice, évangile: conférence de Careme 1985 a' Notre Dame de Paris: texte intégral et complément*, 1985.

In his exposition of Justice in the World, Arrupe wished to follow up the Synod of Bishops and work towards ensuring that its purpose was achieved. He wanted to propose practical ways and means of actively helping to bring about justice.[79] He stresses that the statement of the third Synod of Bishops in *Justice in the World* is not the adoption of a theoretical position: it is a call to action.[80] Whereas the First Vatican Council had spoken of signs, the Second Vatican Council preferred to speak of witness. It is, Arrupe emphasizes, our love for one another which makes the church a symbol. When Christians genuinely live according to the Christ's gospel of love—and love presupposes justice—the demand that the church should live according to the Spirit which gives it life, becomes convincing. Life is experienced best through witness, through Christians.[81] God's word, Arrupe continues, is mainly witness. The people of God must witness to the salvation which God has revealed.[82]

The mission of the church is to preach the Gospel but to preach as Christ did, not simply through words, but through action. It is not simply a matter of talking about it: one must live and die for it.[83] The Gospel is a message of love. But love demands justice. The Gospel is therefore also a message about justice. Arrupe emphasizes that actions, not simply words, are necessary. At the same time, more than action: life itself. *Word, action and life* are what make up witness. Witness is, first and foremost, life. The dynamism in this type of witness is enormous. It is not relayed through power. It reveals the values which transform people's lives. It can bring about radical changes in society as much as in individuals which power cannot achieve. Why do saints have followers, Bergson asks ? They demand nothing. But men and women act. All that the saint needs to do, is to exist.[84]

If the teaching of the church is to be effective, it must according to Arrupe, make people act. It must be confirmed by life, by those who live according to the Gospel. This is not easy. The example of a Christian life, a just life, will be followed by many and serve as an inspiration for many. But it will also be a symbol which raises opposition. Christ himself was such a symbol and the servant is not superior to his master.[85]

In Arrupe's view, it is through suffering that the just or righteous man will often bear witness. To bear witness by one's life is to place that life in the service of an ideal, no matter what it costs. To bear witness by one's life is to be ready to lose it. This is why those who have given their lives for the Christian ideal are called martyrs. They are God's witnesses par excellence. The Prophet is a witness, a witness on behalf of justice. A prophet is one through

---

[79] P. Arrupe, Witnessing to Justice, 1972, 6.
[80] Arrupe, op. cit., 5.
[81] Arrupe, op. cit. 8.
[82] Arrupe, op.cit., 8 f.
[83] Arrupe, op. cit., 9.
[84] Arrupe, op. cit., 10.
[85] Arrupe, op. cit., 11.

whom the Holy Ghost speaks, interpreting the signs of the times and by virtue of this revelation, calling upon the people to act in a certain way. This prophetic role is not limited to the institutional and hierarchical church. *Lumen Gentium* maintains that God's people can also take part in the prophetic work of Christ.[86]

The Lord sends us (Arrupe says) prophets to help us on particularly difficult parts of our way or to awaken us from our sinful slumber or to reveal to us our evil acts or to point out wrongful attitudes from which we must free ourselves or to indicate necessary tasks which we must do, things which require radical changes in our life. We need these things to be pointed out to us because we would otherwise never think about them. This is especially so in the case of questions of justice, which sometimes appear to us as problematic and unthinkable. In a world which is stained, as indeed it is, by the grave sin of injustice we need prophets to show us with clarity, energy and courage, the new ways of righteousness and justice which mankind must follow.[87] According to Arrupe, Christians are called to witness to the Gospel message of justice, love and peace in the context of the contemporary world.[88]

On the one hand, there is increasing awareness of human dignity and rights and of the need for unity, solidarity and peace. Power and dynamic forces—scientific, technological, economic, social and political—intensify and strengthen this awareness by bringing human beings closer to one another. On the other hand, we see common and clear violations of the basic rights of individuals, groups and whole nations. The world is scarred by profound and scandalous inequalities in the distribution of material resources, power and responsibility. Unjust systems and structures reduce countless people to a state of submission and tend to prolong and even increase these inequalities. This state of affairs leads people to violent and destructive conflicts and even threatens to throw the world into a global war. The Synod of Bishops says that the contemporary world is marked by the "profound sin of injustice" and "opposes by its perversity the Creator's plan." Today, it is not simply a few individuals but the greater part of mankind which has fallen victim to these injustices. In this context it is the duty of the church and all Christians to witness on behalf of justice with greater urgency. It is a part of the church's mission to witness on behalf of justice and to do it through its life and through the personal and common lives of all Christians.[89]

According to Arrupe, when we speak of witnessing on behalf of justice, we mean Divine Justice as revealed by God Himself in the Old and New Testaments. In the Old Testament, the Synod says, "God reveals Himself to us as the liberator of the oppressed and the defender of the poor, demanding of mankind, faith in Him and justice for our neighbour." In the New Testament, God

---

[86] Arrupe, op. cit., 12.
[87] Arrupe, op. cit., 13.
[88] Arrupe, op. cit., 16.
[89] Arrupe, op. cit., 17 f.

reveals himself to us in Christ Our Lord: in His life and message. And what is Christ's message ? It is that Christian love for our neighbour and justice cannot be divorced from one another. It is by dedicating our lives to such ideals as the liberation of the oppressed, the defence of the poor, love and concern for mankind as brothers and sisters of Christ and our own flesh and blood, that we can witness on behalf of justice, according to Arrupe. We must make it clear for the world through our life's witness that it is an integral part of the Christian vocation to establish a social order "based upon truth, built upon justice and inspired by love" as *Gaudium et Spes* expressed it during the Second Vatican Council.[90]

Arrupe explains human rights in the following way. Discrimination is a direct challenge to the Christian view of human beings. Human dignity, the unity of the human race and the equality of human beings is the essence of the Christian Gospel which proclaims our common origin, our common aims, our common salvation and our common fate. Discrimination on the basis of race, colour, standards of living or religion is alien to the attitude of Christ. We must treat all people the same, without discrimination, irrespective of their sex, race, colour, faith or social position. There is suport for efforts towards the emancipation of women.[91]

Arrupe maintains that if Christian witness on behalf of justice is to be effective, it must be a common witness. Christians cannot be divided in their witness. Ecumenical cooperation should involve all aspects of our witness. Serious theological study and reflection is required to promote a clear basis for a common Christian witness and involvement in the social field.[92] In order to defend fundamental human rights and promote justice, peace and freedom, we must cooperate with all people, even with non-Christians who according to the Synod employ just means to bring about a more just and more humane world. The Pontifical Commission Justice and Peace and the World Council of Churches contributed to the development of this ecumenical cooperation especially through its joint committee for society, development and peace (SODEPAX). From one point of view, Arrupe's exposition and application of the Synod of Bishops' document *Justice in the World* is nothing more than an appeal to implement human rights in both their individual and social dimensions. Justice embraces demands for human rights. Where there is justice, human rights are implemented. Where it is lacking, human rights are violated. Justice and human rights cannot be separated. They are two sides of the same coin.

Declaration of Human Rights

A declaration demanding the defence of human rights was issued on 23 October 1974 by Paul VI and the Synod of Bishops. When the document was shown

---

[90] Arrupe, op. cit., 18.
[91] Arrupe, op. cit., 31.
[92] Arrupe, op. cit., 59 f.

to the Pope, he asked for it to be distributed in his name and that of the bishops. The declaration speaks of the right to life, the right to eat, socio-economic rights, political and cultural rights and the right to religious freedom.

In the Gospel, the Bishops observe, we find the fullest expression and clearest reason for involvement in the preservation and promotion of human rights. Human dignity is based upon the image of God and its reflection in each and every member of the human race. The bishops draw attention to those rights which are specially under threat today. The right to life is threatened by abortion and euthanasia, through torture and war. The right to eat is threatened by starvation and hunger.

Socio-economic rights are threatened by the concentration of economic power to a few nations and by multi-national corporations, structural imbalance in trade relations, lack of balance between economic growth and economic distribution, unemployment and by patterns governing the global consumption of resources.

Political and cultural rights require that indiviuals can influence their fates; that they can participate in the political process in a free and responsible way; that they have free access to information, freedom of expression and of the press,; that they have right to education and can determine what education their children are to have. The bishops reject the denial of rights on the grounds of race.

The right to religious freedom reflects human dignity as it is recognized by the word of God and reason. It is denied by certain political systems which try to prevent religious worship, religious education and the vocation of the priesthood. We call upon all governments (the bishops say) to eliminate every kind of discrimination.[93]

This document from the Synod of Bishops shows that the main emphasis of the presentation is placed on social, not individual rights. It calls for changes in the socio-economic and politico-cultural spheres. These are prerequirements for people in the Third World to be able to live a life of human dignity. Their fidelity to the Gospel message, leads the bishops to act on behalf of human rights. *The promotion of human rights forms a part of the preaching of the Gospel.* For the bishops, human rights are primarily something which involves changes in social and economic structures and relations. The declaration is completely in accord with the demands made by CELAM at Medellin in 1968 and by the 1971 Synod of Bishops in its document *Justice in the World.* If during the Cold War which followed in the wake of the Second World War, human rights primarily meant individual rights, in the deepening conflict between the poor and rich world, these rights mean social rights and the right to life.

---

[93] 1974 Synod of Bishops, Statement on Human Rights and Reconciliation, Origins 4 (November 7, 1974) 318–320. 1974, Bischofsynode, Botschaft über Menschenrechte und Versöhnung, Herder Korrespondenz, Monatshefte für Gesellschaft und Religion, Heft 12, 28 Jahrgang, Dezember 1974, 624–625. S. H. Pfurtner provides a commentary on the call of the 1974 Synod of Bishops for human rights in Die Menschenrechte in der römisch-katholischen Kirche in Zeitschrift für evangelische Ethik 1/1976 35 ff.

5.5 Justitia et Pax and Human Rights

With the setting up of the Pontifical Commission Justitia et Pax in January 1967, Paul VI carried out the wish expressed by the Second Vatican Council in the pastoral constitution *The Church in the modern world.*

The Commission's mandate was to persuade God's people to carry out His call to promote development, justice and peace in the world. The Commission was a Pontifical one. It was set up by the Pope and answerable to him. Its secretariat formed part of the Roman Curia, the central administration of the Holy See.

The Commission attempted, on the basis of the instructions given by the Second Vatican Council, to cooperate with other Christian churches and denominations, especially with the World Council of Churches. The Pontifical Commission and the World Council of Churches created a joint committee for development, justice and peace (SODEPAX) with a secretariat in Geneva.

The regional and national conferences of bishops all over the world were asked to establish or authorize comparable bodies to Justice and Peace within their respective territories. They formed, as it were, a circulatory system for the justice and peace initiative not simply within the Catholic church but also ecumenically by linking up with other Christians by means of SODEPAX and with other people of all religions and ideologies as well as with temporal organizations. All this complex structure was made to serve God's human family.

Justitia et Pax was concerned, among other things, with human rights. It was to its chairman, Cardinal Maurice Roy that Paul VI addressed *Octogesima adveniens* in 1971 which took up inter alia the human rights issue. Justitia et Pax was responsible in *The Church and human rights*, 1975 for a collective documentation, concerning the church's view of human rights.

In 1988, Justitia et Pax held a symposium in Rome on *human rights and the church.* J. Joblin of the Gregorian University gave a historical survey of the church and human rights with an eye to future developments and Walter Kasper presented the theological foundation of human rights.

The following account examines two publications about human rights, which were inspired by Justitia et Pax.

The Church and Human Rights 1975

The aim of the document *The church and human rights* which deals with the human rights issue from a Christian perspective, is to invite reflections and criteria to be submitted to the national Justitia et Pax commissions.[94] Its intention is to encourage national Justitia et Pax commissions to involve themselves

---

[94] The Church and Human Rights Pontifical Commission Justitia et Pax 1975 5. This document is also available in German as Die Kirche und Menschenrechte Arbeitspapier der Päpstlichen Kommission Justitia et Pax 1976.

in the defence and promotion of human rights at the national and international levels.[95]

First of all, Justitia et Pax undertakes a historical survey of pontifical documents on the basis of how the issue of human rights is treated in them.[96] The analysis of *Rerum novarum* was carried out at the beginning of the 1970s and it was therefore natural, given the socialist criticism of Western emphasis on the individual nature of human rights, that Justitia et Pax should draw attention to *Rerum novarum* and claim that this encyclical looks upon human rights as social in character by viewing them in their social context. According to Justitia et Pax, the social aspect of human rights is also asserted in *Quadragesimo anno*. There is a connection between these rights and the social and economic conditions required for their implementation. Justitia et Pax was influenced by current discussions when it sought to reconstruct the linkage of human rights with the Catholic social tradition. The 1960s were a reaction to the liberal and individualist interpretation of human rights, characteristic of the 1940s and 1950s. The question arises to what extent this interpretation of *Rerum novarum and Quadragesimo anno* are really based on these documents, as originally presented, and how far it is a projection of the discussion in the 1970s when Justitia et Pax embarked on its interpretation of the two social encyclicals. There is no reason to examine this issue in more detail. It suffices to state that it is highly probable that that is a grain of truth in both suppositions.[97]

Pius XII's emphasis on human rights during and after the Second World War, was principally determined by his fight against dictatorship, first in the form of fascism and nazism and later in the form of communism. Given this background, Justitia et Pax showed that Pius XII's interest was chiefly concerned with individual human rights. It is a question of preserving the dignity of the individual person.[98] Justitia et Pax notes both the social as well as the individual aspect of the human rights, emphasized by John XXIII and Paul VI in their social document. Not only individuals but also peoples have rights to development in the social and economic sphere as well as in the human sphere.[99] The Synod of Bishops in 1974 regarded human rights in the same way as Justitia et Pax, as a consequence of the Gospel. All three aspects are to be found in *Evangelization of the modern world* i.e. individual and social rights,together with the right to life and the right to be fed.[100]

Justitia et Pax emphasizes that the Catholic church draws attention in its social teaching to the importance both of people's individual rights and their social rights. The commmission thus reflects the situation within the Catholic church, in which liberation theology in Latin America not least, gave prominence at the beginning of the 1970s to the Third World perspective on human

---

[95] The Church and Human Rights 1975 9.
[96] Op. cit., 10–12.
[97] Op. cit., 13–15.
[98] Op. cit., 15–17.
[99] Op. cit., 17.
[100] Op. cit., 18–19.

rights. The basic human right—the right to food and sustenance—can only be satisfied in a society which has just social and economic structures. This is the prequirement for individuals to be able to shape their own lives freely.[101] The basis of human rights in Catholic social teaching is the natural law.[102] Starting from the Catholic church's social teaching during John XXIII and Paul VI, Justitia et Pax shows that the three aspects of human rights—the individual, social and Third World aspects—are adequately accounted for and that in the official social doctrine of the church, there is a balance between them.[103]

Justitia et Pax interprets the Catholic church's exertions on behalf of human rights as part of its mission of striving for justice and love which in turn form an integral part of the evangelical message. Thus human rights are justified in terms of the Christian gospel and receive their legitimacy from it. It is this which explains both the Catholic church's exertions on behalf of human rights and the ultimate reason for their exertions. The gospel is both the starting point and the goal of the Catholic church's actions on behalf of human rights. This action, according to way Justitia et Pax views matters, is thus purely occasioned by religious reasons.[104] According to Justitia et Pax, human beings have a dignity which is the foundation and starting point of the UN declaration of human rights. This dignity is based on the fact that human beings are reflections of God: they are created in God's image. Thus human rights are deduced from human dignity which in turn is derived from the fact that human beings are created in the image of God. There are three components involved in this theological argument: *human rights—human dignity—the reflection of God.* Human beings can therefore never be treated as an instrument for the welfare of others: they are ends in themselves.[105] Justitia et Pax emphasizes repeatedly that human rights have both a private and general aspect and that they encompass both the individual and society.[106]

After making various historical observations, Justitia et Pax considers pastoral aspects of the human rights issue.[107] One reason for the intensified work on human rights was the 25th anniversary of the UN declaration in 1973 which Justitia et Pax and the World Council of Churches celebrated jointly.[108] According to Justitia et Pax, violations of human rights can arise from economic and political situations and these violations are combatted by eliminating the economic and political factors which produce them. This way of arguing is designed to point out the connection between individual and social aspects of human rights.[109] The Catholic church, through its local and national bodies,

---

[101] Op. cit., 20–21.
[102] Op. cit., 20.
[103] Op. cit., 21–28.
[104] Op. cit., 31.
[105] Op. cit., 34.
[106] Op. cit., 36 f.
[107] Op. cit., 40–61.
[108] Op. cit., 47.
[109] Op. cit., 53.

contributes constructively to the campaign for human rights by studying the various factors which lead to violations and by indicating the mechanisms which cause human rights to be set aside.[110] According to Justitia et Pax, it is important to pay attention to the interaction between human rights and the society in which they operate, so that a balance can be achieved between the individual and collective aspects of these rights.[111]

Human Rights and the Church 1988

In his introduction to the Justitia et Pax symposium in Rome in 1988, *John Paul II* draws attention to the connection between human rights and peace which was the main theme of *Pacem in terris* 1963, the church's fundamental document on human rights which was issued 15 years after the declaration of human rights in 1948.[112] John Paul II speaks of the apostolate for human rights. He supports those who are involved in this type of service. It is his hope that this apostolate will communicate more widely the teaching of *Pacem in terris* and the principles in the declaration of human rights.[113]

Joseph Joblin begins his lecture on *The Church and Human Rights: Historical Overview and Future Outlook* by stating that human rights in the Western World are primarily individual in character whereas in the socialist world they are primarily collective. In the non-European world, the idea of human rights is often completely alien.[114] The church has altered its attitude to human rights: it no longer rejects them but is one of their most enthusiastic protagonists.[115] Pius VI condemned the declaration of the rights of man and citizens of 1789, which he considered as madness.[116] The French Revolution was anti-religious and it was this that led Pius VI to condemn the declaration of 1789. The revolution tried with this declaration to create a completely secular society, devoid of any religious foundation.[117]

According to Joseph Joblin, the idea of human rights is rooted in the Classical and Judaeo-Christian traditions and the civilization which came about through their confluence. It considered the human being as a power in relation to the external world. Human beings had the capacity to reflect over their own situation.[118] John XXIII bridged the gap between believers and non-believers

---

[110] Op. cit., 54.

[111] Op. cit., 58.

[112] Human Rights and the Church, Historical and Theological Reflections Conferences presented at an International Colloquium organized by the Pontifical Council for Justice and Peace Rome 14–16 November 1988, 1990 6. This document is also available in French: Les Droits de l'homme et l'église, Réflexions Historiques et Théologiques Conseil Pontifical Justice et Paix. Relations présentées à un Colloque international organise à Rome du 14 au 16 novembre 1988 par le Conseil Pontifical Justice et Paix 1990.

[113] Human Rights and the Church 1990, 9.

[114] Op. cit., 11.

[115] Op. cit., 13.

[116] Op. cit., 15.

[117] Op. cit., 34.

[118] Op. cit., 18.

in the Western world. The unifying bond was cooperation for the common good and not the reasons behind such cooperation. The starting point was the recognition of the inviolable, equal and responsible person: in other words, human integrity. All of us have a duty to obey our conscience and for this reason. civil society must recognize people's right to follow their conscience.[119] In all human beings, conscience is the source of rights.[120]

Human rights imply a recognition of a common moral authority. They are a symbol of future hope. However as Walter Kasper begins his lecture on *The Theological Foundation of Human Rights*, there is a need for a normative basis for human rights. In the concentration camp, Jews, Christians and Marxists were, for different reasons, opponents of an inhuman totalitarian system but they were unable to formulate the metaphysical reason for this moral position.[121] The historical origin of human rights is particular, but their universal validity requires some basis on which to rest. Because of their particular historical origin, both the concrete view and concrete implementation of human rights are interpreted in different ways according to the historical context in which these rights arise. There are different human rights traditions: the Western liberal human rights tradition, the social human rights tradition of Marxist origin and the The Third World conception of human rights. *Human rights can be misused with the aim of serving one's own interest.* They are then subordinate to reasons of state or party. They are used to serve the ideological underpinning of certain interests and privileges.[122]

The inviolability of human rights means that they are unconditional and absolute.[123] Human rights, Kaspar maintains, are in part an expression of liberation from old orders and in part a protest against new types of enslavement. They contain normative elements.[124] When Kant provides a foundation for the independence of morality, he proceeds from the assertion that human beings are never means, but are always ends in themselves. This gives human beings a special dignity in relation to other values. The idea of human dignity is something to be found in human beings. In it, something unconditional and absolute is revealed. It is because human beings as moral beings are representatives for the absolute, that they have a right to human dignity.[125] The idea of human rights based upon human dignity, Kasper stresses, was first discussed by the Catholic church in John XXIII's encyclical Pacem in terris.[126] The pastoral constitution *Gaudium et Spes* also expresses the view that human rights are based upon the dignity which human beings are given by God.[127]

---

[119] Op. cit., 39.
[120] Op. cit., 40.
[121] Op. cit., 48.
[122] Op. cit., 49.
[123] Op. cit., 50.
[124] Op. cit., 51f.
[125] Op. cit., 52f.
[126] Op. cit., 53.
[127] Op. cit., 54.

Human rights have their origins in the Biblical idea that human beings are created in the image and likeness of God. The Biblical tradition is later combined with the doctrine of natural rights. Thomas Aquinas underlines the dignity of human beings and anticipates the modern formulation of human dignity. The theology of the doctrine of natural rights has developed since the beginning of modern times. Political consequences were derived from it. *Bartolomé De Las Casas used the doctrine of the natural rights of human beings to argue against Spanish colonial policy.* A Christian tradition of human rights existed according to Kasper independently of the modern human rights tradition. Pius XI and Pius XII bring it into play in their encyclicals and pronouncements against fascism (*Non abbiamo bisogno,* 1931), national socialism (*Mit brennender Sorge,* 1937) Marxism (*Firmissimam constantiam,* 1937) and communism (Divini redemptoris, 1937, *Pius XII's Christmas message* 1942).[128] The problem was no longer rationalism and liberalism but totalitarianism. Faced with the threat to human freedom from the totalitatian systems, the church chose the side of freedom and defended human dignity.[129]

In contrast to the liberal tradition of human rights with its roots in the enlightenment, the Christian tradition, according to Kasper, asserts that human rights are both individual and socio-cultural.[130] Human rights precede and go beyond the state and society; they are not given to the individual by the state and society. They come with human beings' very existence. They are recognized and carried over by the state and society into the sphere of positive law. They are based upon human beings' God-given existence.[131]

Kasper then proceeds to deal with the problem of basing human dignity upon natural law and theology by asserting that human rights within theology are based, either upon natural right or upon Christology. The natural law foundation is to be found especially in texts before the Second Vatican Council. Human dignity is derived from the very nature of human beings, their possession of reason and free will. Divine law is inscribed in the hearts of the heathen. They can understand the Will of God by listening to the voice of their conscience. The foundation of human rights upon natural law provides them with a universal validity. But in the Concilium texts, these ideas of natural law are supplemented with a theological, Christological argument.[132]

Human rights are given a theological basis by starting with the theology of creation. Human dignity is seen as being based upon the fact that God created human beings in the divine image. God is reflected in human beings. However this being, created in the likeness of God, is ensnared by sin. Even the sinner, however, has respect for human rights. *The theological ideas are placed on a Christological plane.* God becomes a human being in Christ and bestows on

---

128 Op. cit., 55.

129 Op. cit., 55 f.

130 Op. cit., 56.

131 Op. cit., 58.

132 Op. cit., 59 f.

166

mankind a unique dignity. Gaudium et Spes maintains that through the Incarnation, whereby God became a human being in Jesus Christ, God unites Himself with all mankind.[133] Through the Holy Ghost, Christ's salvation is transferred to us. The dignity of the new human being is given by the Holy Ghost. In Jesus Christ, all those natural differences which are to be found between people lose their alienating and discriminatory character. There is neither Jew nor Greek, neither bondman nor free, neither man nor woman. All are one in Jesus Christ. All human beings are called to this universal dignity by God's child. From this theological basis of human rights, it follows that a commitment to human dignity and rights is an integral part of the Gospel witness. This is the main point in Walter Kasper's analysis. He points out that this approach is apparent in the document of the Synod of Bishops, *Justice in the world* 1971 and in Paul VI's written statement *Evangelii Nuntiandi* (To Preach the Gospel) 1975 and was continued by John Paul II in the encyclical *Redemptor Hominis* (The Redeemer of mankind) 1979. According to Kasper, the theological-Christological foundation of human rights is superior to the natural law foundation from an ecumenical standpoint since it is also acceptable to Protestants.[134]

When human rights are given a Christological foundation, they are then based on the central ideas of Christianity and not on the least common denominator. The shift in the activities of the church towards non-European cultures, Kasper holds, gives the the Christological foundation some advantage over the natural law foundation. Europe has increasingly distanced itself from Christianity and has become pluralistic.[135] It is important to point to Jesus Christ as the concrete categorical imperative and the concrete universal. The Christians bring what is human forward into the light just as Grace does with nature. Mother Teresa's human commitment which springs from a profound belief in Christ, is evident also for non-believers.

Walter Kasper argues both for a natural law and a Christological approach to human rights. His reason is that both standpoints are to be found in both the documents of the Second Vatican Council and the teaching of John Paul II.[136] There is an inner connection between both ways of giving a foundation to human rights. The dignity of human beings is recognized, not only by reason, but through the divine revelation. The human mystery only becomes clear in the mystery of Jesus Christ. God reveals the human being wholly and fully in Jesus Christ. The old principle that Grace does not corrupt Nature but brings it to completion, is confirmed.

Kasper holds that the differences between the Orthodox, Catholic, Lutheran and Reformed traditions when it comes to giving a foundation for human rights, spring from the fact that people view the relationship between Nature and Grace differently. This diversity is also present in the way of defining the

---

[133] Op. cit., 60.
[134] Op. cit., 61.
[135] Op. cit., 62.
[136] Op. cit., 63.

relationship between temporal and eschatological salvation and between human welfare and Christian salvation.[137] Kasper stresses that the Gospel is not some trivial Utopia. It is a source of light and strength for acting in the world. Commitment to human dignity and rights is an integral part of the witness to the Gospel.[138]

Kasper means that only religion can secure the survival of the modern idea of human rights since modern secular society is incapable of doing so. Modern society needs for its own sake a foundation of legitimacy which is independent of the society itself. The human mystery receives in Jesus Christ its eschatological meaning[139] God revealed in Jesus Christ that the meaning of human existence is to serve others. Human rights require to be interpreted in the light of Christian love for our fellow human beings.[140]

5.6 John Paul II and Human Rights

John Paul II was elected Pope on 16 October 1978. His election meant that the Catholic church began to spotlight human rights because of Karol Woytola's Polish background. His own experience had been formed by the Catholic churchs confrontation with the communist state and the individual's lack of liberties and rights. It was therefore natural that he used his platform as leader of the Catholic church to campaign on behalf of human rights. His activity in this sphere was one of the factors which paved the way for the collapse of the Soviet empire.

The human rights theme recurred in the Pope's addresses and messages at the start of his Pontificate. In the UN he raised the matter in his message on the thirtieth anniversary of the declaration of human rights on 2 December 1978. In Puebla, he touched on it in his address of 28 January 1979. The theme recurred in his first encyclical *Redemptor Hominis* of 4 March 1979. During his first visit to Poland as Pope, he raised the question of human rights in a speech on 2 June 1979. He naturally analyzed the human rights issue in his address at the UN in New York on 2 October 1979, at UNESCO in Paris on 1 June 1980[141] and in a letter in connection with the Helsinki document on 1 September 1980. He turns to the question of apartheid on 7 July 1978. He deals with human rights in a speech during his third visit to Poland on 8 June 1987 and in a speech before the Council of Europe on 8 October 1988.

In certain respects, above all from the start of the 1980s, John Paul II has very little new to add, in his analysis of the the theme of human rights, to what he had said earlier. To avoid repetition, there is therefore no point in dealing

---

[137] Op. cit., 64.
[138] Op. cit., 65.
[139] Op. cit., 67.
[140] Op. cit., 68.
[141] Jean Paul II en France mai–juin 1980, 1980 98–107.

with it in this investigation. John Paul II represents a *Christocentric humanism* in his view of human rights.[142] He provides a Christological foundation for human dignity and human rights.[143]

The Polish situation particularly in the period 1978–1980 (although also afterwards) forms an important background to John Paul II's campaign for human rights. There is therefore good reason for beginning our presentation with a sketch of John Paul II's role in developments in Poland.

Justitia et Pax published a series of pamphlets with the title *The Social Teaching of John Paul II*. They dealt with the social dimensions or aspects of John Paul's addresses during the first years of his Pontificate. The texts or extracts from the texts were published with a commentary. The themes which are treated, tell us something about Justitia et Pax's focus of interest. The first seven pamphlets analyzed the following themes: *1) General aspects of John Paul II's social teaching and the use of the expression "the church's social doctrine" 2) the human person and social structures 3) Religious freedom 4) The theme of liberation 5) Human work 6) The person,the nation and the state and 7) Human rights.*

John Paul II and Poland

The new Pope John Paul II wished to celebrate the nine hundredth anniversary of the martyrdom of his predecessor, Stanislaw the Holy, on 8 May 1979. Stanislaw had been bishop of Cracow. Already in December 1978, John Paul sent a special Christmas letter to his previous archdiocese in Cracow in which he spoke of the importance of the myth of Stanislaw the Holy in Polish culture. He wrote that in the person of Stanislaw the Holy, we can perceive a defender of the most basic human rights upon which human dignity rests. The religious legend was transformed into a source for the mythological legitimization of the campaign against violations of human and civic rights in Poland.

John Paul II arrived in Poland on 2 June 1979. Before the assembled communist leaders headed by Party Secretary Edward Gierek, he said that it was the mission of the church to make human beings conscious of their rights and duties. Peace can only be based upon respect for basic human rights which include the right for a nation to liberty and to the creation of its own culture. His message to the Communist power élite and their chief, Edward Gierek, was that the church's role was not simply cultic. He challenged the Marxist claim that religion is an expression and cause of human alienation. The church's evangelical mission in life, which cannot be separated from its sacramental mission, is to defend human rights. To carry out its role, the church has to be free. Furthermore, Poland has agreed to this by signing the universal declaration of human rights.

---

[142] O. Höffe u.a. Johannes Paulus II und die Menschenrechte. Ein Jahr Pontifikat 1981, 76–81. The same book is avaliable in French: O Höffe et. al., Jean Paul II et les droits de l'homme, 1980.
[143] Op. cit., 81–87.

The first Pontifical mass was held in Warsaw on Victory street (a place until then used exclusively for state functions) and was broadcast by television the length and breadth of the country. One of the places set apart for the official rituals of the communist state was transformed into a holy place for the Catholic ceremony. For the majority of the Polish people, it was no longer "their" place to which "we" are sometimes invited. For the first time, it became *our* place where *our* Pope as representative of *our* church celebrates the mass with *us*. Around a million people participated in the first Warsaw mass with young people predominating. The last Pontifical mass was held in Cracow on 10 June and attracted a crowd of 2.5 to 3 million people, the largest in Polish history.

The Pope was received with gifts from various groups and individuals. Many observers described the direct social consequences of this visit as a purification. The crowds were also unexpectedly disciplined An independent observer wrote that the Papal visit would affect the very core of national consciousness.

The regime tried to exploit John Paul's homecoming as a way of securing legitimacy. The official propaganda tried to present the visit as proof of the Pope's approval of the communist regime.

The Pope's visit changed Poland. Already at the first service in Victory street in Warsaw, he pointed to the link between the Polish nation and Catholicism and challenged the temporal definition of the Polish nation. It is impossible to understand the history of the Polish nation without Christ. If we throw away this key to understanding our nation (said the Pope), we risk a basic misunderstanding. We do not understand ourselves. It is impossible to comprehend this nation without Christ. During his first visit, the Pope placed Polish history in the context of Catholic mythology and touched upon many other important contemporary questions such as national sovereignty, the European roots and orientation of Polish culture, civic rights, human dignity and the value of work.

He also put forward another idea in his acts of worship which was seldom discussed in the official media in Poland. He explained that Christianity must once more take part in the creation of Europe's spiritual unity. Economic motives alone cannot achieve this. Europe cannot cease from striving after its fundamental unity and must turn to Christianity. The issue of European unity was tabu in Poland. The accepted view was to create instead a picture of Poland closely allied to the Soviet Union. The idea that European unity should be based upon a common Christian background must have sounded like sacrilege to official ears.

On 7 June 1979, in Auschwitz, he spoke of the place as the Golgotha of our times and affirmed the church's commitment to human dignity and civil rights. John Paul II pointed out that his first encyclical *Redemptor Hominis* dealt with human rights.[144] Millions of people came of their own volition and without the promptings of the state to celebrate their Pope. They saw that citizens were

---

[144] Johannes Paulus II Homilie bei der Messe im Konzentrationslager Auschwitz-Birkenau (7.6.1979) in Johannes Paulus II und die Menschenrechte 1981, 117–121.

capable of organizing society without the state. Their fear of the state was correspondingly diminished and at the same time, their consciousness which focused on the personality of the Pope, developed. John Paul II breathed new life into symbols for the nation, Catholicism and civil society which were accepted as genuine elements of identity by the Poles. The awareness that the national community can be defined outside the communist state, filtered through to all sections of society, including the working classes. Merely through the influence of the Pope's visit, Polish workers attained a new level of self-identification as members of a wider community organized round such accepted symbols as the Pope, the Black Madonna, the Catholic church and the common national heritage. This new consciousness formed the first step towards formulating the positive programme developed in the period 1980–81.

John Paul II became the central figure of national identity and the country's indisputable moral authority. This resulted in a loss of social position for the communists holding power. On his first visit to Poland in June 1979, John Paul spoke about human rights. He gave the Poles a new self-respect and renewed faith.

On his third visit to Poland after Gorbachev had begun his campaign on behalf of *glasnost* and *perestroika*, John Paul II demanded in the presence of General Jaruzelski, on 8 June 1987, the implementation of the UN charter of human rights in Poland. Jaruzelski wished to exploit the Pope's visit to Poland for his own political ends. However, John Paul did not accede to his wishes but instead openly supported Solidarity. In 1987, the Polish socialist party declared that it felt greater solidarity with the social teaching of the church than with Marxism.

John Paul II's visit to Poland rapidly became the focus for campaigns for human rights which were directly critical of the totalitarian communist system. Developments in the Soviet Union beginning in 1985 enabled him during his third visit to agitate more openly on behalf of human rights and the workers' right to organize themselves in trades unions than had been possible during his two earlier visits. Jaruzelski had wanted to use John Paul's visit in June 1983 politically in giving his government international legitimacy, in demonstrating his political correctness for the Soviet Union and in improving relations with USA and Western Europe.

Activist priests such as Henryk Jankowski and Jerzy Popieluszko received popular support because of the violation of human rights by the Polish authorities. The Catholic church was the single most significant defender of human and civil rights in Poland since the Second World War. In connection with the rise of Solidarity in August 1980, the Second Vatican Council's statement that one of the basic human rights was the right of workers to be able to organize themselves in a trades union, was cited. The strikers took their ideology from the Polish Catholic church's idea that every human being has certain fundamental rights.

References

John Paul's addresses in Poland are to be found in John Paul II Return to Poland, The Collected Speeches of John Paul II, 1979.

There is a comprehensive literature about John Paul II's role in the developments in Poland around 1980. The journalist T. Garton Ash provides a social and political analysis of the Polish revolution in The Polish Revolution Solidarity 1980–82, 1983. J. Kubik tackles the Polish revolution during the 1970s and early 1980s from an anthropological perspective in The Power of Symbols against the Symbols of Power, the Rise of Solidarity and the Fall of State Socialism in Poland, 1994. Historians, journalists, sociologists and political scientists write about the same historical events from other points of view. Kubik is a cultural anthropologist and specializes in the popular aspect of oppositional movements and the culture of Solidarity. Another informative source about the Polish revolution is B. Törnqvist Plewa in The Wheel of Polish Fortune, Myths in Polish Collective Consciousness during the First Years of Solidarity, 1992. Like J. Kubik, she shows how national myths have played an important role in mobilizing societies. They are relived in the national consciousness. M. Walsh touches on the Polish revolution in John Paul II, A Biography, 1992. This is a chronologically presented and readable biography. In contrast to G. Williams, The Mind of John Paul II, which ends with 1980, Walsh studies developments up to 1994. Williams, however, gives a more profound and thorough portrait of John Paul II than Walsh. The latter is a nimble-fingered writer who along with Brian Davies has also presented the Pontifical social texts in Proclaiming Justice and Peace. 1991.

Message to the UN Secretary General on the Thirtieth Anniversary of the Declaration of Human Rights on 2 December 1978

John Paul II continually makes reference to human rights in his social teaching. After the message he sent on the thirtieth anniversary of the declaration of human rights, to the UN Secretary General on 2 December 1978 and less than two months after becoming Pope, John Paul II once more took up the theme of human rights in his opening address to the CELAM conference on 28 January 1979 and devoted a chapter to it in his first encyclical, *Redemptor Hominis* published on 4 March 1979.[145] It is the central theme of his address to the General Assembly of the United Nations on 2 October 1979.

He also returned to this theme in many other talks and addresses. This showed how much his mind was preoccupied with the question of human dignity. Human rights form the basis of his remarks to ambassadors when they present their credentials and of his messages to various international organizations. Great emphasis was placed on it during his apostolic journeys.[146]

It seems reasonable, first of all, to present a condensed account of the main ideas of the important Papal documents dealing with the theme of human

---

[145] RH 17. The social sections of RH are to be found in M. Walsh and B. Davies eds Proclaiming Justice and Peace, 1991. The Latin text is available in AAS 71 (1979) 257–324. The ensuing references are to paragraph 17 of the encyclical.

[146] A good selection of human rights documents from the beginning of John Paul II's Pontificate can be found in O. Höffe u.a. Johannes Paulus II und die Menschenrechte, 1981.

rights. Thereafter we shall present an analysis, drawing together our conclusions.

John Paul II's message to the Secretary General of the United Nations on the thirtieth anniversary of the declaration of human rights began by pointing out that for the Holy See, *human rights are to be found in the Gospel message.*[147] Who can today deny that individuals and states violate human rights: such rights as the right to be born, the right to life, the right to work, the right to peace, the right to liberty and social justice and the right to participate in the decisions affecting peoples and nations? What can be said when we witness various forms of collective violation such as racial discrimination directed at individuals and groups and the use of physical and psychological torture against prisoners or political dissidents? The basis of human rights is the dignity of man. The UN declaration says the same. The basis of justice is the recognition of the intrinsic value of all human beings. Human rights have their source in personal dignity. By respecting this dignity, the rights are effectively protected. For the believer, all rights derive from the intrinsic value of human beings which is ultimately based on God.[148] Rights give rise to obligations. We must respect in others the rights which we demand for ourselves.[149]

Speech at the Opening of the Latin American Bishops' Conference at Puebla on 28 January 1979

John Paul II asserted that he was not unaware of the problems of human rights in Latin America. As bishops (he said), you cannot avoid being involved in these issue.[150] It is in accordance with the mission of the church to defend human beings. The parable of the good Samaritan underlines the importance of attending to human needs. Christ also says in the judgement scene in the New Testament that he identifies with the sick, the imprisoned, the hungry and the lonely who are given a helping hand. *The Gospel shows that justice is part of the evangelical mission of the church.* John Paul II cites his predecessor, Paul VI 's *Evangelii Nuntiandi* of 1975. Evangelization is incomplete if it does not take into account the interaction between the Gospel and the actual concrete life of mankind, both personal and social.[151] When the church acts on behalf of human rights, it serves mankind.[152] The church agitates on behalf of human rights from its evangelical commitment. The church wishes to remain inde-

---

[147] Paths to Peace: A Contribution, Documents of the Holy See to the International Community, 1987, 81.

[148] Op. cit., 82.

[149] Op. cit., 83.

[150] The Puebla address is to be found in John Paul II in Mexico, His Collected Speeches, 1979. It is numbered according to a combination of Latin and Arabic numbers. The present reference is to III.1.

[151] EN 29. EN is to be found in M. Walsh and B. Davies (eds.) Proclaiming Justice and Peace, 1991.

[152] III.2.

pendent of competing political, economic and social systems. It is only interested in the human being as such.[153]

It is with deep sorrow that the church looks upon the massive violations of
human rights taking place in all parts of the world. We call out, John Paul II
says, "Show respect for human beings. They are created in the image of God.
"[154]

The Encyclical Redemptor Hominis 4 March 1979

In *Redemptor Hominis*, John Paul II as the new Pope, formulates his vision of
humanity and the church. He shows how Christology, soteriology, anthropology and ecclesiology interact with one another. They presuppose and entail
one another. For John Paul II, human dignity is a precondition of true humanity. His view of the church is Christocentric. *In its affirmation of Christ, the
church discovers its identity.* Human beings are the Way of the church because
Christ identifies with them, redeems them and calls them. John Paul II looks
upon the church as the people of God on their historical journey. Just as Paul
VI had already stressed in *Evangelii Nuntiandi,* 1975, John Paul II draws attention to such elements of the social doctrine of the church as human value or
dignity, solidarity and justice. The social order must serve humanity. This is
also the goal of the common good.[155]

John Paul II, as the private person Karol Woytola, had contributed to the
anthropological issue in his monograph *The Acting Person*, 1979. Human
rights are closely linked to anthropology. John Paul II alludes to UN activities
on behalf of human rights. Because the majority of states have ratified their
commitment to this goal,this is a guarantee that human rights will remain a
fundamental principle in the work on behalf of human welfare.[156] This problem is closely linked to the church's mission in the modern world. Peace grows
out of respect for the inviolable rights of human beings, just as war springs
from violating these rights and brings with it further more serious violations of
them.[157] If human rights are violated in various ways, it is a result of other
underlying factors. Modern programmes and systems must be revised in the
light of mankind's inviolable rights.[158]

The Declaration of Human Rights associated with the establishment of the
UN organization aimed at distancing us from the last world war´s terrible experiences and at creating the foundation for a continuous assesment of programmes, systems and regimes from the standpoint of human welfare or the
person in the community. It must be a basic ingredient of the common good to

---

[153] III.3.
[154] III.5.
[155] John Paul II, Die Würde des Menschen in Christus. Die Antrittsencyklika Redemptor Hominis
Papst Johannes Paulus II Mit einem Kommentar von Bernhard Häring, 1979.
[156] RH 17.
[157] RH 17.1.
[158] RH 17.2.

174

establish the essential criterion which can be applied to all programmes, systems and regimes. Failure to do so will lead inevitably to human suffering. Violations of human rights go hand in hand with violations of the rights of nations.[159] John Paul II holds that social programmes, systems and regimes are to be judged *according to the extent that they promote or impede the implementation of human rights.* By human rights, he means both individual and social rights. This emerges from the fact that he places human beings in society i.e. human beings living with one another in a community, at the very centre and not individuals who are isolated from one another. The goal is to achieve the common good in society. Programmes, systems and regimes are means of attaining this end.

Totalitarian forms of government have claimed to act on behalf of a higher good, namely that of the state, but experience has shown that this was often merely what was good for some particular party identified with the state. Such governments limited the rights of their citizens and denied recognition of inviolable human rights as these have been formulated internationally in midcentury. The question is whether the acceptance of the declaration of human rights also entails the practical implementation of its spirit. Everyday life in society often conflicts with human rights.[160]

It is the job of those in power to uphold the common or general good in society. This is what gives those in power their rights. These latter rights can only be understood on the basis of respect for human rights. *The common good which the power of the state serves is attained when all citizens have their rights guaranteed.* When this last is lacking, it leads to a dissolution of society with citizens in opposition to those in power or to a situation of repression, violence and terrorism. The principle of human rights is one of the most profound matters in the domain of social justice and it is a measure for testing how far social justice has been implemented in the life of political communities.[161] Human rights are regarded thus as an aspect of social justice and *the existence of social justice is a test of whether human rights have been concretely enforced.* Social justice and human rights are mutually dependent. They are two sides of the same coin.

This analysis shows that if one side of individual and social human rights is emphasized by John Paul, then it is the social aspect which is given priority. His own experiences were derived from a communist country, namely Poland, and although he clearly rejected Marxism, he also stressed that individuals do not exist in a vacuum but exist, as part of a social context, in a society. His social doctrine combines personalism and sociocentrism. The latter was developed by the communists while Mounier and Maritain were responsible for personalism.

---

[159] RH 17.3.
[160] RH 17.4.
[161] RH 17.4.

Address to the 34th General Assembly of the United Nations, 2 October 1979

John Paul II displayed his positive appreciation of the Declaration of Human Rights when in the introduction to his address, he held that it was an undoubted milestone on mankind's road to moral progress.[162] This declaration had been composed when terrible revelations of the Second World War such as Auschwitz were still fresh in mind. Millions of people had paid for this declaration with their suffering and the sacrifice of their lives. The price must not be allowed to have been paid in vain. If the truths and principles to be found in the document are forgotten, ignored or lose their self-evidence then the noble aim of the United Nations can be threatened by new destruction. This will happen if the Declaration of Human Rights is allowed to fall under the sway of political interests. This is often no more than a one-sided desire for profit and progress or a thirst for power irrespective of the needs of others. It is not compatible with the noble spirit of the declaration. Political interest in this sense, the Pope says, sullies the noble and difficult task of the UN to work on behalf of the good of all humanity.[163]

Every analysis must begin from the assumption that although each person lives in a specific concrete social and historical context, that person possesses a dignity which must never be diminished nor destroyed. Instead, if a genuine peace is to be brought about, it must be respected and guaranteed.[164] Permit me, says John Paul II, to name some of the most important rights which are universally recognized: our right to life, freedom and security; the right to food,clothing,housing,healthcare,rest and recreation; the right to freedom of expression and the right to freedom of education and of culture; the right to freedom of thought, to freedom of conscience and to religious freedom, along with the right to manifest our religion whether individually or in communion with others, generally or privately; the right to choose our way of life, to begin a family and to enjoy all those things which are necessary for family life; the right to property and work, to adequate working-conditions and to a just wage; the right to associate and meet freely; the right to freedom of mobility, to immigration; the right to nationality; the right to participate politically and the right to take part in a free election to determine what political system is to govern the people to whom we belong. All these human rights taken together constitute the essence of human dignity. They satisfy the basic needs of human beings, the exercise of their freedoms and their relations to their fellows. They

---

[162] John Paul II's address to the UN on 2 October 1979 is to be found in John Paul II, Pilgrim of Peace, The Homilies and Addresses of His Holiness Pope John II on the Occasion of His Visit to the United States of America, October 1979, 1979 and in John Paul II, The Pope speaks to the American Church, John Paul II's Homilies, Speeches and Letters to Catholics in the United States 1992. The material in the UN address is broken into sections numbered from 1 to 23. Our references here are to this system of numeration. 7.
[163] 9.
[164] 12.

are always concerned with man; they are always about the full human dimension of humanity.[165]

The first threat to human rights comes from the distribution of material goods. This distribution is often unfair and unjust both at the level of individual communities and also globally. Different forms of inequality in the ownership and enjoyment of material goods can often be explained by differing historical causes and circumstances. While these circumstances can reduce the moral responsibility of people today, they cannot prevent situations of inequality from continuing to be characterized by injustice and social inequality. *It is necessary*, the Pope stresses, *for human beings to be aware that the economic tensions between countries and in the relations between states and even between whole continents, contain major ingredients which involve the erosion or violation of human rights.* Among these ingredients are the exploitation of labour and many other abuses which affect human dignity. The criterion to be applied in comparing different social, economic and political systems is the humanitarian one: how far is each respective system able to reduce, impede or eliminate, as far as possible, the various forms of human exploitation and instead ensure for human beings, through their work, not only a just distribution of material goods but also a participation in guaranteeing that their dignity is respected and maintained throughout the whole process of production and in the social life surrounding this process. It must never be forgotten that although human lives are dependent upon material resources, human beings must be their master and not their slaves.[166]

The gap between rich and poor, John Paul II concludes, is not only a serious symptom in the life of each community. The same can be said of the gaps between countries and regions of the earth. The only way to bridge these gaps between rich and poor areas is through cooperation between countries.[167] Social rights and the poor world's right to life are emphasized at least as much as individual human rights in the Pope's address to the United Nations.

Human Rights in the UN, Puebla and Redemptor Hominis

We shall give a seven-point summary of John Paul II's position on human rights on the basis of our previous remarks about his address to the UN, Puebla and *Redemptor Hominis*.

First of all, John Paul II views the defence and promotion of human dignity as an integral part of the mission of the church. The church's involvement in human rights is a direct consequence of the Christian Gospel. It is based on our witness for Jesus Christ. The Pontiff looks upon human rights work as a step in the church's mission of evangelization. In this, he continues with the standpoint already adopted by his predecessor Paul VI.

---

[165] 13.
[166] 17.
[167] 18.

Secondly, John Paul II regards human dignity as the basis of human rights. This view had also been shared by John XXIII in his efforts on behalf of human rights. It was expressed in written form in *Pacem in terris*. The Catholic church and the UN Declaration of Human Rights shared the conviction that human dignity was the foundation of human rights. In contrast to the UN, however, the Catholic church gave this conviction a theological motivation. John Paul II held that human dignity has its source in God the Father and is revealed in Man's brotherhood in Jesus Christ. Thus for him human rights rest primarily upon a Christological foundation.

Thirdly, John Paul II accords human beings priority and as a result this priority carries over to the position of human rights in every political system or programme. Awareness of human rights is a powerful force for change and tranformation in all social systems.

Fourthly, John Paul II looks upon respect for human rights as a basis of peace. Peace is dependent upon respect of human beings' inviolable rights. He interprets the universal declaration of human rights adopted after the Second World War as a manifestation of a renewed desire for peace after the experiences of war. Human dignity was systematically violated in the course of the war. Peace must be based upon justice. The unjust distribution of material goods is a threat to peace. The most apposite illustration is the gap between the rich and poor worlds. Underdevelopment implies a systematic violation of human rights and creates dangerous threats to world peace. For John Paul II, there is a clear connection between peace, human rights and development. He supports the right to life in the Third World. So did Paul VI in his encyclical *Populorum Progressio*, 1967 but subsequent developments led John Paul II to sharpen this demand.

Fifthly, John Paul II emphasizes the importance of UN work to define human rights. He has confidence in, and supports UN efforts in the sphere of human rights. Within its organizational framework, judicial instruments for human rights are created. The Pope is committed to seeing that they are ratified by as many nations as possible.

Sixthly, for John Paul II respect for human rights is the foundation of the legitimacy of power. Political power assigns human beings central importance. The interests of the state and of a particular party, however, must be distinguished. The state must guarantee the dignity both of the individual person and the people as a whole. At the same time, the state cannot claim to be the ultimate value.

Lastly, John Paul II states firmly that justice is the principle underlying and guiding the existence of the church. Human rights also apply within the church.

References

John Paul II's expositions concerning human rights are available not only in English but also in German. In the latter language may be noted Johannes Paulus II Die Menschenrechte Texte von Johannes Paulus II Päpstliche Kommission Justitia et Pax 1982. The rights of woman and women are the subject of an apostolic letter of 15 August 1988. John Paul II Mulieris Dignitatem On the Dignity and Vocation of Women, 1988.

There are a number of instructive monographs analyzing the place of human rights in John Paul II's thinking. Among them are P. I. André-Vincent, Les Droits de l'homme dans l'enseignement de Jean Paul II, 1983; T. Herr, Johannes Paulus II und die Menschenrechte. Neue Wege der katholischen Soziallehre?, 1982; O. Höffe u.a. Johannes Paulus II und die Menschenrechte, Ein Jahr Pontifikat, 1981; John Paul II, The Social Teaching of John Paul II 1979–1982, Volume 3: Religious Freedom presented by R. Heckel, 1980; John Paul II, The Social Teaching of John Paul II, 1979–1982 Volume 7: Human Rights presented by G. Filibeck, 1981.

Summary

After the Second World War, the Catholic church emerged as a defender of human beings and human rights in society with new arguments taken from John XXIII and the Second Vatican Council. Paul VI's Eastern policy with its emphasis upon step-by-step action enjoyed both successes and failures. Its greatest success was the Holy See's support for Basket Three of the Helsinki Act dealing with Human Rights. Its greatest failure occurred in Czechoslovakia where the position of the church remained difficult under a repressive regime. The Holy See intensified its efforts on the human rights issue in the wake of the Helsinki meeting of 1975.

John Paul II, after his election as Pontiff on 16 October 1978, became perhaps the foremost champion of human rights. The source of his expositions on human rights can be found in his stress upon human inviolability and his insistence that human beings cannot be reduced to a mere object of political power. Human rights formed an integral part of his policy on Eastern Europe. During his first pilgrimage to Poland in June 1979, he spoke passionately about human rights. These rights were also the main theme of his address to the General Council of the United Nations in October 1979. John Paul II also linked human rights, human culture and efforts on behalf of peace in his address to UNESCO at their headquarters in Paris in 1980.

For the Pope, the church's proclamation of fundamental human rights was primarily a defence of human beings and not a defence of the church's own institutional interests. It was the job of the church to fight on behalf of human rights in Chile, South Korea and in the Philippines as well as in communist countries. The issue went beyond the Cold War. John Paul II's campaign on behalf of human rights was based on an anthropology which emphasized the nature of the human being as a responsible moral agent. John Paul II believed that the church had an obligation to challenge the Yalta imperialistic system's moral legitimacy by means of the church's evangelical campaign for basic human rights, in which the Polish Pope would play a leading role.

John Paul II sharpened the Christian criticism of Marxist-Leninism. Christ can never approve of treating human beings merely as a means of production. He also proclaimed that respect for human rights is a pre-condition for the internal unity of societies in general. With the emergence of Solidarity in August 1980, reference was made to the Second Vatican Council which underlined that the right to form trades unions was numbered among the fundamental human rights.

5.7 The Holy See and Racism

The rejection of racism and apartheid is a recurring theme within the Catholic church. It stems from the pronouncements of such Pontiffs as Paul VI and John Paul II, official delegations appointed by the Holy See and *Justitia et Pax*. This rejection was stimulated by the state of affairs primarily prevailing in South Africa.[168] Justitia et Pax was behind two publications dealing with the issue. The first appeared towards the end of the 1970s and bore the title *The Struggle against Racism Some Contributions of the Church.* The second was published at the end of the 1980s and was entitled *The Church and Racism Towards a More Fraternal Soiciety.*

It is natural to arrange the chapter disposition in accordance with these two publications. First of all, however, a concrete illustration of racial discrimination is given by reference to Catholic reactions to the apartheid system in South Africa.

Catholic Reactions to the Apartheid System

Apartheid was the key question concerning justice in the African continent. It was first seriously introduced when the Nationalist Party came to power in South Africa in 1948. The Dutch Reformed Church provided a biblical justification of governmental policy by claiming that the Afrikaaners were the chosen people of God. Although this church in 1974 came to reject the idea that the black population must remain in a permanently inferior and subservient position, it continued to claim biblical support for separate development and the retention of the race system. A minority within the Dutch Reformed Church questioned apartheid. This scepticism was centred at the Christian Institute established in 1963 by C. F. Beyers Naudé who had a leading role in the Dutch Reformed Church. He was the leader of South Africa's Christian Institute up to 1977. A number of the churches of the black and coloured communities were also linked to the Reformed church family. Allan Boesak, President of the World Alliance of Reformed Churches worked for the condemnation of apartheid by the many Reformed churches throughout the world.

Archbishop Desmond Tutu also took part in the campaign by non-white Protestant clergy against apartheid. The South African Catholic archbishop, Denis Hurley supported the South African church council and the Christian Institute from the 1960s onwards. The South African Catholic bishops con-

---

[168] 22/5 1974, 25/8 1977, 13–20/3 1978, 22/8 1978, 8/8 1983, 7/7 1984 Paths to peace: A Contribution, Documents of the Holy See to the International Community, 1987, 100–102.

demned apartheid in 1957, 1960 and 1962 but the church in general lent support to race discrimination. Catholic seminaries remained segregated until 1963. It was only ten years later that the Catholic church came out in opposition against segregated schools. It opened the white parish schools for black pupils in 1976.

The student demonstrations in black Soweto in June 1976 changed race relations in South Africa for good. The demonstrations and the resulting army and police repression sent shock waves throughout the Catholic church. In February 1977, the conference of South African bishops issued a declaration admitting that the Catholic church had fallen behind in witnessing for the Gospel in issues relating to social justice. The declaration promised to desegregate church institutions. It also criticized police brutality during the Soweto rebellion.[169]

In their *1952 statement on race relations*, the Catholic bishops make no mention of apartheid by name. The statement is reformist in tone. The bishops condemn race discrimination. They propose that the whites should gradually incorporate blacks in their society.[170] The race problem is complex, say the bishops. It depends on the fact that the majority of non-Europeans, especially the Africans, have not reached a level of development which would justify their integration in a homogeneous society. Although the majority of non-Europeans are still underdeveloped there are many well-qualified people who can participate to the full in social, political and economic life. There is a group of non-Europeans at different stage of cultural development of whom the majority are quite unprepared for participating in social and political life, based on what is usually called the Western standard.[171] There are rights which derive from the nature and constitution of human beings. Among these rights is the right to human dignity. Colour discrimination is an attack on the natural right of non-Europeans to human dignity.[172]

Between 1948 and 1957, legislation was passed which distinguished whites and blacks. Different educational systems were introduced for whites and blacks. Mixed marriages and social contacts were forbidden and separate residential areas were instituted. In their 1957 statement, the bishops condemn apartheid as an evil because it preserves white supremacy at the cost of black rights. The statement is opposed to separate development. It makes a moral appeal to the whites and is reformist in tone. Since 1952, segregation in the name of apartheid has been more clearly defined and more stringently applied. Integration is unthinkable. Apartheid is the only possible solution. The basic principle of apartheid is the preservation of what is called white civilization. White supremacy is not compatible with justice and the teachings of Christ.[173]

---

[169] Social Justice and Race Relations within The Church 1977 in C. Villa-Vicencio Between Christ and Caesar 1986 232–234.
[170] 1952: Statement on Race Relations in A. Prior ed Catholics in Apartheid Society 1982, 167.
[171] Op. cit., 168.
[172] Op. cit., 169.
[173] 1957: Satement on Apartheid in op.cit., 170.

The evil of apartheid leads to attacks upon love and justice. Human beings are injured and injustice is committed when the practice of discrimination is introduced as the supreme principle in the welfare state, the ultimate law from which everything else derives. If the principle of apartheid is condemned as evil, this does not mean that perfect equality can be introduced in South Africa. People cannot participate fully in the same political and economic institutions before they have much in common in terms of culture. All social change must take place gradually. The state must promote the welfare of all its citizens.[174] No other change is able to preserve that order without which there would be no society, no government, no justice and no common good. The message to white Catholics is the following: many of our schools, seminaries, convents, hospitals as well as our social life in general are marked by segregation. In the light of Christ's teaching, this situation cannot be tolerated for ever. The time has come for that change of heart and practice which the law of Christ demands. Apartheid has an evil and anti-Christian character. It spawns injustice and increases bitterness.[175]

In a *pastoral letter in 1966,* the bishops maintained that it is a violation of human dignity to prevent someone by virtue of their race or nationality from choosing their own way of life and to restrict their choice of work, their right to freedom of movement, their place of residence and their freedom to raise a family. If certain laws make the exercise of these rights unnecessarily difficult or impossible, all legal means must be used to change them.[176] In 1972, due to the influence of the Second Vatican Council and Latin American liberation theology, the tone is sharpened. South African legislation is described as having dehumanizing effects and the church's responsibility for the poor is mentioned. Trades union rights, a minimum wage and other welfare measures are recommended.[177]

After 1968, the black South African student organization was created under the leadership of Steve Biko. It borrowed ideas from the civil rights movement in the USA in order to devise a black theology relevant to the needs of blacks in South Africa. Between 1968 and 1974, there was a rise in political consciousness among the blacks of South Africa. The bishops were forced to take heed of this phenomenon of black consciousness. In 1974, Bishop Butelezi delivered a statement about black consciousness and human rights.[178] The movement for black consciousness can serve God by demanding recognition as well as those rights planted in every human being by God. Failure to believe that these rights have been given by a superhuman authority and that they give every human being holy protection under divine law, entails that they lack a secure foundation. These rights have been given by God, not simply to secure

---

[174] Op. cit., 171.
[175] Op. cit., 172.
[176] 1966: Pastoral letter in op. cit., 180.
[177] 1972: A Call to Conscience addressed to Catholics in South Africa in op. cit., 181.
[178] 1974: Bishop P.F.J.Butelezi: Black Consciousness and Human Rights in op. cit., 184.

182

a better and happier life now, but also because without them it is difficult for a human being to be truly human, to serve God and other human beings and to live up to one's human dignity.[179]

In a *statement in 1977*, the bishops made their hitherto most outspoken judgement about the political situation. The majority of black South Africans are not only poor but oppressed. Christ's Gospel is a means of human liberation. There is support for ideas of black consciousness.[180] The bishops express the conviction that the only solution to racial tensions is to grant full citizenship and human rights to all people in the Republic, not upon the basis of colour but upon that common humanity about which Our Lord has taught us.[181]

The most powerful churches in South Africa were Protestant, in particular Dutch Reformed. The Catholic church made few statements about the race situation prior to 1950 but thereafter and especially after the Second Vatican Council, its position has been clear. Just as the English-speaking churches reacted vigorously to the apartheid policy after the Nationalist Party's victory in 1948 so the Catholic bishops spoke out clearly. Apartheid is un-Christian. The Catholic church was essentially black. Black Catholic priests adopted a militant standpoint with regard to the race issue. The conference of the Catholic bishops of South Africa in 1957 held that the church disapproved of apartheid because it embodied an unjustifiable principle of discrimination. What was needed was a recognition of the right of all races to develop with a view to gaining full citizenship, something which apartheid denied. Already in 1952, the same conference of bishops condemned apartheid. They held that the apartheid legislation was discriminatory. The bishops discussed human rights. The State must not act against these rights. In 1957, apartheid was again condemned by the Catholic bishops. In both 1952 and 1957, apartheid was described as something evil.

References

The pronouncements of the South African bishops on race discrimination and apartheid are to be found in A. Prior ed. Catholics in Apartheid Society, 1982. Among the monographs analyzing churches in general in South Africa, there is J. W. de Gruchy The Struggle in South Africa, 1986. The Catholic church is specially discussed in G. Abraham, The Catholic Church and Apartheid. The response of the Catholic Church in South Africa to the first decade of National Party rule 1948–1957, 1989.

The Struggle Against Racism

Roger Heckel was under-secretary in Justitia et Pax and was responsible for drawing up the book *The Struggle Against Racism: Some Contributions of the Church*, 1979. Selected parts of this book will be presented here. The UN

---

[179] Op. cit., 185.
[180] 1977: The Catholic Bishops' Conference in op.cit., 186.
[181] Op. cit., 187.

celebrated the twenty-fifth anniversary of the Declaration of Human Rights in 1973 by proclaiming a decade of action dedicated to combatting racism and racial discrimination. Paul VI supported these efforts of the UN.[182] The church teaches the equality of all human beings and is opposed to all attempts to deny this equality. The church is interested in all programmes and initiatives for exposing racial discrimation. The Holy See wishes to work together with other Christian denominations in tackling this issue.[183]

In 1965, the General Council of the United nations ratified the international convention on the elimination of all forms of racial discrimination. Race discrimination in the form of apartheid in South Africa, reduced the black population to the status of second-class citizens.[184] The programme for combatting racism consists in promoting human rights, eliminating racism, opposing racial discrimination and in eliminating racist regimes.[185]

The various departments within the UN along with special committees took part in the campaign against racism and apartheid during the first half of the 1970s. The world conference on measures for fighting racism and racial discrimination which was held in Geneva from 14 to 25 August 1978, evaluated what was done.[186] However, the tensions caused by ethnic pluralism in many countries had to be distinguished from racial conflicts. Racism often involves a certain component of domination.[187] During the Second Vatican Council, John XXIII and Paul VI stressed the equality and equal value of men, women and peoples.[188] In 1966, the Holy See signed the international convention on the elimination of all forms of racial discrimination. Paul VI gave his moral support to a decade devoted to efforts in fighting racism and racial discrimination.[189]

In 1974, he received the special committe on apartheid and stressed the church's doctrine on the equal value of men and women.[190] In his address to the diplomatic corps on 14 January 1978, Paul VI took up the issue of human rights and specifically named South Africa, pointing out the structures and attitudes which had to be altered.[191] When the Holy See participates in the campaign against racism, Heckel emphasizes, it is particularly interested in promoting what it means to be a human being in the fullest sense. The Secretary-General of the United Nations pointed out at the Geneva conference on racism on 14 August 1978, that laws are not enough in combatting racism. Racial discrimination has its roots not only in organized society but in the

---

[182] R. Heckel, The Struggle against racism: some contributions of the Church, 1979. 1 f.
[183] Op. cit., 2.
[184] Op. cit., 3.
[185] Op. cit., 4.
[186] Op. cit., 4 f.
[187] Op. cit., 5.
[188] Op. cit.,7.
[189] Op. cit., 8.
[190] Discrimination denies Christ's message in Paths to peace: A Contribution, Documents of the Holy See to the International Community 1987, 107–109.
[191] R. Heckel, op. cit., 8 f.

hearts of men and women.[192] Philosophy, ethics and religion have an important role to play. They concentrate on the origin and nature of human beings at a level which is beyond the area of scientific research and the methods which are available to science.[193]

The Christian doctrine of man has evolved on the basis and in the light of the revelation and in continuous contact with human expectations and experiences. In *Gaudium et spes,* the Second Vatican Council emphasized that all human beings are created in the image of God; that they have the same nature and origin and are redeemed through Christ; and that they have the same divine calling and purpose. There is a fundamental equality between all human beings which must be recognized. All human beings are not equal as regards physical, intellectual or moral capacity. But any kind of social or cultural discrimination with respect to fundamental personal rights which is based on sex, race, colour, social conditions, language or religion is incompatible with God's purpose.[194]

In his address to the diplomatic corps on 14 January 1978, Paul VI held that for those who believe in God, all human beings—even the least privileged—are sons of the Universal Father who created them in His image and guides their purpose and mission with love. The brotherhood of all men is a consequence of God's fatherhood. This is a key point in Christian universalism which it shares with other great religions. It is an axiom incorporating the highest human wisdom of all ages which is dedicated to promoting human dignity. For a Christian, no human being is excluded from the possibility of being redeemed by Christ and of enjoying the same mission and purpose in the Kingdom of God. Those who accept the Gospel, therefore, can never deny the fundamental equality of all human beings in the name of race or ethnic group superiority, even although physical, intellectual and moral differences may exist. Heckel holds that the texts from the Second Vatican Council and Paul VI base the Christian doctrine of humanity upon the mysteries of the creation and salvation through Jesus Christ. This is the source of its stability. By reflecting upon these mysteries, it discovers a youthful vitality.[195] The inheritance which the Holy See brings to the dialogue with institutions in world society is that suggested.[196]

The Holy See views itself as an expert on the subject of humanity. At international conferences, it proclaims the Christian view of human beings. This is combined with an open attitude towards research and further study. It helps the church to be receptive towards questions and experiences which lead it to a deeper understanding and formulation of its own doctrine. Racism is the product of many factors in civilization.[197] The Holy See attacks the problem from

---

[192] Op. cit., 10.
[193] Op. cit., 12.
[194] Op. cit., 12 f.
[195] Op. cit. 13.
[196] Op. cit. 14.
[197] Op. cit. 15.

an ethical and religious point of view and exposes the common root of aggression and sin.[198]

In South Africa, as was earlier noted, the conference of Catholic bishops in 1977 affirmed that it was time to hasten the promotion of black people to responsible functions and high positions within the church, encouraging them to do so in order that the church's multicultural nature in South Africa is clearly profiled.[199] In the USA in 1976, the Catholic bishops maintained that members of every racial and ethnic group have an immeasurable value. Racial antagonism and discrimination are among the most persistent and destructive evils in the nation. The most widely known victims of this discrimination are Spanish Americans, black Americans and American Indians.[200] Thanks to the law and the courts, the bishops continue, there has been progress in latter years in removing a number of social, political and cultural structures which underpin racism. The church must continue its efforts to make its institutional structures models for racial justice and strive to eliminate racism from the hearts of the faithful by reminding them of what it means to be the sons and daughters of God and brothers and sisters in Christ.[201] Apartheid in South Africa is rejected and the civil rights movement in the USA receives the support of the national conferences of bishops.

John Paul II, at his inaugural Mass in October 1978, had this to say:
"Be not afraid. Open the doors wide for Jesus Christ. For His redeeming power opens the borders of states and of economic and political systems and the wide field of culture, civilization and development. Be not afraid. Christ knows what there is in human beings. He alone knows it."[202]

Roger Heckel deals with the Holy See's attitude to the race issue during the 1960s and 1970s. He does this mainly by presenting representative documents or extracts from them, which reflect the Holy See's way of arguing. The church's particular contribution in this respect, is the moral and religious approach to the problem. The disadvantage of this way of tackling the problem is that the discussion tends to deal with theoretical issues and does not dwell on an analysis of reality. It fails to take account of how principles work in everyday practical life.

The Church and Racism

In 1988, Justitia et Pax came out with a new publication on the race question, entitled *The Church and Racism, Towards a More Fraternal Society*. In what follows, we shall present some sections from this work.[203] *Racist* ideologies

---

[198] Op. cit. 16.

[199] Op. cit. 24.

[200] Op. cit. 25.

[201] Op. cit. 26.

[202] Op. cit. 28.

[203] In Washington D.C., the US Catholic bishops published Catholic Church, National Conference of Catholic Bishops, Brothers and Sisters to us: US bishops pastoral letter on racism in our day, 1979.

are rooted in the reality of sin which has existed from humanity's beginning. The word means consciousness of the biologically determined superiority of one's own race or ethnic group which has evolved above all through the practice of colonization and slavery.[204]

The first great wave of European civilization was followed by a massive destruction of pre-Columbian civilizations and a brutal enslavement of their peoples. Indians and blacks were enslaved. Their work was exploited.[205] A racist theory was developed to justify these actions.[206] Bartolomé de Las Casas aligned himself on the side of the Indians. His work is one of the first contributions to the doctrine of universal human rights based upon personal value independent of ethnic or religious affiliation.[207]

During the eighteenth century, a racist ideology was developed in opposition to the ideas of the humanist philosophers who had worked for the dignity and liberation of black slaves, who were mere commodities in a shameless and widespread trade. The racist ideology sought support in natural science. In addition to differences in physical characteristics and skin colour, it attempted to demonstrate an important difference of an inherited biological nature, thus showing that the oppressed and enslaved peoples belonged to inferior races with regard to their mental, moral and social qualities. Towards the end of the eighteenth century, the word *race* was used for the first time to classify human beings biologically. In the nineteenth century, historical civilizations were interpreted in biological terms as engaged in a conflict between strong and weak races with the latter genetically inferior to the former. The decadence of great civilizations was explained by reference to their degeneration i.e. the mixture of races weakened the purity of their blood.[208]

Such ideas gained support in Germany. The national socialist party made a racist ideology the basis of its political programme, with the aim of physically eliminating those who belonged to "inferior races". This party was responsible for one of the greatest acts of genocide in history. It struck particularly at the Jewish people but other groups like the Romanies (Gypsies) and those who were handicapped or mentally ill were also victims.[209] In addition to Nazi racism, the fate of the Armenians after the Great War and in more recent times that of the Cambodian people deserve also to be noted. The memory of such crimes must never be allowed to fade. Younger generations must learn the extremities of which persons and societies are capable when they fall prey to the power of hatred.[210]

According to Justitia et Pax, the most obvious contemporary form of racism was institutionalized racism. This type of racism was sanctioned by the consti-

---

[204] The Church and Racism, 1988, 9.
[205] Op. cit., 10 f.
[206] Op. cit., 11.
[207] Op. cit., 11 f.
[208] Op. cit., 13 f.
[209] Op. cit., 14.
[210] Op. cit., 15.

tution and laws of a country. It was justified by an ideology of the superiority of people with a European background to those who are non-white or who are of African or Indian origin. Such was apartheid in South Africa. It could be supported by biblical interpretations. Characteristic of this regime was the radical segregation pervading large sectors of ordinary life, and applying to black, Indian and white people, with only the latter minority wielding political power and treating themselves as masters within major regions of the territory. All South African were defined with reference to the race to which they were officially assigned. A number of people thus became second class citizens with respect to higher education, housing, work and public services.[211]

Ethnocentricity is a very widespread attitude in which a people has a tendency to defend its identity by denying that of others; it refuses to recognize that they are fully human. This behaviour corresponds to a need to protect values, beliefs and customs in one's own society which appear to be threatened by corresponding values in other societies. The presence of others is only tolerated provided they can be assimilated in the dominant culture.[212] Social racism can reveal itself when poor peasants are treated without regard for their dignity and rights, expelled from their land, exploited and kept in a situation of economic and social oppression by powerful landowners who benefit from the indifference or active cooperation of the authorities. This is the new type of slavery which is common in the Third World.[213]

There is a spontaneous racism, Justitia et Pax continues, which criticizes foreign immigrants. It is characterized by superficial nationalism and can lapse into racial hatred. Such attitudes are based on an irrational fear brought about by the presence of others and the confrontation with what is unfamiliar. They aim at denying others the right to be what they choose or indeed to be in "our country".[214] Anti-semitism has been the most tragic form of racist ideology in the present century. Attempts are made to keep the anti-semitic race myth alive. Anti-Zionism must be distinguished from anti-semitism. It calls into question the state of Israel and its policy.[215]

John Paul II emphasized for the UN special committe against apartheid on 7 July 1984 that the creation of human beings in the image of God gives to each person a pre-eminent value. It underlines the fundamental equality of all human beings. This equality is given the aspect of brotherhood through the incarnation of the Son of God. The church looks upon reconciliation through Jesus Christ as the basis of human rights and duties. Every form of racial discrimination is absolutely unacceptable.[216] John Paul II is an advocate of Christological humanism. His vision of man is built round Christ.

---

[211] Op. cit., 17 f.

[212] Op. cit. 20.

[213] Op. cit. 21 f.

[214] Op. cit., 22.

[215] Op. cit. 23.

[216] The system of apartheid contrary to the dignity of individuals and whole communities in Paths to Peace: A Contribution Documents of the Holy See to the International Community, 1987, 109–111.

Justitia et Pax points out that all human beings created in the image of God, have the same origin and are intended to constitute a single family according to God's design in the beginning. The present and future unity of mankind is typologically affirmed in the first human being. Adam is a collective singular. It is human beings who are the image of God. From the first couple arose the human race.[217] The New Testament confirms anew this revelation of the dignity of all human beings, their fundamental unity and their obligation of brotherhood since they are all redeemed and brought into one fold by Christ. Christ has united Himself with every human being. He alone perfectly manifests God's presence under those human conditions to which he submitted. For this reason, Christ is the new Adam, the prototype of a new humanity. The work of reconciliation and atonement is universally carried out by God in Christ. It is not merely intended for the Elect. It is the whole race of Adam which is involved and which is recapitulated in Christ.[218] The Catholic church anchors its anthropology on the creation and on reconciliation through Christ.

It is the task of the church to be the people of God, here in the world. The church is charged with proclaiming and bringing about the unity of humanity despite any ethnic, cultural, national, social or other division which may exist, thus showing that all such divisions are abandoned in the cross of Christ. In this way, the church is able to contribute to the promotion of the brotherly coexistence of all peoples.[219] In *Sollicitudo Rei Socialis*, 1987, John Paul II stresses that this leads to efforts for solidarity between rich and poor. Peace is the fruit of solidarity between peoples and nations.[220] Justitia et Pax concludes that it is the task of Christians to work with others for brotherhood and solidarity between races. Racism can only be destroyed by getting at its ultimate root: the human heart. It is from the heart that just or unjust behaviour springs. People can be responsive to the Will of God or shut themselves off, in an egoism dictated by fear or the instinct of domination. To indulge in racist thoughts and to entertain racist attitudes is a sin against the Gospel of Christ which holds that my neighbour is not simply a person from my own tribe or group or from my background, my religion or my nation. My neighbour is every person I encounter.[221]

The task of the church is carried out through the witness of the lives of Christians: respect for foreigners, the acceptance of dialogue, mutual assistance and cooperation with other ethnic groups. The world needs to see this among Christians to be convinced by the Christian message.[222] *The Church and racism* issued by Justitia et Pax is a fundamental document regarding the church's view of racism. Besides analyses and definitions, it also contains ap-

---

[217] The Church and Racism 1988, 28.
[218] Op. cit. 29.
[219] Op. cit. 31.
[220] Op. cit. 33.
[221] Op. cit., 34.
[222] Op. cit., 35.

peals for action. However like Heckel's *Struggle against Racism* it keeps to a theoretical level and does not descend to examining concrete historical situations where human rights are applied or violated.

Concluding Comparison

The gap between the theoretical and the concrete factual aspects of the human rights issue was occasionally a problem in the Catholic church. Ecclesiastical documents which deal on a general level with human rights and which reflect the opinion of the official Catholic church in the form of the Vatican, fail to touch on the ambivalent role played by the national Catholic church with respect to the human rights movement in dictatorship's Argentina in the period 1976–1983. Instead of putting the eloquent ecclesiastical words and principles concerning human rights into practice, the majority in the Argentinian church did not lend their support to such rights. Here one notes a discrepancy between statements at international and national levels and what actually happens at the level of concrete reality within the national church. The main reason for this attitude was very obvious; namely the Argentinian national church endeavoured to avoid coming into conflict with the representatives of the dictatorship, with the risk of reprisals if it did so.

In Poland, the relationship between theory and actual practice took another form. In the Polish case, it would be wrong to speak of a gap between them; rather it was more a question of agreement. John Paul II was at the forefront of both the national and international Catholic church in demanding human rights in opposition to the totalitarian communist power élite, in fearless disregard of acts of revenge and other consequences. The Catholic-inspired human rights movement in Poland functioned as a "snow-plough" against the Soviet system. The outcome as far as human rights in the Polish nation and church were concerned, was the opposite to what happened in the case of the Argentine people. In Poland, the Catholic church's efforts on behalf of human rights, paved the way for the fall of communism whereas in Argentina the lack of effort by the Catholic church led to the preservation of the dictatorship.

These two illustrations of the implementation and non-implementation of human rights in concrete historical situations shows that the Catholic church's efforts provide examples of diametrically opposed attitudes.

The Catholic church's attitude with respect to developments in South Africa was more akin to that displayed in the Poland than to that in the case of Argentina. At the same time, each national development was naturally unique and original. However in South Africa, in contrast to the situation in Poland and Argentina where Catholics formed a majority, the Catholic church was in the position of a minority. In South Africa, it was protestants and protestants of the Reformed church who were in the majority. We shall return to the Reformed church in South Africa when we deal with human rights within the World Alliance of Reformed Churches. Moreover what was at stake in the South

190

African case was not primarily human rights in general, but certain of these rights which contradicted racism and apartheid. In South Africa, the Catholic church hastened to adopt a clear stance in opposition to racial segregation and thus to those in power. The Catholic bishops condemned racism and apartheid, with their attack directed against the exponents of the apartheid system who had held political power in the country since 1948.

5.8 The Concilium and Human Rights

After the Second Vatican Council there were traditionalists and reformists within the Catholic church as well as various groups adopting a mixture of views. From the beginning of the 1970s, the moderates' main organ of expression was Communio while the reformists put forward their views in the journal Concilium from the mid-1960s. Theologians such as Hans Küng and Edward Schillebeeckx were members of the circle associated with Concilium. Various issues of the journal were devoted to human rights. In 1979 there appeared an issue on *the church and human rights* and 1990 saw an issue devoted to *ethics in the world religions and human rights*. The latter year also witnessed an issue of Studia Missionalia devoted to *human rights and religions*. The perspective was widened from being concerned with the church and human rights to one preoccupied with the world religions and human rights. One of the important factors contributing to this development was the so-called Interreligious Dialogue.

Between the issue about the church and human rights and that about ethics in the world religions and human rights, two others were discussed which were linked to the same problem, namely *the church and racism* and *unemployment and the right to work*. The present chapter with its four sub-headings appropriately follows this arrangement of the material.

The Church and Human Rights 1979

In the introduction to the issue devoted to the theme of *the Church and human rights*, 1979, it is maintained that human rights are an important aspect of justice and humanization. The universal relevance of human rights is a God-given opportunity, a Kairos for the church.[223] Human rights leads to the question of anthropology, the Christian view of mankind and to Christology i.e. who is Christ.[224]

Wolfgang Huber, the Protestant theologian, who together with H. E. Todt published *Menschenrecht—Perspektiven einer menschlichen Welt* 1977, writes about *human rights—an idea and its history*. According to Huber, the concept of human rights has in modern times been developed as an instrument for

---

[223] A. Müller and N. Greinacher (eds.) The Church and the Rights of man, Concilium 124, 1979 VII.
[224] Op. cit., IX.

criticism and for conferring legitimacy. Pertinent authorities responsible for discharging social and political power are examined critically from the viewpoint of human rights. Existing regimes receive legitimacy and justification on the basis of human rights so that the difference between given social conditions and the demand for human rights is as little as possible.[225] Freedom, equality and participation constitute the foundation of human rights. They reflect the slogan of the French Revolution: freedom, equality and fraternity.[226] Freedom, equality and participation, Huber stresses, create the concept of human rights. Understood in this way, this concept is close to the Christian faith. The view that all human beings are the children of God leads to the view that the fundamental rights in society are the same for all of us. The inviolability of human beings derives from the theological conviction that men and women are justified before God by faith alone. Huber's approach of basing human inviolability upon the doctrine of justification through faith is essentially Lutheran as far as the theology of human rights is concerned. However the issue concerns the universality of human rights. On the one hand, human rights depend upon historical conditions; on the other hand, they constitute a universal human law.[227] Huber avoids adopting either particularism or universalism in his view of human rights. Instead he asserts that these rights are both particular and universal. The hope of a universal community of law finds its expression in human rights. For Christians, this community is an image of the the universal community which they call the Kingdom of God.[228]

The Reformed theologian, *Jan Millich Lochman* poses in his Concilium article the question *Ideology or theology of human rights? The problematic nature of the view of human rights today* Church communities look upon human rights as Kairos for the church.[229] According to Lochman, the special task of the church is to proceed from such rights for others and to defend our fellow human beings' rights.[230]

The Catholic theologian *S. H. P. Pfürtner* deals with the theme of *human rights in Christian ethics*. The violation of human rights is obvious to each and every one wherever human beings are reduced to the level of humiliated, enslaved or despised people.[231] In Catholic circles, John XXIII devoted a serious discussion to the term human rights in *Pacem in terris*, 1963. This encyclical was therefore cited as the first declaration of human rights produced by Papal authority. Thereafter Paul VI made use of the phrase human rights. In the Protestant world, the term arose out of the meeting of the World Council of Churches in Amsterdam in 1948.[232] In Pfürtner's interpretation of events, it has

---

[225] Op. cit., 2.
[226] Op. cit., 6.
[227] Op. cit., 8.
[228] Op. cit., 9.
[229] Op. cit., 11.
[230] Op. cit., 17.
[231] Op. cit., 57.
[232] Op. cit., 60.

192

become clear for the churches that the issue of human rights is essentially a question about human beings as human beings—human beings by virtue of their very humanity—human beings who embody human dignity—human beings with the right to live as human beings among their fellows. Slowly, people in the church realized that human rights also embrace God's concern for men and women.[233] The churches are given a social task of great importance, namely to promote awareness of human rights and respect for them. This means to promote a feeling for human rights in a spirit of solidarity and cooperation.[234]

The Chilean priest *Segundo Galilea* gives an analysis of *the church in Latin America and the campaign for human rights*. In Latin America, human rights are the rights of the poor. 1) For the majority, the problem is to be human. 2) The church's campaign for human rights is primarily concerned with the rights of workers, peasants and the indigenous peoples. It is a question of the right to work, to earn a minimum wage. 3) The church is in the process of donning the mantle of the church of the poor, but this not the case everywhere. 4) In Chile, the church gave support to Marxists who were persecuted and humiliated. 5) In Latin America, the principal relationship of importance is no longer that of church-regime but that of church-people. The church must remain free and adopt a prophetic role in opposition to the state if it does not wish to lose all relevance among the people.[235] For Galilea, human rights are primarily social rights.

The Church and Racism 1982

An issue of Concilium in 1982 dealt with white racism directed against coloured people.[236] Black theology is a reaction to racist religion in the USA since the 1960s.[237]

The theologian *Johannes Brosseder* who has ecumenism as a speciality, writes about the *the World Council of Churches' programme for combatting racism*. The first step towards this programme was taken at Evanston in 1954. The segregation of human beings on the basis of race, colour or ethnic origin was condemned as contrary to the Gospel and the nature of the Christian church.[238] The conference on church and society at Geneva in 1966 rejected ethnocentricity in the churches and Christians were encouraged to oppose the myths of racial superiority and racial inferiority. There were demands for the equal participation of all racial and ethnic groups in the life of the society in which they lived. At Uppsala in 1968, racism was condemned because it con-

---

[233] Op. cit., 61.
[234] Op. cit., 62.
[235] Op. cit., 104 f.
[236] G. Baum and J. Coleman (eds.) The Church and Racism Concilium 151 1982 151, 1982 VII.
[237] Op. cit., VIII.
[238] Op. cit., 25.

flicted with Christian belief. Racism rejected the effects of Christ's act of reconciliation and atonement. Through His love, all human differences lose their significance. Racism denied the humanity shared by men and women, as well as the belief that all men and women are created in the image of God. Racism falsely asserted that our true significance is to be found in our racial identity rather than in Jesus Christ.[239] The Uppsala conference held that there was need to develop a programme.[240] These and other actions led to the establishment of the Programme to Combat Racism in 1969 for the next five years. The aim was to make those suffering from racial oppression more aware and to help them to organize themeselves. Liberation movements could be supported.[241] In 1975, a Faith and Order discussion about *racism in theology and theology against racism* was held. An important issue was that of investments in South Africa.[242] This was discussed in a publication edited by Ans van der Bent entitled *World Council of Churches: Statements and Actions on Racism 1948–1979* (1980). The analysis of the human rights issue in general and of racism in particular as expressed within the ecumenical movement with its organ in the World Council of Churches displays the close ideological connection between this movement and the Catholic reformist circle associated with the journal Concilium.

In his article, *the Catholic church's campaign against racism,* the social historian *Roger-Henri Guerrand* deals with the same theme as Johannes Brosseder but is specially concerned with Catholicism.[243] The Catholic church does not exhibit a programme similar to the World Council of Churches' Programme to Combat Racism. Although racism was rejected as a matter of principle, no systematic attempt was made to counteract it in practical terms. Another way of putting is to say that the Catholic church lacked a counterpart to the Programme to Combat Racism of the World Council of Churches.

Deotis Roberts presents what was to be the theological answer to racism in the *article A Creative Response to Racism: Black Theology.* This theology expresses Christian belief in black experience for all black Christians.[244] Blackness is concerned with the awareness of belonging to the Afro-American heritage. It is more a matter of consciousness than of black skin. It has to do with a new self-definition, a different kind of self-understanding and a feeling of value and self-respect. Jesus is presented as a radical. He is seen as the oppressed or as a suffering slave because of his involvement in the liberation of the oppressed. Atonement is not simply vertical, it is also horizontal. It embraces understanding of what God does in the world to liberate human beings. He unites with them in the struggle for liberation. This means to to oppose power structures which dehumanize life. It embraces a political

---

[239] Op. cit., 26.
[240] Op. cit., 27.
[241] Op. cit., 27 f.
[242] Op. cit., 28.
[243] Op. cit., 25–30.
[244] Op. cit., 35.

and social justice view of faith which resists institutional and cultural manifestations of oppression based on race.[245] Black theology is a theology of protest.[246]

Unemployment and the Right to Work 1982

The fact that Concilium discusses the theme of right to work in its pages shows that human rights are considered to be social as well as individual in nature. The issue of Concilium concerned contains a significant amount of empirical material. The data collected illuminates the theme of unemployment and the right to work.

The Jesuit and social ethicist, *Friedhelm Hengsbach* provides an analysis of the question of *the church and the right to work*. He points out that the Second Vatical Council's constitution *The church in the world today* in its philosophical and rational approach to the problem,does not seek to base its argument upon natural law but upon the Bible and the pastoral approach to the problem which corresponds to the actual context of people's lives. This latter approach had long been adopted in the Francophone world under the slogan: Look, judge, act. In an analogous way, Hengsbach's aim in his article, is to present campaigns carried out or supported by the church.[247] The right to work is emphasized in *Gaudium et Spes*.[248] John Paul II published a whole encyclical dedicated to work.[249] Hengsbach's commentary to *The Church in the World Today* is obviously intended to apply to all later church documents, including *Laborem Exercens*.

Ethic of the World Religions and Human Rights 1990

A special issue of Concilium in 1990 contains a number of essays which deal with *human rights in the great world religions*. In their introductory remarks, the editors, Hans Küng and Jürgen Moltmann note that it would be of some importance if the great world religions could agree about basic ethics and about the fundamental rights of man.

A member of the institute for ecumenical research linked to the University of Tübingen, *Karl Josef Kuschel*, in one article dealt with *world religions, human rights and the humane*. It is essentially a review of a colloquium held in Paris from 8 to 10 February 1989 at the invitation of the Goethe Institute and UNESCO. The Secretary-General of UNESCO used this opportunity to stress

---

[245] Op. cit., 39.
[246] Op. cit., 40.
[247] J. Pohier and D. Mieth (eds.) Unemployment and the Right to Work Concilium 160, 1982, 40.
[248] GS 26.1 and 67.1 in M.Walsh and B.Davies (eds.) Proclaiming Justice and Peace, 1991.
[249] LE in Op. cit.

the importance of the world religions for the UNESCO programme *Education for Human Rights*. The differences between religions did not rule out the search for common values.[250]

The main contribution came from *Hans Küng*. Judaism was represented by *Eugene B Borowitz*, Islam by the Parisian historian *Muhammed Arkoun*, Indian religions by the Professor of Religious Study *Bithika Mukerji* from Benares university, Buddhism by the philosopher *Masao Abe* from Kyoto university and finally Confucianism by the philosopher *Liu Shu Hsien* from the Chinese university in Hong-Kong. The contributions from Borowitz[251] and Mukerji[252] as well as that of Küng[253] were published in Concilium.

Küng's argument was based on the following assumptions. 1) Historically religions had fostered not only peace but also war. 2) Each religion considers itself as the true religion and thus draws a line between itself and other religions. 3) A conversation between religions about truth is only fruitful if each of the religions is prepared to indulge in self-criticism. 4) Every religion has its own criterion about what is true and false. Are there not certain general criteria by which one might judge religions?[254] In Küng's view, the human—the truly human—is such a criterion. Only a religion which promotes humanity can be a true and good religion. If a religion spreads inhumanity, it is a false religion.[255] True religion is the fulfilment of true humanity. 1) What is truly human must be based upon the absolute and is not some superstructure placed above concrete religions. 2) In the name of religion, human dignity and human rights are violated, hate and violence are inspired and destruction is caused. 3) It is possible to base humanity on the particular tradition of every religion. According to Kuschel, the participants at the Paris Colloquium were agreed on these three points.[256] Hans Küng dealt with the theme *towards a world ethic of world religions—basic questions for contemporary ethics in a global context*. Why should individuals and groups, Küng asks, behave in a truly human way?[257] Human beings can live truly human lives, moral lives, without religion, but they cannot provide a justification for the universality in the moral demand. The categorical thou cannot be derived from finite human existence. Why not commit inhuman actions if it is in one's own interest to do so and if there is no transcendent authority which unconditionally applies to all?[258] In the prophetic religions—Judaism, Christianity and Islam—it is that sole unconditional in everything conditional, that which we call God, which can justify the universal nature of the ethical demand. Religion is thus the foundation of morality for its

---

[250] H. Küng and J. Moltmann (eds.) The Ethic of World Religions and Human Rights Concilium 1990, 97 f.
[251] Op. cit., 25–33
[252] Op. cit., 70–78.
[253] Op. cit., 102–119.
[254] Op. cit., 98 f.
[255] Op. cit., 99.
[256] Op. cit., 100.
[257] Op. cit., 103.
[258] Op. cit., 113.

practitioners.[259] The fundamental ethical demands in the religions are based upon humanity. They are agreed about certain fundamental ethical requirements.[260] All the world religions demand: do not do unto others that which you would not wish them to do unto you. Alternatively, do unto others as you would that they would do unto you.[261]

The Reformed theologian *Jürgen Moltmann*, who like Küng is one of our time's most widely read theologians, writes on *Human Rights, The Rights of Humanity and the Rights of Nature*. Moltmann distinguishes between four groups of rights: 1) protective rights such as the right to life, liberty and security; 2) rights to liberty such as the right to freedom of religion, opinion and freedom of association; 3) social rights such as the right to work, the right to sufficient nourishment and a right to a home; and 4) participatory rights such as the right to co-determination in political and economic life.[262] According to Moltmann, human rights suffer from anthropocentrism. They must be in harmony with the rights of nature—the earth from which, with which and in which human beings live. Human dignity cannot be fulfilled by human rights at the expense of nature; there must be harmony with nature. If human rights cannot be integrated with the rights of nature then they cannot lay claim to universality.[263]

5.9 The Mission and Human Rights

The Catholic mission had for centuries been confronted with the world religions. In 1990, the subject of human rights was introduced as a new component in the dialogue between the Catholic church and the world religions and this was reflected in Studia Missionalia published by the Missiology faculty of Gregorian university in Rome. A special issue was devoted to *Human Rights, Christianity and other Religions*.

Mariasusai Dhavawony writes about *Mother Teresa's mission of love on behalf of the poorest among the poor*. This mission is thus seen as a result or expression of human rights.[264] *Maurice Bormanns* gives an analysis of *human rights in a Moslem environment*.[265] The universal declaration of human rights in Islam is reproduced. It was supported by the Islamic Council in Europe.[266] The latter item is interesting because it tends to show that human rights are essentially a Western conception and when they are introduced in Islam, it is Western Moslem influences which inspire this declaration. *Human rights in*

---

[259] Op. cit., 114.
[260] Op. cit., 116.
[261] Op. cit., 117.
[262] Op. cit., 122.
[263] Op. cit., 122.
[264] Human Rights, Christianity and other Religions, Studia Missionalia, 1990, 135–158.
[265] Op. cit., 253–276.
[266] Op. cit., 277–302.

Hinduism and Buddhism are also thoroughly treated.[267] *Jacques Vermeylen* writes about socio-political and total liberation, on liberation theology and the Biblical theme of exodus.[268] *Joseph Joblin* reflects upon *human rights and marginal peoples, the responsibility of religions in the face of the refugee problem.*[269]

The essay on Mother Teresa is summarized in the following words which can serve to conclude this section on the Catholic mission and human rights. "Mother Teresa's work for the poorest of the poor has received world-wide recognition. She is considered as one of the most admired of Christians because her mission represents a message about God's love for the unwanted, the abandoned and the homeless. She is the bearer of Christ's love wherever the poor or neglected are to be found. She communicates the spirit of Christ in her work, because she is committed to creating stores of love, friendship, understanding and peace. Christ communicates and lives His life in that of her and her missionaries and through them He is alive in the slums. The poor, seeing them, are drawn to Christ and invite Him to enter their homes and lives. Mother Teresa would say that the credit is not due to her but to God. But she also likes to maintain that God needs our assistance; He needs us as instruments in carrying His love to the poor and in placing the love expressed by the poor before Him."[270]

5.10 USA the Bishops and Economic Rights

Both the bishops in Canada and those in the USA issued a letter calling for economic rights. We shall deal with the USA text as an example of this type of rights within the Catholic church.

Jimmy Carter was deeply committed to the programme for human rights during his period as President from 1977 to 1981. He held that USA had a unique role in promoting human rights internationally.[271]

The Catholic church had been involved in the human rights issue in the USA from the Second World War onwards. This had an effect on American foreign policy.[272] It also influenced domestic policy.[273] This was most clearly seen in the American Catholic bishops' letter on the US economy and its demand of justice for all. This pastoral letter aroused great attention and had political consequences.

---

[267] Op.cit., 303–376.
[268] Op. cit., 49–78.
[269] Op. cit., 391–491.
[270] Op. cit., 155.
[271] J. Carter, Human Rights: Dilemmas and Directions. Transformation 1984 1(4), 2–5.
[272] J. R. Formicola, The Catholic Church and Human Rights: its role in the formulation of US policy, 1945–1980, 1988. W. D. Mscamble, American Catholics and Foreign Policy: Past Limitations Present Obligations. America 1979 141(18) 370–372.
[273] W. Nicorski, Democracy and Moral-Religiou Neutrality: American and Catholic Perspectives Communio: International Catholic Review, 1982, 9(4), 292–320.

The American Catholic bishops' letter on economic rights was published with the title *Economic Justice for All Pastoral Letter on Catholic Social Teaching and the US Economy*, 1986. An interesting discussion of the substance of this document is to be found in C. R. Strain (ed.) *Prophetic Visions and Economic Realities, Protestants, Jews and Catholics Confront the Bishops' Letter on the Economy*, 1989. In his contribution to the discussion, Larry Rasmussen, a social ethicist at Union Theological Seminary in New York and a successor to Reinhold Niebuhr, maintains that the Catholic bishops fail to cast any light on questions about structural power in the American economy and therefore rely upon an unrealistic moral illumination to bring about change. The pastoral letter is utopian. It underestimates the power of social sin to lay obstacles in the way of progress and overestimates the possibilities of achieving the general good through upbringing and education.[274]

The breach between liberal and conservative acdemics became clear in the discussion which followed the publication of the American Catholic bishops' pastoral letter on economic justice. *G. E. McCarthy* and *R. W. Rhodes* the conservative and radical reactions to the pastoral letter in *Eclipse of Justice Ethics, Economics and the Lost Traditions of American Catholicism*, 1992.

According to the Catholic bishops, human rights are a minimum condition for life in a community. According to Catholic teaching, human rights embrace not only civil and political rights but also economic rights. Society as a whole, working through public and private institutions, has the moral responsibility to enhance human dignity and protect human rights. The government has the main responsibility in this area. In a democracy, the government is a means through which we can act together to protect what we deem important and to promote our common values.[275] According to the bishops, the time has come to implement economic rights, to have wider participation in economic power and to make economic decisions more accountable to the common good.[276]

The biblical emphasis on union and community shows that human dignity only can be attained and protected in solidarity with others. In Catholic social teaching, respect for human rights and a strong feeling of both personal responsibility and community responsibility are therefore combined.[277] Economic rights are secured by creating a social order which guarantees minimum conditions for human dignity in each person's economic sphere.[278]

In the American context, with its traditional emphasis on individual human rights, the Catholic bishops make a powerful appeal on behalf of social rights and are dedicated to implementing them with the same determination as in the case of individual rights. A balance must be struck between social and individual rights. The bishops maintained that in the prevailing American situation

---

[274] C. R. Strain (ed.) Prophetic Visions and Economic Realities, Protestants, Jews and Catholics Confront the Bishop' Letter on the Economy. 1989, 134 f.
[275] Economic Justice for All, 1986 XI.
[276] Op. cit., XII.
[277] Op. cit., 41.
[278] Op. cit., 49.

individual rights had an advantage. For this reason, they demanded economic rights for all and the participation of all American citizens, even the poor, in economic power.

References

As earlier pointed out, since the Second Vatican Coucil there is a conflict in the Catholic church between reformists and traditionalists. Concilium is a channel for the views of the former while the Communio is associated with the latter. It is the reformists who voice their opinions in J. A. Coleman and G. Baum (eds.) Rerum Novarum, One Hundred Years of Catholic Social Teaching, Concilium, 1991. They put forward their views about society and social development from the perspective of the encyclicals from Rerum Novarum onwards. J. A. Coleman was Professor of Religion and Society at the Jesuit theological college in Berkeley, California and G. Baum, educated at the New School for Social Research in New York, was professor of theology and social ethics at McGill University, Montreal, Canada.

The Catholic social encyclicals from 1891 to 1991 are discussed thematically by representatives of the Catholic Left in the USA in J. A. Coleman (ed.) One Hundred Years of Catholic Social Thought, Celebration and Challenge, 1991. Analytical attention is also paid to the human rights perspective of these social documents.

Coleman's book on a century of Catholic social thought which is published by Orbis is the diametric opposite of G. Weigel and R. Royal's study of Catholic social thought issued by Ethics and Public Policy, Washington D.C. and entitled Building the Free Society, Democracy, Capitalism and Catholic Social Teaching, 1993. The Catholic social encyclicals from Rerum novarum to Centesimus annus are discussed chronologically, encyclical by encyclical, by representatives of the Catholic Right in the USA. George Weigel was president and Robert Royal vice-president of the conservative Ethics and Public Policy Center in Washington, which was funded by major American financial interests.

In the USA, expositions of Catholic social teaching in general and Catholic views of human rights in particular were given by both the Catholic Left and the Catholic Right. While the former tended to emphasize social rights as much as individual rights, the latter preferred to give individual rights priority. Reformists and traditionalists extracted quite different ideas from Catholic social doctrine, using it for divergent aims and interests. Criticism of the pastoral letter of the American Catholic bishops on economic rights was, however, much more evident among the traditionalists than in the ranks of the reformists. Michael Novak, also attached to the Ethics and Public Policy Center in Washington, was extremely deft in presenting nearly everything the Catholic authorities said as though it were in agreement with his own liberal ideal. For light on this, see his later book The Catholic Ethic and The Spirit of Capitalism, 1993 along with several of his earlier workers.

The young American social ethicist Michael J. Schuck in Chicago has published a monograph analyzing Catholic social doctrine in the course of several centuries, That They Be One: The Social Teaching of the Papal Encyclicals, 1740–1989. It was published by Georgetown University Press in 1991. The Jesuits at Woodstock Theological Center associated with Georgetown University form an ideological counterforce to the Catholics at the Ethics and Public Policy Center in the same city.

The German counterparts to the American books of Coleman and Weigel-Royal are J. Müller and W. Kerber (Hrsg) Soziales Denken in einer zerissenen Welt, Anstösse der Katholischen Soziallehre, 1991. This book was also issued in connection with the centenary of Rerum novarum. In time for the centenary, John Paul II published Centesimus annus. The market economy is a recurring theme in the analyses to be found in the German book. The collapse of communism rendered the planned economy out-of-date and attention was now completely devoted to the market economy. Müller-Kerber's worker also contains a chapter on human rights.

There is a fairly extensive literature dealing with the Catholic church and human rights, sometimes from a wider perspective and sometimes examining more specific issues.

The wider perspective is to be found in J. M. Aubert Human Rights: Challenge to the Churches, Theology Digest 1986 33(1); P. de la Chapelle, La déclaration universelle des droits de l'homme et le catholicisme. Lettre liminaire de René Cassin; préface de Jean-Yves Calvez, 1967; F. Hafner Kirchen, Kirchen im Kontext der Grund- und Menschenrechte, 1992; E. O. Hanson, The Catholic Church in World Politics, 1987; J. Langan, Human Rights in Roman Catholicism, Journal of Ecumenical Studies 19:3, 1982; G. Putz, Christentum und Menschenrechte, 1991; M. Reuver (ed.) Human Rights: A Challenge to Theology, 1983; M. Schooyans, The Place of Human Rights in Catholicism, Lumen Vitae, 1980, 35(2); and L. Swidler and H. O'Brian (eds.) A Catholic Bill of Rights, 1988.

Particular aspects of human rights within Catholicism are illuminated by P. Hebblethwaite, Human Rights in the Church, Journal of Ecumenical Studies, 1982, 19(2); P. Lenvai (Hrsg) Religionsfreiheit und Menschenrechte, 1983; J. Neumann, Menschenrechte auch in der Kirche? 1976; and M. Pilters und K. Walf (Hrsg) Menschenrechte in der Kirche, 1980. These latter publications discuss the questions of women in the church, celibacy, freedom of religion and the church as employer.

5.11 Concluding Reflections

Prior to the Second Vatican Council, the Catholic church stressed that human rights have a natural law foundation. Thereafter human rights were given both a natural law and Christological basis.

In the wake of the Cold War, human rights in the eyes of the Catholic church meant first and foremost individual rights. Their very definition was part of the campaign against totalitarianism in the shape of communism. It was important to stress the liberty of the individual. As the conflict between East and West became overshadowed by the polarization between the industrial countries of the North and the underdeveloped nations of the South, social rights and the right to life were assigned an equal importance in the arguments of the Catholic church to that given to individual rights. Before individuals can make use of their liberty, they must possess a minimum of social security and be able to satisfy their hunger.

There is a discrepancy between the advocacy of human rights as an ideal and the church's actual concrete conduct in the matter of human rights. The best illustration is dictatorship's Argentina. The church leadership in general was silent about the grave violations of human rights, out of fear for their own security.

There was also, however, a clear agreement between proclaimed principles and concrete action. Poland offers the best example of this. John Paul II through his attitude about human rights issues helped to smash the communist social system. The demand by the US Catholic bishops for economic rights, provides another example. The bishops worked towards the attainment of a welfare society in the USA and were prepared to pay the price for adopting a clearly Left-wing point of view on the issue of economic rights.

The weakness in the Catholic church's attitude on human rights issues is that it consistently gives priority to statements of principle and is less keen as a church to be enmbroiled in concrete issues where it has to adopt some specific position. Individual Catholic church leaders such as Archbishop Oscar Romero in San Salvador could do this, but by so doing he attracted the suspicion of the central leadership of the church.

The picture of the Catholic church and human rights after the Second World War is, however, complex rather than simple. There are developments in different directions but certain tendencies can be discerned.

A major issue for the church leadership in Rome was to hold the church together and avoid becoming identified with political movements of various kinds. The Catholic church wished to put forward its own clear ideological profile. Conflicts about human rights were perceived very differently depending upon whether they were viewed from a central, regional or national point of view. The situations in the various Latin American countries provide the best example of this. It can explain why opinions about the church's actions in supporting human rights differed widely depending upon the perspective adopted in viewing these actions. The potential conflict between centre and periphery was clear in the case of human rights issues.

PART 3

Evangelical and Orthodox Christianity

CHAPTER 6
Human Rights and the World Council of Churches

6.1 Introduction

The French Protestant churches, in contrast to the Catholic church, came out in support of the French Revolution. The Catholic church viewed human rights as the product of enlightenment and as an expression of a lay view of the world. Later on, it accepted the ideology of human rights and provided theological justification for their defence. The relevant classical document is *Pacem in terris*, 1963.

Human rights had figured in the programme of the World Council of Churches ever since its inception in 1948. They were seen as part of the church's mission to preach the Gospel in word and deed. The WCC was inspired to action, above all by Frederick Nolde who had been one of the architects of the UN Declaration of Human Rights in 1948. Ever since the conference in San Francisco in 1945 which gave rise to the UN, he worked on behalf of human rights within the new UN as the representative of the churches and non-governmental organizations. He became the first director of The Churches in International Affairs, CCIA, in the newly established World Council of Churches. CCIA took part in helping to draw up the UN Declaration of Human Rights, notably in ensuring the inclusion of the Article dealing with freedom of religion. The definition of human rights derived essentially from the liberal human rights traditions of France and the USA during their respective revolutions in the eighteenth century. It is chiefly concerned with rights to liberty and the rights of the individual. This was the prevailing attitude at the inauguration of the World Council of Churches.

Critics of the liberal human rights tradition held that it divorced political freedom from economic structures and from those social, institutional and ideological patterns which are determined by these structures. In the wake of the UN international conventions on economic, social and cultural rights and on civil and political rights in 1966, the Fourth General Assembly of the World Council of Churches took place in Uppsala in 1968. The statements from the meeting reflected these new developments at the UN. The rights of the individual cannot be divorced from the struggle on behalf of an improved standard of living for the underprivileged in all nations of the earth. Individual rights have to be counterbalanced by social rights. In 1948, individual rights were treated as a precondition for the rights of society as a whole. However developments had taught the World Council of Churches that collective rights, peoples' rights and national rights have a legimate place in the understanding of human rights. The individual is part of society.

The UN declaration of human rights gave priority to liberal ideas of human rights before socialist ones. The conventions in 1966 were intended to restore the balance. The inter-relation between human rights and evil social structures increasingly attracted attention. Political structures were often instrumental in the dehumanization of large sectors of the population. Human rights were used as a tool in the Cold War and there was criticism of this.

The World Alliance of Reformed Churches and The Lutheran World Federation were the first to initiate study programmes dealing with human rights, the first dating from the General Assembly in Nairobi in 1970 and the second from the the General Assembly at Evian in 1970. In 1971, the World Council of Churches followed in their footsteps at Addis Abeba. The Central Committee stressed that collective and social rights were just as important as individual rights. The implementation of social rights was necessary in order that oppressed people, whether in industrialized countries or in the Third World, should attain their liberty.

6.2 Human Rights in the World Council of Churches
From Amsterdam 1948 to Uppsala 1968

The first General Assembly of the World Council of Churches in Amsterdam in 1948 emphasized the importance of the churches involving themselves in the issue of human rights, particularly the question of freedom of religion. They passed a declaration of freedom of religion which stressed that all human beings have a right to decide their own faith and religious affiliation; that all human beings have a right to express their religious beliefs in divine service in church, in education and in action and to proclaim the consequences of their beliefs for social relations; that all human beings have the right to come together with others and to organize themselves for a religious purpose; that every religious organization has the right to decide what course of action to adopt in achieving its ends.[1] Religious freedom was at the very heart of the discussion of human rights at Amsterdam. This theme continued to dominate the deliberations of the World Council of Churches during the 1950s and 1960s in the shadow of the Cold War. Its criticism was principally directed at the lack of freedom experienced by churches and Christians in communist Eastern Europe.

---

[1] W. A. Visser't Hooft (ed.) The First Assembly of the WCC held at Amsterdam, August 22 to September 4, 1948 (1948), 96–99.

The Second General Assembly of the World Council of Churches at Evanston in 1954, maintained that the protection of human rights is important when totalitarianism restricts the liberties of human beings and institutions, and denies the God-given rights which according to God's will, are given to all men and women. A system of justice which defends the rights and dignity of human beings is fundamental. A section of the Evanston report is devoted to the protection of human rights.[2] Evanston pursued the ideas which had been launched at Amsterdam and emphasized the importance of upholding individual rights in totalitarian states. By this was meant primarily the situation of Christians in the communist dictatorships.

At the Third General Assembly of WCC in New Delhi in 1961, attention was paid not simply to individual rights whether civil or political, but also to economic, social and cultural rights. The object in mind was the work on the conventions within the framework of the UN which took place in 1966. Among those participating in this work was the World Council of Churches working through CCIA. In order to uphold human rights in both the senses indicated, international laws which work, are needed. [3] At New Delhi, social rights are given a new emphasis alongside individual rights. A new era had dawned in the history of the World Council of Churches which was concerned with achieving a balance between the individual and social components in human rights. Underlying this development was the fact that in addition to the polarization between East and West, there was now a new conflict between the industrialized countries of the North and the underdeveloped countries of the South. This had an effect upon the way in which human rights were viewed so that attention was paid to their social dimensions such as the right to life. Where the possibility of survival is non-existent, it is not particularly meaningful to speak of individual and social rights.

The World Conference on church and society which was held at Geneva in 1966 encouraged the churches to call upon their governments to ratify and implement the various UN conventions on human rights. The church must step forward and defend brotherhood without discrimination and emphasize the unity of mankind.[4] The Fourth General Assembly of the World Council of Churches in Uppsala, 1968, held that the application of social justice required recognition of the innate dignity of human beings and of equality between people of all races and nations. Human rights cannot be maintained in a world of obvious inequalities and social conflict. Human attitudes have to change. Christians and Christian churches should set an example in their respect for human dignity, equality and freedom of thought, also in their writings. People's active involvement in development, reconciliation and social work ought

---

[2] W. A. Visser't Hooft (ed.) The Evanston Report The Second Assembly of the WCC 1954 (1955), 140–141.

[3] W. A. Visser't Hooft (ed.) The New Delhi Report. The Third Assembly of the WCC 1961 (1962), 276–277.

[4] M. M. Thomas and P. Abrecht (eds.) World Conference on Church and Society, Geneva.

to be encouraged and supported as a way of showing worldwide solidarity. The churches must contribute to channel this involvement. The protection of human rights is a prime task for the entire world community and the implementation of these rights is not unwarranted interference.[5]

Social justice was the key concept at Uppsala and human rights were treated from this perspective. This meant that the social dimension of these rights which had already been highlighted at New Delhi, in 1961, and at Geneva in 1966, were followed up in greater depth at Uppsala in 1968. Human rights were not simply seen as individual rights, but also as social rights. The balance between both aspects of human rights ideology was attained by means of the instrument of social justice.

Frederick Nolde and Human Rights 1948–1969

Frederick Nolde was professor at the Lutheran Theological Seminary in Philadelphia, USA and served as Director of CCIA from 1946 to 1969. He published a number of books and articles on human rights. Among them can be noted *Free and Equal*, 1968 which deals with the ideas and history of efforts to protect internationally the rights and dignity of people. Nolde points out the role played by CCIA in this historic process. His publications also include F. O. Nolde (ed.) *Toward World-Wide Christianity* 1946 and F. O. Nolde *The Churches and the Nations*, 1970.

Nolde was convinced that Christians should not only develop convictions about questions relating to the world community. They should also take action to see that they were implemented. If the Christian minority in the world was to have an effect upon international events, its ecumenical bodies had to influence international decisions whenever and wherever they were made. This was not to be confined to a very general level; it had to take concrete form. No political project, however, could be presented as something absolute when Christians became politically involved. No society can be identified with the Kingdom of God. At most, it can foreshadow certain aspects of that Kingdom. Politics is a necessary pursuit but it is subject to the laws of relativity. The Kingdom of God may be used as a measure by which it may be judged. This judgement is continually being altered since circumstances change. Christian belief can be made visible in political action. Obedience to the Gospel requires such an expression of belief. In the ecumenical movement, so-called "middle axioms" were considered to bridge the gap between general ideas and the concrete particularities of politics. Officially this view, which can be traced to the ideas of J. H. Oldham in the 1930s, has never been abandoned within the ecumenical movement.

Since Nolde was the main figure in the World Council of Churches' human rights work prior to the Uppsala meeting of 1968, it is appropriate to devote

---

[5] N. Goodall (ed.) The Uppsala Report, 1968. Official Report of the Fourth Assembly of the WCC, Uppsala, July 4–20, 1968. (1968), 64–65.

some attention to him during the first twenty years of this organization's history. One suspects that for Nolde human rights meant principally individual rights and he campaigned on their behalf against the communist system. The Churches in International Affairs, CCIA, was given consultative status on the UN Human Rights Commission. The churches in the ecumenical movement made increasing use of CCIA as a medium through which their voices could be heard. Nolde became CCIA's representative.[6] Mrs. Eleanor Roosevelt represented the USA in the human rights work of the UN. Réné Cassin was the French delegate. Frederick Nolde was the representative of the non-governmental, independent organizations.

CCIA was concerned with the religious, philosophical and political components in a planned international instrument for human rights. It was keen that such an instrument should reflect a fundamental attitude with respect to human rights which was acceptable from a Christian standpoint. It emphasized that governments could not guarantee human rights but could only recognize those rights which human beings possessed.[7] CCIA's interest was not confined to religious liberty, although it was in this area that its chief competence was to be found.[8]

Human rights in society belong to the very origin of humanity. 1) Since human beings are created in the image of God, it follows that all of them, irrespective of colour, race, nationality, culture and sex have the same innate value. Furthermore freedom derives from this equality of value in the eyes of God. 2) This view of the value of human beings was demonstrated and given a more profound basis in the historical act whereby God reconciled the world with Himself through Jesus Christ. 3) The Christian vocation comprises those means by which Christians respond to God and reflect God 's purpose for them in society.[9] This is the theological interpretation of human rights accepted by CCIA and Nolde, as CCIA's representative. He linked human rights both to creation and salvation and held that these rights are not granted to human beings by governments but are intrinsic to humanity. Their source is God Himself. Christians and non-Christians demand the implementation of human rights in society, particularly freedom of religion, although their arguments may differ. From a Christian position, Nolde provided a theological justification of human rights but he is prepared to accept that those believing in other world religions, as well as non-believers, may offer other arguments for such rights. What unites all human beings, is the demand that human rights should be put into practice in society.

Individual rights, especially freedom of religion, were at the centre of CCIA's and Nolde's attention. When freeedom of religion was defined within

---

[6] F. O. Nolde, Free and Equal. Human Rights in Ecumenical Perspective. With Reflections on the Origin of the Universal Declaration of Human Rights by C. H. Malik, 1968, 35.

[7] Op. cit., 38.

[8] Op. cit., 39.

[9] Op. cit., 66.

the framework of the UN human rights work, representatives of non-Christian religions were also present. The Islamic delegates were important. For the first twenty years of the World Council of Churches, human rights meant primarily individual rights but after 1968, social and collective rights and the right to life were taken seriously. The beginning of the shift towards a wider, more social conception of human rights can be seen already in 1961 but the real breakthrough for the social dimension of human rights occurred in 1968. The economic, social and cultural rights were the subject of their own convention in 1966 and this reflected a shift in the view taken of human rights as a result of the emphasis placed on them by the socialist states and by Third World agitation concerning the right to life. This development became fully effective within the World Council of Churches after Uppsala in 1968.

6.3 The World Council of Churches and Racism

Programme to Combat Racism 1969

Racism is contrary to Christ's Gospel. In the ecumenical movement, it is looked upon as sinful. Between 1925 and 1968, there were some 30 pronouncements directed against racial discrimination.[10] J. H. Oldham published his book on Christianity and the race problem in 1924. He pointed to the economic and political roots of racism.[11] Racial segregation within a few churches threatened to compromise the church as a whole.[12] The dominant issue between 1933 and 1945 was national socialism in general, and anti-Semitism in particular. The leaders of the ecumenical movement often protested against the persecution of the Jews. Efforts were made to help them to flee. The realization that one of history's greatest crimes—the systematic extermination of six million Jews—had been committed in the name of racial purity, came too late.

The World Council of Churches created a secretariat for race relations and ethnic relations which in the period 1960–1968 dealt with the problem of racial discrimination in a number of studies. It sponsored an ecumenical consultation at Mindolo in Zambia in 1964. The resulting report had the title *Christians and race relations in South Africa*. The economic system in South Africa was based upon race. There were great inequalities between racial groups with respect to welfare and income. This created social conflicts. Economic power was in the hands of the white minority. Christians were restricted in their economic dealings and were unable to follow their calling. This created frustration. [13]

The Programme to Combat Racism, PCR, was set in motion during the

---

[10] Ecumenical Statements in Race Releations, 1965.
[11] J. H. Oldham, Christianity and the Race Problem, 1924, 44.
[12] Op. cit., 263.
[13] Christians and Race Relations in Southern Africa. Report on an ecumenical consultation, 1964.

Fourth General Assembly in Uppsala in 1968. The Assembly viewed white racism as the idea that human beings of European origin are superior, and above all, superior to blacks. This was then taken to justify white dominance, white privileges and white exploitation of the coloured peoples.[14] The murder of Martin Luther King, the main speaker of the General Assembly, only a few months before, brought the ecumenical movement face to face with the nature of racism. From 1969, the WCC Programme to Combat Racism was engaged in confining the damage caused by racism and preparing ways of effectively fighting it.

The world had witnessed the apartheid system in South Africa sentencing Nelson Mandela to imprisonment for life. It had not only heard Martin Luther King's speech in Washington on his great dream of true community between the races in the USA of the future; it had also seen the bullets which had killed him. PCR's task was to express the solidarity which the World Council of Churches felt for those oppressed because of race, to organize research projects geared to practical action and to serve the churches in instructing their own members about racial justice etc. For W. A. Wisser't Hooft it was clear that people in the the ecumenical movemenet were not conscious of the irrational factors in racism and that there was failure to note the economic factors behind racial injustices. According to him, the issue was whether Christians were prepared to pay the price of racial justice and equality at local level.

The plan for an ecumenical programme to combat racism was devised at a consultation on racism held at Notting Hill, London in May 1969. It was based on the Uppsala meeting's insistence that the churches must be ready to combat racism wherever it appeared. After the General Assembly, the Central Committee was given the task of sketching a programme for the elimination of racism. The Notting Hill consultation challenged member churches in WCC to apply sanctions against companies and institutions which practised racism, in order to persuade governments to adopt a similar policy of economic sanctions. This would promote justice and give support to resistance movements which sought to eliminate the political or economic tyranny which make racism possible.[15]

Peoples of various colours suffer from the effects of racism on every continent. Best known were the situation of the black majority in South Africa, that of Afro-Americans in USA and that of the Indians in various Latin American countries. The struggle against racism was a stage in the struggle for a global community, including global development. White racism meant an accumulation of welfare and power in the hands of white people. Many religious bodies in the white Northern world had enjoyed the advantages which came from a racially oppressive economic system. In the ecumenical movement, there were

---

[14] N. Goodall (ed.) The Uppsala Report, 1968 (1968) 241 f.
[15] Statement of the Consultation on Racism, London May 19–24, 1969. in J. Vincent, The Race Race, 1970, 97 f.

a number of churches which derived benefit while others had suffered from such systems.[16]

PCR was a programme for practical action which was combined with studies. The central committee of WCC decided to set up the programme at its meeting in August 1969. It would run for five years and had at its disposal a special department within WCC. A special fund was set up to fight racism. Contributions could be given to liberation movements.[17]

The most important project in the field of action-oriented research was the symposium on Barbados and the publication of its report *The Situation of the Indian in South America*. The symposium was held in 1971 at the centre for multiracial studies at the University of the West Indies. The participants were restricted to qualified anthropologists and ethnologists, many of them from Latin America. To participate, first hand experience of work with Indians, was required. The symposium participants backed a declaration demanding the liberation of the Indians, the so-called Barbados declaration. The symposium report and declaration pointed out that the Indian issue was part of the colonial situation in Latin America and that the solution of the problem was appropriately to be treated within the context of transformation in Latin America.[18]

The conviction that racism is a perversion of Divine Creation and an obstacle to the preaching of the Gospel is widespread among the churches. The programme to combat racism is documented in Ans van der Bent *Breaking Down the walls: Statements and Actions on racism 1948–1985, PCR Information* 1986. The increasing involvement of the ecumenical movement in the struggle against the evil of racism is illustrated by personal witness in A van den Heuvel *Shalom and Combat. Struggle against Racism*, 1979.

Background: USA and South Africa

In the USA, slavery which was the basis of the cotton-growing South, was the first stage of racism. It was the need for labour which determined the relationship between blacks and whites. In 1860, there were in the so-called slave states of the South, 8 million whites and 4 million blacks, nearly all of the latter, slaves. The American Civil War marked the end of slavery. After it, racism developed in two different forms. In the Southern States, the emancipated slaves became agricultural workers, while segregation continued. Racism was often built into the laws of the individual states. It was first in 1953 that a federal law was introduced which forbade segregated schools. In the Southern States, the blacks continued without any political rights. In order to vote in the USA, it is necessary to register and the blacks were dis-

---

[16] Plan for an Ecumenical PCR in E. Adler, A Small Beginning, An assessment of the first five years of the PCR, 1974, 86–91.
[17] An Ecumenical PCR in J. Vincent, The race Race, 1970, 99–105.
[18] The Situation of the Indian in South America 1972. The Barbados Discussion, International Review of Mission, Vol LXII, No 247, 1973.

couraged from registering by various threats. Employers, for example, could threaten to dismiss black workers if they registered to vote. As late as 1963, there was a campaign to get the blacks in the Southern States to register and to support those who were threatened with unemployment because of the campaign.

In the Northern States, the emancipated slaves and their descendants found themselves consigned to urban ghettos where they functioned as a reserve working force. The laws of the Northern States forbade discrimination on the basis of race, but in practice, a racist society with differing conditions for black and white, also emerged there. It was the result not of laws and regulations but of what one might call informal discrimination, where the blacks were placed at the bottom of the American social ladder. Discrimination and its consequences were first described in detail by Gunnar Myrdal in his famous book *An American Dilemma*, 1944.[19] A black middle class has clearly emerged in the USA but the vast majority of blacks are still underprivileged. They have poorer housing, poorer schools, inferior education, higher unemployment etc than the whites.

Such was the background to the civil rights movement with its illustrious leader Martin Luther King Jr. It is vividly portrayed by Taylor Branch in *Parting the Waters, America in the King years*, 1953–63, 1988.

References

White racism is challenged by James Cone in Black Theology. He defines black theology as a form of liberation theology in A Black Theology of Liberation, 1970. Black Theology is placed in a long term historical context in Gayraud S. Wilmore, Black religion and Black radicalism, An Interpretation of the Religious History of Afro-American People, 1993. In For my people. Black Theology and the Black Church, 1984, James H. Cone provides a theological interpretation of the civil rights movement and other race related issues arising from it. Black Theology—A Documentary History, 1966–1979 (1979) published by G. S. Wilmore and J. H. Cone interprets black theology as a theological, religious, social and political movement and contains many contributions on civil right and black power as well as attacks on white religion.

The programme to combat racism was global in character but it was specially relevant to South Africa.[20] South Africa's Nationalist Party came to power in 1948 having been elected by the white minority on a platform of apartheid dedicated to preserving white power and privileges. Once in power, a whole series of racist laws were introduced, including segregated schooling, a prohibition on Africans taking part in trades unions, segregated housing for the different races etc. Above all, political repression followed the mass-mobilization against the pass laws and other racist laws carried out in the 1950s by the

---

[19] For the effects of this book in the USA, see W. A. Jackson, Gunnar Myrdal and America's Conscience, Social Engineering and Racial Liberalism, 1938–1987, 1990.
[20] PCR:1970–1973 E R Vol XXV No 4 1973.

anti-apartheid organizations led by the African National Congress (ANC). ANC was banned in 1961 and was forced to go underground.[21]

An important aspect of the South African situation was the mining industry's massive need for labour which led to an extensive migrant worker system i.e. the recruitment of people from their home villages to work in the mines for periods of three months. This system allowed the mine owners to pay their workers wages which lay under the existence minimum on the argument that their families were looked after at home in the villages. The African workers were not treated as a civilized workforce and in South Africa, the trades union movement developed among the white workers partly along racist lines. The whites feared that their wages would be undercut by competition from the huge African labour reserve. For that reason, they wished to force through regulations which would prevent Africans from doing more advanced jobs. As a result of the compulsory resettlement of more than two million blacks which began in 1960, around half of the African population was packed together in the Bantustan areas which covered 13% of South Africa. The remaining 87% was made up of white South Africa. But even in white South Africa, there were more Africans than whites. They were needed as a labour force.

ANC clearly declared that the struggle in South Africa was about political power. It demanded an undivided South Africa with the dissolution of Bantustan and equal rights for all South Africans, irrespective of race, to vote in elections to a parliament where representation was not along racial lines. In certain church circles, attempts were made to provide an ideological justification of South African racism.

The Sharpville massacre in which the South African police killed 69 and wounded 180 black men and women who were peacefully demonstrating against the pass laws, led to the *Cottesloe Consultation* (1960) between the World Council of Churches and its member churches in South Africa. The statement from the consultation indicated that there was agreement about rejecting all unjust discrimination but no agreement about the apartheid system.[22] The joint statement with far-reaching recommendations was passed by more than 80% of the votes of the South African delegates. The rights of blacks to own land, to have equal opportunities on the labour market and in education and to play a part in government, were underlined. In principle, there could be no objection to non-white representation in parliament.[23] The three Dutch Reformed churches which viewed apartheid as the only realistic solution and believed it to be defensible from a Christian standpoint, left the World Council of Churches after the consultation. Their cooperation with the white racist structures became obvious.

In 1974, there was a report from NGK (Nederduitse Gereformeerde Kerk)

---

[21] ANC-African National Congress (South Africa) 1971.
[22] The Cottesloe Consultation Statement 1961 in C. Villa-Vicencio, Between Christ and caesar (1986), 211 f.
[23] Mission in South Africa—Consultation Report 1960, 31 f.

entitled *Human Relations and the South African Scene in the Light of Scripture* which gives an expressly Biblical and theological justification of apartheid.[24] The church was accused of heresy by WARC, the World Alliance of Reformed Churches in 1982. Many churches rejected apartheid as a sin against the word of God, a heresy (WARC 1982)[25], a status confessionis (Lutheran World Federation, 1977).[26] The Central Committee of the World Council of Churches in 1980 condemned apartheid as a sin, a perversion of Christ's Gospel. Its advice through PCR was for member churches and institutions not to invest in South Africa (1972), to oppose white immigration to South Africa (1972), to refuse bank loans (1974)[27] and to apply comprehensive sanctions (1980). All these were measures directed against the apartheid system in South Africa.

References

There is a large literature on the political and church struggle for liberty in South Africa. Among the standard works are G. Bindman (ed.) South Africa Human Rights and the Rule of Law, International Commission of Jurists, 1988; J. W. de Gruchy, The Church Struggle in South Africa, 1990; and C. Villa-Vicencio, Trapped in Apartheid, A Sociological Theological History of the English-Speaking Churches, 1988.

Apartheid

Within the World Council of Churches, efforts were made to halt investments and break off commercial relations with South Africa and other African countries. PCR supported this proposal in New York in 1972. Later the same year in Utrecht, the Central Committee of the World Council of Churches came to a decision about investments and bank loans. Foreign investments in South Africa were designed to strengthen the white minority regimes in their oppression of the majority of the population. Investments in institutions which prolong racism should cease. The countries intended were South Africa, Namibia, Zimbabwe, Angola, Mozambique and Guinea-Bissau. [28]

In 1980 the Central Committee of WCC appealed to its member churches and all Christians
- to explain that apartheid is a sin which perverts the Gospel
- to encourage and support the South African Church Council and the churches in South Africa in pursuing their prophetic calling and in demanding a basic change in the political system and to continue to express solidar-

---

[24] J. H. P. Serfontein deals with this church and apartheid in his monograph Apartheid, Change and the N. G. Kerk (1982).

[25] WARC 1982, Racism and South Africa, Statement adopted by the General Council in Ottowa on 25 August 1982 in J. de Gruchy and C. Villa-Vicenzio, Apartheid is a Heresy. 1983, 168–173.

[26] LWF 1977 South Africa: Confessional Integrity in op. cit., 160–161.

[27] The WCC and Bank Loans to Apartheid, 1977. Appendix 87. See also E. Miltz, Bank Loans to South Africa Mid-1982 to End 1984, 1985.

[28] Resolution on Investments and Bank Loans, Utrecht 1972 in B. Sjollema, Isolating Apartheid: Western Collaboration with South Africa, Policy Decision by the WCC and Church Responses, 1982, 57 f.

ity and communion with all those in the country who were fighting for a more just society.

- to press governments and international organizations to implement sanctions against South Africa, including an investment halt, an end to bank loans, a weapons embargo and oil sanctions with a view to isolating it
- to cease all financial engagements, whether direct or indirect, in activities which support the apartheid regime.[29]

The Nationalist movement in South Africa originally made use of the political ideology of apartheid as a liberation mythology to foster Afrikaner resistance to British imperialism. When British power declined, it served to underwrite the oppression of the majority of the people in South Africa. The myth of unity was a defence of ethnic solidarity. This theme was developed by L. Thomson in *The Political Mythology of Apartheid*, 1985.

Racism in Theology and Theology Against Racism 1975

From 14 to 20 September 1975, a consultation on racism was arranged by the Faith and Order Commission and the Programme to Combat Racism, PCR. The report was called Racism in Theology, Theology against Racism. The consultation set out to contribute to the theological treatment of problems arising in connection with the ecumenical movement's fight against racism. The aim was not simply to take account of current expressions of racism but also to try to get at its roots and causes. Racism is a characteristic of economic and political structures.[30]

The consultation begins by indicating what it believes is involved in the concept of racism. There is racism when human beings, on account of their race, are relegated to a group whose freedom of movement, whose choice of work, whose place of residence etc is subject to restrictions. There is racism when groups of people, because of their race, are denied effective participation in the political process and are forced to obey governmental edicts which they are powerless to influence. There is racism when racial groups within a nation are excluded from normal channels of attaining economic power by being denied educational opportunities or entry to certain trades or professions. There is racism when the national state's policy is to make use of a racial group's labour on the nation's behalf but, at the same time, fails to allow the group to participate in the national state's affairs. There is racism when people's identities are abused by stereotyping racial and ethnic groups in books, films, the mass media, interpersonal relations and in other ways. There is racism when people are denied the law's protection on account of their race and when the state authorities use their power to protect the interests of the domi-

---

[29] Resolution on Comprehensive Sanctions against South Africa, Geneva 1980 in op. cit., 59 f.
[30] Racism in Theology, Theolgy against racism, Report of a Consultation organized by The Commission on Faith and Order and the PCR, 1975 1.

216

nant group at the expense of the powerless. There is racism when groups or nations continue to derive advantages from regional or global structures which are historically related to racist assumptions and actions. [31]

The consultation then passed to linking racism with the church and theology. Ideas about the people of God and about the notions of election and predestination which are closely connected to them, have been used to justify the white race's expansion and privileges. The white people's emigration to North America or to Africa, has been compared with the Children of Israel's arrival in the Promised Land. Through a kind of typological identification, people already living in these countries were seen as the new Caananites who were divinely ordained to submit to the white Christians and serve them. The idea of election was based upon a literal translation of certain Biblical ideas which were used to read into the Genesis narratives a fundamental inequality between the races. A static view of Creation allowed one to treat this assumed inequality as something given, as a natural law. The eschatological aspect of the belief that women and men are created in God's image, was lost sight of.

The picture of Western man is reflected in our view of Jesus. Much that is derived from European and American culture has coloured artistic representations of Jesus and many things from the same source have been read into the New Testament regarding Jesus' personality and behaviour. He has become the white Jesus who is alien and unrecognizable to people in Africa, Asia and other places. The view of the Bible has been distorted through an emphasis on the individual and his or her spiritual needs. This has led to the development of Christianity as a private religion. Revivalist movements have largely emphasized the individual and his or her eternal salvation. The church has become a communion of reconciled individuals. Moral teaching has laid stress on individual justification and has been preoccupied with the ethics of the individual. The Christian community's common witness and service as the salt of this world, has receded into the background. An incapacity to see and deal with the structural and institutional elements in the life of the churches, has developed. [32]

The consultation drew attention to the unconcious roots of racism. There are psychological mechanisms involved in it. Through the psychological mechanism of repression, our fear of the unknown, our guilt, shame, anxiety are driven into our unconscious, that which is sometimes called the shadow of the conscious self. The dark races have often been scapegoats for unknown and repressed fears in white society. Racism becomes a normal and unremarkable element, not only in the behaviour, but also in the belief of Christians. [33]

Having shown that racism is to be found everywhere in society, the consultation notes that Christian witness rejects racism. Racism is a sin which separates us both from God and from our fellow human beings. Racism is a sin

---

[31] Op. cit., 3 f.
[32] Op. cit., 5 f.
[33] Op. cit., 6.

committed not only by individuals but by churches and communities. The term collective sin is correct inasmuch as it draws attention to the extent to which racism has permeated churches and communities, thereby becoming a part of the fabric of ordinary life. The churches have taken for granted the separation of people according to colour and the existence of barriers between people of different races.[34]

The consultation discussed the struggle against racism and the search for a just society. Institutional racism is the structural aspect of our collective sin. In a racist society, racist ideas have been codified in a system of positive laws and regulations or are manifested in patterns of behaviour.[35]

Institutional racism takes different forms today. Sometimes racism is openly institutionalized and legalized. Legal measures underpin the separation of races and the domination and exploitation of one race by another. Racist theories or ideologies are used to justify legal measures of this kind e.g. apartheid in South Africa. In other countries, the racist element in legislation is more hidden. Racism is also present in international relations. The industrial and economic development of the rich countries is based to a large extent upon the exploitation of other countries particularly through the unequal profit which follows from the exchange of goods and the use of the cheap labour which is available in Third World countries. The struggle against racism involves a radical analysis of the international economic order.[36]

The consultation points out that there is a link between the campaign for justice and the problem of power. The experience of the civil rights movement in the USA provides an example of how black Americans were able to organize themselves to eliminate legal support for racism. By means of non-violent actions based on the Christian principle of love, Martin Luther King and his associates organized an effective strategy for social change.[37]

The consultation emphasizes the collective aspects of human rights. No individual person is free to stand aside self-righteously from the evil of racism. All our actions are influenced by the structures in which we live and for that reason they will sometimes have racist elements.

Racism—A Historical Profile

Before and during the Second World War, the main problem was the extermination of the Jews. After the war, the central issue was the policy of apartheid in South Africa. The Nationalist government introduced apartheid in 1948. In the same year, the World Council of Churches, holding its first General Assembly in Amsterdam, spoke out against racial discrimination.[38]

---

[34] Op. cit., 6 f.
[35] Op. cit., 9.
[36] Op. cit., 10.
[37] Op. cit., 12 f.
[38] Man's Disorder and God's Design. Report of the Assembly. Appendix (1948).

218

In USA in 1954, it was ruled that segregation in schools was contrary to the Constitution. The same year, WCC at its second General Assembly at Evanston, asserted that every form of segregation based upon race, colour or ethnic origin is contrary to the Gospel and is incompatible with the nature of Christ's church.[39]

In 1960, the massacre at Sharpville took place and ANC was declared illegal. The member churches of WCC in South Africa held *a consultation at Cattesloe* and declared that they were united in rejecting all unjust discrimination. No-one who believes in Jesus Christ may be excluded from a church on the grounds of race and colour. The spiritual element within all people who live in Christ must become visible in action such as shared communion and witness.[40] Albert Luthuli received the Nobel Peace Prize in 1961. The third general assembly of WCC in New Delhi emphasized that the church is called to act on behalf of racial justice. Wherever oppression, discrimination and segregation occur, the churches must identify themselves with the oppressed races in their struggle to achieve justice.[41]

In 1964, the leader of the ANC was sentenced to life imprisonment in South Africa. The same year, *the Mindolo consultation* on race relations in South Africa took place. For Christians, the issue of violence as the only remaining alternative arose.[42] In 1965 Martin Luther King received the Nobel Peace Prize and Malcolm X was murdered.[43] The following year, a world conference on church and society was held in Geneva. At that conference, it was stated that the white race dominates the world economically and politically. This domination prevents the development of human community, both nationally and internationally. Christians must see that every pattern of domination is destroyed. Changes in personal attitudes are important but only structural change and that alone can create a pattern of justice in which the dignity and freedom of all human beings is secure.[44]

1968 was the year in which Martin Luther King was murdered. It was also the year when the Fourth General Assembly of the WCC took place in Uppsala. At that meeting, it was emphasized that racism is a denial of Christian faith. Racism denies the efficacy of the act of attonement and reconciliation of

---

[39] W. A. Visser't Hooft (ed.) The Evanston Report, The Second Assembly of the WCC 1954 (1955), 158.

[40] Mission in South Africa—Consultation report 1960 31.

[41] W. A. Visser't Hooft (ed.) The New Delhi Report, The Third Assembly of the WCC 1961 (1962) 103.

[42] Christians and Race Relations in Southern Africa. Report on an Ecumenical Consultation. 1964, 12–13. Violence, Nonviolence and the Struggle for Social Justice, ER Vol. XXV No. 4, 1973.

[43] A comparison of the two men is given by J. H. Cone in Martin & Malcolm & America, A Dream or a Nightmare, 1993. In contrast to the conventional view that the the visions of America put forward by the two Afro-American leaders clash with one another, Cone holds that they in fact converge at the most profound level.

[44] M. M. Thomas and P. Abrecht (eds.) Christians in the Technical and Social Revolutions of Our Time. World Conference on Church and Society, Geneva July 12–26, 1966. The Official report (1967) 204.

Jesus Christ whose love removes the significance of all human differences. It denies our common humanity in the Creation and our belief that all human beings are created in the image of God. Racism falsely asserts that we discover our significance in terms of racial identity rather than in Jesus Christ.[45] It was the pronouncements against racism from Amsterdam 1948 to Uppsala 1968 which led to the creation of the Programme to Combat Racism. The establishment of this unit was the logical conclusion to a development which had begun already at the very beginning of WCC. The campaign against racism could be traced to the pre-history of the World Council of Churches and had been initiated by J.H. Oldham in *Christianity and the Race Problem*, 1924. Within the mission movement, he had experienced the dangers of the white man's demand for supremacy. As a result, he had become one of the pioneers of the emergent ecumenical movement and bequeathed the campaign against racism as an important item in his legacy to this movement. Because the churches participated in racial discrimination, the campaign was about the integrity of the church and the credibility of Christian witness.

6.4 The World Council of Churches, Peace and Women

Human Rights and Peace 1970

A consultation on Christian concern for peace was held at Baden, Austria from 3 to 9 April 1970. It was sponsored by the committee for society, development and peace (SODEPAX). The committee was set up by the World Council of Churches and the Pontifical Commission Justitia et Pax as an instrument for ecumenical cooperation in the promotion of international social justice. In section four, the consultation discussed *human rights and world peace*. There, it was maintained that there is a fundamental connection between peace and human rights which is based upon justice. Structures which deny human beings their rights and dignity, prevent the implementation of justice. Peace cannot be attained as long as there are injustices which deny fundamental human rights. The consultation dealt with a series of subjects related to human rights.[46] The consultation linked human rights to justice. In this analysis, the social dimension of human rights was underlined.

For the consultation, the most serious violations of human rights were to be found in the oppression of the black majority in South Africa and of blacks and other ethnic minorities in countries such as USA and Australia. In South Africa, oppression and tyranny were legalized and institutionalized in political ideologies. In other places, a hidden oppression was embedded in an exploitative economic, social and political system. In Latin America, a totali-

---

[45] N. Goodall, The Uppsala Report 1968. Official Report of the Fourth assembly of the WCC, Uppsala July 4–20, 1968 (1968), 65.
[46] Peace—The Desperate Imperative. The Consultation on Christian Concern for Peace. Baden Austria, April 3–9 1970 (1970) 51–72.

tarian system had come about which built on the subjection of the rest of the population to a ruling class, leading to a continual violation of human rights.[47] The task is to bring about as far as possible the implementation of human rights throughout the social and economic structures of society as a whole. The goal is equal opportunities with respect to the labour market, health, housing, education and leisure.[48] Many underdeveloped countries, according to the consultation, found themselves in a situation of economic, political, social and cultural dependence. Even aid can be used to increase this state of dependence and for that reason, it is important to emphasize the importance of multilateral aid treaties and the need for cooperation between equal parties. [49]

As God's creation, nature displays a finely adjusted biological balance. Measures which risk disturbing this balance are a threat to the human environment. A correct use and economic administration of global natural resources, the consultation maintained, are especially urgent tasks for the churches since they look upon these resources as given by the Creator. All human beings, in present and future generations, have a legitimate right to the collected resources of the world.[50] The pollution of air, water and earth which accompanies material, technological and industrial development, are a threat to the necessary preconditions for human life and put at risk humanity's chances of surviving. Effective measures, the consultation emphasizes, must be taken swiftly to prevent environmental pollution before it reaches a point of no return. Scientists and leaders of industry have become aware of their moral responsibility for producing means which can further disturb the ecological balance. We cannot allow the economic interests of a few people to steer developments which can seriously injure the human environment.[51]

Woman has the same right as man to develop her gifts and personality. In several countries, women belong to the underprivileged. The legislature is largely composed of men. Even when women enter working life, they are often less well paid than men for the same work. This, the consultation states, is a social injustice.[52] The protection of human rights requires a new political and social order, both nationally and internationally.[53]

This document from the consultation at Baden, Austria in 1970 is extremely far-sighted. This is not primarily because it speaks of the linkage between human rights and peace as being one of mutual interdependence. What is far-sighted is that the document emphasizes not only social and economic rights at the national and international level; it also points out the need to implement ecological rights and equal rights between women and men. In the case of the

---

[47] A. M. Thunberg (ed.) Rättvisa och fred, En ekumenisk rapport 1971, 62.
[48] Op. cit., 74 f.
[49] Op. cit., 75.
[50] Op. cit., 76 f.
[51] Op. cit., 77.
[52] Op .cit., 78.
[53] Op. cit., 79.

latter issue, the document anticipated a trend which emerged much more significantly in the 1980s. Human rights in general are a product of justice and social rights in particular grow out of social justice.

Human Rights and Women During the 1970s

In 1974, the World Council of Churches organized *a consultation on discrimination against women* in West Berlin. Philip Potter, a coloured minister from Haiti, was the sole man at the consultation. His presence was due to the fact that he was Secretary General of WCC. In his address, he drew attention to the close link between sexual discrimination and racism. Sexual discrimination was defined as an attitude, action or institutional structure which systematically assigns a subordinate role to a person or group on the basis of sex. The word *sex* only needs to be replaced by the word *race* to obtain a definition of racism. The starting point of Potter's address was some words from the first General Assembly of WCC in Amsterdam. The church as the body of Christ is composed of men and women, who were created as responsible persons to praise God and do His will.[54] God's purpose with men and women is that they should, through their difference, complement one another. Men and women have been created to exist as persons in a relation, different but equal. They are to take part in the same task of fulfilling the Divine Creation as God's co-workers in bringing about the good of all.[55] Potter emphasizes that sexual discrimination, like racism, is a sin. It is only in Christ that we can be transformed into authentic persons as men and women. However, our life in Christ must be manifested in our lives together in church and community. Potter's hope is that the consultation will be a stage in the process towards achieving a fuller humanity as women and men.[56]

The UN Assistant Secretary-General Helvi Sipilä pointed out that existing differences between men and women were mainly to be found in the following areas (a) education (b) working life (c) legislation pertaining to marriage and inheritance (d) participation in the decision-making and administration of society. In order to achieve equality, the attitudes of both men and women must be altered. Men must see women as equal partners. Women must accept their new role as responsible citizens.[57] Equality with respect to the law and the constitution means little if there is no equality in reality.[58]

One address threw light on the status of women in Third World countries during the 1970s. In Africa, women are dominated by men. Polygamy is legal in many countries. In monogamous marriages, man is seen as head of the family. 60 to 80% of agricultural work in Africa is carried out by women. Of

---

[54] Op. cit. Sexism in the 1970s. Discrimination Against Women. A Report of a WCC Consultation, West berlin, 1974 (1975), 27.
[55] Op. cit., 30.
[56] Op. cit., 33.
[57] Op. cit., 37.
[58] Op. cit., 38.

222

the 80% of Africans who are illiterate, the majority is made up of women. The illiterate in Latin America are estimated to form a third of the inhabitants and most of them are women. The patriarchal system is dominant in Asia, as in Africa and Latin America. Man is the head of the family.[59]

The consultation on sexual discrimination which was held in West Berlin in 1974, made the following recommendations with respect to human rights. The liberation of women cannot be divorced from other kinds of discrimination and oppression. It is an integral part of the liberation of humanity as a whole. The liberation of women is not an end in itself but a means for achieving the liberation of all human beings from some form of oppression. The different forms of oppression include racism, apartheid, colonialism and neo-colonialism.[60]

The theme of women and human rights is a recurring one in the World Council of Churches. It was discussed anew in documents of 1979. Once again, racism and sexual discrimination were placed on a par and the status of women in Third World countries was analyzed. In the latter case, special attention was paid to sexual exploitation. Violations of the human rights of women and children were common in Latin America. Assaults on women and children were a problem, not only in the Third World, but also in the developed part of the world. Assault on women was said to be a question of power.[61]

6.5. Human Rights and Christian Responsibility— St. Pölten 1974

Preparations

The Central Committee of the World Council of Churches which met at Addis Ababa in 1971, issued a memorandum on human rights. The churches were encouraged to put pressure on their governments to create national channels which could deal with human rights complaints and simultaneously help to secure the protection of these rights. The Central Committee recommended the Commission of the Churches on International Affairs (CCIA) to take the initiative in arranging a consultation as a way (1) of directing the attention of member churches to human rights (2) stimulating them to greater awareness about the problems involved and (3) providing guidelines for appropriate future action in this sphere.[62] The Central Committee of WCC thus wanted to inspire ecumenical reflection and ecumenical commitment in the field of human rights. The aim was to use CCIA as an instrument for forming a church

---

[59] Op. cit., 74–77.
[60] Op. cit., 111.
[61] Op. cit. Human Rights: WCC Documentation 1979. See also the Report of Conference on Women Human Rights and Mission 1979.
[62] Central Committtee of the WCC. Minutes and Reports of the Twenty-Fourth Meeting at Addis Ababa, January 10–21, 1971 (1971) 66–71.

view on the issue and for inducing the member churches to active involvement in the World Council of Churches' human rights programme.

At its meeting in Utrecht in 1972, the Central Committee of the World Council of Churches issued a report, as well as further recommendations, concerning human rights. The main theme of the proposed consultation was how human rights conceptions are related to cultural, socio-economic and political conditions in different parts of the world. The emphasis was on discovering more effective means for international cooperation in the implementation of human rights.[63] There was a trend away from a predominantly liberal individualistic interpretation of human rights and towards a social interpretation of them as collective rights. This was evident at the meeting in Utrecht in 1972. The struggle for human rights was a stage in liberation from the exploitation of human beings, whether the exploitation was political or economic, or whether it occurred in the industrialized countries or in the Third World. The incentive to moving away from the purely liberal interpretation towards the collective view of human rights, was the UN conventions on economic, social and cultural values in 1966. This view made a breakthrough at the Geneva conference of WCC in 1966 and at the Uppsala meeting 1968 and was followed up at Utrecht in 1972.

At the meeting of the Central Committee of the World Council of Churches in Geneva in 1973, CCIA presented a proposal for *a consultation on human rights and Christian responsibility.* The Central Committee accepted a draft programme for such a consultation.[64] The plan was to try to achieve a new understanding of human rights which went beyond the traditional view of them as individual human rights and which paid particular attention to the needs of the underdeveloped peoples. On the twenty-fifth anniversary of the UN Declaration of Human Rights on 10 December 1973, Cardinal Maurice Roy, the president of the Pontifical Commission Justitia et pax, and Philip Potter, the Secretary-General of the World Council of Churches, issued a joint statement. The declaration challenges us to campaign for a truly human world. Every human being, irrespective of race, religion, class or nationality, has the right to enjoy quality of life.[65]

Long before the St. Pölten meeting, arrangements were made for national and regional seminars, study groups and consultations on the theme of human rights. The background material was produced at these meetings or published directly by CCIA and circulated among the churches as part of the preparations for the meetings. The material was duly filed and placed in the archives at the WCC library in Geneva, providing the source on which the following presentation builds. The preparatory material shows how one approaches human

---

[63] Central Committee of the WCC. Minutes and Reports of the Twenty-Fifth Meeting at Utrecht, August 13–23, 1972 (1972) 147–149. CCIA Reports 1970–1973 (1974) 81 f, 107 ff.

[64] Central Committee of the WCC. Minutes and Reports of the Twenty-Sixth Meeting at Geneva, August 22–29, 1973 (1973) 206–214. CCIA Reports 1970–1973 (1974) 83 ff, 11–117. CCIA Reports 1974–1978 (1979) 15 f.

[65] CCIA Reports 1970–1973 (1974) 85 f.

rights in different ways in different parts of the world, as well as showing how stress is laid upon the theological aspect of these rights. Already at the preparatory stage of the consultation, one was aware that human rights could not simply be treated from an individual perspective: it was also necessary to view them from cultural, socio-economic and political viewpoints in both the developed world and in the Third World. Special emphasis was laid upon the traditions and structures in the developing countries. The aim was to counterbalance individual rights with the social and collective rights, as well as with the Third World's right to exist.[66] The individual interpretation of human rights is no longer uppermost. The Gospel is understood as a call to individuals in the world to be instruments for humanization, liberation and change. What is at stake, is how the churches are to show their concern for individuals as members of a larger society.[67]

The preparatory material contains respective chapters on Africa,[68] Asia[69] and Latin America.[70] Chapters are also devoted to the socialist[71] states in Europe and Western Europe.[72] The arrangement of the material shows that the main emphasis is on human rights in the Third World. With respect to Eastern Europe, it is held that human rights take different forms depending on whether they are considered from a bourgeois liberal or socialist standpoint. The right to the private ownership of the means of production is the foundation of bourgeois government, while the elimination of this right is the foundation of socialist regimes. The foundation for human rights is thus the removal of private ownership. In the socialist system, the right to work is a primary political freedom and right.[73]

In the section dealing with Asia, the following theological views were put forward by *a Korean*. Human rights must be related to a given socio-political and cultural environment. They deal with human beings in society. Humanity, conceived purely as an individual, is a meaningless category when we are speaking about human rights. Human rights are unique because they show the rights for human beings living in relation to others. For the Christian, the emphasis must be on the right of others, in a given society, to live a life worthy of a human being. Human beings' justification for existence is to show their relation to their Creator and in Him, their relation to their fellow human beings. Human alienation from the Creator has led to broken human relations. It is the responsibility of human beings to defend and promote human rights because they are not their own self-given rights but are given by God

---

[66] Human Rights and Christian Responsibility Preparatory Documents for the St. Pölten Conference WCC CCIA (1974) (Br 280.428 H 88 r Copy 1) 8.
[67] Op .cit., 13.
[68] Op. cit., 15–29.
[69] Op. cit., 30–33.
[70] Op. cit., 34–57.
[71] Op. cit., 58–67.
[72] Op. cit., 68–75.
[73] Op. cit. 59. The Meaning of Human Rights and the Problem They Pose ER no 2 April 1975, 141.

Who created human beings in His image.[74] Human rights must be created and developed in the context of human beings' differing environments although their common essence consists in their having been created in God's image. Rights are determined by the society in which human beings develop their personality. Thus human rights can only be defined relatively, in terms of the different socio-economic, political, cultural and historical contexts. Depending on the socio-economic and political processes and ideologies, the ways in which human rights develop, will vary. To defend human rights is to liberate humanity, that is to say God's image, in the world of dehumanizing forces. In order to liberate themselves from the dehumanizing effects of political manipulation, technocratic and structural injustice, negative ideological propaganda, religious dogma and the status quo of institutions, human beings require to develop their creativity, their critical capacity. An important aspect of the church's educative task must be the transformation of human consciousness and will.[75] This Asiatic way of arguing is an example of how human rights are given a theological basis or are legitimized theologically. Theological ideas are intertwined with what is basically the Western ideology of human rights. Human rights are presented as simultaneously universal and relative: they are given with human existence and are dependent upon the surrounding environment.

The first section of the second series of preparatory material for the human rights consultation deals with human rights from a theological perspective.[76] The Swede *Gustaf Wingren*, as well as the Englishman *David Jenkins*, contributed[77] to this discussion. Their expositions helped to stimulate ideas about human rights in the run-up to the conference. David Jenkins, earlier the director for the Humanum Studies at the WCC, emphasizes that the churches' commitment to human rights i.e. the right to be fully human, can be derived from the Christian Gospel.[78] However, he contests whether the idea of human rights is Biblical. The Bible is scarcely concerned with human rights. On the other hand, it is concerned with human potentialities and with divine activities and human responses to these.[79] God has given us the possibility of being human. We are created to be human. We have an inalienable right to be so. Taking account of the concerns of all is therefore related to being human.[80] Jenkins, as a theologian, is prepared to affirm human rights to the extent that they entail increased humanity.

---

[74] Signum A Preparatory Documents 30.
[75] Op. cit., 31.
[76] Human Rights and Christian Responsibility 2nd Series of Preparatory Documents for the St. Pölten Conference WCC CCIA (1974) (Br 280.428 H 88 ri copy 1) 3–27.
[77] Op. cit. 12–15. See also ER no 2 April 1975.
[78] D. Jenkins, Human Rights in Christian Perspective Study Encounter no 2, 1974, 1.
[79] Op. cit., 2.
[80] Op. cit., 3.

The Consultation

The international consultation on *human rights and Christian responsibility* was held at St. Pölten in Austria from 21 to 26 October 1974. Fifty people from thirty countries participated in the consultation. There were people from East and West, North and South. They came from capitalist societies and socialist societies, from very rich countries and from extremely poor countries; they came from independent countries and from those which had been colonized. There were men and women of many races: priests, theologians and lay people. The Protestant, Anglican, Orthodox and Roman Catholic traditions were all represented. [81] At St. Pölten, two types of working groups participated. *The first type of working group* concentrated on a) right to life and work b) the right to equality c) the right to national sovereignty, to self-determination and international community and d) the increase in the number of political prisoners and refugees. [82] The *second type of working group* concentrated on 1) equipping the local and national churches to identify human rights violations and to protect victims 2) equipping regional ecumenical organizations and the WCC for the more effective defence and promotion of human rights 3) promoting greater international, ecumenical understanding and cooperation in the defence and implementation of human rights.[83]

The group which worked with the right to life and work, pointed out that the majority of human beings in Asia, Africa and Latin America do not only live in industrialized urban areas but in the countryside. Their right to meaningful work and an existence based on the cultivation of the soil, is violated by national and international economic and financial systems. The right to farm cannot be protected without basic agricultural reforms in Third World countries. The right to a peasant or small farmer existence is related to rights for other exploited groups such as women, children and Indians. The prevention of child labour must be followed up with measures to alter hard economic realities where children are condemned to work in order for the family to survive. [84]

The group which dealt with the right to equality maintained that Christian involvement is based upon three aspects of Christian belief, namely

– that human beings are created in the image of God
– that in the Creation and Incarnation, human beings are bound together as brothers and sisters
– that the life of Jesus Christ gives the lives of human beings meaning in their relations to one another.

---

[81] Human Rights and Christian Responsibility Report of the Consultation St. Pölten Austria 21–26 October 1974, WCC CCIA(1974) 1.
[82] Op. cit., 3.
[83] Op. cit., 4.
[84] Op. cit., 36.

Human dignity and human solidarity with all other human beings is based on these foundations.[85]

This is a theological justification of equality. The Gospel emphasizes the value of all human beings in the eyes of God; salvation through Christ which gives human beings their true worth; love as a inspiration to action; and love of our fellow human beings which is the practical expression of an active belief in Christ. Human beings are inviolable because they are created in the Divine image and receive personal salvation through the death and resurrection of Jesus Christ, the Son of God.

In his address, the chairman of the consultation and CCIA, the Swede *Olle Dahlén*, asks if Christians—given the struggle for survival of million upon millions of people—ought not to stress economic and social rights. We call them collective rights because they affect large groups of people and whole nations.[86] At St. Pölten, emphasis was laid upon giving priority to collective rights, as opposed to individual rights. Social, economic and cultural rights were said to be the foundation of personal liberty. When economic, social or cultural rights are infringed, the causes must be identified and removed.[87]

The Anglican theologian, *David Jenkins*, pointed out that the campaign for human rights shows that we are involved in structures and actions which promote or allow the violation of rights. The campaign for human rights (he continued) is humanity's struggle to achieve freedom for human potential.[88] Jenkins' *first* thesis is that the campaign for human rights does not involve any theological justification. His *second* thesis is that the campaign for human rights is part of God's struggle for men and women created in His image and is part of His judgement concerning the inhumanities of societies and institutions. The campaign and demands for human rights are thus to be understood as protests against something dehumanizing and against the limitations imposed upon freedom and development. Human rights are related to relations and possibilities for human development.[89] Jenkins' *third* thesis is that every Christian approach to human rights requires a realistic appreciation of possibilities and actions in the light of solidarity in sin and within an eschatological framework. The ultimate source of human alienation and human beings' inhumanity towards other human beings, is conceived as sin. This sin is expressed in the alienating structures of society.[90]

The St. Pölten consultation was a prelude to the debate about human rights at the Fifth General Assembly in Nairobi in 1975. At this consultation, stress was laid upon social rights and the right to life. This depended on where the emphasis in the matter of human rights was placed in socialist and Third World countries. It was opposed to the capitalist world's unilateral emphasis on indi-

---

[85] Op. cit., 39.
[86] Op. cit., 11.
[87] Op. cit., 49.
[88] Op. cit., 29.
[89] Op. cit., 30 f.
[90] Op. cit., 32.

228

vidual rights. Already at the first major special meeting of the World Council of Churches on human rights in 1974, the shift from individual to social and collective rights is clearly visible. Among the more significant factors accounting for this change, were the development in the Third World and the fact that the Third World had taken over the leading responsibility within the WCC. The St. Pölten consultation started out with the assumption that emphasis should be placed on cultural, socio-economic and political rights. It thus fulfilled the intentions of the meetings at Geneva in 1966, Uppsala 1968 and Utrecht 1972.

Reactions

The Ecumenical Review, the main journal of the World Council of Churches, held that an important contribution at the St. Pölten consultation was the linkage of human rights with economic-political structures.[91] A whole number of this journal was devoted to the theme of human rights. In it, we find articles such as David Jenkins *A theological inquiry concerning human rights: some questions, hypotheses and answers*—his consultation address—Julio Barreiro *In defence of human rights*, Alice Wimer *One step on a journey*, Burgess Carr, *Biblical and theological basis for the struggle for human rights*, Gustaf Wingren *Human rights: a theological analysis*—his contribution to the preparatory work for the consultation—Edward Rogers *The right to live*, Victoria M Chandran *In Christ no male or female* and the East German contribution *The meaning of human rights and the problems they pose*.

After the St. Pölten meeting, a report documenting the proceedings was published with the title *Human Rights and Christian Responsibility*, which brings together various reactions to the consultation. They show traces of Cold War polarization between capitalism and communism and of the conflict between the industrialized and developing countries, between the First and Second Worlds and the Third World. In Dimas Almeida's contribution *Human rights and the liberation of human beings without rights* it is asked whether our campaign for humanity, for life, for land and for the future, is not the necessary and right response to God's own engagement in the struggle.[92] The question is also raised whether the theological approach to human rights ought to start from the liberation of the oppressed. The theological thought in the Old Testament takes as its starting point the exodus. Exodus means liberation from captivity, liberation for the future and for life. In the New Testament, Christ is celebrated as a liberator. A theology of human rights must start from the concrete theology of liberation. It must present the universal meaning associated with this freedom as a universal human right and the future of this freedom as a new humanity. It is not easy today to speak of the church in this liberation process initiated by God. It is often linked to countries which have a social system which represents violence and injustice in the world. The church ends

---

[91] Editorial ER no. 2 April 1975, 93.
[92] Human Rights and Christian Responsibility CCIA Background Information 1975/No 8, 3 f.

up on the side of the oppressors and is unable to live up to the Easter message which it preaches. For this reason, many who work for the liberation of humanity, expect nothing of the church. Social criticism of the system which oppresses people inevitably becomes a criticism of the religion of this society. This criticism is insufficient to get the stagnating church to adopt the role of prophet and liberator. Jesus Christ is the source of the liberating truth. He criticizes the church from within.[93]

The Christian community's campaign on behalf of human rights and its commitment to the liberation of people who have been deprived of their rights presupposes, according to Almeida, a community which is free of any alliance with the forces of oppression. Where the Christian community is silent when confronted with situations which prevent people from being human, it confers sacramental authority on situations of oppression, thus alienating itself from its Master, from Whom it derives its own justification for existence. The transformation from a stagnant to a prophetic church cannot take place without an identification with that Christ who died and rose again and with His mission in the world. With this alienated starting point, it is impossible to read the Scriptures through the eyes of the poor, of those who have been deprived of their rights or of the oppressed and simultaneously make the Bible a religious book or a code for moral principles. The oppressed, the humiliated have discovered Jesus, the true liberator, the creator,not of promised or potential freedom, but of a concretely occurring freedom. To fight for human rights is to fight for those whose lives are at a sub-human level. The Christian community exists, above all, for the hungry because they should see in the deeds of Jesus Christ the concrete liberation from their situation.[94] Almeida's contribution contains a plea for a human rights theology which is a variant of liberation theology. Its starting point is Christology and not natural law. The essay is a genuine embodiment of a Third World perspective on human rights.

In a critical intervention from José L. Casal on *What Cubans expect from St. Pölten*, it is pointed out that 7 delegates at the conference came from Latin America, 3 from Africa, 4 from Asia and 2 from the Middle East. This meant 16 delegates in all from Asia, Africa, Latin America and the Middle East in contrast to 27 delegates from Europe. Four regions of the world had only 16 delegates whereas a single region—Europe—had 27 of whom 6 came from East Europe and a single country, the United Kingdom, had 4. The socio-political realities from which the delegates came, influenced their analyses of human rights.[95] At the same time, the consultation make a clear distinction between rich and powerful capitalist countries and exploited, humiliated peoples. It also showed the link between collective and individual rights and the dependence of human rights upon socio-economic and political factors. Although the consultation stressed these points, a question remained about its

---

[93] Op. cit., 5 f.
[94] Op. cit., 6.
[95] Op. cit., 26, 28.

own position. It was unclear. On the one hand, problems relating to human rights were understood to have socio-political and economic implications; on the other hand, no socio-political and economic solutions to such problems were mentioned.[96] In this intervention, there is a critical assessment of the St. Pölten consultation from the socialist bloc. There is a failure to do justice to the socio-economic side of human rights.

In *Ulrich Scheuner's* contribution entitled *human rights in the ecumenical discussion,* it is pointed out that the goal of the consultation was to achieve a balance between individual and social rights. This was also the central problem in the discussion of human rights within the ecumenical movement.[97] The Western viewpoint stresses the independence of the individual and sees in fundamental rights a bastion of legal guarantees which protect the individual against arbitrary political actions and restrictions on the part of the state. This view limits the state's use of power and political discrimination against persons and groups. Such ideas are an expression of individualism and can be combined with social conditions required to guarantee human existence. This view is not applicable in situations where the fundamental needs for life, work, housing and education are matters of primary concern. The individual view has its limitations. The door for demands for social rights must be kept open. In *the communist world,* human rights are not an expression of individual freedom, but must be seen as the collective demands of those groups who are denied their rights in the social system of the non-socialist world. The aim of these rights is to satisfy the social needs which can be achieved by transforming a social system. According to the Marxist view, basic rights are guaranteed by the state through the implementation of social requirements. Social and economic rights are placed in the forefront while intellectual rights have a more subordinate role. Individual rights can indeed be an obstacle to the realization of the social programme. It is the attainment of social rights which is of prime importance.[98] In the case of the *Third World countries*, the view put forward is not a uniform one. Social rights such as the demand for work, a share of material welfare and protection of their cultural inheritance occupy the foreground of attention. Given their needs and relatively declining living standards, it is understandable that the realization of such social guarantees is given priority. The fulfilment of their social demands is not directed at their own states but against international society or the rich nations. Their demands concern relations between states. They are about social equality between peoples. They are related to the attainment of a new economic world order. The author holds that this goes beyond the framework of collective rights.[99]

According to Scheuner, the theological discussion within the ecumenical movement, should see the individual in the context of the commandment to

---

[96] Op. cit., 27.
[97] Op. cit., 31.
[98] Op. cit., 35 f.
[99] Op. cit., 36.

love, which places less emphasis upon our own right and more upon our duty towards our neighbour.[100] It is necessary for the definition of human rights to go beyond the liberal tradition but at the same time it must not set it aside. The social rights must be included in this definition. Human rights must not be watered down by general demands for greater justice. Individual and social aspects of human rights must be seen as belonging togther and as mutually dependent.[101] The task of the churches is to work for a form of human rights implementation which embraces economic improvements without losing contact with issues such as intellectual freedom and the right to deviate from the dominant political view. These two aspects of human rights belong together.[102] Emphasis on these points is designed to rule out superficial individualism and collectivism, when it comes to defining the meaning of human rights. It is clear that it rules out the communist states' way of dealing with human rights. Freedom of the individual and political pluralism cannot be surrendered in order to attain some fixed social goals. Human rights are also distinguished from work with social justice. Although human rights have a social dimension, they cannot lose contact with the individual. From this viewpoint, it is doubtful if the concept of human rights should be introduced in dealing with the relation between nations, states and peoples and in the work on behalf of a new world order.

The Definition of Human Rights

Ludwig Raiser reacts to the ecumenical discussion of human rights and stresses that the the limits of human rights must be clearly set out. He holds that, otherwise, there is a risk that the concept of human rights becomes fuzzy and that in the end it is cheapened by linking it with every demand for a just political or economic order or with the fixing of certain definite socio-political goals. Thus the demand by the developing countries for a just economic world order—no matter how urgent it certainly is—is not properly part of the theme of human rights.[103] Ludwig Raiser calls for a clear distinction between the discussion of social justice on the one hand and ideas about human rights on the other. The former is wider than the latter. In order to retain a clear conception of human rights and not allow the idea of human rights to become blurred, it is important to separate clearly the wider and narrower areas of discussion.

CCIA opted for the wider definition of human rights and refrained from

---

[100] Op. cit., 38.
[101] Op. cit., 39.
[102] Op. cit., 40. U. Scheuner originally published his article in Ökumenische Rundschau 24 Jahrgang Heft 2 April 1975, 152–164.
[103] L. Raiser Menschenrechte in einer gespaltenen Welt Erwägungen zum Stand der ökumenischen Diskussion Evangelische Kommentare No. 4, 1975, 203. The jurist, Ludwig Raider, belonged to the synod of the Evangelical church in Germany in the period 1949–1973. He develops his views on human rights exhaustively in L. Raiser Vom rechten Gebrauch der Freiheit, Aufsätze zur Politik, Recht, Wissenschaftspolitik und Kirche, 1982, 119–201. His son is Konrad Raisser, who is General Secretary of the World Council of Churches.

adopting too narrow a notion. Human rights issues, whether political, economic or religious, are interrelated. They must be tackled as a whole. It is misleading and dangerous to speak of human rights divorced from their context and without a basic understanding of the socio-economic, political and cultural realities in the world in which we live. Human rights are used as a political weapon, as an ideal for self-realization based on hostile images.[104]

6.6. Human Rights at Nairobi 1975—Presuppositions, Content, Effects

The General Assembly at Nairobi

The international consultation on human rights and Christian responsibility at St. Pölten in Austria approved a series of formulations which might serve as a list of major human rights projects for the churches' work. Furthermore it developed strategic programmes of action for the implementation of human rights. In June 1975, CCIA gave its approval to the St. Pölten report and forwarded its recommendations to the General Assembly in Nairobi in December 1975. In other words, St. Pölten made a contribution to the General Assembly which CCIA presented in a series of reports and documents: among them is to be found the right to life and work, basic social, economic and cultural rights.[105]

The General Assembly at Nairobi from 23 November to 10 December 1975 took place in the wake of the Helsinki agreement which was reached in August of the same year. The work carried out on human rights at St. Pölten provided a basis for discussions. In other words, the St. Pölten report and the Helsinki agreement formed the main basis for the discussion on human rights at Nairobi and much attention was devoted to the content of the documents from both these meetings. Church delegates from Latin America, Asia, Africa and the Middle East testified to flagrant violations of human rights and expected the General Assembly to devote attention to their situation. No rights are possible without fundamental guarantees for life, embracing the right to work, to adequate nourishment, to guaranteed health care, to reasonable housing and to education designed for the full development of human potential. The violation of individual rights takes place in the context of society and within social structures. The campaign for human rights, including the individual ones, is at bottom a campaign for the liberation of whole society as a whole. Human rights are not simply a humanitarian affair. Such rights have a clear political meaning and political implications. The shift from individual rights to social and collective rights which could be noted at St. Pölten in 1974 was maintained and made its breakthrough at Nairobi in 1975.

---

[104] CCIA Reports 1974–1978 (1979) 6.
[105] CCIA Reports 1974–1978 (1979) 18 ff.

We can summarize what Nairobi had to say about the meaning of human rights in three points. *First of all*, the General Assembly was aware that human rights cannot be divorced from issues which are at the root of human rights violations. *Secondly*, it knew that the violation of human rights occurs in the context of society and within social structures and that the campaign for human rights, including the individual ones, is at bottom a campaign for the liberation of society as a whole. *Thirdly*, human rights are not merely a humanitarian matter but have a clear political meaning and political implications. The General Assembly helped to raise the political dimensions of human rights to a conscious level, recognizing that the lack of such awareness allowed human rights to be misused in ideological struggles and political conflicts. The churches reached a consensus about the content of human rights. The General Assembly drew up their conclusions in six points as recommended at St. Pölten. Among these are to be found the right to life and personal dignity. The Nairobi meeting confirmed increasing ecumenical unity about human rights.

During the first decades of the World Council of Churches, the greatest attention had been paid in the human rights issue to the question of freedom of religion. With a deeper social awareness, freedom of religion lost this preeminent place and became part of the WCC's integrated human rights ideology, in which there was a balance between individual and collective rights. On the theological plane, Nairobi had the following to say about human rights. God wishes a society in which all can enjoy human rights. All human beings are created in the image of God and are equal in His sight. Jesus Christ has combined us, one with the other, through His life, death and resurrection so that what concerns one of us concerns us all.[106] Human rights are theologically based both upon the creation and upon Christology. All human rights are approached within the theme of the framework of injustice and the struggle for liberation emphasizes that they are placed within a socio-economic and socio-political perspective. They are seen in their social context, nationally, regionally and internationally.

Background Information 1975

CCIA was the World Council of Churches' special instrument for work on human rights. Both before and after Nairobi, it had the special task on behalf of WCC of implementing human rights. The Commission on World Mission and Evangelism was also involved in the human rights issue. CCIA presented some background material in the form of a series of brochures, inter alia on *human rights from 1975 in Africa, the Middle East, Lebanon, The West Bank, Korea, Campuchea and Vietnam, the Philippines, the Pacific, New Caledonia, El Salvador* and a host of other regions and countries. This background mate-

---

[106] D. M. Paton ed Breaking Barriers—The Official Report of the Fifth Assembly of the WCC Nairobi, 23 November–10 December 1975 (1975) 97–119, 169–179. CCIA Reports 1974–1978 (1979) 20–29, 187 f.

rial is concerned with strengthening the churches' instrumental apparatus, the practical approach to human rights and the advisory group for human rights within CCIA—HRAG—which we shall deal with later.

The CCIA reports on *human rights in Korea*[107] and *El Salvador One Year of Oppression*[108] show that when the military take control of the government and civil administration, the scope for human rights is reduced. When the causes to human rights violations were studied, it was discovered that one of the factors leading to repression, torture and political murder, is the militarization of societies and political institutions. CCIA held a workshop on militarism and human rights at Glion, Switzerland from 10 to 14 November 1981, to discuss the relationship between these two realities. The conclusions of the meeting were published in *Militarism and Human Rights*, 1982. The workshop pointed to the increasing spread of militarism in the industrialized world, the phenomenon of paramilitarization i.e. the integration of civilians into the apparatus of oppression and the adoption of remarkably similar national security legislation in many countries. The consultation was held in order to study in greater detail the relationship between militarism and human rights and to bring together prominent experts in the field. Papers were presented on militarism and human rights, and on the relationship between them. Other papers dealt with militarism, technology and human rights;the international trade of repression and superpower intervention in the Third World; national security doctrines and their influence on militarism and human rights; human rights, militarization and underdevelopment in the Philippines; militarism and human rights in Puerto Rico.[109]

The Background Information was designed to supply the churches and other church-associated institutions and groups with diverse documentation, studies and analyses of issues of importance for the ecumenical movement. Several were related to human rights. In other words, the human rights component was very prominent in CCIA's background information.

The Implentation of the Helsinki Act 1977

The final act of the conference on security and cooperation in Europe, the so-called Helsinki agreement, was signed on the first of August 1975 by 35 states in Europe and North America. The so-called third basket dealt with humanitarian problems.

In 1976, Philip Potter,the Secretary-General of the World Council of Churches, invited the churches to a discussion about the Helsinki Final Act. He wanted to find out how they looked upon the application of the Helsinki act and raised the following five questions. 1) In what ways is the Helsinki declaration studied in your churches? 2) Can you identify practices and procedures

---

[107] Human Rights in the Republic of Korea CCIA Background Information 1979/1.
[108] El Salvador One Year of Repression CCIA Background Information 1981/1.
[109] Militarism and Human Rights CCIA Background Information 1982/3.

in your society which contradict the spirit and letter of the Helsinki declaration? 3) What opportunities has your church to assist in illuminating obscurities, to study and understand the Helsinki declaration in your country and its implementation., particularly with regard to freedom of thought, freedom of conscience, and freedom of religion and belief? 4) What actions does your church take or plan to take in this respect? 5) In what sense does your church envisage further international cooperation among churches of the signatory nations in order to ensure a more effective implementation of the Helsinki declaration? What role do you wish the World Council of Churches to play here in the light of the initiative by the European churches, the Lutheran World Federation, the World Alliance of Reformed Churches and other ecumenical and denominational groups and congregations?[110] The CCIA contacted the member churches in the signatory states about the agenda and their participation at the meeting. Around thirty representatives of churches in North America and Europe met in Montreux, Switzerland from 24 to 28 July 1976 for discussions. The member churches' answers to the Secretary-General's circular of 19 March 1976 functioned as a basis for the discussions.[111] The colloquium made a recommendation to the central committee of the World Council of Churches in August 1976 that CCIA's capabilities with respect to human rights should be strengthened and that an advisory group on human rights should be set up within CCIA.[112]

A second colloqium was held in Montreux from 12 to 15 July 1977 which brought together representatives of the member churches in those states which had signed the Helsinki Final Act and of the conference for European churches, the National Council of Churches in the USA and the Canadian Council of Churches. The colloquium was sponsored by CCIA. The consultation reiterated the conviction of the St. Pölten consultation that the emphasis of the Gospel is upon the value of all human beings in God's eyes; upon Christ's work of atonement and reconciliation which has given human beings their true dignity; upon love as a motive for action; and upon love of our fellow human beings which is the practical expression of an active belief in Christ. Christology is the theological starting point and goal in dealing with the issue of human rights, not the creation and natural law. This is symptomatic of the theological arguments about human rights within the ecumenical movement. The outcome of the second Montreux colloquium was a proposal to establish The Churches' Human Rights Programme for the Implementation of the Helsinki Final Act.[113] The working committee of the programme held its first meeting at Cartigny, Switzerland in 1979.

The Helsinki Act was signed in August 1975. Governmental representatives

---

[110] ER Vol. XXVIII no. 4 October 1976, 443. CCIA Reports 1974–1978 (1979), 163–166.
[111] Central Committee of the WCC. Minutes of the Twenty-Ninth Meeting. Geneva 10–18 August 1976, 10–15.
[112] ER Vol. XXVIII no. 4 October 1976 456. CCIA Reports 1974–1978 (1979), 167–174.
[113] CCIA Reports 1974–1978 (1979), 175–183, ER vol. XXX no. 1 Jan 1978, 59–64

opposed each other at the follow-up meetings in Belgrade in 1977 and Madrid in 1980 by putting forward views of human rights—individual as opposed to social rights—which conflicted. A compromise was reached around 1983 in Madrid. The third follow-up meeting began at Vienna in 1986. Within the World Council of Churches, CCIA became responsible for the programme of implementing the Helsinki Act. Consultations were held. The main topic for discussion was human rights issues and human rights violations. The programme dealt with the relation between human rights and security and with confidence-building measures.

6.7 The Human Rights Advisory Group 1977

At the meeting of the Central Committee of the World Council of Churches in 1977, the proposal was put forward to set up an Advisory Group on Human Rights, HRAG, which would deal with WCC's global involvement in the human rights field.[114] This advisory group for human rights was created within CCIA to help the commission to monitor trends and tendencies with respect to human rights and to propose actions for implementation, situations to be followed up and studies to be carried out. It would give added depth to CCIA's work in the field of human rights.

The human rights group began its work in 1978[115] and met in Copenhagen in 1979 and in Glion in 1981.[116] It brought together expertise on human rights, emphasized the interdependence between individual and society and the interrelationship between the universality of human rights and the concrete political conditions under which societies exist. The establishment of the human rights advisory group was a step in strengthening the churches' instrument for dealing with human rights.

Report on the Human Rights Programme 1980

The Advisory Group on Human Rights met for the first time in Copenhagen from 30 September to 4 October 1979. It received written reports on the human rights situation in Latin America, Bolivia, Brazil, the Caribean, Cuba, Africa, Angola, Australia, USA, Canada, the Philippines, USSR, Rumania, Italy and East Germany.

Within the human rights advisory group, there was a discussion of theologi-

---

[114] Central Committee of the WCC. Minutes of the Thirtieth Meeting. Geneva 28 July–6 August 1977 (1977) 106–109. Report on Human Rights WCC Central Committee Geneva Switzerland 28 July–6 August 1977 Document No. 13. Cf. Recommendations on Human Rights WCC Central Committee Geneva Switzerland August 10–18, 1976 Document No. 21. CCIA Reports 1974–1978 (1979), 31–38, 43–51.

[115] Progress Report on Human Rights WCC Central Committee Kingston Jamaica January 1–11, 1979 Document No. 13, 3 f.

[116] CCIA Reports 1979–1982 (1983), 26 ff.

cal aspects, trends in human rights issues, strategies for ecumenical solidarity and human rights education. In *Report on the Human Rights Programme,* 1980, the conclusions drawn by the advisory group were summed up:

1) *Integrated Approach*: it emphasized the ecumenical consensus which had been achieved in the 1970s, the significance of both individual and social rights, the interaction between the universality of human rights and the concrete political conditions in which societies live a conflict-filled existence. It is necessary for the church to be a church for others engaged in the struggle for human rights.

2) *Barriers to implementation* The difficulty in implementing human rights is that the fundamental causes are not simply at the level of individual morality but are of a structural nature. The injustice of the present international economic structures produces an unequal distribution of welfare which results in poverty, unemployment and emigration. The transnationalization of production and distribution affects national development which results in an inability to govern. The military-industrial complex promotes the militarization of societies by means of the doctrine of national security as well as the militarization of international relations leading to a doctrine of global security which in turn generates a risk of nuclear war.

The Human Rights Issue and the Human Rights Movement 1981

The human rights advisory group´s second meeting was held at Glion, Switzerland from 2 to 7 March 1981. The background and preparatory material for the meeting as well as the report of the meeting itself was published in J. Zalaquette *The Human Rights Issue and the Human Rights Movements Characterization Evaluation Propositions A Decade of Human Rights in the Work of the WCC Report from the CCIA Human Rights Advisory Group* 1981.

What had happened during the 1970s, was that representatives of different philosophies and religions either began to formulate their own human rights views or else emphasized the connnection between their respective traditions and human rights. The weakness with the liberal theory of human rights is that it does not sufficiently stress the individual's social dimension. Marxism held that a person can only achieve freedom in solidarity with others. Human rights are based upon demands for social and economic equality. In Christian tradition, human beings have a transcendent dimension—they go beyond the state—and the individual has a fundamental dignity. This means that civil and political rights have as much weight as economic, social and cultural rights. According to the presentation of the problem in The Human Rights Issue and the Human Rights Movement, the liberal tradition overemphasizes the individualistic view of human rights while the Marxist tradition overemphasizes the social view of human rights. By contrast, the Christian tradition maintains a balance between these two perspectives. It is an interesting interpretation of the churches' contribution to the human rights debate. It indicates a third approach to the issue. Human rights are not granted to human beings by the state but are given by God when He created mankind in His own image. This way of reasoning in terms of an individualist and Marxist approach to human rights is reminiscent of what I pointed out in Church and Society in the Modern Age 1995, namely that the churches in their view of society find themselves placed between capitalism and socialism and draw attention to both individual and social elements in their view of society and in their interpretation of society's role and function.

At Glion, attention was drawn to the influence of economic systems upon human rights. Despite various efforts, little progress has beeen made in founding a new international economic order. Children and workers are the main victims of the status quo. International companies tend to defend the old order. Environmental abuse, the weapons race and problems caused by new and uncontrolled technology are examples of causes of human rights violations. Further development of ecumenical strategies in the field of human rights is concerned with the rights of peoples and minorities to their own culture and language, the continuation of colonial domination and the political use of religion.[117]

6.8 Human Rights and Latin America

Torture in Brazil

Brasil was under military rule from 1964 until 1985. Like similar governments in Argentina, Chile and Uruguay, the Brazilian military regime permitted the systematic torture of its political opponents. Torture was the most feared weapon in the well stocked arsenal of oppression which held not only activists, but also the population at large, in its grip. The military introduced laws pertaining to national security which created an alibi for the violation of civil rights and allowed the torturers to go unpunished. J. Dassin ed. Torture in Brazil, A Report by the Archdiocese of Sao Paulu 1986 with a foreword by Philip Potter, the Secretary-General of the World Council of Churches, is a report on human rights violations by the military regime. Potter stresses that torture is the most grim and barbaric crime which can be committed against a human being. The book is a report on an investigation within the field of human rights. It is an examination of the political oppresssion which was directed against thousands of Brazilians who were treated by the military as opponents of their regime. Torture was an important constituent in the military system of justice in Brazil. The proceedings at political trials held in military courts show that the judicial authorities were aware that torture was used in the pre-trial interrogations and investiga-

---

[117] Reports of the CCIA Human Rights Advisory Group Glion Switzerland March 2–7, 1981 in J. Zalaquette The Human Rights Issue and the Human Rights Movement 1981, 61 f.

tions and that the evidence which emerged was considered legally valid even although the defence was able to demonstrate how the confessions had been extracted under duress.

Human Rights Office for Latin America 1973

The world was shocked by the brutality of the coup carried out by General Augusto Pinochet in Chile in 1973 in removing the constitutionally elected President, Salvador Allende. The coup was followed by a systematic hunt after opponents. Hundreds of thousands became the victims of torture, execution, disappearance and exile. This pattern of events was repeated in the coup in Uruguay in 1973, in Paraguay in 1974 and in Argentina in 1976. In Central America, the repression led to civil war, waged against the Somoza regime in Nicaragua in 1976. During the coup in Chile in 1973, the Latin American churches appealed to the World Council of Churches for assistance to receive the thousands of refugees brought about by this event. It led to the creation of The Human Rights Resources Office for Latin America—HRROLA. The task of this office was to support the churches in Latin America in defending and promoting human rights. HRROLA came into existence after the coup in Chile in 1973 as part of the Justice and Service section of the World Council of Churches. The office cooperated with CCIA. HRROLA was given the task of assisting the churches in Latin America in their work of defending human dignity, of giving moral support to these churches and of providing information about the human rights situation in the region. The disappearance of people in Peru during the 1980s was the highest in the world.

Consultation on Human Rights and the Churches in Latin America, 1973

From 25 to 28 February 1973, a consultation was held on *human rights and the churches in Latin America*. The situation was said to constitute a challenge for the churches. When we speak of the liberation of human beings in Latin America, we must not forget how urgent it is to develop an effective strategy for dealing with violations of human rights, in both their individual and collective forms. Within this context of the struggle for liberation, the consultation proposed that the World Council of Churches should 1) create a special programme for the defence of human rights in Latin America or expand and stregthen existing WCC programmes in this field 2) collect information and documentation about human rights violations and channel it to the relevant bodies dealing with this issue 3) channel help as effectively as possible to political prisoners, refugees and their families.[118]

---

[118] CCIA Reports 1970–1973 (1974), 118–122.

The Santiago Declaration 1978

An international symposium on *The Dignity of Man: his Rights and Obligations in Today's World* met in November 1978 in Santiago, Chile. The Catholic church in Santiago acted as host and representatives of churches, international organizations and humanitarian associations from different parts of the world participated in the meeting. The symposium noted that thirty years had passed since the proclamation of the declaration of human rights and that it still served as an ideal which all peoples and nations should strive to live by. It is a source of encouragement to all those throughout the world, who work for a true humanism. The declaration of human rights proclaims the basic ideas of all human beings and societies, ideas which can be shared by people of all races, creeds and convictions.

According to the symposium, the idea of human rights has become the supreme value which sums up the development of human beings and society. For this reason, humanity has reached a deeeper and broader awareness that these rights must be implemented. In spite of what has been done, the declaration is still more of an aspiration than a reality. There are obstacles to human efforts to become fully human.

- In many of the UN member states violations of human rights occur;
- many governments have introduced systems which diminish human value and often try to justify different forms of institutionalized violence and torture by reference to the interests of the state.

All human rights are invisible and dependent upon one another. People can only enjoy freedom and justice if conditions are created in which they can exercise their civil and political, as well as their economic, social and cultural rights. Abuse of civil and political freedoms is not simply a direct violation of human integrity and dignity; it also constitutes a serious obstacle to a sound process of development. In the same way, abuse of economic, social and cultural rights makes the attainment of civil and political rights impossible. The fact that innumerable people live under inhuman conditions is a violation of human rights. It is related to the unjust international order. The attainment of a new international economic order is therefore crucial for the promotion of human rights. In making this point, social and collective rights are clearly given equal status to individual rights.

The symposium issued the Santiago Charter. It expressed the conviction that recognition of the dignity and rights of all human beings is the basis of justice and peace in the world, because we believe that every human being has the right to be a person. The integrity of personality was dependent upon reasonable human living conditions and thus upon social and economic conditions. Among the signatories of the declaration were several well known Catholic champions of human rights such as Cardinal Raul Silva Henriques of Santiago,

Chile and Cardinal Paulo Evaristo Arns of Sao Paulo, Brazil. Other signatories included Roger Heckel from the Pontifical Commission Justitia et Pax and the theologian José Miguez Bonino. co-president in the World Council of Churches.[119]

The Mission and Human Rights

In addition to CCIA, the Commission on World Mission and Evangelism was involved in the human rights issue. This was shown in an issue of International Review of Mission for 1977, which was devoted to human rights just as a special number of The Ecumenical Review in 1975 had been. The theme was analyzed from the viewpoint of the mission churches. Freedom means not only freedom of religion but also freedom from hunger, want and fear. Human rights are at the very core of the liberating Gospel of Christ.[120] Violation of human rights were specially common in Latin America. [121]

The Protestant Latin American theologian José Miguez Bonino wrote an article entitled *Whose human rights* ? In the declaration of human rights of 1789, there is talk of equality and universality. In USA, however, it became clear that Indian men and later black men, were not included among the ranks of men who had been created equal. The situation was still worse in regard to Indian women and black women. The proclamation of human rights at the end of the 18th century concerned the embodiment of the aspirations of one particular social group, namely the bourgeoisie. The shift towards universalism is first expressed in the UN declaration of human rights of 1948.[122] The churches look upon the human rights campaign as being based upon belief. They have tried to find a firm theological foundation for universality in human dignity and rights. Theology has been based upon the doctrine of creation and/or the doctrine of salvation. Human beings who are God's creation and formed in His own image, form a basis for the rights of all. The incarnation, God's love manifested in the death and resurrection of Christ, indicates a Divine commitment to humanity which underlines the infinite value of every human being. According to Bonino, the struggle for the humanity of every human being is the visible sign of the true church. [123] In Latin America, Indian rights are the litmus test of a society's capacity to function. The rights of the poor and defenceless measure the health of the nation. The test of the universality of justice is the condition of the poor. The condition of the Indians shows the inhumanity of Latin American society.[124] The fundamental human right is the right to a life worthy of a human being. The meaning and content of the churches'

---

[119] The Charter of Santiago in M. Reuver ed. Human Rights: A Challenge to Theology, 1983, 59–61.
[120] Editorial International Review of Mission LXVI no. 263 July 1977, 215 f.
[121] Op. cit., 218.
[122] Op. cit., 221.
[123] Op. cit., 222.
[124] Op. cit., 223.

commitment to human rights, even at the more formal legal level, is to be found in the defence of a humane life for the humblest people in society.[125]

In his article, Bonino points out the potential conflict between universalism and particularism in the conception of human rights, as well as indicating the two main theological alternative foundations for human rights, the one based upon the creation and natural law and the other upon salvation and Christology. However, he does not come out in favour of one of these alternatives. Within the World Council of Churches, the main theological approach to human rights was based upon Christology, whereas the Roman Catholic Church first adopted this approach after the Second Vatican Council without, however, relinquishing its traditional natural law position originating in scholastic theology. The main point in Bonino's line of argument is to ask whose interests and aims are served by human rights in different concrete situations. He wishes to get away from a purely theoretical and abstract treatment of human rights and approach them from a practical level, by looking at the way they function in real life. The concrete example he considers, is that of the Indians in Latin America..

6.9 Interdenominational Study Project on Human Rights 1979

Introduction

Various religious denominations tried to discover in their own theological roots a basis for church involvement in the human rights issue. Global denominational associations like the World Alliance of Reformed Churches and the Lutheran World Federation carried out studies. In 1979, CCIA offered its services as coordinator of *an international study project on the theological basis of human rights*. This project was supported, not simply by CCIA, but also by a number of denominational groups such as the Lutheran World Federation, the World Alliance of Reformed Churches and the Pontifical Commission Justice and Peace. As its primary goal, the project chose an inner search for a deeper theological understanding of human rights on the basis of each denominational perspective. Secondly, the various ways of approaching the problem should lead to a common ecumenical understanding.

In addition to the World Alliance of Reformed Churches and the Lutheran World Federation, the preparatory committee of the Panorthodox Council, the Pontifical commission Justice and Peace, the Baptist World Alliance, the Anglican Consultative Council and the Reformed Ecumenical Synod took part in the study. Each of the participants contributed to the discussion. One example is a discussion which took place in Geneva from 21 to 22 April 1983 between the World Council of Churches and the Reformed Ecumenical Synod about the

---

[125] Op. cit., 224.

biblical and theological basis of human rights. The report *Res Testimony on Human Rights* formed the basis for the resulting exchange of views.

A number of the denominational groups such as the Lutheran World Federation and the World Alliance of Reformed Churches proceeded to stage two. They compared ways of approaching the problem and picked out common elements as well as points where there was disagreement. An interdenominational consultation bringing together Reformed, Lutheran and Orthodox theologians was held in Geneva in 1980 and resulted in a report, published by the Lutheran World Federation and entitled *How Christian are Human Rights ?*. The verdict of this gathering was that since there is no long tradition concerning theological positions on human rights, it will perhaps be easier to attain a future common theological platform with respect to human rights.

CCIA collected examples of theological reflection emanating from Christians and churches involved in the human rights struggle. They were published in *Human Rights: a Challenge to Theology*. This publication contains theological studies relating to human rights. It was produced for the interdenominational study project on the theological basis of human rights. The authors were theologians and Christians who were themselves involved in the campaign for human rights. They try to communicate the insights into their beliefs which their involvement has given.[126]

After this introduction, it is natural to arrange this section dealing with the interdenominational study project directed by the World Council of Churches by analyzing the three main documents which the project gave rise to, or is associated with.

How Christian are Human Rights? 1980

An international working conference *on the theological foundations of human rights* was held from 30 April to 3 May 1980 in Geneva. Professors in law and theology met to discuss the approaches of Reformed, Lutheran and Orthodox theology and to try to harmonize them. Background papers and conclusions were presented in the volume E. Lorenz ed. How Christian are Human Rights? 1980.[127]

Jürgen Moltmann describes different churches' theological approach to human rights in *Christian faith and human rights*. He holds that the St. Pölten consultation managed to balance the one-sided Western ideas about human rights by beginning with the right to life. From 1948 to 1960, freedom of religion was central to church activity and the theological work on human rights. Since 1960, another theme has emerged at ecumenical meetings. Voices of the Third World condemned racism as a serious violation of fundamental human rights. The rights of the individual were linked to the struggle for im-

---

[126] Progress Report on Human Rights WCC Central Committee Kingston Jamaica January 1–11, 1979 Document No. 13, 5, Appendix III 1 f.
[127] E. Lorenz ed. How Christian are Human Rights LWF 1980, 5.

proved living standards at Uppsala 1968. Stress was laid upon economic, social and cultural human rights. The history of liberty in Western Europe has little to say about this. How are individuals to attain their rights to liberty if they cannot find the economic and social possibilities to allow this. In the Third World, interest is fixed not upon the freedom of the press, but upon the right to life. For this reason, the St. Pölten report, like the Roman Synod of Bishops, gives precedence to the right to live, the right to food and nourishment and the right to work in the catalogue of human rights. A shift takes place in the ecumenical discussion from the Western liberal view of human rights which gives less prominence to social rights to the Third World's right to life. The ecumenical human rights discussion shows an openness and flexibility among Christians who have to live in situations fraught with contradiction. The church becomes the church for the world through its relation to human rights. The discussion of social problems takes place within the framework of human rights. Moltmann holds that the Christian contribution to thinking about human rights must start from human dignity and humanity. It is here that he discovers the theological basis of human rights. Moltmann locates this starting point in the Roman Catholic, Lutheran and Reformed tradition. Human dignity arises through the fact that human beings are made in God's image. The incarnation of God as a human being, sheds new light on the picture of human beings and their dignity. Christian theology holds that human dignity originates in what is shared by God and human beings without excluding other religious or humanist bases of human rights. God's image means full communion with God.[128]

The American Lutheran theologian, Carl E. Braaten, presented a talk entitled *Toward an ecumenical theology of human rights*. He pointed out the two dimensions of God's revelation through the law of Creation and the Gospel of Redemption and he raised the question of how these could be kept together in creating an ecumenical theology of human rights. He holds that the thing that combines them, is to be found in the eschatological view of Christian belief. Work on behalf of human rights can be interpreted as earthly signs of the justice of the Kingdom of God. The Gospel bears witness to this for the world on the basis of the justification which God guaranteed through Jesus Christ. Human rights are not simply about law and order but also about Jesus' message about the Kingdom of God. The Kingdom of God has two dimensions. The vertical dimension of the Gospel allows us to encounter God's absolute transcendence. The horizontal dimension of the coming Kingdom speaks of the meeting with Christ in the form of the person of our neighbour, with his or her needs. The task is to combine the vertical line of justification by faith alone with the horizontal line in the form of the Kingdom which strives for justice in an evil world. God's love for Christ's sake and commitment to human rights for humanity's sake, are combined in the picture of what God does for the the

---

[128] Op. cit., 11–23.

world in the history of Jesus Christ. The God who is involved in the struggle for human liberation from hunger, misery, oppression, ignorance and from all the powers of sin and evil, is none other than the Father of Jesus Christ who reconciles the whole world with Himself. The reign of Divine Justice revealed in the work of Christ is God's total and final power to secure at last the fulfilment of human rights which are often denied and only partly realized under the conditions of earthly existence. [129] Braaten overcomes traditional Lutheran theology's division between the two Kingdoms with human rights being assigned to the Kingdom of this world by linking his ideas to modern exegetics and developing an ecumenical theology of human rights based upon the perspective of the Kingdom of God. At the same time, he bases this theology upon justification through faith alone and gives it a Christological focus.

The conference indicated theological ways of approaching human rights in its conclusions and recommendations. 1) All theological pronouncements about human rights derive from Christian anthropology which holds that human beings are created in the image of God: it is this nature of humanity which constitutes its inviolable dignity. 2) Given this common view as starting point, it is then possible to choose a variety of ways of approaching human rights: one way is to start with the Creation and treat the sources of the recognition of human dignity and fundamental human rights as located in humanity's natural law. Another approach is based upon the experience of God's covenant with His people. The story of the biblical covenant is a presentation of human dignity and basic human rights. The new covenant in Christ reveals God's justice and justifies human existence. A further approach is to take the sinner's justification through the grace of God as a starting point for the basis of their freedom and thereby derive human beings' responsibility for their fellow humans in the world. 3) Three areas require further theological research and discussion. a) The view that human beings are created in the image of God b) the relationship between the justification of the sinner and the Kingdom of God c) the relationship between creation theology and natural law 4) the struggle for the recognition and implementation of human rights takes place in a world which is no longer God's good creation nor the Kingdom of God. Human rights relate to the violation of human dignity and the setting aside of human rights. We do not share the humanistic optimism of the Enlightenment which gave rise to the first formulation of human rights in Europe and America. Since human beings are created in God's image but are at the same time sinners, human rights are formulated to counteract the degrading conditions of this world. From the struggle for human rights emerges the duty to work for a world which respects human dignity and which can survive.[130]

---

[129] Op. cit., 49–51.
[130] Op. cit., 84–86. Report of a Limited Research Project on Theological Basis of Human Rights.

Human Rights a Challenge to Theology 1983

Theological reflection and the campaign for human rights derived its material, not from Europe and North America, but from Latin America, Asia, Africa and the Pacific. The expressions for theological reflection about human rights came from the Third World. The Third World theologians in EATWOT, at their conference in New Delhi in 1981, maintained in a statement entitled *The challenge of reality to theology* which was published in *Human Rights: A Challenge to Theology*, 1983, that they looked with a certain hope on pressure for a new international economic order and the demand for an effective North-South dialogue. The congregations of Christians and other faiths have, through their commitment to the poor and oppressed, shown that religion is not some opium of the people. The ties between the oppressed of the Third World and the exploited minorities in the rich countries have become deeper. The Third World theologians are encouraged by the development in the First World of the Feminist Movement, the search for new life styles, the ecological defence of nature, the anti-war and anti-nuclear weapons organizations and the network of solidarity with the Third World's cause.

Traditional Western theology has stimulated personal spirituality and the expansion of mission but it has not been capable of responding to the social problems of the First World and the challenges of the Third World. In the eyes of the Third World, this theology has been alienated and alienating. It has failed to inspire the struggle against the evils of racism, sexual discrimination, capitalism, colonialism and neo-colonialism. Traditional theology has not involved itself in the real drama of the people or spoken in the religious and cultural idiom and style of the masses in a meaningful way. It has remained largely academic, speculative and individualistic, paying little attention to sin's social and structural aspects. The Bible itself has not always been used to express the liberating Gospel of Jesus Christ. Often it has been employed to give legitimacy to Christian participation in oppression and to bless the dominant race, class or sex. Theology has often been incapable of carrying on a dialogue with other world religions in such a way as to be enriched by the centuries of wisdom and deep spiritual experience of their adherents.

In order to create a theology which is relevant for the life of our people, a new perspective is necessary. In the Third World, attempts have been made to develop a theology based upon Biblical reflection on the struggle for liberation. Social analysis is a fundamental element in a theology of liberation. Without an adequate understanding of society, theologians are unable to interpret God's Will for our societies and for our time. The starting point of the Third World theologians is the struggle of the poor and oppressed against all forms of injustice and oppression. Christian involvement in this struggle requires a new starting point for theological reflection. This participation is belief in action and the manifestation of Christian commitment which constitutes the first act of theology.

In the fight against oppression, God appears as the saving God who acts in history. Racism is a form of oppression, particularly in South Africa where for many blacks, Christianity is the religion of the oppressors and has long supported the existing ideology of apartheid. When blacks fight to restore their humanity, both through their struggle against the socio-political structures of apartheid and through their challenge to the distorted picture of Christ, God is drawn into the struggle against racism and theology cannot ignore this dimension of God's presence. The oppressed are the presence of the Crucified God. But Christ arose from the dead and proclaimed victory over the forces of evil and death. In the struggle of the weak and powerless for light and life, the resurrection of Jesus is an historical experience and the resurrection of those who have been trampled in the dust can begin.

Poverty and oppression in the Third World brings about the deaths of millions through hunger, sickness and oppression. Many people also lose their identity, dignity and personality. The poor and oppressed fight not only for a better economic standard but also for freedom and dignity, life and full humanity. In the Third World we find the dialectical tension between life and death manifested in various ways. To believe in the God of life is to believe in love, justice, peace, truth and human wholeness. It is also to condemn the causes of the dehumanization of our people and to fight against the systems which diminish and crush the lives of so many.

We cannot separate God from the Kingdom of God. The Kingdom of God is the Kingdom of life. By bringing about the Kingdom, Jesus also introduced the sign of life. He healed the sick, fed the hungry, restored the outcast and released the imprisoned. He came to give life and life more abundantly. The Kingdom of life is revealed above all in the resurrection of Jesus. The resurrection means that new life and new humanity is formed in the victim's struggle against injustice, even in their death. To be a follower of Jesus, is to witness to his life, death and resurrection. Discipleship encourages participation in the struggles of the oppressed for the transformation of social structures and the renewal of cultures.[131]

The liberation theology which was developed within EATWOT and which has been sketched above on the basis of the statement Reality's challenge to theology is from one standpoint the Third World's theology of human rights, the right to life of the poor and oppressed. This theology interprets the situation of the oppressed in Asia, Africa and Latin America but also points to liberation and redress. There is a way out of humiliation, and faith is a power which allows us to escape from hopelessness.

---

[131] M. Reuver ed. Human Rights: A Challenge to Theology 1983, 30–36. R. O'Grady writes on the the church's human rights work in Asia in Bread and Freedom Understanding and acting on human rights 1979.

Res Testimony on Human Rights

The purpose of *Res Testimony on Human Rights* is to promote human rights within the Gospel perspective of justice and love. It has emerged from the American Reformed tradition and formed a basis for discussions between the World Council of Churches and the Reformed Ecumenical Synod in Geneva in April 1983. A chapter of this document deals with human rights in a world perspective and we shall review the main points it raises. Human rights are related to the situation of the Canadian Indians, the Indians in the USA, the peasants of South and Central America, Roman Catholics and Protestants in Northern Ireland, guest workers in the Netherlands and West Germany, the Solidarity movement in Poland, black and coloured people in South Africa, Palestinians in the Middle East, Christians in Sri Lanka and in Russia etc. In Western democracies, parents are denied the right of freely choosing an education for their children, workers are prevented from joining trades unions which share their religious convictions and minority groups are excluded from participation in welfare society. Historically, human rights have been violated through the persecution of the Christians in the Roman empire, the Crusades against the Infidels in the Middle Ages, the activities of the Inquisition, the wars of religion, Western Colonial imperialism, the Slave Trade, contemporary dictatorships and the Nazi extermination camps.

At present, it is a matter of supporting the campaign for God-given human rights on the basis of the Bible. The church cannot identify its view of human rights with those human rights ideologies which have their roots in Western individualism (capitalism) or in Eastern collectivism (communism). This is because the Kingdom of God relativizes all temporal kingdoms. The church must distance itself from all social systems and assess them on the basis of the norms of God's word, proclaiming the gospel of justice and reconciliation to the world in which we live and are called upon to serve. The doctrine of individualism declares that free and sovereign people are the fundamental entities and building blocks in society. According to Scripture, persons are important but as individuals they are not the only thing of importance. Human rights are more than individual rights because human beings are always part of a living network of interpersonal relations. No man is an island. Human beings are social in nature. Our lives are interwoven in a social fabric in the form of a social order. Individualism underestimates the collective character of human life. It atomizes human beings and encourages the fragmentation of society. It lacks social substance. There is a fundamental unity in the human race which constitutes the basis for the exercise of human rights. Collectivism attacks human rights. It recognizes a solidarity within the human race but it takes it too far by proclaiming a united people while simultaneously setting class against class and undermining the Biblical notion of unity and solidarity. It creates an institutional megastructure and makes the interest of this structure the ultimate measure of all other things in life. Individualism and collectivism abandon the Biblical idea of differentiated responsibility in society. No temporal institution—whether the City State of antiquity, the medieval church, the modern state, the workers' party or the transnational corporation—may be treated as absolute or deified. Collectivism always has a tendency to transform a certain social organization into a virtually omnipotent superstructure, bestowing on it a messianic and suprahistorical role which Scripture reserves for the Kingdom of God alone. By politicizing life, governmental collectivism tends to mould political rights according to one form and either to dictate the conditions according to which other human rights may be exercized—at home, in school, in church, in art, in science, in the media, in journalism—or to suppress them.

Individualist and collectivist societies replace Divine Sovereignty by some form of human autonomy embodied in some form of state absolutism. Both ideologies must be judged in accordance with the word of God. Both theories coincide in the fact that they distance themselves from the sovereignty of God. Neither individualism nor collectivism is a true friend of human rights. The former looks after personal liberties but neglects justice and equality for all. Collectivism looks after law and order and the distribution of welfare. But it falls badly short when it comes to freedom and responsibility. Although the aims of individualism and collectivism diverge, they do converge in the bureaucratic state. They both create societies which are controlled from the top down. The Biblical vision of a pluralistic society goes up in smoke. There is another type of society which is based neither upon individualism nor upon collectivism. It constitutes a third way, a society which allows pluralism. This society is based upon the Bible. It is rooted in the Judaeo-Christian tradition. It gives expression to human rights. It is based upon a reformed view of the world. The pluralistic view of society contains two fundamental dimensions. First, there is the idea that by virtue of the order of Creation we discover the meaning in our lives within the framework of different spheres of activity, each and every one of them having its own divinely devised identity and integrity (such as marriage, the family, divine service, politics, art, science, journalism). Secondly there is the aspect of so-called denominational pluralism—the recognition that we,as a consequence of our fall into sin and as a fruit of our salvation, live in a religiously divided world with different communities of faith (Protestant, Catholic, Jewish, Islamic, Hindu and Buddhist) and that human rights, religious liberties and the freedom of all such groups to express their convictions openly must be satisfactorily satisfied. These are the fundamental contours of a pluralistic vision of life.[132] Thus the North American vision of a good society is given legitimacy by the Reformed Synod.

---

[132] RES Testimony on Human Rights The Reformed Ecumenical Synod 1983, 16–25.

6.10 The World Council of Churches and racism in the 1980s

Barbara Roger's book *Race No Peace without Justice* is a critical assessment of a global consultation on Churches responding to Racism in the 1980s which was held in the Netherlands from 16 to 21 June 1980. The issues discussed included the rights of the native peoples in areas dominated by European settlers, problems concerning immigrant workers, national security doctrines and their abuse by racial minorities and a series of regional questions embracing the untouchables in India, Moslems in the Philippines, the Indians in America, the arabs in Israel, blacks in the USA and the key issue of the white minority regimes in South Africa. The consultation resulted in a statement which is to be found in the book.

The report *Churches responding to Racism in the 1980s* contains the reports of various working parties. Racism is sinful. It must be openly opposed by Christians and the church. There is a contrast between the church's prophetic role and racism in some ecclesiastical structures. Often the churches reflect their social environment and the weaker groups of society, including those who are racially oppressed, have no place in the leading roles of the church or in its decision-making processes. Racism has an economic basis. The dominant economic system in the world is concerned with promoting self-interest, greed and the interests of the white race. This system exploits natural and human resources in the form of the peoples of the Third World. In the process they are reduced to the status of impersonal units. This is seen most clearly in the case of so-called migrant workers. They lack the security of citizenship or trades union membership and often the supportive presence of their families. The lives of such workers are tailored to the economic demands of an exploitative and soul-destroying system. The doctrines of national security result in an intensification of racial discrimination and racial oppression. They provide obstacles to changes in an unjust status quo and allow the preservation of power structures.[133]

6.11 Human Rights at Vancouver 1983

The General Assembly at Vancouver

The sixth General Assembly of the World Council of Churches took up the issue of human rights. It was noted that violations of human rights took place in the majority of societies. Economic domination and unjust social structures suppress people's socio-economic rights such as the fundamental needs of

---

[133] Churches responding to Racism in the 1980s, 1983, 78 ff. Statement from the International Consultation on the Churches' Response to Racism in the 1980s in the Netherlands (1980) in A van der Bent, Breaking Down the walls, WCC's Statements and Actions on Racism 1948–1985 (1986), 74 ff.

families and societies and the rights of workers. The meeting also addressed itself to the denial of fundamental human rights as the basis of a doctrine of national security, and the denial of the right of workers to set up trades unions which represent their interests.[134] Vancouver lists a series of rights, among which occur in addition to those accepted at Nairobi the following: the right to peace, the right to protection of the environment, the right to development. Individual rights and their violation is placed in the context of society and its social structures. Human rights cannot be divorced from major questions such as peace and justice.[135]

The World Council of Churches Programme for Human Rights

The aim of human rights work within the World Council of Churches was to create preconditions for an effective implementation of human rights. First of all, efforts were made to identify the actors involved. Thereafter there was the question of devising a methodology. The main activity of the WCC human rights programme was located within CCIA. However, nearly all programmes within WCC have elements which directly or indirectly are relevant to human rights. For example, human rights form part of the Commission on the Churches' Participation in Development (CCPD). A major part of CCPD's programme is concerned with the defence and protection of people's rights. These matters were discussed in CCPD publications such as *To Break The Chains of Oppression, The Poverty Makers* and *Towards a Church of the Poor.* The growing awareness of the role of transnational corporations in the systematic denial of human rights is apparent in *Transnational Study.* CCPD coordinated a study of political ethics which tries to formulate the role of the churches in the development of an ethos for national and international politics with the aim of implementing human rights.

The shift within WCC from the individualist aspects of rights and freedom of religion to one where social rights are also considered, is exemplified in the book *Workers' Rights are Human Rights* 1981 by A. A. Evans. This was a co-production between Idoc International in Rome and CCIA in Geneva. In the process of development, the Roman Catholic church and the ecumenical movement in the form of the World Council of Churches came together. The author of the book came from ILO, the international association of trades unions in Geneva. An example of the international labour organization's work within the field of human rights is G. Da Fonseca's *How to file Complaints of Human Rights Violations, A Practical Guide to Intergovernmental Procedures,* 1975. This re-orientation from individual to social rights including the rights of workers is also apparent in another Idoc work, namely E. and M. Weingärtner, *Human Rights is more than Human Rights: A Primer for Churches on*

---

[134] D. Gill ed. Gathered for Life Official Report VI Assembly WCC Vancouver Canada 24 July– 10 August 1983 (1983), 88–89.
[135] Op. cit. 140. CCIA Reports 1983–1986 (1987) 28.

Security and Cooperation in Europe. Erich Weingärtner was a specialist on human rights and the human rights programme within WCC where he was responsible for several human rights publications. Among them may be noted E. Weingärtner, *Behind the Mask Human Rights in Asia and Latin America An Inter-regional Encounter,* 1988. He worked earlier within Idoc in Rome and transferred later to become Executive Secretary in CCIA.

6.12 The World Council of Churches and South Africa

Within both WCC and the Roman Catholic church, human rights all too easily became a subject for argument on a theoretical and abstract plane. The World Council of Churches, however, was saved from becoming completely immersed in theoretical arguments thanks not least to its involvement in the struggle against apartheid in South Africa. This became the principal test case for WCC 's concrete agitation on behalf of human rights. The campaign against racism which had its own programme within WCC, was not marginally involved in actions on behalf of human rights but in fact served as the foremost sphere of application of human rights. In South Africa, the ecumenical movement was engaged on behalf of the victims of injustice and their struggle for liberation. Racism was condemned as a sin and its theological justification was rejected as heresy. The twenty-five year old struggle against apartheid was celebrated by the publication of Pauline Webb's *A Long Struggle The Involvement of the WCC in South Africa,* 1994.

Apartheid denied the majority of the inhabitants of South Africa citizenship and fundamental human rights. As a result, there were serious attempts at Uppsala 1968 to formulate a theology directed against racism. It was a question of a genuine theology of struggle. Apartheid for its part had been given a theological defence. Philip Potter, the Secretary-General of WCC in the period 1972–84, led the campaign against racism which had been initiated by his predecessor Eugen Carson Blake, Secretary-General 1966–1972 and earlier active in the American civil rights movement with Martin Luther King. Since white racism attracted PCR's main attention, South Africa occupied centre stage. The South African government claimed to defend "Western Christian civilization" with its policy of apartheid. This claim challenged Christian faith and theology. The campaign against apartheid developed into a religious struggle. This explains the intensity of WCC's involvement. South Africa was home to an ideology which built apartheid on the basis of its vision of a Christian civilization.

Ever since the Cottesloe consultation of 1960 on the heels of the Sharpeville massacre which had occurred earlier the same year, Beyers Naudé the white South African prelate of the Reformed denomination and leader of the Christian Institute, had shown sympathy with the WCC's negative attitude towards apartheid. The World Council of Churches, despite the opposition of the apartheid regime, thus had support within South Africa not simply from the black and coloured population, but also from whites. In 1977, the South African government issued a ban on both the Christian Institute and its director, Beyers Naudé. The South African government accused the World Council of Churches which economically supported the liberation struggle in South Africa, of being a communist-infiltrated terrorist organization. It was claimed that weapons had been purchased with money sent by WCC. No less a person than Visser't Hooft, the Secretary-General 1948–66, however, could indeed imagine situations of oppression where Christians co-operated to eliminate a tyrannical rule. Visser't Hooft did not exclude armed struggle. In this he was in the company of no less than Jean Calvin, John Knox and Dietrich Bonhoeffer.

The close connection between the World Council of Churches' programme against racism and the liberation struggle in South Africa was apparent at the meeting of the General Assembly at Vancouver in 1983, where Desmond Tutu, then Secretary-General of the South African church council, Allan Boesak and several representatives of ANC took part. The complete openness displayed by the South African church leaders in their remarks, showed courage. They were the objects of threats and restrictions by the apartheid regime. Boesak criticized racial supremacy which was justified theologically. As early as 1979, Allan Boesak had sent a *letter to the Minister of Justice in South Africa*. The reason for this was that the South African church council had given support to civil disobedience and the Minister of Justice had issued warnings. He maintained that ministers of religion and churches must keep out of politics and devote themselves to their task of preaching the Gospel. Boesak pointed out that the Gospel which the churches were called upon to preach, concerned not simply human beings' inner life, but the whole of their existence. Christians must show obedience to God's word also in political life. They must obey God more than men. Human laws must be subordinated to the Word of God. Where justice is lacking, the government can no longer derive its authority from God but in fact is in conflict with God. In this situation opposition to a government is justified and becomes a duty.[136]

In 1985 and 1986, 150 South African theologians published a theological commentary to the political crisis in South Africa which became known as *the Kairos Document*. In it, the theological defence of existing racist conditions in South Africa was criticized. It was principally directed against a theology which treated the apartheid state as legitimate. The Kairos Document came to be considered as a prophetic tract for our times.[137] In the so-called Rustenburg Declaration of 1990, the South African churches admitted that they were to blame for the legitimization and support of apartheid. Simultaneously, they rejected apartheid as sinful. Racism was thus condemned just as the regime

---

[136] A. Boesak to the South African Minister of Justice 20 August, 1979 in A. Boesak, Walking on Thorns, The Call to Christian Obedience (1984), 58–65.

[137] The Kairos Document in W. H. Logan ed. The Kairos Covenant Standing with South African Christians 1988, 2–47.

was in the process of dismantling the apartheid system. The churches' delay in rejecting apartheid as sinful encouraged the government to hold on to it.[138]

The World Council of Churches' involvement in South Africa in the campaign to implement human rights by fighting racism and apartheid, was exemplified in a several numbers of PCR Information reports and background papers. They often bore titles directly linked to the situation in South Africa: *Bank Loans and Investments in South Africa: A Survey of actions taken by churches and groups in relation to WCC policies 1979/No 3, The Churches Involvement in Southern Africa 1982/No 14, South Africa in Crisis 1983/No 17, Southern Africa: The Continuing Crisis 1985/ No 20, The Challenge to the Church A Theological Comment on the Political Crisis in South Africa The Kairos Document and Commentaries Special Issue 1985, Southern Africa— The Harare and AJ-Gams Declarations: A Call for Freedom and Independence for South Africa and Namibia 1986/No 23, From Cottesloe to Cape Town Challenges for the Church in a Post-Apartheid South Africa 1991/No 30.* The documentation on the World Council of Churches' involvement in human rights violations in South Africa also includes J. Mutambirwa *South Africa the Sanctions Mission Report of the Eminent Church Persons Group* 1989.

6.13 Summary

The culmination of human rights activities in the World Council of Churches during the 1970s depended upon a number of factors, not least upon grave violations of human rights. The Pinochet regime in Chile is a good example of the latter.

There was a growing insight that human rights are not only related to individuals but are also linked to social, economic and political structures. Between Uppsala 1968 and Vancouver 1983, human rights linked to social, economic and cultural structures had highest priority within the World Council of Churches. Between Amsterdam 1948 and Uppsala 1968, human rights had primarily been about individual and religious liberty. In the period 1948 to 1968, human rights were principally a matter of individual rights but from 1968 onwards, they came just as much to be linked to evil social structures, not least in the Third World.

Theologically, human rights were related to both creation and salvation. Their basis was both creation theology and Christology. Human beings had been created in God's image and Jesus Christ restored the Creation after the Fall. Involvement in human rights can be seen as an extension of the view of the church as a redeemed community. The work on behalf of human rights is included in the liberating Gospel. The principal line of development in theological arguments for human rights is not the creation-theological, natural law

---

[138] The Rustenburg Declaration in L. Alberts and F. Chikane, The Road to Rustenburg The Church looking forward to a new South Africa 1991, 275–286.

one, but the salvation—historical and Christological one. In an increasingly religious and politically pluralistic world, the Christological basis of human rights was more designed to reflect the standpoint of the churches than its natural law counterpart. For this reason, the World Council of Churches adopted this approach. It was also accepted by Roman Catholic Christians after the Second Vatican Council although the Catholics continued to retain the natural law argument for human rights which was derived from Scholastic theology.

Another notable feature of human rights theology within the World Council of Churches is its contextualization. The question was raised: about the interests and purposes which human rights serve in differing social, political, economic, cultural and religious connections. Human rights functioned as an instrument serving differing interests in differing contexts. This influenced the theological arguments and the meaning attached to human rights varied.

The circumstances noted did not, however, alter the main line of development as regards human rights within the World Council of Churches. A change of emphasis from individual to social and collective rights took place in the period which is the object of analysis in this monograph.

There was a latent conflict in the ecumenical discussion of human rights between a more person/individual oriented view of human rights and one which was more oriented towards society. The latter resulted in demands for social justice quite generally. According to the exponents of the individualist standpoint this was to stray from the domain of human rights. This dialectic between the two human rights ideologies must not be overshadowed by the shift from the individualist to the social conception of human rights which took place within the ecumenical movement. Both conceptions were to be found side by side from the end of the 1960s, counterbalancing one another. But there was also a certain friction between them.

Exegetic research created a foundation for the formulation of an ecumenical theology of human rights. This was adopted not only by confessions with full membership in the World Council of Churches but also by the Roman Catholic Church. This human rights theology had its starting point in the Biblical perspective of the Kingdom of God and was clearly Christological in character. A reduction in human rights violations was a sign of the coming of the Kingdom of God and this had been made possible by the Christ's act of atonement and reconciliation.

A noteworthy feature of the issue of racism and human rights within the World Council of Churches is that the perspective was completely dominated by apartheid in South Africa while the civil rights movement in USA and the struggle for freedom in East Germany remained in the background. It may be asked why the campaign against apartheid so totally dominated the scene, whereas the liberation struggle of the blacks in the USA and the issue of freedom of conscience and freedom of thought in Communist Eastern Europe did not command corresponding interest within the World Council of Churches.

The explanation would seem to be that the American church communities enjoyed a strong position within the World Council of Churches and consequently exerted considerable influence on the choice of items on WCC's agenda. As regards East Germany, the World Council of Churches was keen not to endanger the German churches' opportunities. For pastoral reasons, it preferred to keep a low profile on human rights issues. Another factor which contributed to the strong emphasis on apartheid in South Africa was that this system had been given a theological basis in a way which had no parallel in USA or East Germany. An apartheid theology had been devised and apartheid was justified on the basis of the fundamental document of the Christian religion, namely the Bible.[139] This explains the phrenetic involvement of the World Council of Churches against apartheid. It is heresy. On the basis of the doctrine of Creation and Salvation, it is shown that apartheid is without foundation. Instead it is in diametric opposition to basic Christian teachings.

References

The sources of the above presentation of human rights in the World Council of Churches are to be found in official documentation in the form of reports from the General Assemblies, Central Committee meetings and from the meetings and consultations of their subsidiary organs. This is supplemented by WCC and CCIA reviews of their activities.

The development of the human rights issue has been traced at six General Assemblies as reflected in their documentary proceedings. W. A. Visser't Hooft, the first Secretary-General of WCC, was responsible for the publication of the three first reports, The First Assembly of the WCC 1948 (1948), The Evanston Report 1954 (1955) and The New Delhi Report 1961 (1962). N. Goodall was responsible for the publication of The Uppsala Report 1968 (1968), D. M. Paton for Breaking Barriers Nairobi 1975 (1976) and D. Gill for Gathered for Life 1983 Vancouver 1983 (1983).

The ongoing work within WCC has been reviewed in written form through reports from the Central Committee and of particular importance for the present investigation are those which cover developments during the later part of the period under investigation. The ten Formative Years 1938–1948 WCC (1948), The First Six Years 1948–1954 WCC (1954), Evanston to New Delhi (1961), New Delhi to Uppsala 1961–1968 (1968), D. Johnson ed. Uppsala to Nairobi 1968–1975 (1975), Nairobi to Vancouver 1975–1983 (1983) and T. F. Best ed. Vancouver to Canberra 1983–1990 (1990).

CCIA was the organization which had a special responsibility for human rights and in its reports concerning its activities there are extensive accounts of action on human rights issues. The Churches in International Affairs CCIA/WCC Reports 1970–1973, 1974–1978, 1979–1982, 1983–1986, 1987–1990.

Research on the World Council of Churches and Human Rights is still in its infancy. However a number of monographs dealing with this theme have been published: N. Richardson, The World Council of Churches and Race Relations: 1960–1969 (1977) and W. Weisse. Südafrika und das Anti-Rassismus—Programm Kirchen im Spannungsfeld einer Rassengesellschaft (1975). Another related work is P. Webb ed. A Long Struggle The Involvement of the World Council of Churches in South Africa (1994).

CCIA and PCR specialized in human rights. Ans J van der Bent has published a short history of CCIA in Christian Response in a World of Crisis A brief history of the WCC's Commission of the Churches on International Affairs (1986) which also throws

---

[139] C. Villa-Vicencio, The Theology of Apartheid, 1982.

light on its human rights activities. E. Adler writes on PCR in A Small Beginning An Assessment of the first years of the Programme to Combat Racism (1974). B. Sjollema, Isolating Apartheid. Western Collaboration with South Africa: Policy Decisions by the World Council of Churches and Church Responses (1982) provides information on apartheid in South Africa and the churches' opposition to apartheid. Valuable views on CCIA's work are presented by Ninan Koshy in Churches in the World of Nations International Politics and the Mission and Ministry of the Church (1994).

Two informative works on human rights within the ecumenical movement have been published within the framework of CCIA's background information, namely J. Zalaquett The Human Rights Issue and the Human Rights Movement Characterization Evaluation Propositions A Decade of Human Rights in the Work of the WCC Report from the CCIA Human Rights Advisory Group 1981 and E. Weingärtner Human Rights on the Ecumenical Agenda Report and Assessment 1983.

Zalaquett provides a broad presentation of the human rights issue from the Second World war to the beginning of the 1980s on behalf of CCIA within the World Council of Churches. He points out that non-governmental organizations,among them the churches, play a central role in the movement for human rights but at the same time he consistently takes a broad view of the human rights issue.

Two publications have been intimately linked to human rights work within different parts of the World Council of Churches but simultaneously contain useful analyses of this work. First of all there is M. Reuver ed Human Rights: A Challenge to Theology. This work was published in association with Idoc International in Rome and CCIA. Secondly there is T. Tschuy, An Ecumenical Experiment in Human Rights A Publication of the Human Rights Programme for the Implementation of the Helsinki Final Act 1985. This programme has been sponsored by regional ecumenical bodies.

Documents originating with and views about the ecumenical movement's campaign against racism are to be found in K. M. Beckmann Anti-Rassismus Programm der Ökumene (1971) and G. Bassarak/G. Wirth Herausforderung des Gewissens über den ökumenischen Beitrag zum Kampf gegen den Rassismus (1977). A. van der Bent devotes a chapter of Commitment to God's World A Concise Critical Survey of Ecumenical Social Thought 1995 to the World Council of Churches' way of dealing with racism.

CHAPTER 7

Human Rights and the Lutheran World Federation

7.1. Introduction

The development in the treatment of human rights within the Lutheran World Federation took place at several different levels. Human rights were discussed partly at general assemblies and central committee meetings and partly at consultations and symposia. In addition, there was an ongoing theological discussion of the issue in relation to various types of meetings. The disposition of the present chapter is purely chronological. The first document which is analyzed, is linked to a symposium on Christianity and human rights which took place in connection with the 20th anniversary of the UN declaration of human rights. The symposium is reflected in an issue of Lutheran World 1968. The second document noted is U. Duchrow *Two Kingdoms—The Use and Misuse of a Lutheran Theological Concept* 1977. This book, together with A. Duchrow *Lutheran Churches—Salt or Mirror of Society? Case Studies on the Theory and Practice of the Two Kingdoms Doctrine* 1977, originates with a consultation in Geneva in 1976. Duchrow's first book forms the initial and concluding section of his second book. The third main document considered is also linked to a consultation in Geneva in 1976. It is entitled *Theological Perspectives on Human Rights*. The fourth main document analyzed is J. Lissner and A. Sovik eds. *A Lutheran reader of Human Rights* 1978. *How Christian are Human Rights?* forms the fifth main document and arose in the course of interdenominational study work within the framework of WCC. The sixth principal set of documents to be analyzed includes W. Hubert and E. Tödt *Menschenrechte Perpectiven einer menschlichen Welt* 1977, M. Honecker *Das Recht des Menschen* 1978 and W. Pannenberg *Anthropology in Theological Perspective* 1985. The seventh main document to be considered is M. Garreton *On the Problem of Human Rights Today: Human Rights and the Social Crisis* in Human Rights Concerns LWF March 1979. The eighth main document analyzed is E. Lorenz ed *The Debate on Status Confessionis Studies in Christian Political Theology* 1983. The book originated with a symposium arranged by the Lutheran World Federation in Geneva in 1982. The ninth and final set of documents consider women's human rights as they are discussed in *Women's*

259

Human Rights 1984 and *Women in the Lutheran Tradition* 1991. Both these books arise from meetings arranged by the Lutheran World Federation.

As has been stated, it is natural to deal with the documents above and other documents linked to them in chronological order. A major feature in the historical background to work on the human rights issue within the Lutheran World Federation has been the difficult situation of Lutherans in communist East Germany. The question of human rights was coloured by the meeting of East and West in the shadow of the Cold War. At Evian in 1970, the Lutheran World Federation paid special attention to the human rights situation in Brazil and South Africa. In both regions, there were violations of human rights. The Lutheran churches agitated against conditions in both Brazil and South Africa. The human rights issue in Chile became acute after the overthrow of the democratically elected socialist Allende government and the Pinochet dictatorship's brutal seizure of power by means of a military coup in September 1973.

7.2 The Human Rights Situation in east Germany

In GDR, the church tried to find its way in a socialist society where religion was banished to the private sphere and the church was unable to contribute to the good of the people. The church tried to find a path between opposition and opportunism.[1] After the Second World War, 90% of the population belonged to the church.[2] GDR (1949–90) was the only communist system in which Protestantism was the dominating religious force. The evangelical church had 14.2 million members in 1946, 10.1 million members in 1964 and 6 435 000 members in 1986. In Berlin-Brandenburg, the church lost more than half of its members between 1962 and 1987.[3] The communists in East Germany advocated freedom of thought and freedom of religion and the divorce of church and state.[4] Christians and communists could work together to rebuild Germany, even if their motives had different origins. Both wished to bring about justice and peace. Religion was pronounced to be a matter for private conscience. The reason for this attitude on the part of the Marxists was that they needed support in the transition from capitalism to socialism and the church was judged to be a possible supporter in this task. The communist party assumed that the majority of the population was religious.[5]

The state ran the schools and the church was responsible for religious education. Within the church, there was opposition to what Otto Dibelius called a

---

[1] H. Dähm, Konfrontation oder Kooperation? Das verhältnis von Staat und Kirche in der SBZ/ DDR 1945-1980 (1982) 7.
[2] Op.cit. 11.
[3] S.P. Ramet ed Protestantism and Politics in Eastern Europe and Russia, The Communist and Postcommunist Eras 1992 40 f.
[4] H. Dähm, op.cit. 20.
[5] Op.cit. 21.

purely politically determined unified school.[6] The school syllabus was to have a Marxist-Leninist basis and the school has a predetermined view of life as its goal. It was claimed that Marxism-Leninism offered a scientifically based explanatory model which accounted for natural and social events without need for additional theological interpretation. Marxism-Leninism emerged as a scientific world view. It was a materialist view of the world. Marxism-Leninism is atheist in character. It is incompatible with the Christian religion.[7] The teaching personnel in school were charged with introducing their pupils to this materialistic outlook. When the East German state laid claims to a monopoly on education based upon materialism and atheism, it encountered the opposition of the church. The content of education did not correspond to the convictions of the majority of the people.[8] In the conflict about the goal of the school, the communist state stood for Marxism-Leninism and excluded religious types of interpretation. The conflict led to the issue of freedom of thought and conscience which was guaranteed by the constitution.[9]

From 1954, the state offered young people leaving school a secular youth dedication ceremony. This would be preceded by question periods devoted to life, nature and society. All this was a stage in building society. Parents, independently of denominational background, were able to send their teenagers to a secular youth dedication ceremony. Participation was voluntary. The church replied that an evangelical Christian could not participate in a secular youth dedication ceremony. Children who are submitted to a practice which is contrary to confirmation, cannot be confirmed. The same was true of Catholics who were unable to take part in a secular youth dedication ceremony because it rested on a materialistic basis. Could one prepare oneself for communion and at the same time take part in a course of unbelief? Can one attend the holy sacrament and simultaneously deny God? On this question, there could be no compromise.[10] In the sphere of education and upbringing, there was a lasting conflict between church and state in East Germany which had its roots in differing anthropological and ethical-moral positions; as a result, it was unsolvable in principle. At the practical level, some partial accommodation was possible. Christians could accept the socialist state and social order, even if it often entailed situations which were difficult from the viewpoint of conscience and belief. There was, however, freedom as far religious rites were concerned. Divine services could be celebrated, baptisms could be carried out, holy communion could be celebrated, marriages could take place in church and religious funerals could be held. Children were also able to prepare for confirmation although obstacles existed. Religious supervision was given in schools up to 1967. The teaching of Christian doctrine was transmitted increasingly via

---

[6] Op.cit. 30.
[7] Op.cit. 36.
[8] Op. cit. 37.
[9] Op.cit. 42.
[10] Op.cit. 52 f.

the church.[11] Church property in the form of land was not collectivized and church buildings remained in the church's possession. This was quite different from the situation in the Soviet Union where the Russian orthodox church's total wealth was confiscated. The churches in East Germany were allowed to levy a church tax in the form of voluntary financial contributions from congregation members. The churches also enjoyed a certain tax exemption.[12]

This assertion is valid for the period 1949–1968. This period coincided with the epoch in the history of human rights after the Second World War in which the main emphasis was on individual rights and freedoms, including freedom of religion. The focus of attack was upon places like East Germany where complete freedom of conscience and thought was lacking.

The churches in East Germany gave the World Council of Churches' programme against racism their full support. The aim was to achieve economic, social and political justice for oppressed ethnic groups.[13] The churches' campaign against racism became a sphere of application for the implementation of general human rights.[14] However within the East German educational sector, there was an ineradicable conflict between the goal of fostering socialist citizens and the constitutionally guaranteed right to freedom of belief and conscience.[15] The theologian Günter Krusche distinguished between the individualist aspect of the First World's concern with human rights, the social aspect favoured by the Second World and the structural aspect emphasized by the Third World. These aspects were not incompatible. Krusche advocated this view within the Lutheran World Federation.[16]

7.3 Christianity and Human Rights

At a symposium arranged by the Lutheran World Federation in connection with the twentieth anniversary of the UN declaration of human rights, the declaration was examined from the viewpoint of Christian theology and ethics. This predilection was reflected in an issue of Lutheran World which was devoted to the theme of human rights 1948–1968.

The theologian *Trutz Rendtorff* reflected upon the theme of *freedom and human rights*. He pauses initially to consider a number of points. *First of all*, he observes that human rights are a fundamental ethical factor in the modern world. The problem, however, is that little of their content is in fact implemented. There is a not inconsiderable gap between ideal and reality.[17] *Sec-*

---

[11] Op. cit. 98.
[12] Op.cit. 99.
[13] Op.cit. 141,
[14] Op.cit. 142.
[15] Op.cit. 144.
[16] Op. cit. 144f.
[17] Op.cit. T. Rendtorff Freedom and Human Rights- Theological Reflections on the Declaration of Human Rights in LW Vol XV No 3 1968 178.

ondly, he states that human rights have an authority of their own. No political, philosophical or religious view can lay exclusive claim to human rights. They cannot be founded upon Christian revelation. Thus their legitimacy is not derivable from Christianity although they tend to share the same goals as Christian thought.[18] Thirdly, he points out that conservative Lutheran thought looks upon human rights with profound scepticism. Such rights recognize no higher authority such as God: as far as they are concerned, human beings are the supreme authority. They represent humanity's liberation from God. Human rights are based ethically entirely upon human beings, whereas from the viewpoint of Lutheran anthropological pessimism, this is unseemly. In the eyes of the latter, Man is exclusively a sinner. This argument also shows, however, that human rights protect human beings from themselves as upholders of the power structure.[19] *Fourthly* Rendtorff maintains that human rights have a dual aspect, liberating human beings from authorities and protecting them against the threat of destruction.[20]

Rendtorff goes on to consider some further points. He emphasizes *firstly* that human rights are rights to liberty. They are primarily concerned not with freedom in general but with human beings' concrete liberties as citizen and individual. The aim is to build a world in which human beings can enjoy their liberty. Freedom leads to the destabilization or collapse of old social orders. But no order can claim to be final for human beings in their search for self fulfilment.[21] *Secondly,* he points out that human rights are rights to life. The declaration of human rights shows traces of its roots in the developed part of the world. It belongs to the North and not to the South. It is the problems of the developed peoples which find expression in it. It is not formulated from a concern about our daily bread and the threat from hunger. For this reason, the conquest of hunger in the world must be given its proper place in human rights.[22] *Thirdly*, he shows that human rights are rights to peace. Without peace, human rights cannot be promoted and the encouragement of human rights leads towards peace. Where human rights control the individual and social development of life, structures of peace are created.[23]

Trutz Rendtorff conceives human rights in their widest sense. For him, they coincide with what contemporary theology has to say about human beings and society.[24] His analysis of human rights from a theological standpoint, however, shows signs of being a product of the Cold War conflict between West and East and the polarization between the Industrialized world and the Underdeveloped one, North and South. For Rendtorff, human rights do not spring from Christianity although he indicates points of contact between them.

---

[18] Op.cit. 179.
[19] Op.cit. 179f.
[20] Op. cit. 181 f.
[21] Op.cit. 182f.
[22] Op.cit. 184.
[23] Op. cit. 185.
[24] Op. cit. 187.

7.4 The Lutheran Doctrine of Two Kingdoms

The Lutheran World Federation was sponsor to a consultation on the Lutheran doctrine of two kingdoms from 26 to 28 June 1976 in Geneva. Since understanding of this doctrine lies behind the Lutheran view of society and human rights, there is reason to devote some attention to it. According to Ulrich Duchrow, Luther did not formulate a unique doctrine about the two kingdoms. His thinking includes aspects which point in different directions. Luther, however, rediscovered a dualism in the Christian tradition which went back to the New Testament. Divine power is engaged in a struggle with the forces of evil, the Kingdom of Evil, to the very end of time. God struggles against the forces of evil in every dimension of creation, with the aim of establishing His Kingdom. God equips human beings with reason so that they can organize and bring order to social conditions. God exerts His temporal power by means of reason and His spiritual power through salvation in Christ. For His twofold rule, God makes use of institutions established by human reason- ecclesia, politia, oeconomia. These institutions are designed for different dimensions of human life but all serve God's loving will which is to fight evil. God's twofold rule, the spiritual and the temporal, and the human institutions designed for this task, are in Luther's theology neither opposed to one another nor independent of one another but complement each other and are interrelated.[25]

According to Duchrow, Luther never formulated a systematic theory about the two kingdoms or about God's twofold rule. The two kingdom doctrine, as it came to be formulated, was about two different spheres of life, a personal inner sphere and a personal, external sphere. This dualism was developed by representatives of liberal Lutheranism such as the jurist Rudolph Sohm, the theologian Ernst Troeltsch, the politician Friedrich Naumann, the sociologist Max Weber and the ethical thinker Wilhelm Herrmann, at the end of the nineteenth century. The saving love of Christ was reserved for the individual's private sphere. Both spheres of life became independent. Luther's two kingdom doctrine was set out and explained from this viewpoint.[26]

Ulrich Duchrow, on the other hand, gives an exposition of the two kingdom doctrine which is clearly critical of turn-of-the-century liberal theology. Duchrow is keen to unite both aspects of God's rule of the world, whereas these remained two separate areas of life in the eyes of the liberal theologians. The attitudes of those representing Protestant culture led to religion being removed from social life. Duchrow's aim is the opposite, namely to apply religion to social life. This aim makes him keep the two kingdoms together. The close links between religion and society is the frame of reference which determines his interpretation of Luther. The theme of the two kingdoms and the twofold rule is extremely complex. It raises the question of the relationship between

---

[25] U. Duchrow, Two Kingdoms-The Use and Misuse of a Lutheran Theological Concept (1977) 3 ff.
[26] Op. cit. 12 f.

God, the individual, society and the world. The idea of two kingdoms and the twofold rule is one of the great attempts in human history to promote a theological understanding of human experience in its totality. This idea is rooted in specific historical conditions.[27]

Duchrow formulates a typology linked with Max Weber's ideal types. They do not describe a concrete historical case. They are heuristic aids to understanding and assessing certain ways of thinking or attitudes to the extent that they apply a two kingdoms doctrine. In the case of historical facts, there are normally different types operating simultaneously, either in particular mixed circumstances or at different levels and in various groups in churches and society.

Type 1: the two kingdom idea is used to support an adjustment to existing power structures without a critical evaluation of them in the light of Christian criteria or of reason.

Type 2: the two kingdom idea is used to support a dualistic adjustment to existing power structures without an evaluation of them in the light of Christian criteria or of reason.

Type 3: the two kingdoms idea is used to support participation in God's struggle to make powerholders take account of universal, long term human interests in all relations affecting their lives and liberty.[28]

Duchrow develops the following line of argument. An erroneously applied two kingdoms doctrine was challenged by a theology and practice which proclaims Christ's dominion over all aspects of life. What Duchrow has in mind here, is the Barmen declaration formulated by the Reformed theologian, Karl Barth. If the church is to be able to participate in God's struggle against the forces of evil and their effects in the world, it must itself be aware of how far the church is an object for the forces of evil in a given situation. Luther and the reformers were able to see in reason a principle for understanding and promoting the general good of all. However today, reason is no longer viewed in terms of the good, the true and the beautiful. Reason is an ambivalent tool. It can be used to promote powerful private interests. Churches and theologians must avoid becoming tools of those in power.[29] Duchrow points to Augustine's vision of history. The church father depicts history on a gigantic canvas, as the battle between two groups (civitates), one ruled by the Devil, the other ruled by God. In the contemporary epoch, the two are, however intertwined in a way which is not readily distinguishable for the human eye. Modern social theories are connected to the classical theological tradition. Marxist theory defines history as a struggle between classes. In Latin American liberation theology, one finds a formulation of dependence theory. According to this, national and international orders are not in balance. They form a pattern where the periphery is controlled by the power centre.[30] Dualism between the two kingdoms, Duch-

---

[27] Op. cit. 28.
[28] Op. cit. 29.
[29] Op.cit. 31f.
[30] Op.cit. 33f.

row contends, leads to the church ending up with a ghetto existence which emphasizes individual salvation. The church does not sanction the socio-economic processes but condemns them as evil.[31]

Duchrow summarizes by saying that Luther's doctrine of the two kingdoms illuminates the twofold strategy applied by God in His struggle in history against the forces of evil, as well as His cooperation with human beings and their institutions in bringing about justice in the world. The two kingdoms doctrine must not be allowed to lead to the division of life into separate spheres or compartments of which some fall outside the competence of the Gospel or church. The question at issue is the following. Is this doctrine used to sanction private interests and to support existing structures of power or does it make Christians into true followers of Christ?[32]

The exposition and application of the two kingdom doctrine within Lutheranism has consequences for conceptions of human rights. If life and society are divided into two separate spheres, hermetically sealed off from one another, human rights end up outside the sphere of action of the Gospel and become an entirely secular matter. If on the other hand, life and society are kept together in one total conception then everything in human experience—and this includes human rights—is linked to the Gospel. The dominant trend in postwar Lutheranism, drawing on the experience of the Nazi epoch which is illuminated in a series of case studies,[33] is to avoid the notion that certain sectors of life and society follow their own laws independently of the Gospel. This trend explains the strength of commitment to human rights at both a theoretical and practical level within the Lutheran World Federation.

7.5 A Theological Perspective on Human Rights

The General Assembly of the Lutheran World Federation at Evian in 1970 helped to stimulate reflections about, and the study of human rights issues. The meeting unexpectedly paid attention to the church's role in the world and gave socio-political matters a higher priority than ever before. The General Assembly met to discuss the theme *Sent into the world* and the third section dealt with *Responsible participation in contemporary society*. The General Assembly at Evian marked a turning point in the history of Lutheranism. The question was no longer *if* but *how* the church should become involved in the promotion of human rights and social justice. The meeting gave rise to a range of studies and activities dealing with human rights within the Lutheran World Federation. Its study commission decided steps should be taken to assess critically and pro-

---

[31] Op.cit. 41.
[32] Op,cit. 56.
[33] U. Duchrow ed. Lutheran Churches- Salt or Mirror of Society? Case Studies on the Theory and Practice of the Two Kingdoms Doctrine 1977. U. Duchrow Hrsg Zwei Reiche und Regimente Ideologie oder evangelische Orientierung? Internationale Fall und Hintergrundstudien zur Theologie und Praxis lutherischer Kirchen im 20. Jahrhundert 1977.

mote concrete aspects of the churches' social-ethical responsibility. Evangelization cannot be divorced from social action and the church cannot be divorced from society. A special unit within the studies department was named the project field for peace, justice and human rights.

A parallel event took place within the World Alliance of Reformed Churches dating from the meeting of its General Assembly at Nairobi in 1970. In the Lutheran movement, the development resulted in a consultation on human rights at Geneva from 29 June to 3 July 1976. The proceedings are documented in *Theological Perspectives on Human Rights*. One issue raised concerned the significance of such characteristic aspects of Lutheran theology as ecclesiology and the doctrine on the two kingdoms for a theological understanding of human rights. The *first working group* dealt with theological issues within the human rights domain. The *second working group* addressed the question of human rights in different cultural, social and political systems. This included such questions as the tension between individual and social rights, the role of human rights in the process of humanizing society, the relations between human rights, peace and the ecological crisis. The third working group was concerned with the churches' responsibility for implementing human rights. Attention was devoted to the importance of power and powerlessness in the implementation of human rights.[34]

Theological Questions Within the Human Rights Sphere

Human rights are first and foremost a question of ethics and morality, even if the goal should be their incorporation in the law. Human rights are concerned with human beings only as human beings, that is beings exposed to many threats from the will to power and the domination of the state or from political and economic forces. Human rights cannot be implemented unless the social conditions and political structures are simultaneously justly organized.[35]

Three types of rights are distinguished: the rights to freedom and protection, the rights to equality, the rights concerning participation.[36] The task is not to deduce human rights from specifically Christian premises. They are rights which concern all human beings, even those who neither live nor wish to live according to the Gospel. In the Lutheran tradition, they can be treated as phenomena within God's temporal kingdom. Temporal human values are not to be given a Christian legitimacy. To speak theologically of temporal human rights does not exclude that they require to be interpreted through faith. The right to liberty is not given to human beings by governments or societies but is part of their essential humanity. It is a transcendental factor.[37]

---

[34] Theological Perspectives On Human Rights Report on an LWF Consultation on Human Rights Geneva June 29-July 3 1976 (1977) 7.

[35] Op.cit, 11.

[36] Op.cit. 12.

[37] Op. cit. 13.

Respect for human beings' inviolable dignity has a more profound meaning. We believe that God justifies Sinners i.e. forgives their sin and receives them through Grace into His communion. Through God's action, human beings receive a position and dignity which does not depend at all upon their own qualities and over which states and societies are not permitted to exercise control. We see that the recognition of the dignity of human beings agrees with the position which God guarantees human beings through justification. The equality of all human beings is derived by the Christian from the doctrine that human beings are created in God's image. Given that all human beings are equal in the sight of God, it follows that all have equal value. Rights relating to equality correspond to the position God assigned to human beings in the creation and then again in the salvation. Within the church as the Body of Christ, all human beings are called brothers and sisters. Even in the sphere of God's temporal kingdom, human beings must show through their lives according to the law, that they are called to be the image of God. Human beings belong to a larger unit, namely humanity, of which individuals and groups are part, independently of their particular natures, qualities and social position. They are to be legally assured of the opportunity of participating through an active life and by assuming responsibility for the shaping of society and the human environment.[38]

There are parallels or analogies between what is valid in the Christian community and what we require to abide by within the sphere of temporal human rights. There is a difference between the justice which is applied in the Kingdom of God and the justice which is applied in temporal human law. The latter has its limitations and cannot attain through legal compulsion, things which emanate from love and hope. To communion with Christ belong faith, love and hope which are creative and inspirational in their effect. Temporal law can only be based upon reason.[39] Efforts to implement human rights easily lead to a sense of hopelessness and surrender. Christian faith gives hope and encouragement by virtue of God's promises.[40] God's word sharpens our insight into reality. It attempts to make us see with clarity and to look critically when we behold imperfection in human organization and perceive human fallibility due chiefly to our egoism and tendency to assert our own rights at the cost of our neighbour's.[41] The Gospel can be a source of motivation and guidance in concrete discussion of human rights.[42]

The *first working group* relates human rights to the individual but also maintains that they cannot be realized independently of the social and political context. In other words human rights have both individual and social dimensions. The first working group emphasizes that from a Lutheran viewpoint

---

[38] Op.cit. 14.
[39] Op. cit. 15.
[40] Op.cit. 16.
[41] Op.cit. 17.
[42] Op. cit 18.

human rights are temporal and are based in the temporal kingdom: they are valid for members of other religious faiths, non-Christian and Christian. But the same group interprets human rights theologically as being based on the doctrine of justification.

Human Rights in Different Cultural, Social and Political Systems

Despite all the differences with respect to interpretation and implementation, human rights are concerned with the humanity of individuals and human beings in general. Their codification is an expression for, and a result of, this striving after greater humanity. The implementation of human rights is subjected to influence from existing socio-economic, cultural and historical conditions. It is local and specific. This local and specific aspect of their implementation must not raise questions about the universal validity of human rights. They are there to serve the whole of humanity. There are certain fundamental rights such as the right to life and to personal inviolability, in particular freedom of thought, conscience and religion, as well as the right to equality between men and women, children and old people, the right to participate in society and in political and economic decisions and the right to cultural identity and national self determination.[43]

In European and Anglo-Saxon traditions, human rights are conceived as individual rights. In the socialist tradition, human rights appear as social rights and social equality. In Africa, social rights are related to the context of the family and the tribe. Human rights coincide with the rights of the group. In Latin America, human rights are implemented via the encompassing society. Common elements can be uncovered in individual and social rights. a) There is a shared conviction that fundamental human rights must be respected by every political system b) Every society must not only guarantee social rights for their citizens but must also makes social demands on them. c) The right to personal economic initiative must be limited by the rights of society. The rights of individuals are limited by the rights of others. The modern state has responsibility for securing the material basis of its citizens. Freedom (the inviolability of the individual), equality (the person as social being) and participation are not contradictory rights but constitute elements which belong together.[44] Failure to satisfy the fundamental needs (food, medical care) of individuals, groups and peoples leads to a loss of respect for human dignity and for human rights. The implementation of human rights is to be understood as a process of humanization.[45]

Our responsibility for the lives of future generations is violated when the earth's resources are meaninglessly exploited and wasted, when nature is disturbed and the basis of future life is destroyed.[46] Ecological issues make it

---

[43] Op. cit. 19.
[44] Op. cit. 20f.
[45] Op.cit. 21.
[46] Op.cit. 22.

clear that human rights can only be discussed from a unified viewpoint. A full implementation of human rights can only occur in a world which deserves the epithet *human* and in which the ecological balance is maintained. The pollution of air and water, effects of scientific and technological development, the result of urbanization and industrialization etc have consequences for conditions in society necessary to guarantee human rights for every individual. The biblical message teaches human beings to look upon themselves as part of creation. Human rights can be so interpreted that they justify human beings' demands on their natural environment. This is to misunderstand human dignity which is given in the creation. This dignity compels human beings to arrange and preserve the earth for all living things around them and only to use their rights in accordance with the living needs of nature so that the biosphere remains unharmed.[47]

The *second working group* presents human rights as something ambivalent. They are universal with regard to their validity but local with regard to their concrete implementation. Other working groups by means of analyses, try to bridge the polarization between individual and social rights. At the most profound level, they coincide. This attitude reminds one of the ecumenical movement's attitude to capitalism and socialism. Other working groups finally incorporate ecological rights in the picture as a variant of human rights.

The Churches Responsibility for Implementing Human Rights

As an illustration of church activity in the field of human rights, the work carried out by *The Christian Institute of South Africa, The South African Council of Churches* and *The Southern Christian Leadership Conference* are cited.[48] The church defends justice. The church's mandate includes ensuring that those in power are responsive to God's law for the way in which they influence persons and societies. The churches fulfil their mission in the field of social justice by 1) making themselves aware of injustices and their causes in their own society and at an international level, carrying out investigations and collecting relevant information in the field 2) relating this matter to their creed, upbringing, lay work and communication and using relevant methods for increasing awareness 3) seeking wide co-operation with individuals, groups and organizations which are striving after the same goals in this matter.[49] Every holistic strategy to protect and extend human rights for individuals and folk groups involves a spreading of power which allows the underprivileged to protect their rights through the establishment of a balance of power. To give power to the powerless is ultimately in the interests of everyone. The powerless acquire a new sense of dignity and worth while the powerful are liberated from the arrogance and insensitivity of power. Examples of church activities in

---

[47] Op.cit. 24.
[48] Op.cit. 28.
[49] Op.cit. 30.

270

this area are PCR and Catholic support for the base congregations in North East Brazil.[50] The Lutheran World Federation consultation has in *its third working group* adopted a wide definition of human rights work to include work on behalf of social justice.

7.6 Lutheran Exposition of Human Rights

The Lutheran World Federation human rights programme resulted preeminently in two publications. The first—*Theological perspectives on Human Rights 1977*—has already been presented and analyzed. The second was *A Lutheran Reader on Human Rights* which was published in 1978 by J. Lissner and A. Sovik. The aims of this programme went back to the demands which had been raised by the General Assembly at Evian in 1970. These aims were to support member churches in the study of the universal declaration of human rights and in theologically reflecting about the foundation of human rights, to prepare and process material to help the member churches to promote and implement human rights and to evaluate the possibilities of international action in this domain. *A Lutheran Reader of Human Rights* contains mainly documents from Lutheran churches reacting to the Lutheran World Federation's consultation in Geneva in 1976. The contributions are coloured by theological traditions and socio-political circumstances in different churches and countries. Important aspects of the Lutheran World Federation's official attitude to human rights is reflected in the statement of the General Assembly at Dar Es Salam in 1977.

From Evian 1970 to Dar Es Salam 1977

The human rights process within the Lutheran World Federation was inaugurated at Evian in 1970 and produced visible results at the General Assembly at Dar Es Salam in 1977. The General Assembly at Evian took place against the background of human rights violations in Brazil. The meeting was switched from Porto Allegre to Evian.[51] Human rights were treated as an expression of justice in the world. Social justice, human rights and world peace were presented as correlative concepts.[52]

Human rights in Dar Es Salam were dealt with against the background of the situation in South Africa, the massacre in Uganda and the security conference in Helsinki. The aim was to cooperate with all good forces to bring about an increased humanity. It is significant that the Lutheran World Federation at

---

[50] Op.cit. 31.
[51] U. Duchrow und W. Huber (hrsg) Die Ambivalenz der Zweireichlehre in lutherischen Kirchen des 20. Jahrhunderts 1976 199-202. K.O.Nilsson (ed) Evian- före och efter (1971) 18 ff.
[52] The Evian Assembly 1970: Resolution on Human Rights in J. Lissner and A. Sovik (eds) A Lutheran Reader on Human Rights LWF Report (1978) 1-3.

its General Assembly in Dar Es Salam in 1977, gives priority to social rights and the right to life in the Third World. They are mentioned before individual rights. In contrast to the division into individual rights to liberty in the Western industrial nations and social rights in the East European socialist states, the General Assembly emphasizes in its decision on human rights that its aim is to surmount the conflict and asserts that both types of right are indivisible at the deepest level. Human rights violations can be brought to an end by spreading power and by creating just structures and systems at a national and international level.[53]

The Theological Basis of Human Rights

Torleiv Austad, the Norwegian social ethicist, writes about *the theological basis of human rights*. He points out that the wish was expressed at Nairobi in 1975 that human rights should be given a theological basis. Theologians are not agreed about this question. Some give human rights a natural law basis while others give them a Christological basis. The more sophisticated our notion of human rights becomes, the more one approaches complex questions about social, political and economic justice in society. It is unclear what is included in human rights. The issue also involves the question of individual rights versus social rights.[54] Austad points out three standpoints with respect to the theological basis of human rights. The Anglican, David Jenkins, maintained that human rights do not require any theological justification but are an integral part of human existence. The Lutheran, Trutz Rendtorff, bases human rights upon human nature. The Reformed theologian, Jürgen Moltman, bases human rights upon God's dominion over human beings and His demands on them. These rights reflect God's steadfastness as regards His covenant. Human beings have a dignity because they have been created in the likeness of God. Human rights, whether individual or social, are based on human beings' likeness to God. The different human rights declarations reflect natural rights thinking. This is the case beginning with the Stoics and continuing through the American Declaration of Independence of 1776, the French Declaration of Human and Civil Rights of 1789 until we come to the UN Universal Declaration of Human Rights of 1948. The latter declaration represents an ethical minimum based upon natural law and clothed in common human experience. The UN conventions on economic, social and cultural rights—both dating from 1966—also base individual and social rights upon human nature. The Helsinki conference of 1975 relates individual freedom of conscience to the inviolable dignity of human beings and thus to natural law.[55]

---

[53] The Dar Es Salam Assembly: Resolution on Human Rights in op.cit. 53-54. The situation in South Africa constitutes a *status confessionis*, E Lorenz ed. The Debate on Status Confessionis Studies in Christian Political Theology (1983) 5, 11.

[54] J. Lissner and A.Sovik (eds) in Op.cit. 55.

[55] Op. cit. 56 f.

Einar Molland bases human rights upon a law which is inscribed in the heart of every human being. Christians and non-Christians thus have in natural law a common platform on which to base human rights. In short, he adopts the same position as David Jenkins. Human rights is based on one of the best things known to human experience through the ages. Austad asks what the relationship is between views of human beings in the sphere of human rights and views of man in Christian belief. He holds that the human rights declarations lack a definite view of humanity but nonetheless suggest certain postulates. They speak about human beings' inviolable dignity. Human identity involves the capacity to realize oneself and assume responsibility. Human beings are free, with a dignity based upon nature and reason. This view of man is part of the humanistic tradition and is in accord with the Enlightenment view of human beings as free, independent and rational beings. Human beings are also social beings who assume responsibility for their neighbour and society. Human beings have the capacity to fight against injustice, violence, oppression and poverty.[56] When this view of human beings is compared to the Christian one, one discovers differences. According to Christian understanding, human beings are created in God's image in order to believe in God. Human beings are not autonomous creatures with rights but servants of God and the servants of their neighbour. The laws and benefits of society are not based upon human nature but upon an expression of the Creator's will and generosity. Towards God, human beings have nothing to show apart from their hostility to God and their errors. Only through faith in Jesus Christ can human beings become what they were created to be: children of God. Christian ethics is based upon the belief that God has called human beings to serve their neighbours. In the human rights declarations, the radical view of sin which characterizes the Christian view of man, is lacking. The conclusion which Austad draws from his analysis is that there are obvious differences between the view of man present in the declarations of human rights and that of Christianity. The FN conventions of 1966 draw attention to the distinction between individual and social rights. Here it is a question not simply of the individual's rights against the state but also the state and society's responsibility for human beings and human society. Human rights were extended to apply to nations, ethnic groups and international society. Human rights concern both the individual's relation to society and society's relation to the individual.

In the Bible, ideas corresponding to human rights, are lacking. In the Golden Rule, we encounter not rights and demands based upon human nature but responsibility and service to our neighbour. Christian ethics is altruistic. The twofold commandment to love and the ten commandments are not rights based upon human nature.[57] Austad refuses to treat human rights as absolute and as divine laws. From a theological standpoint, the foundation, meaning and function of human rights have to be understood relatively and not absolutely. They

---

[56] Op.cit. 58f.
[57] Op. cit. 60f.

can be interpreted in various ways. It is a question of general ethics and not one of eternal truths in the Christian sense. There are, however, certain points of contact between human rights and Christian ethics. This is entirely natural since they have sprung from the Christian, humanistic tradition of the West. It is important from a theological standpoint that they are practised within an altruistic framework. What is crucial is not to emphasize our own rights but to be concerned about the life of our neighbour. Christian ethics in the Bible emphasizes the support of the weak, the poor and oppressed persons and groups. Human rights can function as a way of hindering evil and ensuring goodness and justice. Understood in this way, human rights have an important task in God's continued work of creation and maintenance of life in the world. According to Austad, there is a close relationship between human rights and Christian ethics. The right to life is the fundamental human right. The right to life is based on the idea that life is a gift of God. Because of this, Christian ethics requires us to emphasize the importance of our neighbour's life and of our own life. From the Christian viewpoint, all human beings have the same value because they are created in God's image and are objects of God's love in Jesus Christ. Human rights lack such a basis, but non-Christians can work together with Christians so that all human beings have the same value.[58] Austad holds that Christians are able to interpret human rights in the light of of their belief in God and the commandment to love their neighbour. However the humanization of the world is not the same as its evangelization.[59]

Torleiv Austad's arguments about the relationship between Christian ethics and human rights cannot be said to express the standpoint of the Lutheran World Federation. On the other hand, it is hardly conceivable that basic theological reflections about the question of human rights would be be conspicuously published in an official final document from this denominational group if they contradicted the Lutheran World Federation's view of the relationship between Christian faith and human rights.

Luther and Human Rights

Luther's doctrine of two kingdoms has been an important starting point for the exposition of human rights within modern Lutheranism. Ulrich Duchrow, who is active in Geneva and Heidelberg, is a prominent authority on how this doctrine of two kingdoms is treated within theology. He has demonstrated this in several works including *Christenheit und Weltverantwortung Traditionsgeschichte und systematische Struktur der Zweireichlehre* 1979 and *Die Ambivalenz der Zweireichlehre in lutherischen Kirchen des 20. Jahrhunderts* 1976.

Marc Lienhard, Professor of Ecclesiastical History in the Faculty of Protestant Theology at Strasbourg was engaged in various connections to write about human rights. First of all, he published *Luther and human rights* in *Revue*

[58] Op. cit. 62 f.
[59] Op.cit. 64f.

274

d'Histoire et de Philosophie Religieuses 54:1, 1974. This article was translated into English and is to be found in *A Lutheran Reader on Human Rights*. As a Luther scholar, he was entirely familiar with the Lutheran inheritance of ideas and related it to the problem of human rights in a monograph on Luther. It appeared in English in 1982 with the title Luther: Witness to Jesus Christ. Thereafter he broadened his perspective so that it applied to Protestantism and human rights and the fruit of this later work is to be found in *Human Rights Teaching UNESCO 2:1* 1981.

As the basis of his analysis, Marc Lienhard mainly relies upon the writings of Luther dating from the period 1520–1530 which deal with socio-political questions as well as extracts from Luther's exegetical works. The rights of freedom of belief and conscience belong to an absolute level. At the level of temporal existence, it is a question of relations between people and things and the rights corresponding to them. Both types of rights derive from God's action on behalf of His creation. The prince is obliged to respect fundamental human rights because they are included in God's work which creates and protects human life. According to Luther, a Christian accepts that his own rights are in danger but he watches over and defends the rights of his or her neighbour.[60] The Peasants' revolt enabled the peasants to defend what they considered to be their rights. However Luther opposed them. The peasants identified their struggle with the Gospel message and looked upon their enterprise as a kind of crusade. Human beings cannot, however, defend themselves by revolting and simultaneously consider this as being in agreement with the Gospel. Human beings cannot bring about justice for themselves. Suffering and the Cross constitute the Christian's law and nothing else. The peasants cannot in the name of the Gospel seize what they consider to be their right by force.[61] Luther's chief principle was that Christians must be prepared to surrender their own rights on behalf of others.[62]

Human Rights from a South African Perspective

Like all the other churches in South Africa, the Lutherans were required to declare their position with respect to the dominant system of racial segregation. In 1975, the Evangelical Lutheran churches in South Africa issued a declaration in Swakopmund in Namibia, the so-called *Swakopmund declaration* which rejected the apartheid system. It is improper to accept churches which are ethnically segregated. [63] Those who approve racial segregation as a guiding principle in the life of the churches deprive themselves of discipleship. God's grace is open to all independently of racial status.[64] We (the au-

---

[60] Op.cit. 66-70.
[61] Op.cit. 75.
[62] Op.cit. 80.
[63] Op. cit. 48.
[64] Op.cit. 49.

thors of the Svakopmund declaration continued) are convinced that the church includes people of all nations, races, cultures and traditions, called and gathered together as God's united people, to which all belong in one and the same way. The church is not a community of undifferentiated people but a community of those who, though different, hold fast to the same gospel. Christ's body is broken and divided when one teaches that the church must be structured along ethnic, racial, cultural or traditional lines. Those who are not prepared to allow a preacher in his congregation to proclaim the Word and administer the sacrament because he is of a different race, thus destroy the evangelical mission of the priest and the unity of the church.[65] The South African political system, because of its discrimination of certain parts of the population and its concentration of power in the hands of one race, is not consistent with the gospel of God's grace in Jesus Christ. The system is an impediment to discipleship. It must be changed with the help of all Christian citizens in South Africa.[66]

The Lutheran churches' rejection of the apartheid system in South Africa is sharp, unambiguous and clear. It adopts the same line as the Catholic church, the World Council of Churches and the World Alliance of Reformed Churches. For all of them, apartheid is a flagrant violation of human rights.

Human Rights from an East German Perspective

The dividing line between East and West ran through Germany and human rights were correspondingly coloured by this division. In what follows, we shall try to establish how Lutherans in Germany dealt with the problem of human rights in relation to their faith and how they related human rights to theology.

The socialist view of human rights was based on Karl Marx's view of man. "Man is not an abstraction dwelling in the individual person. Its reality contains a collection of social conflicts." Thus human beings cannot be human beings without the society in which they live and to which they are related. Human rights in the Marxist sense are the legal expression of the objective and independent elements in a given specific historical situation. Socialist human rights form a complex system of economic, cultural, ideological and political rights: the right to work, the right to education and so on. Fundamental socialist rights aim at the freedom of the individual which can only be guaranteed and attained through the freedom of society.[67] The socialist interpretation of human rights on the basis of Marx, was the norm in East Germany and was presented by *Hans Schäfer* in an article on *the view of Man in the declaration of human rights*.

In an article on *universal human rights, Manfred Stolpe* holds that in East

---

[65] Op.cit. 50.
[66] Op.cit. 51.
[67] Op.cit. 133.

Germany, one tries to achieve a balance between civil and political rights on the one side and economic, social and cultural rights on the other. In certain states—and by this he would appear to allude to Western states, including West Germany—only civil and political rights are effective.[68] Stolpe considers the human rights issue from an East German perspective and it is hard to think that many people in the West would agree that civil and political rights worked effectively in East Germany. Stolpe holds that the interpretation and realization of human rights in East Germany must be understood by always recalling the experience of the violation of human rights which took place during the Nazi epoch. During this period of German history, it became clear that individual rights could only be guaranteed when collective rights were preserved. The socialist labour movement paved the way for seeing individual rights and duties as part of society.[69]

Günther Krusche made several contributions to the Lutheran World Federation dealing with human rights from an East German perspective. One article was entitled *Normativeness and relativity of Human Rights*. He maintained that whether one adopts an individualistic or social interpretation of human rights, there is unanimity that what is at stake is to preserve Man's essential humanity and human dignity.[70] According to socialism, individuals cannot realize their own existence by themselves, but only in society. Human beings are dependent on their fellow human beings in society. They cannot attain their rights at the cost of the rights of others, but only together with them. They cannot realize their individuality outside of society but only within it. According to Christianity, human beings do not live merely for themselves; they cannot keep their lives egoistically to themselves. Instead they discover themselves to the extent that they devote themselves to others. The welfare of others is a measure of their own humanity.[71] Krusche draws attention to points of contact between the socialist and Christian view of human beings and society. As regards the basic issue they are closely related but their motivations are different. Individual rights and the rights of others must be counterbalanced.[72]

Krusche holds that the UN declaration of human rights reflects an individualist-liberal view of the individual and society. Marxist-Leninist ideology proceeds from the assumption that the interests of the individual and society coincide. It follows that social concerns have priority over individual ones. Conflicts between the individual and society are ruled out.[73] Marxists and Christians can co-operate despite their ideological differences. They have different starting points but both wish for the welfare of mankind.[74] For the Christian,

---

[68] Op.cit. 180.
[69] Op. cit. 183.
[70] Op.cit. 107.
[71] Op.cit. 113.
[72] Op.cit. 114.
[73] Op.cit. 118.
[74] Op.cit. 120f.

however, solidarity has its roots in the Cross and cannot be identified with Marxist arguments. Krusche rejects talk of ideological co-existence. A feature of Christian discipleship is always to stand up for the weak and the unfortunate. But Christians and Marxists have different views about who are the weak and unfortunate in society.[75]

Krusche in presenting his views cannot be said to provide a theological legitimacy for a socialist view of human rights. Neither on the other hand, can he be said to reject the socialist dimension of human rights. He shares the Marxist view of the UN declaration of human rights which looks upon it as the product of an individualistic view of man and society. He makes a point, however, of underlining the ideological difference between Christians and Marxists when it comes to motivating social rights.

Another article by *Günter Krusche* is entitled *Human Rights in A Theological Perspective A Contribution from the GDR*. It was also published in *Lutheran World* in 1977. In it, he raises the basic issue of the conflict between the universal validity of human rights and particularism in their attainment and implementation.[76] Krusche hold that despite the emphasis on the class question in East Germany, the question of individuals and their welfare is still ultimately valid, even in the class struggle. However the socialist view looks upon human beings more in terms of social relations than the Western view does. It rightly insists that freedom without justice is a mere parody of human rights, just as justice without freedom sets human dignity at risk. Human rights delineate a domain where humanity can be retained and guaranteed under special circumstances at a given point of time. Universality within particularity is one of the conditions which must guide the Christian struggle on behalf of human rights.[77] The struggle for the implementation of human rights is one arena where God's struggle for human rights takes place. The question is how theology can mediate between the particularism in the implementation of human rights and their universal validity. Via their members, the church is involved in humanity's fight for increased rights, freedom and increased equality, because this fight carries on God's own struggle against the forces of evil.[78] Human rights remind the church of the ultimate struggle between good and evil. In this struggle, the church must make use of its own weapons, namely the word and the spirit of love. Since the members of the church live in the world, it is the task of the church to strengthen and arm them, to inform and motivate them, so that they perceive their mission of serving all human beings. According to Krusche, the church experiences the divine history which comes to meet it in the tension between universality and particularity. Thus it is possible to justify theologically people's involvement in human rights in diverse situations. A path to salvation is offered in the struggle for

---

[75] Op.cit. 124f.
[76] Op.cit. 171.
[77] Op.cit. 172f.
[78] Op.cit 174f.

human rights.[79] Krusche thus anchors the struggle for human rights on the Christian message of salvation. It is not peripheral but is placed at the very centre of Christian belief.

7.7 Theologies of Human Rights

The division of Germany along ideological lines put the issue of human rights into sharp focus. The theological works dealing with human rights which were published reflected these special German circumstances. Some illuminating examples of this are works published by C Ordnung: *Menschenrechte sind Mitmenschenrechte Ein Beitrag zur ökumenischen Diskussion*, 1975; *Die Menschenrechte im ökumenischen Gespräch Beiträge der Kammer der Evangelischen Kirche in Deutschland für öffentliche Verantwortung*, 1979. When German theologians wrote about human rights, their presentation was coloured by the fact of living in a country where the Federal Republic was contrasted with the DDR. The legal systems and dominant ideologies in both German states were so different that meaningful comparisons were scarcely possible. Theology also developed in different directions.

In what follows, we shall present and analyze the work of certain theologians of whom the first three are directly concerned in developing human rights theologies while the fourth discusses anthropology which forms the basis of every theology.

W. Huber and H. E. Tödt

The aim of the theology of human rights due to *Wolfgang Huber* and *Heinz Eduard Tödt* in *Menschenrechte Perspectiven einer menschlichen Welt* 1977 is to overcome the disintegration of the human rights discussion into separate discussions of legal, philosophical and theological aspects and to bring these perspectives together in a unified view.[80] Huber and Tödt see three opposed groups of interest when it comes to incorporating human rights as a part of international law: the Western bloc, the Eastern bloc and the Third World states.[81] These theologians distinguish between human rights and basic rights. The former are given to human beings *qua* human beings. The latter are given to citizens as members of a community.[82] In the Western bloc, human rights are identical with individual rights to freedom; in the Eastern bloc, human rights coincide with social basic rights; and in the Third World human rights are about peoples' right to self-determination.[83] Three antagonistic conceptions of

---

[79] Op.cit. 176.
[80] W. Huber- H. E. Tödt, Menschenrechte Perspektiven einer menschlichen Welt (1977) 9.
[81] Op.cit. 32.
[82] Op. cit. 38.
[83] Op. cit. 65.

human rights thus find themselves in confrontation: an individualistic conception which is represented by the Western capitalist states, a collectivist conception which the countries espousing state socialism advocate and finally the Third World view that national self-determination comes before guarantees on rights for their citizens. The key ideas behind these opposing conceptions are freedom, equality and participation.[84]

Huber and Tödt distinguish between five theological basic models for the interpretation of human rights.

1. The *first basic model* is when one is concerned to base human rights clearly upon definite theological fundamental assertions or to deduce such rights from them. *Jürgen Moltman* is an example of a thinker who adopts this model. He works for the World Alliance of Reformed Churches and we whall have reason to return to him. Human rights are based upon God's covenant with His people and the divine right vis-à-vis human beings which arises from it.[85]

2. The *second type of basic model* is when a double foundation of human rights is advocated. The second foundation consists in tracing human dignity to the fact that humans are made in the image of God while obligations concerning human rights are deduced from divine commandment. The Second Vatican Council adopts this attitude. *Catholic moral doctrine* is usually based partly upon natural law and partly upon *the revelation.*[86]

3. *The third basic model* refrains from any special theological basis for, or legitimation of, human rights. Martin Honecker whom we shall deal with later, maintains that human rights are not a fruit of Christianity but of historical development. Human rights express a universally natural ethos. Honecker bases ethics upon a general humanity and not upon something specifically Christian. Dogmatics acquires its knowledge from revelation while ethics acquires its knowledge from what is universally human. Human rights belong to ethics. For Moltmann, human rights are not a temporal phenomenon whereas they are for Honecker.[87]

4. *A fourth basic model* proceeds from the observation that there is no basis for human rights—whether philosophical or religious—which can claim universal validity. *Trutz Rendtorff* does not use theology to base and legitimize human rights but to analyze the function of human rights. The theological conceptual counterpart to the function of human rights is *the doctrine of justification.* Just as God's justice is revealed in his unconditional acceptance of the sinner, so human beings receive the title of human being unconditionally.[88]

5. A final basic model proceeds from the question of the analogy and differ-

---

[84] Op.cit. W. Huber Menschenrechte-Christenrechte in Rechte nach Gottes Wort Menschenrechte und Grundrechte in Gesellschaft und Kirche In Auftrag der Synode der Evangelisch -reformierten Kirchen in Nordwestdeutschland herausgegeben vom Landeskirchenvorstand 1989 85.
[85] W.Huber-H.E.Tödt,Op.cit. 65 f.
[86] Op. cit. 67.
[87] Op. cit. 68.
[88] Op.cit. 70f.

ence between theological basic statements and human rights. It does not seek some theological foundation for human rights but the foundation upon which a Christian involvement with human rights depends and according to which these rights can be understood theologically. There is a relationship between the justice which is established in Christ and the law which human beings seek in order to shape their world. This model is adopted by W. Huber and H. E. Tödt.[89]

Three elements are present in human rights: the right to freedom which corresponds to personal inviolability; the right to equality which corresponds to personal dignity; and the right to participation.[90] They are radicalized in Christian faith. 1. Freedom is understood as a quality which derives from human nature.[91] 2. Equality is based, in the Christian community, upon love of one's neighbour.[92] Racism contradicts equality. It is an expression of discrimination. The demand for a new economic world order is a consequence of equality.[93] 3. The right to participation is exemplified in form of Christian community which Paul characterizes with the formula of the church as the body of Christ.[94] The three constituent elements in the fundamental pattern of human rights—freedom, equality, participation- must be induced to integrate. Freedom, equality and participation are relational concepts. They only have meaning in relation to something e.g. the state, society, the international system. These relations are assigned a legal structure which results in a genuine field of reference for human rights.[95] In Western democracies, the temptation is to interpret human rights in a one-sided manner i.e. as exclusively liberal rights to freedom, in order to protect the sphere of private liberty.; this can lead to a defence of the status quo which benefits those who have. In the European peoples' democracies, emphasis is placed upon economic, social and cultural rights. The rights of the individual to personal freedom is interpreted restrictively, because the individual is not recognized to possess any legal position vis-à-vis the state or society.[96]

Using the concepts of analogy and difference, W. Hubert and H. E. Tödt seek to clarify the closeness and distance between the fundamental content of Christian faith and the concept of human rights. There are both similarities and differences between human rights and Christian belief.

M. Honecker

Martin Honecker builds up social ethics around the problem of human rights. Human rights are not simply the rights attached to self i.e. *our own* rights.

---

[89] Op. cit. 72f.
[90] Op. cit. 162.
[91] Op. cit. 163.
[92] Op. cit. 167.
[93] Op. cit. 168f.
[94] Op. cit. 170.
[95] H.E.Tödt Theological Reflections on the Foundations of Human Rights LW 24 (1) 1977 48 f.
[96] Op. cit. 53.

Human rights encompass both our rights and simultaneously the rights of others. The one cannot exist without the other. Human rights are rights which apply to all, independent of pigmentation, race, social position, origin, nationality, religion and ideology. Human rights are based upon that humanity which is common to all human beings. Human rights are not given but are original. They are based upon self-determination and self-responsibility.[97] Some thought needs to be given to the relationship between the humane and Christian faith and Christian ethics. Martin Honecker deals with this matter in his book *Das Recht des Menschen Einführung in die evangelische Sozialethik* 1978. However he arrives at the result that human rights are not based upon a specifically Christian ethic but upon what is humane. He works with an ethic of general humanity upon which human rights is based and not with a special Christian ethic. He reviews in detail the historical development of human rights. Honecker essentially ends up adopting a position close to the the doctrine of natural law.

Honecker notes various ways of arguing theologically with respect to human rights. One model of interpretation proceeds from an analogy between human rights and Christian faith. The gospel of Jesus Christ is the criterion of human ethics. Another model is put forward by Karl Barth and employs a Christological argument. It rejects natural law as a basis for human rights.[98] Honecker raises the objection that the Christological approach can only serve to guide Christians. The Gospel relating to Jesus Christ can only function as a source of knowledge leading to political action for believing Christians. This leads to the danger of Christians becoming opinionated and claiming "to know better".[99] Honecker believes that Jürgen Moltmann's eschatological arguments are closely related to those of Karl Barth. Moltmann refers to the Biblical tradition's forward-looking orientation: this corresponds to the forward-looking nature of human rights. This focus on the future gives, as far as human rights is concerned, a meaning of liberation. Moltmann's theological viewpoint is to be seen in the treatment of human rights adopted by the World Alliance of Reformed Churches. For Moltmann, Jesus Christ becomes the bearer of human rights.[100] Honecker also discusses the model of interpretation which proceeds from the analogy and difference between human rights and Christian belief. It is linked to the two kingdoms doctrine of the reformation. But it rejects any interpretation of the two kingdoms doctrine which implies a sharp distinction between belief and politics. In his critical assessment of this model, Honecker emphasizes the necessity of recognizing the autonomy of the human ethos. Theology cannot itself contribute to the issue of human rights.[101] Honecker gives an exposition of Luther's doctrine of two kingdoms and main-

---

[97] M. Honecker Das recht des Menschen Einführung in die evangelische Sozialethik 1978, 18.
[98] Op. cit. 128-133.
[99] Op. cit. 134f.
[100] Op.cit. 135-139.
[101] Op.cit. 142-149.

tains that for Luther, reason corresponds to the order in the world. Human rights, as univeral demands, require to be in accordance with reason.[102] Honecker assigns freedom, justice and solidarity to an ethical assessment of human rights. They constitute fundamental values.[103]

Martin Honecker concludes that human rights are neither rooted in Christian belief nor possess a specifically Christian meaning or content. This, however, does not exclude a specifically Christian treatment of human rights. Human rights cannot be deduced from Christian belief. They raise the issue of the relationship between a Christian interpretation of the world and a human ethos.[104] Human rights encourage one to participate in a never-ending process of humanizing human conditions and attitudes.

At a consultation held by the Lutheran World Federation in Geneva from 27 to 29 February 1984, Martin Honecker dealt with the question of criteria for public pronouncements or official silence, in cases of human rights violations. He held that due to the complexity of life and the importance of statements about threats to life, a scholarly explanation was of limited significance. The Lutheran World Federation should not overestimate the importance of its scholarly theological work. Such efforts can only be supportive and subsidiary. Honecker does not look to scholarship and science, for the solution to life's problems. More modesty is needed in such matters, even with respect to ideas. Honecker regards his own ideas more as a contribution to pastoral advice and assistance.[105]

Honecker stresses that a church and its members must not remain silent when life and humanity are fundamentally threatened. According to Luther, Christians have the obligation to bear witness for justice in a conflict situation.[106] The discrimination of human beings on the basis of race, colour or ethnic origin (the Aryan paragraph, antisemitism in the Third Reich, apartheid) as *status confessionis*, belong to an ecclesiological category which cannot be directly applied to society in its entirety. If racism is practised or given theological legitimacy within the church (the Aryan paragraph, apartheid) then the church's witness on behalf of the Gospel is called into question. In addition to this, antisemitism and apartheid are evil and harmful—in short, sin—and as such they must be condemned by the churches and Christians.[107] A reason for being silent in special cases is that to do the opposite would injure human beings. If the church is silent, it must in every case be made entirely clear that it does not give its consent to injustice and evil. To be silent because of economic interests is to violate justice, despise humanity and deny the will of

---

[102] Op. cit. 162f.
[103] Op. cit. 171.
[104] Op. cit. 201.
[105] M. Honecker, Criteria for public pronouncements or official silence in cases of human rights violations in E. Lorenz ed. To speak or not to speak, Proposed criteria for public statements on violations of human rights, 1984, 18.
[106] Op.cit. 19.
[107] Op. cit. 20.

God. The church cannot, however, by reference to imperatives in the name of the church and on the basis of the Gospel's demands, participate in the general debate: instead it must employ arguments of common sense type. According to Lutheran teaching *primus usus legis* is binding for temporal life. In order to participate actively, Christians must find concrete manifestations of this law especially in their profession and in their position as Christians in the world. As far as social issues such as human rights are concerned, it is a question of producing reasons for and against. A Christian solution does not exist. One can only draw comparisons between better and worse solutions or between a more humane or less humane solution. If we introduce the Gospel as an authority in the development of social and political goals, we transform relative rules which can always be improved into something absolute. This leads to viewing the world in terms of a theological ideology and prevents necessary compromises in society. Honecker wishes to use the two kingdoms doctrine today in such a way as to prevent politics becoming something absolute and ideological. If this happens, political activity is transformed into an act of salvation.[108]

Honecker holds that the conception we have of the church or theological self-awareness is important when we deal with human rights. What does the church take as its essential i.e indispensable manifestations, its fundamental tasks? Is this confined to divine service and sermon or does it also include public pronouncements? How is this related to the freedom of the laity in the church? Are human rights a matter for the laity? According to Honecker, the church must be quite clear about what is theologically fundamental for its existence, its *esse*, that which the church cannot abstain from. The church has to distinguish between what is beneficial and what is absolutely necessary for its existence as a church.[109] For Honecker, there are more and less serious violations of human rights. The core of human rights concerns violation and destruction of life through torture and through basic infringements of human dignity.[110] Honecker asks on what theological grounds the church bases its defence of human rights? Is it the Gospel or is it, as Honecker holds, from a Lutheran standpoint also the church's responsibility for law (*Primus usus legis*)? In what sense and to what extent can human rights be seen as a human concretization, a realization of the law, which God desires as a support for human co-existence.? In Honecker's view, the church's right to champion humanity should be established on this basis.[111]

Martin Honecker touches on the discussion of the doctrine of the two kingdoms which Ulrich Duchrow in particular initiated at the Lutheran World Federation. In Honecker's view, this doctrine allows one to observe with a good conscience the world around with a watchful eye and rely that it will be preserved by God, without the contribution of Christians, because it is the world.

---

[108] Op. cit. 21f.
[109] Op. cit. 23f.
[110] Op. cit. 25.
[111] Op. cit. 26.

The doctrine of two kingdoms allows us to see the world calmly and objectively. However, it does not permit indifference to the world's misery nor does it approve of evil and injustice. Nonetheless, it prevents a theologization of the world, society, nature and creation. In this respect, the doctrine of two kingdoms is only one of the fundamental differences between God and the world, shared by all Christian churches, providing they do not identify the Gospel with the world. According to the Protestant conception of Christian belief, we must distinguish between law and Gospel, belief and actions, creation and salvation, conscientious involvement and action in the world but must not separate them. Ideal types are hardly ever encountered in reality. They have no significance for understanding and assessing concrete conditions. For this reason, according to Honecker, Duchrow's division into types is intended to encourage (one ought to behave in such and such a way). Duchrow's thesis requires to be tested in each individual case. The instrument (assessment criterion) used by Duchrow i.e. faith (revelation) and reason, normative and contextual theology, power and legitimacy, criticism and adjustment, needs to be further discussed. Questions such as the tasks of individuals, society, the church, political responsibility and the laity require further examination. They have not been solved by Duchrow. Honecker sees the present distinction between the two kingdoms in a twofold sense. 1. The distinction between the two kingdoms frees temporal life from ecclesiastical domination. The world does not take the Gospel as its model; but the law through which God wishes to preserve and protect the world from evil is absolutely valid for, and within, the world. 2. The doctrine of two kingdoms opposes every attempt to transform politics into ideology or to render it absolute. Politics is not an act of salvation. The aim of politics is to preserve peace on earth and to retain an order where human coexistence is subject to law. The theological significance of the two kingdoms doctrine consists in encouraging a distinction between God's acting and speaking via the Gospel and the apprehension of, and responsibility for the world.[112]

W. Pannenberg

The most illuminating analysis of anthropology from a theological point of view is Wolfhart Pannenberg's *Anthropology in Theological Perspective*, 1985 which derives from a work in German. Since anthropology is both the starting point and end point for theologians dealing with human rights, Panneberg's exposition and ideas are of interest for the present investigation.

The theological approach to human beings is based upon the Christian belief about God's incarnation.[113] Dogmatic anthropology has two central themes: God's image as manifested in human beings and human sin. Theology's two anthropological themes—God's image and sin—are also seen to be central for

---

[112] Op. cit. 27 ff.
[113] W. Pannenberg, Anthropology in Theological Perspective, 1985, 12.

the theological interpretation of anthropological studies. To speak of God's image in human beings is to speak of their nearness to the divine, a nearness which also determines their position in the world of nature. To speak of sin is to speak about the divorce from God of human beings who are designed to be one with God. Sin is therefore a contradiction in human beings, a conflict within Man.[114] The conflict between nearness to God and distance from God has repercussions on the whole of religious life. It finds expression in the polarization between what is holy and what is profane. Ideas about the image of God and sin describe the anthropological manifestation of this basic conflict which characterizes all religious life.[115] The nearest we can come to concrete human reality is in the study of history, since it deals with the concrete lives of individuals and the ways in which individuals interact in the historical process. Although abstractions are used in history, it nevertheless comes closer to human life than other anthropological disciplines. The others deal only partial aspects of human reality: biology discusses the special characteristic of human beings in relation to animals; sociology deals with the fundamental forms of social relationships between people; psychology deals with the general structures of human behaviour. On the other hand, history as a discipline presupposes in principle all such aspects in describing human existence in its individual concrete forms. History cannot be the basis of the other anthropological disciplines. History absorbs them all, as component aspects.[116] Panneberg asks if the investigation of anthropological data leads to ideas about the image of God and sin. He also raises the question of whether ideas about conflict with, and distance from God throw light upon empirically derived anthropological phenomena. [117]

7.8 Human Rights and the Social Crisis in Chile

The Chilean sociologist *Manuel Garreton* wrote in the Lutheran World Federation's Human Rights Concerns for March 1979 against a background of human rights violations in his native country. He discusses the issue of human rights and the link between human rights and social crisis.

First of all, he analyzes human rights as an ideology. He distinguishes between individual, political and social rights. In the ideology of human rights, sometimes stress is laid upon equality and sometimes upon liberty. The basis of liberty is the right to private property. Freedom is freedom for the property owner and those with the possibility of becoming property owners.[118] Human

---

[114] Op.cit. 20

[115] Op.cit. 21.

[116] Op.cit. 22.

[117] Op. cit. 21. K. Cronin in Rights and Christian Ethics 1992, 233, develops ideas similar to those of Pannenberg.

[118] M. Garreton, On the Problem of Human RightsToday: Human Rights and the Social Crisis in Human Rights Concerns, LWF, March 1979, 5f.

rights emerge as a large ideology involving different conflicting interests. The ideology is used to represent, justify and legitimize the actions of the various interested parties.

Secondly Garreton presents human rights as a socio-historical value system. They have developed historically as ideas about the good sanctioned by human societies. They are the products of social history generated by social groups in their struggle to strengthen their right to life. The right to life is not reduced to a biological level but is defined in cultural terms. The right to life is always understood as the right to a humane life, a good life, a life of dignity, a life worth living. These values are products of the struggle of social groups; they develop from situations of conflict between human beings and between human beings and nature. They are generated during special periods by social groups who have the capacity to make them universal.[119] Human rights constitute both an expression for the interests of social groups and values which can be made universal and also a framework for the development of social life. Human rights are both values and norms of society.

When human rights are viewed as a socio-historical value system, their history shows a constant dialectical interaction between particularism and universalism. The campaign for the recognition of human rights derives from those sections of society which suffer from some form of social discrimination, from exploitation in the production system or are politically oppressed in some sense. Without denying the universalization of human rights, we can state that human rights claims are always formulated in very concrete terms—they are not at all vague and abstract- in relation to a specific context of discrimination, exploitation and domination.[120] The significant discussions about human rights always take place in period of social crisis.

Thirdly Garreton analyzes human rights in the current crisis. It is a history of conflicts, of demands for democratization; it is a history in which capitalism maintains structures characterized by fundamental injustices.[121] The economic basis of the military regime is to strengthen capitalism which prevents the spreading of welfare. The aim is a free economy. The military, the ruling class, the governmental technocrats and representatives of international capitalism form an alliance in this project.[122] The system's dominance justifies the ideology of national security. The growth of the human rights movement in Chile is to be seen against this background.[123]

For Manuel Garreton, human rights cannot be divorced from the social, political and economic system but must be seen as a function of it. Human rights acquire their contemporary meaning and application where universalism and particularism meet. By allowing a human rights theoretician such as

---

[119] Op.cit. 7.

[120] Op. cit. 8.

[121] Op. cit. 9f.

[122] Op.cit. 11.

[123] Op. cit. 12. The exiled Chilean Lutheran Bishop, Helmut Frenz, is involved in human rights because it is humane. J. Lissner and A. Sovik eds A Lutheran Reader on Human Rights 1978 147.

Garreton to express his opinions in their newsletter, the Lutheran World Federation shows the direction in which ideas on this issue were going within the Federation.

7.9 Apartheid in the Church as Status Confessions

The treatment of the human rights issue not only within the World Council of Churches but also within the Lutheran World Federation was above all determined by apartheid in South Africa. At its Sixth General Assembly in Dar es Salaam in 1977, the Lutheran World Federation declared that the situation in South Africa constituted a status confessionis. On the basis of the Christian faith, the South African apartheid system was rejected.[124] It was decided that the systematic segregation in South Africa was unjust and flagrantly violated human rights.

A consultation was held in Bossey in the spring of 1982 and gave rise to the publication *The Debate of Status Confessionis Studies in Christian Political Theology*. The aim was to stimulate discussion about the theological and ethical implications of apartheid. A series of problems relating to apartheid were addressed at the consultation and in the publication. They showed how complex the apartheid issue was. It was pointed out that the Lutheran churches in South Africa have two roots: mission and immigration.[125] These factors were important in explaining why some Lutheran churches had exclusively white members. The word *apartheid* had come to express an ethical ideology determined by ethnic nationalism. It is insufficient to equate apartheid with racism. The word means "apartness" and is best translated by *special development in accordance with one's particular character.*[126]

The Afrikaner and indigenous white nationalism are confronted with black nationalism. These two ideologies are locked in struggle. The apartheid ideology is not defined as racism but as a specific form of nationalism. Its key element is a people's identity. This ideology becomes sinful when it is combined with racist elements and their consequences e.g. discriminatory behaviour and legislation, homelands and the seasonal worker system. The important element in the apartheid ideology is the concept of people.[127] No church is so closely associated with the ideology of apartheid as the Nederduits Gereformeerde Kerk. In this church, a biblical and theological concept of people and nation has produced apartheid. Church and people are conceived as being virtually identical and the Afrikaner people are looked upon as Israel in the Promised Land.[128] It was further pointed out that in the New Testament, social,

---

[124] Resolution on Southern Africa: Confessional Integrity (Dar es Salaam, Sixth Assembly of the LWF, 1977) in E. Lorenz ed The Debate on Status Confessionis Studies in Christian Political Theology 1983, 11.

[125] E. Lorenz ed op.cit. 24.

[126] Op.cit. 27.

[127] Op.cit. 28f.

cultural and sexual (biological) differences have no significance in the view taken of humanity. The New Testament view is incompatible with the ideology of apartheid. The protest is therefore particularly sharp when a government describes itself as Christian but systematically violates classical human rights.[129] But there was also criticism of stigmatizing South Africa as a status confessionis. The totalitarian regimes in Eastern Europe, but not the apartheid regime in South Africa, were allowed to go free.[130] Are there objective criteria for deciding when political and social injustices must be rejected, not only on political grounds but also on grounds of religious belief? In contemporary Protestantism, human rights are used as a measure for assessing political and economic systems but in the ecumenical discussion, there are conflicting views about human rights. Is the ambivalent human rights criterion comparable to the unambiguous character of the act of confession.[131]

The consultation in Geneva in 1982 presented a number of conclusions and recommendations. Apartheid is a complex phenomenon which must be analyzed from a series of related viewpoints: political, racial, ideological and theological. However, this complexity must not be allowed to obscure the simple truth that apartheid is evil in nature and must be exposed. 1. *Politically* apartheid constitutes *an unjust system of government* which sanctions violations of human rights and suppresses the civil and religious liberties of many of its citizens. 2. *Racially,* apartheid is *a system of institutionalized violence* in which people are subjected to discriminatory prejudice and mechanisms of segregation merely on account of their racial and ethnic identity. 3. *Ideologically* apartheid treats the categories of nation and race as absolutes, *transforming them into a religious phenomenon.* Thereby apartheid becomes a false gospel which assigns religious significance to the national and racial security of a minority to the detriment of the common good. When such a false gospel infiltrates the church, apartheid exposes its true character as heresy. 4. *Theologically* apartheid is intimately linked *to a theocratic view of the world* which is based upon the view taken by certain Christians of the Reformed church of the account of salvation, *election, covenant, people* and law. If one of the dangers of Lutheran social ethics is a dualistic divorce between Divine Law and the Gospel, between creation and salvation, between state and church, a comparable weakness in the Reformed position is the uncritical confusion of these notions. Apartheid destroys those beings created by God. It does so in the name of the Creator and by virtue of the authority He confers. For this reason, Lutheran churches are called by God to profess their faith when faced with an unjust political system which is based upon a heretical and distorted ideology and upon a false interpretation of holy scripture.[132]

---

[128] Op.cit. 34.
[129] Op.cit. 39f.
[130] Op.cit. 41.
[131] Op.cit. 43
[132] Op. cit. 125 f.

The pronouncement from the Sixth General Assembly of the Lutheran World Federation *South Africa: Confessional integrity and the consultation in Geneva* 1982 on the church as status confessionis was a logical consequence of events. In the Barmen declaration of 1934, Christian faith was set in relation to the situation created by national socialism. The situation in South Africa had been on the agenda of the Lutheran World Federation for many years. Since the Evian meeting of 1970, there had been awareness of the ethical aspects of racism, questions about social justice and human rights and of their theological implications. Only an application of the two kingdoms doctrine with its division of reality into two separate spheres could have removed the South Africa issue from the Federation's agenda. But the time when the two kingdom doctrine could be employed in this way, was past. The view was that the South African situation could not be separated from the the proclamation of the Gospel and Christian belief. When apartheid was given a theological justification, the credibility of the Gospel and the church's status as a church was threatened. The situation was seen as analogous to that of 1934. The church membership was split along racial lines, with exclusively white Lutheran churches: a wedge was driven between believers partaking of Holy Communion.

7.10 The Human Rights of Women

In 1979, The United Nations approved a convention on the abolition of all types of discrimination of women.[133] This decision was reached during a period which the UN had labelled as women's decade. As early as 1974, the World Council of Churches had arranged a consultation on the discrimination of women in West Berlin which we have already discussed. Women's rights were also discussed at consultations within the Lutheran World federation. This took place on several occasion during the 1980s in the wake of the UN convention.

The first analysis of womens' rights resulted in a report entitled *Women's Human Rights* 1984 from the Study Department of the Lutheran World Federation. The value of this study is mainly to be found in the fact that it lists a series of issues which are linked to women's rights. Women are often economically dependent on men; they have large families and cannot find a well-paid job. Not infrequently they are forced to undertake the work of two. Work is not divided equally between men and women in the home.[134] Women are often consigned to the home while men go out to work. When women do manage to get a job, it is often because their wages are lower than men's for the same task.[135] It is important that women are released from the fear of physical violence. They too wish to have the freedom to educate themselves and to under-

---

[133] G. Melander ed 1990, 80-92.
[134] Women's Human Rights 1984 12f.
[135] Op.cit. 17.

take different types of work. Within the family, they also wish to enjoy the same rights and freedoms as men.[136] There is a list of rights which are specified as women's rights. Women, however, are not always aware of them.[137] Even if women are knowledgeable about their rights, tradition, culture, customs and religion can act as obstacles. Such is the case in India. There, for example, a woman's consent to marriage is not important. A girl accepts the family's decision. Even if she is consulted, she tends to agree submissively to parental choice. Girls usually accept the system as it applies.[138] Theologically it is held that human beings are created in the image of God. Humanity is comprised of man and woman and mirrors God's being which is both masculine and feminine. One can appeal to God both as Father and Mother simultaneously.[139] However, from a historical perspective, Christianity has often helped to underpin a hierarchical order. The subordination of women has played a central role in theological thought. Both the myth of Creation and certain passages in Paul have been used for this purpose.[140]

The second analysis of women's rights stems from a consultation with women Lutheran theologians at Karjaa, Finland from 18 to 23 August 1991. This resulted in the report *Women in the Lutheran Tradition*, 1992 which was published by the department for mission and development within the Lutheran World Federation. The report contains a number of observations which are relevant to the present enquiry. No less a person than Katarina von Bora, the wife of the reformer Martin Luther, was consigned to exercising her influence domestically, while Luther and his men held forth in the church. Luther was fearful of witches and ordered them to be burned. Thus the Reformation did not really alter the position of women in church and society.[141] The Moravian Brethren placed men and women on an equal footing. Women participated at all levels of congregational work and made their personal contributions. Women and men co-operated in parish work.[142] Lutheran churches, however, are most often ordered along hierarchical lines. It is more common to have ecclesiastical structures built around the office than around the priesthood in general where various services can be combined on an equal footing. Women would appear to have few possibilities within the hierarchical model.[143] At the consultation, arguments were put forward for women priests. All believers are priests and all work together for the Kingdom of God. The idea of the general priesthood finds expression in the image of the church as the people of God. All believers are equal as members of the people of God. The laity and the priesthood of believers coincide. There is no clear distinction between priest

---

[136] Op. cit. 71.
[137] Op. cit. 25 ff.
[138] Op.cit. 47 f, 57.
[139] Op.cit. 30.
[140] Op.cit. 66.
[141] Women in the Lutheran Tradition 1992, 21.
[142] Op.cit. 15.
[143] Op. cit. 44.

and layman, between educated and uneducated, between white and black and between man and woman. God created humanity. He gave the same tasks and the same responsibility to both men and women. They are to be co-creators and to have dominion over the earth. Jesus does not apply standards to women which are different from those he applies to men. He did not assign women one type of office and man another. Christ called upon women to go forth and proclaim the good news. Women played an important role in the life and witness of the young church. A woman was given the task to go and inform the disciples that Christ had risen.[144]

7.11 Theological Re-Orientation

Social involvement within the Lutheran World Federation increased step by step through its coming to terms with Lutheranism's role in Nazi Germany, the political tensions in Europe brought about by the Cold War and the Third World's process of liberation. This social and political involvement led to a theological re-orientation. The dichotomy between the church and the world was overcome. The church is not identical with the Kingdom of God. The world is not identical with the Kingdom of Satan. The struggle between God and Satan is waged in the church and the world. The distinction between the law and the Gospel does not coincide with the dichotomy between the world and the church. Reason is responsible for the world. Love, however, sets limits to reason so that the welfare of our neighbour does not suffer as a result.

The two kingdoms doctrine is so interpreted that the social orders—God's left hand—are not sharply distinguished from the church—God's right hand. The result is that Christian belief provides guidance both in society and in the church. After Hitler, Lutherans could no longer maintain watertight divisions between the two kingdoms. The light of Christian belief is thrown, not only over life in the church, but also over the structures of society.

Within the domain of human rights, it was shown that Lutheranism did not represent some form of social quietism. The dichotomy between the two kingdoms was rooted in a turn-of-the-century theological interpretation of Luther but the social quietism to which it led, was surmounted in the theological work devoted to social justice and human rights within the Lutheran World Federation. The dominion of Christ applied to all areas of life and not simply certain spheres. The sovereignty of God extends to the whole of creation. The Lutheran central doctrine of justification through faith, was given not only an individual but also a social dimension. The responsibility of the church concerns not only spiritual questions but also the shaping of society and human relations within society. This leads to an involvement with human rights.

Apartheid, the relationship between women and men and that between rich

---

[144] Op.cit. 64f.

and poor were put on the agenda of the Lutheran World Federation. Above all, the stance adopted with regard to racial segregation refutes all talk of Lutheran social quietism. The defenders of the turn-of-the-century Luther interpretation saw in this a confusion of the two kingdoms.

7.12 Summary

The Lutheran World Federation involved itself in the implementation of human rights because human life was seen as a gift of God and human dignity was not considered to derive from the state. Human dignity exists independently of whether it is guaranteed by those with political power or not. However, it is the task of those with that power to respect and protect human dignity. The idea of human rights expresses this insight in such a way that it is acceptable irrespective of the religious belief of the individual or lack of one.[145] The purpose of public pronouncements on violations of human rights is to diminish the suffering of those affected, to help to ensuring justice for them and to remind those in power of their responsibility to protect human rights.[146]

Within the Lutheran World Federation, no uniform outlook on the relationship between Christian belief and human rights can be discerned. One is keen to treat human rights as a matter concerning the whole of mankind and not simply something for Christians. This has consequences for the way human rights are treated theologically. Sometimes they are based upon the humane i.e. what is taken to characterize humanity in general. Human rights are also linked both to classical doctrines in Lutheranism such as the doctrine of two kingdoms and the doctrine of justification as well as to the emphasis of modern exegesis on the Kingdom of God in the New Testament. It is therefore possible to speak of theological pluralism within Lutheranism.

Both the individual and social aspects of human rights are stressed, as is their link to the right to life and ecology. However, the social rights and the right to life are increasingly given priority in the Third World. This reflects the shift in social development which has taken place since the mid 1960s. It also reflects the fact that the Lutheran church acted as a people's church in communist East Germany. The goal as far as human rights within the Lutheran World Federation is concerned, is to achieve a balance: a balance between the forces within human beings, between human beings in society and between human beings and nature. Thereby one can make the world a more humane place. Human rights apply to all human beings and their link to Christian belief and Christian theology can take various forms.

Since the Second World War, Lutheranism has been conscious of its social responsibility. This is rooted in the dearly-purchased experiences from the

---

[145] E. Lorenz ed. To speak or not to speak? Proposed criteria for public statements on violations of human rights, 1984, 41.
[146] Op.cit. 45.

Nazi period, as regards Christian responsibility for liberty and justice in the social order. Lutheranism has become aware that it has something to say about both public and private life. This has been displayed in a new way of dealing with the two kingdoms doctrine. It no longer prevents the church from intervening in social life, but tells the church what it must do. The authorities are held to account for how they discharge their responsibilities under God's dominion. Both kingdoms are kingdoms of God. The most striking illustration of the new Lutheran attitude was the campaign against apartheid in South Africa. Apartheid was presented as casus confessionis.

Human rights functioned as a mediating idea in the discussion rather as middle axioms had served within the ecumenical movement. They presented a utopia or a vision of a transformed social order. The ecumenical ideas of a just, sustainable and participatory society put forward a goal to fight for. They drew attention to the latent conflict between ideal and reality. The idea of human rights had a similar function. They present an idea or paradigm in order to criticize the social status quo and to encourage attempts to change it.

References

References to source material on which the present investigation is based, have been presented throughout. The Lutheran World Federation has generated an abundance of documents, whether in the form of statements from the Secretary-General, the executive committee or from the general assemblies, exchanges of ideas at consultations, the reflections of individual theologians or contributions to journals. The Lutheran World Federation has demonstrated its vigorous involvement in the sphere of human rights in the postwar period.

For the sake of completenesss, some further documents may be listed. Southern Africa: Confessional Integrity Preparatory Material for the Lutheran World Federation Executive Committee Meeting Geneva July 13–August 9 1989. Public statements and letters in the Area of International Affairs and Human Rights issued by the Lutheran World Federation 1984–1990 and 1990–1991. This collection of documents is to be found at the library of the World Council of Churches in Geneva. It forms a parallel to the CCIA documents within the World Council of Churches.

E. Lorenz hrsg Widerstand Recht und Frieden Kriterien legitimen Gewaltgebrauchs Studien aus dem Lutherischen Weltbund 1984 is an interdenominational and ideologically critical study with illustrations from a variety of contexts. It is based on the consultation of the Lutheran World Federation of 4–8 January 1982. The issue of power was closely linked to the issue of human rights. In the final analysis, power was a guarantee of the maintenance of human rights. At the same time, power could lead to the violation of human rights.

The Encounter of the Church with Movements of Social Change in Various Cultural Contexts 1977 is composed partly of papers from a seminar at Bossey from 21 to 27 September 1975 and partly of papers from a consultation held at Glion from 4 to 11 July 1976. These documents show that the social consciousness of the 1960s had also begun to influence the Lutheran World Federation. The documents are particularly devoted to the churches' encounter with Marxism.

On the other hand, very little has hitherto been written about the treatment of the issue of human rights within the Lutheran World Federation. Apart from the monographs previously mentioned, a number of other works deserved to be noted here: The Lutheran World Federation Reports 1963–1969 (1979). The Lutheran World Federation

Reports on the Work of Its Branches and Related Agencies 1970–1977 (1977) and From Dar es Salam to Budapest 1977–1984. Reports on the Work of the Lutheran World Federation (1984). These books give full accounts of work within the Lutheran World Federation between the General Assemblies.

In Rights and Christian Ethics 1992, K. Cronin points out that human dignity is derived from the fact that human beings are created in the image of God. Possessing and exercising rights is a vital aspect of this dignity. Being made in the image of God gives a reason for acting morally. This reason is justified on religious grounds.

The German theologian Ulrich Duchrow occupies a prominent, if controversial, place in the theological discussion of social problems within the Lutheran World Federation. He has published a series of works which are relevant to the issue of human rights. In addition to those previously mentioned, there is U. Duchrow, Alternativen zur kapitalistischen Weltwirtschaft Biblische Erinnerung und politische Ansätze zur Überwindung einer lebensbedrohenden Ökonomie 1994. In Duchrow's view, the market economy opposes human rights. Indeed it is a violation of these rights.

CHAPTER 8

Human Rights and the World Alliance of Reformed Churches

8.1 Introduction

The theological work concerning human rights issues was discussed by the World Alliance of Reformed Churches (WARC) at Nairobi in 1970, by the Lutheran World Federation at Evian in 1970, by the World Council of Churches at St. Pölten 1974 and by the Roman Catholic Synod of Bishops in 1974.

Within WARC, an individual theologian, Jürgen Moltmann, played a role in the treatment of the human rights issue in a way which had no parallel in other denominational and interdenominational associations. His theological ideas had a decisive influence upon the position adopted by WARC with respect to human rights.

The human rights issue was discussed at a consultation in London in 1976 organized by WARC. This consultation was partially documented in a publication in German and English on human rights, entitled respectively *Gottes Recht und menschenrechte* and *A Christian Declaration on Human Rights*.

Human rights were discussed at *a consultation in Dublin* in 1978 from an ecumenical perspective. This conference was arranged by the Irish School of Ecumenics and Jürgen Moltmann was one of its theological architects. His aim was to help to lay the ground for an ecumenical theology of human rights. He viewed his work for WARC as a step in attaining this goal. To this end, Moltmann wrote about human rights in various denominational organs. The consultation in Dublin ended in the issuing of a statement.

Jürgen Moltmann worked out a theology of human rights which is particularly associated with two publications, the first in German *Menschenwürde Recht und Freiheit* 1979 and the second in English *On Human Dignity Political Theology and Ethics* 1984. There is reason to believe with these works that he arrived at the ecumenical theology of human rights which he also had sought in the course of his work for WARC.

In 1987 in Geneva, representatives of the Reformed churches held a *seminar on justice, peace and the integrity of the creation* with the subtitle *forms of solidarity: human rights*. The starting point for the seminar was human rights activities within WARC and the World Council of Churches.

The ecological crisis accelerated at the close of the 1980s. It was therefore natural for WARC to choose the rights of nature as a subject for studies and discussions, as well as directing attention to the rights of future generations. These considerations resulted in a proposal to extend the universal declaration of human rights. In 1990, under the editorship of the Reformed theologian Lukas Vischer, WARC published the work *Rights of Future Generations Rights of Nature*.

In WARC, human rights were linked to the extension of the demand for justice and led to two Dutch Reformed churches being expelled from the denominational community at the General Assembly in Ottawa in 1982 because of their attitude towards apartheid. The issue of apartheid was intensively discussed within the Reformed church, both at international and national level. A document illustrating the latter is H. H. Nordholt's *Apartheid und Reformierte Kirche* 1983 which can be traced to the discussions within the Reformed union of churches in Germany, Netherlands and Switzerland, which formed part of WARC.

The study of the theological basis of human rights within the World Alliance of Reformed Churches had political consequences. The young pastor Andrew Young, who was a disciple of Martin Luther King Junior, became involved in this. He supported Jimmy Carter´s candidacy for the US Presidency and took part both in framing and implementing Carter's policies in which human rights occupied an important position. The language of human rights formed an important part of American political rhetoric at the close of the 70s and Jimmy Carter's human rights activism had significant roots in WARC's study of human rights.

It seems natural to arrange this chapter on human rights in WARC on the basis of what has been said above. 1) Divine right and human right 2) understanding human rights 3) human dignity and human rights 4) solidarity and human rights 5) the rights of future generations or the rights of nature 6) apartheid and the Reformed church. As already noted, Jürgen Moltmann´s contribution, whether his papers on this subject on behalf of WARC or his own publications, runs like a red thread through the work on human rights.

The preferred historical background for the treatment of the human rights issue within WARC is the civil rights movement in the USA and the campaign against apartheid in South Africa. These two historical processes help to define the contours of the human rights issue within WARC.

8.2 The Civil Rights Campaign in USA and the Campaign Against Apartheid in South Africa

The civil rights campaign and the Vietnam war became dominant issues in USA politics from the 1960s. The murders of John F. Kennedy, Martin Luther King Jr. and Robert Kennedy, along with civic disturbance and student unrest, presented a picture of a USA with problems. Eugene Carson Blake, later Secretary-General of the World Council of Churches, was active in the civil rights movement. In his eyes, racism was blasphemy. More than 5 000 church members were arrested for their activities in the civil rights campaign on behalf of the Civil Rights Bills. The churches helped to bring about the Civil Rights Act during Lyndon Johnson's administration.

A leading exponent of liberation theology in the USA was Robert McAffee Brown. In *Theology in a New Key Responding to Liberation Themes*, 1978, he maintained that traditional Christianity tended to interpret evil in individualistic terms. Only a minority create problems. If they can be converted, everything will be fine. The insight of liberation theology was that evil is part of the system—it is built into the fabric of society.[1] According to Brown, contemporary America is in need of radical social change. Liberation theology in USA was aligned with black theology and feminist theology. With Martin Luther King's death in 1968, many blacks raised the question of whether the civil rights movement could bring about real social changes for their community. The black power movement was an attempt to break through the structures of discrimination. In *Black Theology and Black Power*, J.H.Cone makes the following point. Jesus proclaims liberation for those imprisoned and fights against all who quietly accept the structures of injustice. If Christ is not to be found in the ghetto but remains in the pleasant life of suburbs, then the gospel is a lie. Christianity is not alien for Black Power. It is Black Power.[2] Cone was doubtful whether King's non-violence strategy would succeed. For him, the choice between violence and non-violence was a decision about a lesser or greater evil. If the system is evil, revolutionary violence is justified and necessary.[3] Since a black revolution in a society of which 90% was white had little chance of achieving results, Cone preached a type of racial ecumenism.[4]

Black theology in the USA and South Africa share a common demand. They look upon political and cultural liberation as the heart of the evangelical message. Their opposition is directed against racism and other forms of oppression. In *Black Theology USA and South Africa Politics, Culture and Liberation* 1989, D. N. Hopkins maintains that what shapes Black theology in USA and South Africa is that both proclaim the Christian message as one of liberation for blacks who fight against racism and for a whole humanity. With a view to the future, an effective Black theology must integrate politics and culture.

Black Theology in USA grew out of the civil rights movement and the Black Power movement. The former started on 1 December 1955 in a bus in Montgomery, Alabama. Rosa Parks, a black woman employee, took a seat on a bus and refused to vacate it when asked to do so by a white man. Her refusal to

---

[1] R. McAffee Brown, Theology in a New Key, Responding to Liberation Themes 1978, 15, 61, 178.
[2] J. H. Cone Black Theology and Black Power 1969, 38.
[3] Op. cit., 56,137,143.
[4] Op. cit., 151.

submit to the Southern segregation laws gave rise to a new generation of black civil protest. Because she was tired after a day's work and because she felt herself wrongly treated, Rosa Parks began a movement in which Martin Luther King Jr. became involved. It soon carried the North American Blacks' struggle for justice far outside the country. For the next 382 days, King and the blacks in Montgomery successfully boycotted the city buses to protest against segregation. An old black woman had got the protest going.

The black church during the 1950s and early 1960s, under King's leadership, played a decisive role in breaking down legal segregation, primarily in the South. It knew that the Christian message was inconsistent with the discriminatory laws on white supremacy. The civil rights movement built on the experiences and work of the National Association for the Advancement of Colored People (NAACP) during the 1940s and early 1950s. It created a new form of protest. Blacks moved out from the courtrooms into the streets. Massive boycotts, sit-in strikes and acts of civil disobedience undermined segregation. At the social level, the civil rights movement demanded full equality for all Americans within the framework of the US constitution. Black faith in the black church gave motivation to the movement.

Black theology developed among black pastors who had participated in King's civil rights movement. These ministers were veterans of civil rights resistance in the South and desegregation activities in the North. They had preached at the funerals of civil rights activists. They had experienced dynamite being smuggled into their churches. According to King's interpretation, the Christian gospel demanded that we love our enemy and influence the moral consciousness of the white supremacists. But by 1966, an increasing group of black clergy found themselves faced with a choice between King's Christian non-violence philosophy, Black power, urban guerillas and Malcolm X's black nationalist philosophy. Black theology emerged from a synthesis between King's Christian message on radical justice and Black power' s black liberation nationalism. Authentic Christianity meant racial justice and black liberation by all necessary means. The Black power movement arose out of the civil rights movement. According to Black power, the latter had achieved little. The poor blacks remained poor. Black power grew in reaction to white segregationist terror in the South.

The young began to ask if the philosophy of turning the other cheek was merely another form of the bowing and scraping which their grandparents had gone through to get something from the white man.

Why must they wear a suit and tie, conduct sit-in strikes and have their bodies beaten to pulp for rights which were guaranteed by the constitution? Why should America give blacks rights which other citizens have enjoyed from birth? Black power showed the resurrection of the spirit of Malcolm X, the contemporary father of black nationalism. He said that the worst crime which the white man had committed, had been to teach blacks to hate themselves. Malcolm X demanded black liberation by all necessary means. Politically, he represented black solidarity and the right to self-determination. Culturally he extolled black pride and Pan-Africanism. Theologically, he defined the white man as the devil. Black pastors had access to a theology which responded to the era of "We shall overcome" with integration but which was irrelevant to the era of "I am black and I am proud". Black pastors had to examine their faith and distance themselves from racist Christianity. Black theology arose in response to the black liberation movement's focus and attack on the white racism. Could blacks continue to persist with a theology of integration—a theology where all power continued to lie in the hands of the whites? Could black identity, culture, history and language be authentic sources for creating theology? What had a blue-eyed Jesus to do with Black power and Black liberation? James H. Cone's *Black Theology and Black Power* was published in March 1969. As previously pointed out, he argued that Black power is the Gospel of Jesus Christ.

Non-violent civil disobedience and black consciousness were behind the growth of Black theology in South Africa. At the beginning of the 1950s, the African National Congress (the foremost voice of black resistance) consisted of both an older liberal wing and a younger, more nationalist one. The younger leadership transformed ANC from the tactics of passive opposition and courtroom verdicts to one of civil disobedience. Tactics altered from appealing to white courts to massive mobilization with boycotts, strikes and marches. In the 1950s, ANC still hoped to bring about black participation in government, without violence. ANC wished for the apartheid laws to be repealed. The transition to more combative tactics was carried out within the framework of a liberal democratic strategy. Behind the social movement towards liberal democracy, there was a liberal Christian world view. Many ANC leaders had been educated at white mission schools. Many ANC leaders were Christians. Whites and blacks were to work together for a non-racist goal.

At the close of the 1950s, young nationalists in ANC began to agree about an African position. They wanted an Africa for Africans and the restoration of stolen land to indigenous African ownership. The goal was black liberation from European ways of thinking and black self-determination. Their goal was a future South Africa governed by blacks. The nationalist group in the ANC saw no difference between radical whites and white liberals. Both represented the whites and aimed at forcing the blacks to accept cultural self-denial. Black nationalists maintained that a genuine and healthy culture and morality compelled the oppressed blacks to value themselves, their history and their culture. The blacks had to go it alone if they were to attain a black governmental majority in post—apartheid South Africa. If the whites lacked minority privileges, they would be absorbed by the blacks. In 1959, the African wing broke away and founded the Pan Africanist Congress (PAC). Its president was Robert Sobukwe, a Methodist lay preacher. Laws prevented mixed sexual relations; they segregated lives; they codified black identity with a pass. PAC organized massive resistance against the pass. This campaign began on 21 March 1960 and led to direct confrontation with the state. All Africans were to refuse to carry passes and to go voluntarily to prison.

At the Sharpville demonstration, the police opened fire, killing 67 blacks, the majority of them shot from behind. World opinion turned against the apartheid regime. Some black leaders went underground. Others went into exile. As at the birth of Black power, the black consciousness movement turned on the hypocrisy of the white liberals, for the most part English-speaking whites. Following the Sharpville massacre, the anti-apartheid scene as far as black Africans were concerned, was characterized by a political vacuum. The blacks found themselves in the grip of fear. Steve Bantu Biko, the father of black consciousness, was the leader of the South African students' organization SASO. It held its first conference in 1969. Integration did not mean the assimilation of blacks into an established system of norms drawn up and motivated by white society. Biko discovered that the whites were those principally responsible for the oppression of the blacks and at the same time were those most active in opposition to this oppression. Biko called this situation one of total white power. In his view, the white liberals played their same old game. They laid claims to a monopoly of intelligence and moral judgement and laid down a framework for black liberation. The white liberals were the worst racists of all because they refused to credit the blacks with the intelligence to know what they wanted.

The Bantustan legislation forced the blacks to move from white areas to segregated black areas in unfertile country far from the cities i.e. far from the centre of power and trade. This displayed the height of white arrogance. Biko maintained that nothing can justify the arrogance whereby a clique of foreigners have the right to determine the lives of the majority. Biko varied Malcolm X's theme that black Americans suffer from self-hatred. The blacks had become a shadow of what is meant by personality.

A theological crisis of identity seized the black church leaders. A black theolgy was needed. Black theology in South Africa created its own theological agenda in response to the racism in white Christianity. Why had God made me black? Was Christianity ever intended for blacks? Why did the blacks suffer because God had created them as non-whites?

References

The literature about the civil rights campaign in USA and the campaign against apartheid in South Africa is vast. In both cases, the churches played a central role. A. J. Reichley in Religion in American Public Life, 1985, devotes a chapter to the development after the Second World War and takes up the leading role which religious leaders played in the civil rights and black power movements. R. E. Luker in The Social Gospel in Black and White American Racial Reform 1885–1912, 1991 deals with the racial issue as reflected in religious life, in the social gospel movement. The book traces the role of American social Christianity's role in race reform in the period between emancipation and the civil rights movement.

L. W. Baldwin discusses the roots of Martin Luther King's work and his legacy in two volumes, There is a Balm in Gilead, The Cultural Roots of Marin Luther King Jr

1991 and To Make the Wounded Whole, The Cultural Legacy of Martin Luther King Jr 1992. James H. Cone provides an illuminating study of the relationship between the civil rights movement and Black power movement in Martin & Malcolm & America, A Dream or a Nightmare 1993. Martin Luther King did not look upon the campaign for human rights as something peripheral to his mission as a pastor bearing Christian witness, but instead saw it as an integral part of that mission. In 1961, he said "I am first and foremost a minister. I love the church and I feel that civil rights is a part of it".

The role of the churches in the South African campaign against apartheid is analyzed by J.W. de Gruchy in The Church Struggle in South Africa 1979 and in C. Villa-Vicencio, Trapped in Apartheid, A Socio-Theological History of the English-Speaking Churches, 1988. The latter tries also to identify the motives which led prominent personalities with quite different views of life and from divergent religious and political backgrounds to involve themselves in the anti-apartheid campaign in a series of interviews published under the title The Spirit of Hope, Conversations on Politics, Religion and Values, 1994.

Among other works which are illuminating for Christianity's role as a social factor in the South African liberation struggle are P. Randall ed. Directions of Change in South African Politics The Study Project of Christianity in Apartheid Society 1971, J. Wallis and J. Hollyday eds. Crucible of Fire, The Church Confronts Apartheid 1989 and S. Rothe, Der Südafrikanische Kirchenrat (1968–1988): Aus liberaler Opposition zum radikalen Widerstand 1989. The latter work is a doctoral dissertaion which analyzes the work of the South African Council of Churches during a crucial period in the campaign against apartheid.

8.3 Divine Right and Human Right

The General Assembly of WARC in Nairobi 1970 called for a theological basis for human rights and a theology of liberation. Jürgen Moltmann introduced this discussion.[5] Through actively taking part in the dialogue between Christians and Marxists, he came into contact with political theology as it was interpreted by J. B. Metz.[6] What was crucial for Moltmann was the transformation of rights, which ensured the freedom of individuals, into duties to liberate those who are deprived of these rights.[7] According to Moltmann, a theology of human rights must start from the theology of liberation.[8] He asks how, on the basis of the ideal of human rights, a concrete utopia can be developed which relates the future of mankind to the political, social and racist injustice of today in order to overcome opposition.[9]

1974 was the crucial year for church action on behalf of human rights. Both the World Council of Churches at St. Pölten, as well as Paul VI and the Roman Catholic Synod of Bishops, had human rights high on their agenda. These events were reflected in WARC's organ, Reformed World.[10] The reformed the-

---

[5] RW Dec. 1971, 348.
[6] A.J. Conyers, God, Hope and History, Jürgen Moltmann and the Christian Concept of History, 1988.
[7] Op. cit., 354.
[8] Op. cit., 355.
[9] Op. cit., 357.
[10] R W Dec 1974, 174 f.

ologians, Jan M. Lochman and Jürgen Moltmann, worked on the collective document on human rights which was to be placed before the member churches of WARC in 1976. In North America, Allen O. Miller took charge of the preparatory work. A noteworthy feature of North American Reformed activities was that the theology of human rights developed under the influence of liberation theology.[11] Liberation theology is defined as an attempt to understand God's salvation in Jesus Christ as containing all aspects of human life in society.[12] Human rights, it is maintained, reflect the fact that human beings are created in the image of God.[13] Liberation theology is presented as a response to oppression—after centuries of oppression, women demand full participation in society just as do the handicapped, the old and the young who are marginalized by social, political and economic systems.[14] Allusion is made to G. Gutiérrez ' *A Theology of Liberation*. Liberation theology and human rights theology are treated as parallel in the North American material. Both wish to promote human dignity.[15]

In the wake of the Helsinki Agreement, which included respect for human rights and which was endorsed by 33 European states as well as USA and Canada, WARC arranged in London in 1976 a consultation on human rights with 21 theologians from six continents. The aim of the consultation was *to summarize the study of the theological foundation of human rights* which had been in progress since 1970 and to formulate Reformed thinking on this issue. Jürgen Moltmann was the main speaker. The meeting led to a statement on theological guidelines for the work on human rights. Its starting point was Moltmann's address.[16]

Moltmann stresses that human rights must be understood within the historical context in which they were formulated and functioned. The North Atlantic states formulated individual human rights in opposition to the fascist dictatorships which lost the Second World War. The socialist states emphasized social human rights by way of criticizing capitalism and the class war. The Third World countries demanded the right to economic, social and political self-determination as a stage in the liberation process from the old colonial powers. The task of theology with respect to human rights was in Moltmann's opinion to base them on God's law i.e. his demands on human beings. The London consultation adopted this thesis from Moltmann and made it its own. It is a matter of coming to the defence of human dignity.[17] The divine demand on human beings is expressed in the idea of God's image. Human rights reflect God's demands on human beings because they are formed to mirror God's image—human beings in relation to one another and to creation. God's image

---

[11] R W June 1975, 268.
[12] Op. cit., 269.
[13] Op. cit., 270.
[14] Op. cit., 271.
[15] Op. cit., 273.
[16] Op. cit., R W June 1976 50 f.
[17] Op. cit., 59.

points to human beings' inviolable dignity.[18] The mistake of liberalism is to ignore the social side of liberty and it is individualism's mistake to ignore social consciousness.[19] As regards the relationship between different types of rights, Moltmann argued as follows. Individual rights do not carry more weight than social rights. There is no conflict between them. The rights of the individual person can only be developed in a just society and a just society can only be based upon the rights of the individual. Collective egoism is as much a threat to human rights as individual egoism.[20] The rights of human beings to steer creation must be counterbalanced by the rights of non-human creation. Thus we cannot merely talk of human beings' rights with respect to the earth; there are also earth's rights with regard to human beings. Moltmann introduced into the discussion what came to be called ecological rights already in the mid 1970s and the demand for such rights was raised again by Moltmann and pursued by WARC at their London consultation in 1976. Economic growth is subject to ecological limits. The struggle for survival must not be carried out at the expense of nature. Ecological death paves the way for the end to human existence.[21]

The London consultation's guidelines drew particular attention to three dimensions of human life which have relevance for human rights: man and woman, individual and society, and human life and its ecological context. In identifying our humanity as creatures made in the image of God, the equality and independence of men and women are underlined as are the equal value and independence of present and future generations in the service of nature.[22] Environmental rights are about the responsible use of earth and nature. To this also belongs the right of future generations to the world.[23]

Following the London consultation of 1976, the theological study of the human rights issue within WARC since its introduction at the General Assembly in Nairobi in 1971, was summed up. This summary took the form of two publications, one in German entitled *Gottes recht und Menschenrechte Studien und Empfehlungen des Reformierten Weltbundes* by Jan Milich Lochman and Jürgen Moltmann, which appeared in 1976 and the other in English, namely *A Declaration on Human Rights Theological Studies of the World Alliance of Reformed Churches*, 1976 by Allen O. Miller

The Czech theologian, Jan Milich Lochman, who was based in Basle and led the theological work on human rights within WARC, wrote the introductory section to both publications. He pointed out that the individual aspects of human rights are dominant in the early ecumenical movement. Human rights defend the interests of citizens as free individuals, free producers and free owners. Individual human rights are criticized by socialists and Marxists for

---

[18] Op. cit., 61.
[19] Op. cit., 63.
[20] Op. cit., 64.
[21] Op. cit., 65 f.
[22] Op. cit., 52 g.
[23] Op. cit., 56 f.

being the rights of the privileged classes. It is a question of creating conditions in society which make it possible for all people to exercise their rights. The rights of society carry more weight than the interests of individuals. In the Third World, human rights are reduced mainly to surviving, achieving an improved balance of life opportunities between the poor and the rich and the elimination of exploitation within national and international frameworks.[24] The ecumenical discussion of human rights takes places against this background.[25] The question was raised in the ecumenical movement about a common theological basis in the Christian campaign for human rights. In what does the specifically Christian contribution to the further development of the human rights issue consist? According to Lochman, answering this question required deeper theological reflection.[26] The theological basis of human rights was what the General Assembly of WARC in Nairobi in 1970 had sought.[27] When human rights are placed in a liberation context, they become a step in the search for greater justice.[28] Lochman reveals new aspects of human rights, notably the following. Like Moltmann, he underlines that the basis of human rights is God's demands on human beings. Human rights form part of the framework of God's covenant with His people and the creation.[29]

Lochman, influenced by liberation theology, places stress on the social dimension in the Christian message and develops later in his book *Reconciliation and Liberation Challenging a One-Dimensional View of Salvation*, 1980 the idea of salvation as reconciliation and liberation. Thus for him, salvation has not simply one dimension: it has a vertical and a horizontal dimension which at the most profound level constitute one entity.

The Spaniard, Daniel Vidal, a theologian influenced by Barth, approached human rights Christologically. Jesus Christ is the revealer of God's law.[30] He is also the revealer of human rights.[31] Human beings have received rights in Jesus Christ, the new human being.[32] *An American theologian* emphasized that only God has rights while human beings have privileges.[33] Rights are gifts from God and duties are the commands of God.[34]

James H. Cone emphasized that Black theology is liberation: it relates the powers of liberation to what is central in the Gospel, namely Jesus Christ. In the Biblical tradition, the focus is upon God's actions in history, which liberates human beings from captivity. What God does, is always related to the liberation of the oppressed. Cone held that God's salvation coincides with

---

[24] Op. cit., 14 f.
[25] Op. cit., 16.
[26] Op. cit., 17.
[27] Op. cit., 18.
[28] Op .cit., 19.
[29] Op. cit., 21.
[30] Op. cit., 42.
[31] Op. cit., 44.
[32] Op. cit., 45.
[33] Op. cit., 56.
[34] Op. cit., 59.

human liberation. This is particularly evident in God's revelation in Jesus Christ.[35] Black theology emphasizes the right of blacks to defend themselves against those who try to destroy them. Black theology is aimed at racism.[36] It is clear that James H. Cone defines Black theology as a variant of liberation theology. But it is not simply an offshoot of liberation theology: it is also a form of human rights theology.

WARC pursued its project on human rights from a Christian perspective, from its General Assembly in Nairobi in 1970 until its consultation in London in 1976. At the forefront was WARC's theology section led by Jan Milic Lochman and two theological committees, one North American and the other European. The WARC study of the theological basis of human rights was initiated at Nairobi in 1970 and summed up at the consultation in London in 1976. In 1971, Jürgen Moltmann delivered an introductory study document and in 1976 a definitive report. By means of these writings, he was able to exercise considerable influence on the study process in WARC. He managed to outline a human rights theology. This human rights theology grew out of the study carried out in the earlier part of the 1970s. The most important contributor to this theology was the Tübingen theologian Jürgen Moltmann. This work in WARC had an important influence on the civil rights movement and Jimmy Carter's administration, as well as on the freedom struggle against apartheid in South Africa, just as theological reflection about human rights was affected by the aforementioned historical phenomena.

8.4 Understanding Human Rights

The theme *Theology and human rights* was discussed at a WARC *consultation in Scotland* in 1978. The driving force behind this work was Jürgen Moltmann.[37] At the thirtieth anniversary of the UN declaration of human rights, a consultation was arranged from 20 November to 4 December 1978 by the Irish School of Ecumenics. The consultation was interdenominational and interreligious. Participants included not only Christians with differing denominational backgrounds but also representatives of non-Christian religions, philosophers and jurists. The aim was to promote the study of, and actions concerning human rights in a world which calls for justice. If the ecumenical ideal is one union of believers serving the world, a new emphasis on belief operating through justice, is necessary.[38]

The question had been raised why religions and ideologies are concerned with human rights and why conversations about human rights take place from

---

[35] Op.cit., 68 f.
[36] Op. cit., 74f.
[37] RW Sept. Dec. 1977, 324 ff.
[38] A. D. Falconer ed. Understanding Human Rights An Interdisciplinary and Interfaith Study., The Proceedings of the International Consultation held in Dublin 1978, 1980 IX.

the perspective of belief. José Miguez Bonino investigated the relationship between Christianity and human rights and showed why Christians are involved on behalf of those who demand their humanity. When social rights entered the picture after the Second World War, it drew attention to the masses—the industrial proletariat in the Northern hemisphere and the exploited masses of the Third World—who had been excluded from the civil rights defined by the bourgeois world.[39] As regards the relationship between the universal and the specific, Bonino maintained that God's universality is expressed in his special concern for the poor, the oppressed, the powerless and the marginalized.[40] The fundamental human rights today are rights to a humane life. Human rights mean the struggle on behalf of the poor and the socially and economically oppressed: it is a struggle for their liberation.[41] If one can speak of a human rights theology in Bonino's writings, then it is one side of his Latin American theology of liberation.

Jürgen Moltmann reviewed the theological studies of human rights which have been carried out in denominational groups and associations and pointed to areas of agreement and disagreement. He called for a deeper theological approach to human rights. He pointed out the change of emphasis which has taken place within the ecumenical movement in thinking about human rights. In the first phase, from 1948 to 1960 attention was primarily fixed upon individual rights. Human rights were mainly understood as freedom of religion in communist Eastern Europe. In the second phase from 1960, social rights and the right to exist entered the picture. This development culminated in 1974 with the St. Pölten consultation and the Roman Catholic Synod of Bishops. Human rights meant primarily the fight against racism.[42] The central concept for Moltmann is human dignity. It is superior to human rights. The starting point of WARC's theological basis of human rights is human dignity. Human dignity is not itself a human right but the source and basis of all human rights. The latter presuppose respect for the individual person's value.[43] Moltmann distinguishes between that part of human rights which applies to human beings in general and is centred around human dignity and theological interpretations of human beings and human dignity which cannot be put forward with any claim to absoluteness but must instead be understood as Christian contributions to the realization of human rights.[44] WARC's theological foundation of human rights bases human dignity upon the fact that human beings are made in the image of God. According to Moltmann, the theological approaches adopted by the Roman Catholic church, the World Council of Churches and the Lutheran World Federation all point in the same direction. Human rights are based upon human dignity and human dignity rests upon the fact that hu-

---

[39] Op. cit., 27.
[40] Op. cit., 31.
[41] Op. cit., 32.
[42] Op. cit., 183–185.
[43] Op. cit., 187.
[44] Op. cit., 188.

man beings are created in the image of God.[45] That human beings are created in God's image is then in the Reformed tradition linked to God's covenant and thereby expresses God's right to human beings.[46] Moltmann holds that the theological contribution consists in basing human rights on God's right to human beings.[47] In mentioning human beings as being created in God's image, God's right with respect to all human beings is expressed. Human rights reflect God's right with respect to human beings because human beings are necessarily God's image in all relationships of life.[48]

The study *Understanding Human Rights* stresses, not the universality of human rights, but their contentual dependence on differing situations. Human rights are concerned with the promotion of the humane within societies and institutions. The international consultation at Dublin in 1978 called for study and action on the human rights front in the following areas: 1) the relationship between civil, political, social, cultural and economic rights 2) the rights of women and 3) the First World's oppression of the Third World in political and economic structures through investment.[49]

8.5 Human Dignity and Human Rights

Jürgen Moltmann published articles on human rights in various journals and publications. His primary forum was WARC's journal, Reformed World. In it are to be found his original and definitive study documents on human rights from a theological perspective, which shaped WARC's theological foundation of human rights. Moltmann was, however, greatly in demand outside his own denomination. He contributed continuously to the ecumenically sympathetic Catholic journal Concilium, cooperating with the Tübingen theologian, Hans Küng. Moltmann's articles were later collected in two books on human rights. The first and shorter version was entitled in German *Menschewürde Recht und Freiheit* and appeared in 1979. The second and more comprehensive work was published in English with the title *On Human Dignity Political Theology and Ethics* and was published in 1984. The fundamental concept which forms the starting point of Moltmann's theology of human rights figures in the titles of both the English and German books, namely *human dignity*.

Moltmann's fundamental theological expositions concerning human rights were published in Reformed World. They were also presented in the Roman Catholic ecumenical publication, Centro Pro Unione 1977 before they were incorporated in his book on human rights in English.[50] Centro Pro Unione was published by the ecumenical centre in Rome, which shares premises with the

---

[45] Op. cit., 189.
[46] Op. cit., 190.
[47] Op. cit., 193.
[48] Op. cit., 194.
[49] Op. cit., 237.
[50] J. Moltmann, On Human Dignity Political Theology and Ethics, 1984, 19–35.

documentation centre IDOC International on the Via S Maria dell' Anima. Both these institutions, like the journal Concilium, have their roots in the reformist spirit which inspired the Second Vatican Council.

Jürgen Moltmann constructs his theology of human rights on the basis of the image of God.[51] In the idea of God's image is expressed the divine demand upon human beings. Human rights to life, liberty, community and self-determination reflect God's demand upon human beings. In all their relationships, whether between one another or as created beings in relation to the creation, human beings are designed to mirror God's image.[52] God's image is made up of human beings in all their relationships in life—economic, social, political and personal. God's image is made up of human beings along with others.[53] The international community can demand that human rights are implemented in the specific individual society. To be created in the image of God is the basis of human beings' right to rule over the earth and their right to community with non-human creation. The right of humans to rule over the non-human part of creation must be counterbalanced by their respect for the rights of non-human creation. To concentrate the necessities of life and the means of production in the hands of a few is an assault upon God's image in mankind.[54] Economic human rights must be brought about without coming into conflict with the rights of environment and within the limits imposed by ecology. To be created in the image of God is the basis for human beings' right to their future and their responsibility for those who come after them. The present must not be exploited at the cost of the future. Egoism is not only a property of individuals and collectives: there is also a generational egoism.[55]

Human rights are abused when they are used ideologically to justify private interests as opposed to other peoples rights. Christian theology uses the word sin to describe the inhumanity of human beings which is shown in continued violations of human rights. Human rights can first be achieved in an inhuman world through reconciliation. Christ is called to present reconciliation's right to bear fruit in the worldwide struggle for privileges and power. By serving reconciliation, Christians contribute to the attainment of all people's humanity. Christian belief does not lead us away from, but into the battle for human rights.[56] There must be a balance between efforts to attain all kinds of human rights—individual, social and ecological as well as the right to life—even if temporarily some particular right may have precedence. The unity which exists between human rights paves the way for a future universally based community between all peoples and nations. The churches overcome their own egoism by serving the whole of humanity in the struggle for human rights.[57]

---

[51] Centro Pro Unione n 11 1977 15.
[52] Op. cit., 16.
[53] Op. cit., 17.
[54] Op. cit., 18.
[55] Op. cit., 19.
[56] Op. cit., 20.
[57] Op. cit., 21.

Moltmann links human rights not only to the creation but also to the acts and life of Christ. His approach is based both upon a creation theology and upon Christology. The humanity which creation gave to the image of God is restored through Jesus Christ. Mankind's likeness to God is restored through the incarnation and thereby human beings recover their lost humanity. Reconciliation re-establishes human dignity and makes human rights possible in an inhuman world.

8.6 Solidarity and Human Rights

A seminar was organized by WARC under the heading *Justice, peace and the integrity of the creation* with the subheading *Forms of Solidarity:Human Rights* from 14 to 25 August at the John Knox Centre in Geneva. For WARC, the issue of justice in the human rights movement was spotlighted at the General Assembly in Ottawa in 1982. There it was decided to deprive two Dutch Reformed churches in South Africa of their membership of WARC until they altered their attitude about the apartheid system.[58]

In the final seminar report, it was held that the human rights situation should be studied within the framework of the WCC project Justice, peace and the integrity of creation. The emphasis upon human rights was related to all three aspects and the violation of human rights has implications for each one of these aspects. [59] The violation of human rights has three roots: economic exploitation, militarization and violations of identities (cultural, sexual and ethical). Exploitation is an expression of inequality with respect to power between groups within a society and inequality between nations. Exploitation leads to suffering.[60] Militarization affects all aspects of life. The role of military values increases. Militarization supports an attitude of confrontation and hostility and presupposes an enduring state of war and a permanent enemy.[61] The cultural identity of one group or nation means that we must accept others' pride in their identity. We must not think of ourselves as having exclusive rights or believe that we alone stand for the truth. Cultural identity becomes something negative if a group's identity is used to exploit another group. It leads to racism, sexism and nationalism.[62] In 1982 WARC declared apartheid to be heresy and the seminar at John Knox Centre in Geneva in 1987 concurred.[63]

Erich Weingärtner, formerly at the documentation centre IDOC International in Rome and at CCIA within the World Council of Churches in Geneva, as a frequent commentator on human rights issues, maintained in a paper that

---

[58] Forms of Solidarity Human Rights 14–25 August 1987 Centre International Reformé John Knox 1988 7.
[59] Op. cit., 11.
[60] Op. cit., 12.
[61] Op. cit., 15.
[62] Op. cit., 22.
[63] Op. cit., 23.

theology has three functions with respect to human rights: to justify temporal morality, to justify human rights action and to be a forum for reflection.[64]

In another paper, it was stressed that the women's movement raises the issue of women's rights. In patriarchal societies, man is the norm-giving type. Even God is interpreted in terms of man as opposed to woman. God is seen as spiritually apart from matter. Matter is viewed as something immoral. The ancient prophets and philosophers were imprinted with this world of ideas and attacked natural religion in which motherhood is worshipped and viewed as the primary source of life. Goddesses were relegated to inferior positions. The patriarchal church is the critical issue for the institutional church. Within its framework, women are refused ordination to the priesthood. Pressure on the church to overcome the patriarchy is caused, not simply by women trying to attain power, but by the call for justice in the church. A rejuvenated church has to represent the people of God, both women and men. It must exemplify in its inner life that justice which it demands in society.[65]

Religion is a powerful factor in culture and society. It plays a key role in defining and giving legitimacy to notions of belief, attitudes and practical actions concerning women. Religion is both a problem in the sense that its structures of domination have oppressed women but also a solution whereby its vision of liberation or equality has created powerful components for social change.[66]

8.7 Future Generations' Rights or Nature's Rights

At the WARC General Assembly in Seoul in 1989, Christian witness from the perspective of the present ecological crisis was discussed. Nature, as well as human beings, has rights. The General Assembly recommended that it should be investigated whether WARC was able to supplement its 1976 human rights declaration with a similar declaration about the rights of God's creation. It had become more and more obvious that the universal declaration of human rights required to be expanded. If humanity's survival is to be assured, our vision must not stop with the rights of human beings. Human rights are only significant if they are placed in the wider context of the rights of creation as a whole. It is a question of what rights are needed by future generations and what rights are ascribed to nature.[67]

In *Rights of Future Generations, Rights of Nature, Proposal for enlarging the Universal Declaration of Human Rights*, 1990 edited by the Reformed theologian Lukas Vischer, these two questions are discussed. What does it mean to speak of the rights of future generations and the rights of nature? A

---

[64] Op. cit., 29.
[65] Op. cit., 60 f.
[66] Op. cit., 65.
[67] R W March 1989 90–97.

number of lawyers and theologians sought to find answers to these questions and thereby carry out the mandate from the WARC General Assembly of 1989.[68] In 1982, the UN General Assembly issued a declaration on the rights of nature.[69] In 1990 the authors to Lukas Vischer's pamphlet put forward a proposal regarding the rights of future generations and the rights of nature at the behest of WARC. Not only human beings but nature itself ought to be given rights. Both living and inanimate matter are God's creation. Nature is not simply a collection of objects which are available to be used in an arbitrary way by human beings.[70] The authors urged the UN to extend its universal declaration of human rights with statements about the rights of future generations and the rights of nature.[71]

Jürgen Moltmann was among the contributors to the pamphlet. He posed a number of problems. Atomic warfare, like biological and chemical warfare, threatens the survival of mankind. Radioactive waste remains active for thousands of years. Threats thus arise from individual states. For this reason, their freedom of action must be limited out of respect for humanity as a whole.[72] Gene technology can manipulate the genetic structures of life. It can destroy humanity and thus constitutes a new danger. In the industrial nations, the limits for the exploitation of non-renewable sources of energy can be exceeded in the present generation. Declarations of human rights bear with them a risk of anthropocentrism if they are not counterbalanced by declarations about the rights of nature. Human dignity must not be achieved at the expense of nature. If nature were to collapse, the preconditions for the future existence of humanity would be snatched away.[73] Economic growth is limited by ecological considerations. A balance must be maintained between economic and ecological justice.[74] Modern anthropocentrism begins from the assumption that human beings exist for their own sake and nature exists for the sake of human beings.[75] Anthropocentrism is the foundation of modern industrial society. In pre-industrial agricultural societies on the other hand, cosmocentrism was dominant. What is needed is a society with rights for all forms of life and for nature. Human laws must be subordinated to universal laws for human life on earth, if humanity is to survive.[76]

In one contribution, the rights of creation are viewed from a theological perspective. The maintenance of human dignity presupposes the maintenance of the dignity of the creation.[77] In another contribution, a declaration on the

---

[68] L. Vischer ed. Rights of Future Generations Rights of Nature Proposal for enlarging the Universal Declaration of Human Rights 1990, 7 f.
[69] Op. cit., 62-68.
[70] Op. cit., 11.
[71] Op. cit., 13 f.
[72] Op. cit., 18 f.
[73] Op. cit., 20 f.
[74] Op. cit., 22.
[75] Op. cit., 23.
[76] Op. cit., 24.
[77] Op. cit., 48–51.

rights of future generations is formulated in ten points: 1) future generations have the right to life 2) they have a right to an unmanipulated, human, genetic inheritance i.e. a genetic inheritance which has not been artificially altered by human beings 3) they have a right to a rich plant and animal kingdom 4) they have a right to fresh air, to an ozone layer in one piece and to sufficient thermal exchange between the earth and space 5) they have a right to unpolluted water and sufficient drinking water 6) they have a right to a fertile earth and healthy forests 7) they have a right to real reserves of non-renewable raw materials and sources of energy 8) they have a right not to be confronted with products and waste from previous generations which endanger their health 9) they have a right to a cultural inheritance i.e. to an encounter with the culture created by earlier generations 10) they have a general right to physical conditions of life which allow them a humane and dignified existence.[78]

8.8 Apartheid and the Reformed Church

The South African Church Campaign—a Historical Summary

Racism existed before the National Party came to power in 1948 but this event symbolized a dramatic change. Apartheid became a system in which African labour was regulated and exploited for the purpose of achieving growth in the white-owned economy. In 1956, the Anglican mission priest Trevor Huddlestone published his book *Naught for Your Comfort*. He maintained that the reasons behind apartheid are evil and essentially non-Christian. The wish is to dominate and thereby preserve racial hegemony.

The Sharpeville massacre in March 1960 marked a turning point. Following it, the leaders of the African National Congress and the Pan Africanist Congress—Albert Luthuli, Nelson Mandela and Robert Sobukwe—were imprisoned. Many blacks went into exile while others went underground. The World Council of Churches helped to arrange the Cottesloe consultation in December 1960. Franklin Clark Fry from the USA, chairman of the WCC Central Committee, led a consultation which was attended by ten delegates from eight South African member churches and five delegates representing WCC. The latter group include the WCC Secretary-General, Visser't Hooft. The delegates from the Nederduitsch Hervormde Kerk were all white. NHK rejected the final document while NGK, Nederduitse Gereformeerde Kerk, supported it. The Prime Minister, Hendrik Verwoerd expressed his personal displeasure at the NGK delegation's behaviour. A number of the church's synods rejected the Cottesloe decision. NGK withdrew from membership of WCC. NGK rejected racial injustice and discrimination in principle but accepted the policy of separate development. NGK became increasingly isolated in its defence of separate development within RES, the Reformed Ecumenical Synod, which is a world

---

[78] Op. cit., 29 f.

wide association of churches which hold fast to the Calvinist denominational documents of the Reformation. NGK was one of the dominant members of the synod.

There are five Dutch Reformed churches: *Gereformeerde Kerk* (GK); *Nederduitse Gereformeerde Kerk* (NGK); *Nederduitse Gereformeerde Kerk in Afrika* (NGK black mission church) (NGKA); Allan Boesak's church *Nederduitsch Gereformeerde Sendingkerk* (NGK coloured mission church) (NGSK); and *Nederduitsch Hervormde Kerk* (NHK). Around 42% of South Africa's white population belongs to NGK and the majority of white leaders in the country were among its members. This along with various other historical factors has made NGK into the single most politically influential church in South Africa. From 1948, the Dutch Reformed Churches defended the apartheid legislation on theological grounds. This justification led to NGK and NHK being declared heretical by WARC in 1982. The white Dutch Reformed churches have not belonged to the South African Council of Churches because of its protest against the policy of apartheid. The white NHK created its own separate black church NGKA. Blacks were excluded from membership in the white NHK. The Gereformeerde Kerk, GK, with its ultra Calvinistic theology was convinced that God had determined that there should be separation between the races. The white Dutch Reformed churches supported special schools for separate races and created a theological form of Afrikaner nationalism during the 1920s and 1930s. Their apartheid theology formed the ideological foundation of apartheid from 1948 when the Nationalist party triumphed. However WARC declared the theological justification of aprtheid to be heresy in 1982 and this pronouncement affected the Reformed racist churches. The problem for the general synod of NGK was how it could give up the theological justifiction of apartheid without calling into question the authority and legitimacy of the state.

The white Dutch Reformed churches had come to symbolize the legitimization of the white status quo, while the black churches legitimized black demands for liberation. The English-speaking churches have adopted a position between the two. By the English-speaking churches is meant those churches of British origin which have become welded together as a result of the ecumenical movement and their common attitude to the racist situation in general and apartheid in particular. The English-speaking churches were opposed to the Nationalist governments race policy. The English-speaking churches—Anglican, Methodist, Presbyterian and Congregationalist—were dominant in the South African Council of Churches and had their roots in nineteenth century colonial expansion. Membership is non-racist in character. The English-speaking churches led the church attack upon the white native nationalist government´s apartheid policy. Black members in the English-speaking churches exerted decisive influence within ANC from the 1930s and within PAC from its foundation in 1959. The Anglican, Z. K. Matthew, played a central role in ANC up to 1960. Oliver Tambo belonged to Huddlestone's congregation in Sophiatown until he was driven into exile. Nelson Mandela was confirmed in the Anglican church but became a practising Methodist in jail. The founding president of PAC, Robert Sobukwe, was a Methodist lay preacher.

In the English-speaking churches, as in the Catholic and Lutheran churches, the view was held that one could not simultaneously claim that human rights are a product of God's Kingdom and at the same time advocate separate development or apartheid in churches which are meant to be the instruments for the attainment of the Kingdom of God in South African society. The church lacks credibility if its adherents defend apartheid.

References

The literature on the topic of churches and apartheid in general and on the Reformed churches and apartheid is considerable. The development of churches' attitude to the apartheid system in South Africa is insightfully sketched in standard works such as J. W. Gruchy The Church Struggle in South Africa 1979, C. Villa-Vicencio Trapped in Apartheid A Socio-Theological History of the English-Speaking Churches 1988 and Z. Mbali, The Churches and Racism, A Black South African Perspective 1987. De Gruchy's presentation is historically descriptive while that of Villa-Vicencio is historically sociological. De Gruchy and Villa Vicencio look at the South African church struggle from a white anti-apartheid viewpoint while Mbali examines apartheid from a black standpoint. Mbali concentrates on WCC's involvement in South Africa.

Villa-Vicencio is more critical in his judgement of the English-speaking churches than de Gruchy. He looks at the socio-economic and political function of these churches in relation to structures of dominance in South Africa in a way which de Gruchy does not. Villa-Vicencio emphasizes that those churches which take part in racial and economic domination cannot wash their hands of apartheid.

Beyers Naudé and South Africa's Christian Institute

Beyers Naudé belonged to NGK and took part in the Cottesloe consultation. He was behind the establishment of South Africa's Christian Institute, an ecumenical organization with the task of promoting dialogue between the native white and English-speaking Christians and of bearing witness for justice and reconciliation between the races in South Africa. This led to him being deprived of his status as minister by his church and eventually to him finally being banned by the state. NGK delegates were prepared to reject the Biblical and theological justification of apartheid by agreeing to the Cottesloe consultation's recommendations.[79] With the exception of Naudé, they later retreated from this position. He was the only one in the NGK delegation who stood firm. Hendrik Verwoerd, later Prime Minister, had been Naudé's teacher in sociology at university. Naudé viewed Verwoerd as a brilliant, well-prepared and disciplined lecturer. His teaching was characterized by uncompromising logic. However, when Verwoerd presented apartheid, he left out important human elements and failed to allow for human aggression, irrationality, mistakes, recognition of error, historical irony or grace and forgiveness.

---

[79] The Cottesloe Consultation Statement 1961 in J. de Gruchy and C. Villa-Vicencio eds Apartheid is a Heresy 1983, 148–153.

Membership in the South African Institute was individual. It gave priority to study and discussion groups, conference, publications and co-operation with ecumenical organizations working for the same ideal. The Institute had a freedom to act which a Council of Churches lacked because of its accountability to its member church. B. Naudé as Director for South Africa's Christian Institute (1963–1977) received considerable international recognition, but was persecuted by white society in South Africa. He was arrested and interrogated and the Christian Institute was declared by NGK to be heretical.

There was conflict between South Africa's Christian Institute and NGK. In 1965, the general synod ordered all church members to withdraw from the Christian Institute. Naudé failed to influence NGK and white Afrikaner Christians and therefore turned more and more to seeking the support of the English speaking Christians. However, he did not acquire enough decisive support to bring about a fundamental social change. For this reason, he made contact with the blacks in their struggle. The Institute helped to formulate a South African theology of liberation which exerted its major influence in the black community. During the Soweto rebellion in 1976, the Institute supported those at the forefront of black protest and protested at the death of Steve Biko after torture. This stance led to South Africa's Christian Institute being declared illegal in 1977.

If Sharpeville in 1960 indirectly gave rise to the Christian Institute, the Soweto disturbances in 1976 led to its closure. The Institute supported the blacks. It was completely on the side of the rebels in Soweto. On 19 October 1977, the government authorities declared the Institute to be illegal and placed a ban on its leader. The witness of the Institute had thus been silenced but it was continued in other forms by the South African Council of Churches which from 1978 was led by Bishop Desmond Tutu. Beyers Naudé became a symbol for resistance and hope, and this was the title of a *festschrift* on his seventieth birthday.

References

The conflict over apartheid is reflected in the life and work of Beyers Naudé, an ecclesiastic belonging to the South African Reformed church. This is analyzed by P. Walshe in Church versus State in South Africa, The Case of the Christian Institute, 1983. For Naudé's life and work, see also C. Villa-Vicencio and J. W. de Gruchy eds. Resistance and Hope, South African essays in honour of Beyers Naudé 1985 and C. Ryan, Beyers Naudé Pilgrimage of Fate, 1990.

The South African Council of Churches's Message to the People of South Africa

South Africa's Christian Institute existed between 1963 to 1977. 1968 saw the creation of the South African Council of Churches which was set up to facilitate co-operation between the churches. Together these two bodies from the end of the Sixties formed instruments of prophetic leadership in the struggle against apartheid. During the 1960s and 1970s, the South African Council of

Churches became an important ecumenical centre. It took up questions of social justice. Along with the Christian Institute, it prepared *The Message to the People of South Africa*. This was published in June 1968 and rejects the ideology of apartheid as incompatible with the Gospel. For the first time in an official church document, apartheid was declared to be a false gospel.

The starting point of *The Message to the People of South Africa* was a total opposition to apartheid. The Gospel of Jesus Christ shows that God in Christ has broken down the walls between God and human beings and between human beings themselves. Christ has overcome the forces which destructively separate people from one another. Race and nationality have no part to play in drawing distinctive boundaries within the brotherhood Christ has established. In South Africa, the races were rigidly segregated. Racial segregation was said by some to be an expression of God's will and was carried out in the name of Christianity. But racial segregation is contrary to the Gospel of Jesus Christ. The first Christians discovered that God created a new community in which differences of race, language, nation, culture and tradition had no power to separate human beings from human beings. In South Africa, racial differences were assigned too great a significance. A belief in the vital importance of racial identity leads to a denial of the tenets of the Christian Gospel. According to the latter, our brothers are not simply those who are members of our particular racial group but the person who comes our way and who is given to us by God. The Gospel requires us to act from a spirit of reconciliation in Jesus Christ. Racial segregation shows a disbelief in the Gospel. The church ceases to be a church if it supports such a policy with the help of the Gospel. The Christian receives his identity from his communion with Christ. In the case of apartheid, human beings are given their identity by being distinguished or separated from others. Apartheid rejects God´s reconciliation in Christ. Apartheid calls what is good, evil. God judges us, not on the basis of our loyalty to a group, but on our willingness to be born again in communion with Christ. If we try to reconcile Christianity with the South African way of life, we shall discover that we have allowed an idol to take the place of Christ. Where the church ceases to obey Jesus Christ, it ceases to be a church. It severs the link between itself and the Kingdom of God. The mission of the church is to make human beings experience God's power in activity, to transform hostility into love between brothers and to express God's reconciliation and forgiveness here and now.[80]

In 1968, the Council of Churches produced *A Message to the People of South Africa* in which apartheid and separate development were said to be in contradiction to Jesus Christ. They denied Christ's work of reconciliation. For those behind the message, apartheid implied a denial of the Christian doctrine on human beings and ultimately its doctrine on God. Apartheid was heresy.

---

[80] South African Council of Churches, A Message to the People of South Africa 1968 in C. Villa Vicencpio Between Christ and Caesar, Classic and Contemporary Texts on Church and State, 1986, 214–216.

NGK and Human Relations in the Light of Scripture

Soweto 1976 was a continuation of Sharpville 1960. Soweto was a symbol of black protest against apartheid. Two years before Soweto, NGK took action on the race issue and paved the way for the disturbances in Soweto. NGK's general synod issued a statement on apartheid, viewed from an overall theological standpoint: it was entitled *Human Relations and the South African Scene in the Light of Scripture*, 1974. NGK treats state and church as distinct institutions, each with its own task. The principal task of the church is to preach the Gospel of personal salvation in Christ. However, the church is also charged with preaching the Word of God in all areas of life and also for the authorities. The church must be an instrument of the Kingdom of God. It must proclaim the dominion of Christ also within the domain of the state. The church's behaviour towards the state must be based on the church recognizing the authorities' competence in other matters. It is not the task of the church to tell the authorities how they are to regulate relations between the different groups in a multi-national and multiracial situation since the Bible gives no clear instruction on this matter. It is the task of the state to maintain general order within its own area of jurisdiction, to regulate for the sake of general order the legal interests of different groups, to fight evil and to maintain and support justice. The state must act in accordance with Biblical norms i.e. love of God and one's neighbour as guiding lines for the exercise of justice. As an institution, the church subordinates itself to the authorities and the law of the state, provided that the legal order is not in conflict with the Word of God. Human rights are the rights which God has assigned human beings as bearers of His image so that they can fulfil their obligations and their vocation as human beings. The exercise of human rights cannot be isolated from the society in which individuals live their lives. Society has collective rights. A political system based upon separate development for different groups of the population can be justified on the basis of the Bible but the Gospel message of loving our neighbour must at all times be the ethical norm for establishing sound relations between peoples. Since Christians are obliged to apply the principles of the Kingdom of God within politics, they must enjoy freedom of political thought and action, exercized in a responsible way in accordance with the Word of God.[81]

In this document, NGK formulates traditional Reformed theology according to which all social life is placed under the dominion of Christ. At the same time, the document from this standpoint undeniably legitimizes apartheid. Separate development does not conflict with the Reformed interpretation of Christianity but is, according to NGK, a logical consequence of it. All churches in South Africa were agreed that human rights are related to the Kingdom of God. Here there is a consensus. NGK reacted to the Christian declaration on human rights which WARC issued in 1976. But NGK found

---

[81] Human Relations and the South African Scene in the Light of Scripture 1974 in op. cit., 22–224.

318

that apartheid was compatible with the maintenance and defence of human rights. This shows that NGK's conception of human rights was given a theologically motivated meaning which deviated from the corresponding interpretation by the English-speaking, Coloured, Catholic and Lutheran churches. The intensity of the theological conflict about apartheid depended principally on the fact that apartheid was looked upon as heresy, not only by the aforementioned national churches, but also by the majority of Reformed churches throughout the world.

The World Alliance of Reformed Churches, NG Mission Church and Racism

NGK on account of its support for apartheid distanced itself from the Reformed churches in WARC as well as from the Coloured Reformed churches in South Africa. This was apparent at two important synods which were held in 1982. That year WARC held its General Assembly in Ottawa. At the meeting, a clear and unequivocal stand was taken against racism in South Africa. It was asserted that the Gospel of Jesus Christ demands a community of believers which goes beyond all confines of race—a community in which love of Christ and of our fellow human beings has surmounted differences with regard to race and colour. The Gospel fights racism which is a form of idolatry. Racism encourages a false sense of superiority; it denies the common humanity of believers, as it does the humanizing and reconciling work of Christ. It systematizes oppression, domination and injustice. The struggle against racism is a task for the church as a consequence of the Gospel. Apartheid in South Africa is a unique challenge for the churches in the Reformed tradition. White Reformed churches have developed the apartheid policy and given that system its theological and moral justification. The division of the Reformed churches in South Africa on the basis of race and colour is defended as a faithful interpretation of the Will of God and of the Reformed view of the church in the world. Such a situation is a challenge to WARC.[82]

At WARC's meeting at Ottawa in 1982, it was explained that God's promises to His world and the the church directly contradict the ideal and practice of apartheid. These promises which were clearly proclaimed by the prophets and brought to fulfilment in Jesus Christ, are peace, justice and liberation. Those churches which have accepted the tenets of Reformed belief, have thereby committed themselves to living as the people of God and to showing in their daily life and service what that means. This commitment demands a concrete manifestation of the community between races, of common witness to injustice and inequality in society and of oneness at the Lord's table. The Nederduitse Gereformeerde Kerk (NGK) and the Nederduitsch Hervormde Kerk

---

[82] WARC 1982, Racism and South Africa, Statement adopted by the General Council in Ottawa on 25 August 1982 in J. de Gruchy and C. Villa-Vicencio eds. Apartheid is a heresy, 1983, 169.

(NHK) did not only accept the apartheid system but took active steps to justify it. They thus abuse the Gospel and the Reformed faith and oppose in doctrine and action the promises they have professed to believe in. For this reason, the General Council defined this situation as one of status confessionis for the Reformed churches. This meant that the issue was viewed as one where it was impossible to have a different opinion, without seriously threatening the essential nature of the Reformed churches and their common kernel of beliefs. Along with the black Reformed Christians, the Ottawa meeting declared that apartheid was a sin. Furthermore its moral and theological justification was a parody of the Gospel. By disobeying the Word of God, it is a theological heresy.[83] Apartheid leads via the racist structures of society to privileges for the whites at the expense of the blacks. Apartheid was institutionalized in South Africa's laws, politics and structures. The General Council excluded the Nederduitse Gereformeerde Kerk and the Nederduitsch Hervormde Kerk from membership in WARC until such times as they had altered their attitudes. As a condition for their readmission, they must be prepared to accept inter alia that black Christians may not be excluded from divine services, in particular from communion.[84]

This document issued by the supreme decision-making body of the family of Reformed churches does not simply reject apartheid in South Africa. It moreover names specifically two white Reformed churches and excludes them from WARC. Apartheid was condemned as a flagrant violation of human rights and as a grave heresy.

The Nederduitse Gereformeerde Sendingkerk (NG Mission Church) followed up WARC's statement on racism and South Africa. For the NG Mission Church in South Africa, apartheid constituted a status confessionis. Apartheid is a sin and any theological justification of it, is a parody of the Gospel. According to NG Mission Church's synod, NGK believed in the ideology of apartheid which is directly contrary to the Gospel message of reconciliation and the visible unity of the church.[85] The national synod rejected the absolutification of separate development when this absolutification broke down the visible unity of the church or led to the foundation of other and different churches. This passage meant that the synod rejected every doctrine which in the name of the Gospel or as an expression of the Will of God sanctions separate development on the basis of race and colour.[86] The branch of the Dutch Reformed church in South Africa which contained coloured people added essentially nothing to what had emerged at WARC's General Assembly in Ottawa several months earlier in the same year. But because of the position it adopted, it made the doctrinal split at the national level in South Africa quite clear.

---

[83] Op. cit., 170.
[84] Op. cit., 171 f.
[85] Nederduitse Gereformeerde Sendingkerk (NG Mission Church) Confession of Faith 1982 in C. Villa-Vicencio Between Christ and Caesar Classic and Contemporary Texts on Church and State, 1986, 241.
[86] Op. cit., 243.

Apartheid and the Reformed Union

The churches in WARC branded apartheid as a heresy. The Reformed churches in Germany along with other Reformed churches in Europe made an attempt to alter the situation in South Africa. The booklet *Apartheid und Reformierte Kirche Dokumente eines Konflikt im Auftrag des Reformierten Bundes* zusammengestellt von Heinz-Hermann Nodholt 1983, formed part of these efforts. It describes the situation for the white and black Reformed churches and covers the South African contacts of the Reformed Union.[87] The Reformed Union was composed of Reformed churches from West Germany, the Netherlands and Switzerland and formed part of WARC.

In *an introductory* chapter, the main contours of the relationship between *apartheid and the Reformed church in South Africa* were sketched. The Nationalist party introduced apartheid as soon as it took power in 1948. This party had close ties with NGK, which was the largest church among South African whites. NGK was deeply involved in the development of the apartheid system. It was one of the bulwarks of this system. The majority of the members of this church were actively committed to preserving the current distribution of power.[88] How is it possible for white South African Christians to call something good which is condemned by other Christians? How can an ethic of apartheid, which Christians all over the world dislike, grow out of Reformed theology? This is a challenge for Reformed Christians throughout the world.[89] NGK prepared the moral and structural foundation for the Nationalist Party's racial policy. It helped to create a conducive atmosphere for the implementation of the apartheid system. Apartheid is derived directly from the Bible.[90] Separate places of residence for whites and blacks are in accordance with the Will of God. The policy of separate development is derived from the Bible.[91] In such a church, there is no room for prophetic protest about unsatisfactory situations in the state and society.[92]

In *one* chapter, the question of apartheid and the *Reformed Union in the West Germany* is discussed. On 7 April 1979, representatives of the Reformed Union in West Germany and NGK met in Frankfurt. The Reformed Union stressed that the church in South Africa must adopt a prophetic role by publicly defending what is right and freedom without racial segregation.[93] In September 1979, the Reformed Union issued a statement about its relations to the Reformed churches in South Africa.[94] Reconciliation in Jesus Christ produces the relation of dialogue between God and human beings and between human

---

[87] Apartheid und Reformierte Kirche Dokumente eines Konflikt im Auftrag des Reformierten Bundes zusammengestellt von Heinz-Hermann Nordholt 1983, 7 f.
[88] Op. cit., 10.
[89] Op. cit., 11.
[90] Op. cit., 12.
[91] Op. cit., 13.
[92] Op. cit., 15.
[93] Op. cit., 37.
[94] Op. cit., 38.

beings themselves. It is the task of the church to proclaim reconciliation, to live in accordance with it and to come to its defence. Our fellow human beings are not objects, but partners. A system of coexistence which is based on the segregation of ethnic groups is the very opposite of reconciliation. Apartheid isolates human beings from each other and denies reconciliation.[95]

In a third chapter, an analysis of apartheid and the Reformed churches in the Netherlands and Switzerland is presented.[96] Finally there is a discussion of apartheid and WARC. In it, it is pointed out that Allan Boesak studied theology in South Africa and the USA. He obtained his doctorate in the Netherlands. His dissertation Farewell to Innocence A Socio-Ethical Study on Black Theology and Black Power 1977 enjoys a status as a standard work on black theology. With the choice of Boesak as President of WARC, the General Assembly displayed its solidarity with the victims of the apartheid system.[97]

Besides his dissertation, Allan Boesak was the author of several theological books. Among them may be noted *Black and Reformed: apartheid, liberation and the Calvinist tradition.* The book contains a collection of addresses which Boesak gave between 1974 and 1983 to various groups including black citizens in South Africa when they organized themselves into a political movement. His literary output also includes *If this is a Treason I am guilty* 1987 and *The Finger of God: Sermons on Faith and Socio-Political Responsibility,* 1982.

The South African Council of Churches and Prayer for Social Change

A Call to Prayer for the End to Unjust Rule of 16 June 1985 is in line with the attitude which the members of the South African Council of Churches—i.e the English-speaking churches—had adopted since 1948 when the apartheid regime came to power. These churches repeatedly condemned apartheid and declared it to be a heresy.[98] Beyers Naudé—the general secretary of the South African Council of Churches—was one of the authors behind *A Theological Rationale and a Call to Prayer for the End to Unjust Rule.*[99] Allan Boesak emerged as one of the sources inspiring the document.[100] It aimed at challenging the churches rather than being a statement of their position. Black Christians supported the document while a number of whites condemned it. The Christians who were prepared to openly set themselves up against the state were in a minority. Calvin was cited. He had asserted that if the authorities request something which is against what God stands for, one should let it pass unheeded.[101]

---

[95] Op. cit., 40.
[96] Op .cit., 60–67.
[97] Op. cit., 74.
[98] A. A. Boesak and C. Villa-Vicencio, When Prayer Makes News 1986, 16.
[99] Op. cit., 17, 20.
[100] Op. cit., 19.
[101] Op. cit., 20 f.

Let us now mention some of the main points in the South African Council of Churches' call to prayer for social change. They point to developments in South Africa in the treatment of non-whites as a flagrant violation of any reasonable concept of human rights. Soweto on 16 June 1976 is South Africa's most remarkable symbol of black resistance. Around 700 people were killed and hundreds were wounded. These events formed a fundamental crisis in South African society which the authorities were unable to solve. They represented a period of resistance which began on 21 March 1960 when police killed 69 people and wounded a further 180 at the Sharpville Massacre. Sharpville was a turning point. Protest hardened into resistance and the blacks were forced to think more sharply and clearly about the need for a fundamental change. In the wake of Sharpville, church leaders from South Africa and world church leaders met at Cottesloes in December 1960 to reject the apartheid system as un-Christian. As a response to this reality, the South African Council of Churches had condemned the racial structures and the economic framework of oppression in South Africa. They conflict with the Will of God as it is made known in the Bible and in ecclesiastical tradition.[102]

The document continues by noting that on 16 June, 25 years after the beginning of resistance, it is right to remember those whose blood has been shed in resistance and to protest against an unjust system. It is also right that Christians show anew their response to a system which all right-thinking people view as unjust. One must pray that God would replace the existing structures of oppression by another system which is just and remove from power those who insist in opposing His laws, replacing them with leaders who will rule with justice and mercy.[103] Among the historically prominent theologians to be cited is, among others, Karl Barth. He spoke of the duty of the church to pray for the state. Such a prayer is impossible without commitment to work for a good and legitimate government.[104] The pronouncements of the ecclesiastical meetings of the Roman Catholic and mainline Protestant churches (with the exception of the Dutch Reformed churches) hold that the present government on account of its structures of oppression is in opposition to the Christian Gospel to which the country's churches try to be loyal. The prayer is that God should remove from His people the tyrannical framework of oppression and the present rulers of the country. The prayer calls for God's rule to be established in South Africa. The invitation from the South African Council of Churches to participate in prayer for a new and just order in the country was sent to Christians and all men and women of goodwill.[105]

A Theological Rationale and a Call to Prayer for the End to Unjust Rule became the subject of comment. Two prominent South African theologians tried to sum up the position with regard to the prayer's significance in a situa-

---

[102] A Theological Rationale and a Call to Prayer for the End to Unjust Rule in op.cit., 25 f.
[103] Op. cit., 26.
[104] Op. cit., 27.
[105] Op. cit., 29.

tion of social conflict. Charles Villa-Vicencio expressed the theological view of the prayer's place and function which he held lay behind *Call to Prayer for Social Change*. He emphasized that prayer is conscious reflection on the place of human beings in life in response to God who is God of the universe and the Lord of history. Prayer integrates the believer's feeling for the divine in his or her social existence. It is a recognition of a God encountered as the very mystery of life in the midst of life.[106] In connection with *Call to Prayer for Social Change, John W. de Gruchy* defined true prayer as a way of relating to God where we begin to discover God's Will rather than our own and submit our affairs to God in relation to what we know of God's purposes. It is not a way of fleeing from reality or the struggle for justice in the world, but is profoundly a path leading to involvement. In their prayers, Christians do not turn away from the world but rather they turn with God to face the world.[107]

The South African Council of Churches believed that the apartheid system violated fundamental human rights and it exhorted South African Christians to pray for the removal of the people then in power and the appointment of a new government. The prayer was used as an instrument in the campaign to bring about radical social change in South Africa.

The Kairos Document

The Kairos document was produced by a group of theologians who called themselves Kairos theologians. The document is aimed primarily at the church as a call for renewal and action. The non-revised version of the document from 1985 is published in Charles Villa-Vicencio *Between Christ and Caesar Classic and Contemporary Texts on Church and State* 1986 and *P C R Information Reports and Background Papers Special Issue Challenge to the Church November* 1985. The second revised 1986 edition is published in W. H. Logan ed. *The Kairos Covenant Standing with South African Christians* 1988. In the foreword of September 1985, the Kairos document is described as a Christian, Biblical and theological commentary on the political crisis in South Africa.[108] In the foreword of September 1986, it is held that the moment of truth—*kairos*—has finally arrived.[109] Since the discussion between September 1985 and September 1986 has presented an opportunity for more profound reflection upon the issues spotlighted by the Kairos document, we shall refer, in what follows, to the content of the second edition of this document. The section which was completely rewritten for the second edition is that dealing with prophetic theology.[110]

The crisis in South Africa is such that one can speak of kairos, a moment of

---

[106] Op. cit., 44.
[107] Op. cit., 99.
[108] The Kairos Document in W. H. Logan ed. The Kairos Covenant Standing with South African Christians 1988, 2.
[109] Op. cit., 4.
[110] Op. cit., 5.

truth, not merely for apartheid but also for the church and all creeds and religions. The theologians responsible for the document try to understand the theological import of this moment in history. The time is ripe for action. A crisis is a moment of truth which shows us who we really are. The crisis shows that the church is split. There are Christians on both sides of the conflict. Does this show that the Bible can be used for any purpose whatever? [111] The conflict in South Africa is between the oppressors and the oppressed. Both the oppressors and the oppressed claim to be loyal to the same church. The church is divided against itself. The theologians behind the Kairos document distinguish between three types of theologians: *state theologians, church theologians and prophetic theologians.*[112]

The South African apartheid state has its own theology, namely state theology. It provides a theological justification of the status quo with its racism, capitalism and totalitarianism. It confers its blessing on injustice, canonizes the will of the powerful and reduces the poor to passivity, obedience and apathy. It misuses theological concepts and Biblical texts for its own political purposes. Romans 13:1–7 is used to give an absolute and divine authority to the state. The idea of law and order is employed to control people. The word communist is used against all who reject the state theology.[113] The law is made up of apartheid's discriminatory laws and order is the institutionalized disorder of oppression. Anyone trying to change this law and order is labelled lawless and subversive. But the law must be just and the order right.[114] The security of the state is more important than justice for state theology. Those who in God's name work to change the unjust framework of society are branded as agitators and rebels. Church leaders are encouraged to restrict themselves to proclaiming the Gospel and not to involve themselves in politics. The state itself adopts a political theology which claims to have Divine approval for maintaining an unjust system of law and order.[115] In state theology, we encounter a God Who historically is on the side of the Boer pioneers,depriving the blacks of their land and giving a majority of the country to His chosen people.[116] The God of the South African state is the Devil in the guise of Almighty God—the Anti-Christ. The oppressive South African regime uses Christianity to justify its evil ways.[117]

Within the framework of church theology, the issue in South Africa is not about personal guilt but about structural injustice. It cannot be dealt with by individual conversions as a result of the proclamation of the commandment to love.[118] In church theology, social analysis is lacking due to the type of faith

---

[111] Op. cit., 7.
[112] Op. cit., 8.
[113] Op. cit., 9.
[114] Op. cit., 12
[115] Op. cit., 13.
[116] Op. cit., 14.
[117] Op. cit., 15.
[118] Op. cit., 19.

and spirituality which has been dominant for centuries. The spiritual life has tended to deal with supernatural things which have little to do with the affairs of this world. Social and political issues have been conceived as worldly matters which have nothing to do with the spiritual matters of the church. Spiritual life has been thought of as something private and individual. Social problems are outside the province of spirituality.[119] This type of belief and spirituality has, however, no Biblical foundation. The Scriptures do not distinguish human beings from the world in which they live. They do not draw a line between the individual and the social or between individuals' private lives and their lives in general. God grants salvation to whole human beings as parts of God's total creation.[120]

From the standpoint of prophetic theology, the conflict is not only about race war. The racist element is certainly present but when viewed more profoundly, the essential aspect of the situation is its tyranny and oppression. It concerns the relationship between the oppressor and the oppresed. The oppressors are advocates of a sinful cause and unjust interests. The oppressed represent the opposing cause and interest, that of justice and liberty. In South African society, there is a structural conflict between those two causes. Structural oppression in South Africa in the form of apartheid will lead to internal conflict. There are those who draw advantage from the status quo and who are determined to preserve it. The system benefits them and provides them with welfare and a high living standard. They wish to ensure that this state of affairs will continue. On the other hand, there are those who do not benefit from the system. They are paid starvation wages; they are separated from their families; they are moved around like cattle and dumped in the homelands to starve. All this is done to benefit a privileged minority.[121] It is not in their interest to allow the system to continue, even in reformed form. They are no longer prepared to be oppressed and exploited. They are determined to change the system radically so that it no longer benefits only the privileged few. They are willing to do so even at the cost of their own lives. They demand justice for all. independent of race, colour, sex or status. It is a question of two conflicting projects and there is no room for compromise. Either there is full and equal justice or there is not. Prophetic theology faces us with a basic choice which admits no compromise. The structures of society must be altered so that human beings are brought face to face with one another as oppressors and oppressed. That is the kairos for South Africa.[122]

The apartheid system is one in which a minority regime elected by a small part of the people has received a mandate to rule in the white community's interest and for its benefit. Such a mandate is totally incompatible with the general good of the people and the aim of every proper government is to pro-

---

[119] Op. cit., 23.
[120] Op. cit., 24.
[121] Op. cit., 29.
[122] Op. cit., 30.

mote the good of its people. To promote the general good is to govern in the interests of the whole people. Because the mandate of apartheid is to govern exclusively in the interest of the whites, rather than in the interest of all members of the community, it ends by not even governing in the interests of the whites. It becomes an enemy of the people.[123] A regime which in principle is the enemy of the people, cannot begin to govern in the interests of the people as a whole. It can only be replaced by another government—one elected by the majority of the people—with a mandate to rule in the interests of the whole people. A regime which has made itself an enemy of the people has thereby also made itself an enemy of God. Human beings are made in the likeness of God and what we do unto the least of them, we do unto God. Love towards both the oppressed and oppressors is displayed by appointing a just regime dedicated to the general good of all the people.[124]

The Kairos document does not in fact concentrate on the tension between black and white but on the tension which exists between an oppressed majority and a privileged minority. The issue is either to change the political order or preserve it. The Lutheran World Federation and World Alliance of Reformed Churches (WARC) criticized the churches for supporting and justifying the apartheid system. The Kairos document points to the opposition between the power élite 's view of reality and the oppressed majority's view of reality. The tension between the élite and the majority runs deeper than the opposition between white and black. The Kairos document is a theological commentary on the South African situation. It offers an interpretation of this situation. It formed part of the liberation struggle in South Africa to uphold a just society. It paved the way for a situation in which human rights—the rights of the majority and not just the rights of the minority—could be implemented and upheld in that country.

Legitimacy and Human Rights in South Africa

The Kairos document maintained that the South African regime lacked moral legitimacy.[125] The issue of the South African regime's legitimacy is the main problem discussed in C. Lienemann-Perrin and W. Lienemann eds. *Political Legitimacy in South Africa* 1988. Contacts were established between the Evangelical church in Germany—EKD—and liberation movements in South Africa after the visit of Oliver Tambo, the President of ANC, to West Germany in Novemeber 1980. A study group on South Africa was set up at the Protestant Institute for Interdisciplinary Research at Heidelberg. It concentrated on issues of political legitimacy and illegitimacy in South Africa. Inspiration and ideas came from EKD and the South African Council of Churches as well as from

---

[123] Op. cit., 31 f.
[124] Op. cit., 32 f.
[125] Op. cit., 31.

the study group on South Africa itself. Ulrich Duchrow belonged to the group. This activity resulted in the book *Political Legitimacy in South Africa.*

The International Commission of Jurists sent a mission to South Africa in 1987 to investigate reports on the oppression of the blacks. The standard of comparison for their judgement was the universal declaration of human rights. They concentrated on trades union rights, discriminatory legislation such as the pass laws, the independence of lawyers, the security system, freedom of speech, human rights in the homelands etc. A final report is to be found in G. Bindman ed. *South Africa Human Rights and the Rule of Law International Commission of Jurists* 1988. The apartheid situation in South Africa is discussed on the basis of the work of the International Commission of Jurists. The cornerstone is the Population Registration Act of 1950. In accordance with it, every individual is classified as belonging to a special racial group. South African citizens receive different rights and privileges according to this racial classification.[126] The International Commission of Jurists came to the conclusion that in South Africa, an undemocratic government, by means of its legislation, has undermined human rights.[127] Apartheid is in itself a violation of human rights.[128]

The Rustenburg Declaration

The national conference of church leaders in South Africa met at Rustenburg in November 1990. It came together at a critical moment as far as change was concerned and issued a declaration, the so-called Rustenburg declaration. In it, it was held that all are agreed that apartheid is a sin.[129] In its intention, its implementation and with regard to its consequences, apartheid is an evil policy. Even if apartheid has been legitimized with the help of the Bible and theology, it is an act of disobedience against God, a denial of the Gospel of Jesus Christ and a sin against the oneness of the Holy Spirit. Some church leaders ignored the evil of apartheid and spiritualized the Gospel by proclaiming the sufficiency of individual salvation without social change.[130] The Rustenburg declaration contained an extensive confession by church leaders of errors committed by them under the South African apartheid regime. They appeal for an end to all discrimination within the church on the basis of sex or race. They call upon the government to repeal all apartheid legislation.[131]

The Rustenburg conference was held when the apartheid system in South

---

[126] Op. cit., G. Bindman ed. South Africa Human Rights and the Rule of Law 1988, 5 f.
[127] Op. cit., 144 f.
[128] Op. cit., 149.
[129] The Rustenburg Declaration Novemeber 1990 in L. Alberts and F. Chikane eds. The Road to Rustenburg 1991, 275.
[130] Op. cit., 277.
[131] Op. cit., 280. For the issue of dismantling the apartheid system, the reader is referred to E. N. Tjönneland, South Africa after Apartheid The End of Apartheid Future Regional Cooperation and Foreign Aid 1992. Another illuminating work is P. Nherere and M. D. Engelbronner-Kolff The Institutionalization of Human Rights in Southern Africa 1993.

Africa faced the prospect of being dismantled and when a new society embodying full respect for the equal value and rights of all human beings could begin to to be built. Through its leaders, the church expressed the hope that it could play a constructive role in the events which were about to take place.

8.9 Summary

The Christian church played an ambivalent political role in South Africa. On the one hand, sections of it—notably NGK—legitimized the ruling class's ideology of apartheid. On the other hand, other sections of the church—principally the English-speaking churches and the Black churches—acted as driving forces for social change and for the elimination of the apartheid system. The church in South Africa worked simultaneously for the status quo and for a change in the dominant social order. NGK was imprisoned in the white, socio-economic structures of South African society and reflected the apartheid ideas of the white ruling class. But there were also churches and individuals Christians who formed the vanguard of radical social reform.

Both wings of the South African church claimed to advocate human rights and to work actively for their implementation. However, they attributed quite different meanings to the concept of human rights and derived different concrete conclusions about its role in South African society.

The church's ambivalent attitude to the white South African apartheid state led however to the eventual victory of the forces of reform. They contributed actively to the dismantling of the apartheid system. Before this, the part of the church which was critical of apartheid had operated under great pressure. The campaign against apartheid provides human examples of moral courage.

References

The journal Reformed World was WARC's main forum for the discussion and analysis of human rights. The 1970s and 80s witnessed an ongoing discussion of human rights from the Reformed perspective. The Reformed Strasbourg theologian J.F. Collange wrote about the churches and human rights in Europe in December 1983. Jürgen Moltmann was a recurring writer on human rights in Reformed World. He functioned somewhat as WARC's representative theologian in this matter. The stance adopted on human rights by the Reformed denomination bears his imprint. WARC's history of theology is sketched in A. P. Sell, A Reformed, Evangelical, Catholic Theology The Contribution of the World Alliance of Reformed Churches 1975–1982, 1991.

Karl Barth played a central role in Reformed Christianity and in various connections, he touches on the issue of human rights. See e.g. K. Barth, The Christian Community and the Civil Community, State and Church: Three Essays ed W. Herberg, 1960. Barth was cited as a theological authority within WARC. He was the forerunner to Moltmann. The Reformed ecumenical synod produced a series of documents which are relevant to the issue under analysis in Church and Nation: Theological Conference Papers (Reformed Ecumenical Synod) 1981. Evangelical Christianity in South Africa is analyzed in Evangelical Witness in South Africa: a Critique of Evangelical Theology and Practice by South African Evangelicals, 1986.

In addition to the books which have already been named as sources for the present work, several additional works which are relevant to the theme of Reformed Christianity and human rights, should be cited. There is for example R. V. Andelson, Imputed Rights: An Essay in Christian Social Theory, 1971. He bases his reasoning on the the Reformed tradition, notably Calvin's *imago dei*. Other works include R. Forbes, Humanism and Human Rights: A Christian View, 1968; S. Greidanus, Human Rights in Biblical Perspectives Calvin Theological Journal 1984 19 (1); K. Hertz, Tutu and Boesak: Liberation Theology as Praxis Mid-Stream 1987 26 (1); P. Marshall-E. Vanderkloet, Foundations of Human Rights, 1981; P. Marshall. Human Rights Theories in Christian Perspective 1983; E. Rogers, Thinking about Human Rights 1978; and G. Spykman, Towards a Biblical View of Human Rights Res Theological Forum 7:1, December 1979.

E. Moltmann-Wendel is a feminist theologian and links this theology with human rights in E. Moltmann-Wendel ed. Menschenrechte für die Frau Christliche Iniativen zur Frauenbefreiung 1974 and the same author's The Women's Movement in Germany, Lutheran World 1975 22 (2).

PART 4

Conclusion

CHAPTER 9

Human Rights—An Inter-Cultural, Inter-Denominational and Inter-Religious Issue

9.1 Human Rights in History

We must distinguish between human rights as a phenomeon in the history of ideas and the actual implementation of human rights. In the latter case, it is important to point out the discrepancy between the formulation of the ideas of human rights and the way in which they are put into practice. Medieval society and Nazism provide good illustrations.

The 1994 Oxford Amnesty Lectures dealt with the theme of *Historical Change & Human Rights* and were given by the historian, Olwen Hufton. In them, it was pointed out that the philosopher and the historian approach the issue of human rights in different ways. The historian tries to capture how human rights were actually put into practice and how they functioned. Having adopted this viewpoint, he then asks what role religion has played in relation to human rights. He is mainly concerned with describing the historical process and the part played by human rights in the events; he is not primarily interested in conceptual analyses of the notion of human rights.

The late Christian medieval period shows how religion was used to violate human rights. The church tried intellectual dissidents and heretics and executed them, often burning them alive. European Jewry was also exposed to cruel treatment. Antisemitism was viewed as a kind of precondition for the creation of a Christian European identity. Lepers were deprived of their rights as human beings. They were banished from human society.

In Nazi Germany, human rights were violated in a way which had never before occurred in an advanced industrial society. There were a number of underlying causes. The absence of powerful protest from the Christian churches was one factor which allowed the holocaust to take place. Unemployment and the economic depression paved the way for a Messiah promising a Utopian vision of national rebirth. Nazism made German blood the criterion for national membership. Nationalism and national identity entered the scene in their most brutal form.

In the medieval treatment of heretics, Jews and lepers, religion played an active role in the violation of human dignity and human rights. In the Nazi extermination of the Jews, on the other hand, religion played a passive role by doing little or nothing. It thereby helped to bring about violations of human rights. Both examples show, however, that religion in practice had not contributed to the implementation of human rights. Religion did not make the world a better place for Jews, heretics and lepers in Medieval times nor did it do much for Jews in Nazi Germany. In these particular cases, it failed to contribute to human well-being and human dignity.

9.2. Human Rights in a Pluralistic World

UNESCO was responsible for conferences on human rights at Maastricht in 1987 and in Middelburg in 1988. The aim was to analyze the relations between human rights as individual rights and human rights as rights associated with a collective, in order to attain better understanding of how these rights were viewed in different cultural, religious and socio-economic systems. The conferences gave rise to published proceedings in the shape of *Human Rights in a Pluralist World, Individuals and Collectivities* 1990 by J. Berting and others. A combination of legal and social science viewpoints dominate the presentation. The book discusses human rights as individual and collective rights as well as religious attitudes towards human rights. It continues with the question of the relationship between social change and human rights and ends with a discussion of the right to cultural identity.

The ideas which were presented at Maastricht and Middelburg at the end of the 1980s are confirmed by the results reached in the present investigation. Human rights, as far as their content is concerned, are essentially determined in a pluralistic world by the cultural and religious context in which they are put forward and applied. This does not rule out that, at a general theoretical level, they are to be found in different cultural and religious traditions. On the one hand, they extend beyond religious and denominational boundaries; on the other hand, the content assigned to them is determined by the local formulation and application. The ethical core expressed in human rights is common for all religions and denominations but the verbal formulations of these rights diverge and their applications have differing outcomes. Universalism and particularism are intertwined in the development of human rights in cultural and religious traditions. In research on human rights, there is some tension between universalism and relativism. Both viewpoints are not necessarily mutually exclusive but can in fact be combined.

Within the field of human rights, the legal approach has long been dominant but it is being increasingly counterbalanced by a social science approach. This is made clear in Bertil Dunér's book *Fria och lika i värde Mänskliga rättigheter i ett samhällsvetenskapligt perspektiv* [*Free and equal in value Human rights from a social science perspective*] 1992. A third variant is the religious studies approach. The aim of the present investigation has been to stress this latter approach to human rights in a pluralistic world without neglecting the legal and social science aspects. It is through the interaction between the different approaches that human rights can be understood as part of the historical process of development from the Nazi concentration camps to the fall of the Soviet empire. Because human rights have many aspects, any interpretation of their function and role in contemporary history must of necessity be multidimensional. Because they have a unique meaning neither within the great religious traditions nor in the interaction between them, a comparative religious studies approach is called for. Pluralism with respect to human rights holds both within the world religions as in the relations between the great religious traditions. The present investigation attempts to contribute to understanding human rights in a pluralistic world from a religious studies viewpoint without in the least calling into question that human rights also have legal and social science aspects. After the end of the Cold War and the fall of the Soviet empire, the polarization between communism and capitalism no longer dominates views of the development; instead the world religions are assigned a crucial significance also within the field of human rights.

9.3 The World Religions and Human Rights

Towards Greater Common Understanding

An issue of the reformist Roman Catholic journal Concilium in 1990 entitled *The Ethics of World Religions and Human Rights* contained a series of articles on human rights in different religions—Judaism, Islam, Hinduism and Buddhism. In the same way, the Catholic mission journal Studia Missionalia in 1990 devoted an issue to *Human Rights and Religions*. What were the factors which explain why attention was paid to this particular problem area? Several can be identified. The demands for a new economic world order was a challenge to the world religions and involvement in human rights was a response to the challenges set by the world situation. J. Gremillon throws light on this issue in *World Faiths and the New World Order A Muslim-Jewish-Christian search begins,* 1977. The shift from the more narrowly defined issue *the church and human rights* which was dealt with in Concilium 1979 to the wider one of *the world religions and human rights* was also a result of globalization and the dialogue between religions. This dialogue is analyzed in A. Camps *Partners in Dialogue, Christianity and Other World Religions*, 1983, L. Swidler ed *Toward a Universal Theology of Religion*, 1987 and in L. Swidler et al. eds *Death or Dialogue From the Age of Monologue to the Age of Dialogue,* 1990. There are substantial descriptions of the great world religions in H. Küng *Christianity and the World Religions, Paths to Dialogue with Islam, Hinduism and Buddhism,* 1986 where Hans Küng responds to these as a Christian theologian. The perspective has widened due to the decreasing distance between people and the increasing dialogue between them. The dialogue be-

tween the religions aims at a deeper, mutual understanding and respect between representatives of different cultures and religions. The boundaries of
world culture have shifted and this has reprecussions on human rights. This
issue is reflected in UNESCO/ International Institute of Philosophy *Ed Philosophical Foundations of Human Rights*, 1986. The trend is towards intercultural, interdenominational and interreligious approaches to human rights.

Concilium is a mirror of the spirit of the times and draws attention to answers by reformist Catholics to various challenges. They react to the issue of
human rights. In Studia Missionalia, *Christians write about human rights in
non-Christian religions*. In 1988, in an issue entitled *Teachers of Religion*, the
journal looked at the conceptual contents of the great world religions as they
have been communicated to us by their original teachers and prophets. Ever
since the 1940s, this journal has studied the cultural and religious situation in
those countries where the Catholic church was involved in missionary work. In
Concilium, in contrast to Studia Missionalia, learned exponents of the non-
Christian world religions are also allowed to state their positions. In its approach, Concilium demonstrates a more open attitude than Studia Missionalia.
It advocates dialogue between representatives of the world religions as well as
practical cooperation on the basis of a common ethical foundation on the human rights issue.

In the introduction to *World Religions and Global Ethics* 1989, the author S.
Cromwell Crawford describes ethics in an independent world and links this to
the world religions. When we speak of a global ethic, we start from the assumption that people are involved in a global society. Biologically, we belong
to a common species. Ecologically, we are a part of the planet's biosphere and
are rooted in the earth's energy system. The representatives of the world religions, because they belong to different traditions, do not simply wish to understand one another but to be enriched through such encounters. When we speak
of a common human nature, we mean certain properties, qualities and energies
which are universal, indestructible and creatively expressed in personal styles.
Human beings are energetic entities and are so structured that they react in a
certain way to external conditions. The world religions represent a variety of
life styles which blossom around the world, each and every one adapted to
different societies and circumstances. According to this way of looking at
things, biology, ecology, religion and ethics thus bring people all over the
world nearer to one another. They discover the unity between mankind and
nature.

In the wake to President Jimmy Carter's human rights campaign, a universal
declaration of human rights based upon the Koran was approved on 19 September 1981 in Paris by Europe's Islamic Council. It says no more than is to be
found in the religious law. Human rights are nothing new; they have always
existed; they are God's gift to us. They can be justified only by that strength
which is to be found in the Law of God. They cannot be understood as natural
laws. A natural right does not belong in a system where everything is ascribed

336

to God, not only in principle but in every concrete instance. Moslems, more than Westerners, emphasize that human rights are a complement to human duties.[1] *Sharia*, Islamic law, is an integrated part of Islam. It is the foundation of *umma*, Moslem society: it is a religious system which does not distinguish between what is Caesar's and what is God's. *Sharia* has been collected and formulated by jurists between the seventh and tenth centuries. It is still binding. According to Islamic jurists, it is capable of regulating the social problems of today.[2]

The representatives for Western Christian tradition and Islamic tradition devoted themselves to an intercultural and interreligious scholarly based dialogue on human rights. A good example of this activity between research scholars belonging to the Western and Islamic tradition is to be found in D. Little et al. *Human Rights and the Conflict of Cultures: Western and Islamic Perspectives on Religious Liberty*, 1988. The work to implement human rights in different societies and cultural contexts was important for the representatives of the religions. Religious dialogue and work on behalf of human rights were parallel to one another. This led to cross-fertilization. Human rights emerged as a practical project for co-operation among the representatives of the world religions. The domain of human rights is also the meeting place between a new Christianity and contemporary humanism.[3]

The concept of Wider Ecumenism will mean not only striving for Christian unity but also unity between all world religions. This issue is discussed in P. Phan ed. *Christianity and the Wider Ecumenism* 1990 and in H. Küng. *Theology for Third Millenium, An Ecumenical View* 1988.

Hans Küng and Human Rights

Hans Küng is an ecumenically minded Catholic theologian who, like Jürgen Moltmann, an ecumenically minded Protestant theologian with whom Küng has cooperated, pursues the human rights issue as an important cooperative project transcending religious boundaries. Both these theologians apply a global and universal view to the issue of the world religions and human rights. Küng's involvement in the dialogue between religions goes hand in hand with his commitment to the idea that the world religions must work together for the implementation of human rights. Their ethics constitute the common link in achieving this goal.

Karl Josef Kuschel, one of Hans Küng's close colleagues at the ecumenical research institute at Tübingen, delivered a report to a symposium held in Paris from 8 to 10 February 1989, on the theme *world religions, human rights and*

---

[1] H. Küng, Christians and the World Religions, Paths to Dialogue with Islam, Hinduism and Buddhism, 1986, 45.
[2] Op. cit., 62.
[3] Viola Francesco Les Droits de l'homme: Point de rencontre entre la nouvelle Chretiente et l'humanisme contemporaine Nova et Vetera 1982, 57 (1) 4–16.

the humane. He pointed out that the situation today has changed. Within Christianity, we can discern a move to recognize the Christian roots of human rights movements and to support the declaration of human rights for genuinely Christian reasons. Human rights are no longer viewed as a rival to a specifically Christian view of humanity but as its inheritance and concrete form. The ever-increasing global linkage of new areas of human existence (in politics, economics, transport and environment) has created unforeseeable consequences for the relationship between the great world religions. Jews, Moslems, Hindus and Confucianists live together with Christians in one and the same city. This development creates a new ecumenical situation and consequently we must reckon with a new challenge.[4] Is there within the individual religions a practical way of behaving which recurs in other religions? Is there a universal ethics of mankind? Are there fundamental convictions, guiding values and basic precepts which people of all the different religions can endorse from the viewpoint of their own tradition?[5]

According to Kuschel, the Paris colloquium took as its starting point the foregoing thoughts. Its theme was the search for an ethic of humanity. Among the sponsors of the colloquium were the Goethe Institute in Paris and UNESCO. Human rights can only be more widely implemented with the support of the world religions and not in opposition to them. The Secretary-General of UNESCO emphasized in his opening address the importance of the world religions for UNESCO's programme *Education for human rights.* The basis of this programme was the publication *International Dimensions of Humanitarian Law,* 1988, which was sponsored by UNESCO and the Henry Dunant Institute in Geneva. Differences between religions does not rule out the search for common values. Unity in diversity was the slogan of the UNESCO programme. A paper by the ecumenical theologian, Hans Küng from Tübingen, served as a basis for the conference. The representatives of the world religions responded to Küng's paper. Every religion has treated itself as the true religion, either in an exclusive way like the prophetic religions of Semitic origin, or in an inclusive way like, in particular, the mystical religions of Indian origin. By so doing, they have excluded the others, ignored them or have absorbed them. A conversation between religions on the issue of truth is only promising if every religion is prepared to indulge in self-criticism. A dialogue between religions presupposes an awareness that the boundary between the true and the false no longer runs between my religion and other religions but within my own religion. Every religion has its own criterion for judging what is true or false. It is a matter of so-called internal criteria. But the question arises if there are not also external ecumenical criteria which can be applied to every religion.[6]

---

[4] H. Küng, J. Moltmann, eds. The Ethics of World Religions and Human Rights, Concilium 1990/ 2 96 f.
[5] Op. cit., 97.
[6] Op. cit., 97 ff.

The question if what is human could serve as a criterion of truth, was raised during the symposium. Küng puts forward the thesis that the human, that is to say what is truly human, is together with the internal criterion of truth, a further criterion of truth for religions. This is so because only religion which promotes humanity, can be a true and good religion. True humanity is a prerequisite of true religion. Humanity is a minimum demand for all religions. Conversely it means that to the extent that a religion spreads inhumanity and inhibits the feeling of identity, meaning and value, it is a false and bad religion. Objections to Küng's thesis included the following: is not the *humanum* the result of European humanism influenced by Christianity—a typically Western criterion which in no way applied to Eastern religions? Is not what is human,as an ecumenically shared criterion, by its nature far too vague to be binding on religions?[7]

Küng met this objection by setting a minimal criterion alongside the maximal one. True religion is the fulfilment of true humanity. Religion is the optimal requirement for the realization of the human. There has to be a religion (as a maximum criterium) if there is to be humanity as an unconditional and universal obligation. There is thus a fundamental dialectical link between religion and humanity. This offered a basis for a budding unity between representatives of the different religions. 1) No representative accepted an independent human criterion as a superstructure over concrete religions. All confirmed that the human must be based upon the absolute. The criterion for the human lost its vagueness whenever one criticized specific violations of the human. 2) All representatives accepted self-criticism as a precondition for dialogue between the religions. All agreed that human dignity and human rights were still abused in the name of their religion. All were agreed that in the religions there was need for action to educate people for humanity. 3) All representatives for the great world religions confirmed in principle the possibility of basing humanity on each religion's own tradition. Humanity was not seen as an invention of the West.[8]

The tasks for the future as the symposium defined them, are threefold. It was a question of creating a universal basic ethic and achieving greater concreteness in ethical and political matters. There was unanimity that the religions should fight for the implementation of human rights. However the political value of this stand needs to be demonstrated.[9]

In the wake of the Paris symposium on the world religions and human rights, Hans Küng gave full expression to his thoughts on the possibilities of creating a global ethic by starting from the world religions in the book *Global Responsibility In Search of a New World Ethic* 1991. He emerged, moreover, as the main architect of *a declaration for a global ethic* which the Parliament of the World's Religions issued in 1993. A global ethic does not reduce the

---

[7] Op. cit., 99 f.
[8] Op. cit, 100.
[9] Op. cit., 101.

religions to an ethical minimum but represents the ethical core or minimum shared by all the world religions today.[10] Perhaps one day, there will be a UN declaration on a global ethic which will give moral support to the declaration of human rights.[11]

In the declaration on a global ethic, it is asserted that a global ethic is to be found in the world's religions. We must treat others as we would wish them to treat us.[12] We must not only live for ourselves but also serve others. We must work for a just social and economic order in which all have the same chance to fulfil themselves as human beings.[13] Religion is often misused purely for the purposes of power politics, including war. The declaration disassociates itself from this by expressing its abhorrence. [14] The morality which is already to be found in the world's religions does not give a direct solution to all the world's problems but it does provide a moral basis for a better individual and global order, namely a vision which can lead mankind away from despair and save society from chaos.[15] A vision rests on hopes, aims, ideals and norms. It is the responsibility of the religions to show that we can keep such hopes, ideals and norms and find a foundation for them and live by them. What the UN declaration of human rights proclaimed at the level of rights, the declaration on a global ethic will confirm and give depth to, from the viewpoint of ethics: the realization of human dignity, the equality of all human beings, their solidarity and dependence upon one another.[16] The religions can bring about a change in inner orientation, in the mental world and in the heart of the people and give life a new orientation. They can offer a fundamental feeling of trust, a basis of meaning, ultimate norms and a spiritual home.[17] Every human being has an inviolable value. All are responsible for protecting this value. Human beings must always be the objects of rights; they must be ends, never means; they must never be the objects of commercialization.[18] There is a well founded principle which has survived in many religious and ethical traditions for thousands of years: what you would not wish done to yourself, do not do to others. Treat others as you would wish to be treated. This ought to be the norm for all areas of life, for families and societies, for races, nations and religions.[19] Every form of egoism ought to be discarded: all selfishness whether individual or collective, in the form of class thinking, racism, nationalism or sexism. We condemn these because they prevent human beings from being truly human.[20]

---

[10] H. Küng and K. J. Küschel, eds. A Global Ethic. The Declaration of the Parliament of the World's Religions 1993, 8.
[11] Op. cit., 9.
[12] Op. cit., 14.
[13] Op. cit., 15.
[14] Op. cit., 17.
[15] Op. cit., 18.
[16] Op. cit., 20.
[17] Op. cit., 22.
[18] Op. cit., 23.
[19] Op. cit., 23f.
[20] Op. cit., 24.

Hans Küng wrote the draft of the declaration for a global ethic at the request of the Parliament for the World's Religions before their meeting in Chicago from 28 August to 4 September 1993.[21] The declaration on a global ethic was not meant to be a new variant of the declaration of human rights but was intended to provide moral support for the UN declaration.[22] The religions' common ethic is seen to be not a new invention but only a new discovery.[23] The sacred writings of the religions provides a maximal ethic while the declaration on a global ethic only offers a minimal ethic.[24]

According to Karl-Josef Kuschel, the Parliament for the World's Religions demonstrates two things 1) the representatives of the world's religions are gathered together at the same moment in time and at the same place; they stand side by side with the same rights and communicate with one another with respect. This removes the demand for the supremacy of one religion over the others. 2) the representatives of the world's religions come from grass root level, that is from the bottom. They do not belong to the religious hierarchies and are not official delegates sent by their leaders. They represent their religions as individuals. The Parliament for the World's Religions has the character, not of an institution, but of a movement. It has the character of a human encounter.[25] The world religions have grown together and at the same time they have come closer to one another. It is especially notable in the larger cities of Europe and North America.[26] A largely monocultural society of European Christian mould has been replaced by a multicultural, multireligious society.[27] Since the world religions live close to one another in the great cities of the world and are not divorced from one another in distant continents, questions arise about interreligious cooperation and a capacity for dialogue. Questions about one ethic for all religions also belong here.[28] In 1993 in Chicago, the Dalai Lama held that every religion is called upon to mobilize within itself ethical traditions and spiritual sources which contribute to the well-being of mankind.[29]

9.4 Human Rights and Religious Values

The book *Human Rights and Religious Values An Uneasy Relationship?* by (among others) the Moslem jurist and human rights expert, A. A. An-Na'im arose from a symposium held at the Free University of Amsterdam from 21 to

---

[21] Op. cit., 43, 48.
[22] Op. cit., 55 f.
[23] Op. cit., 71.
[24] Op. cit., 73.
[25] Op. cit., 81.
[26] Op. cit., 91.
[27] Op. cit., 92.
[28] Op. cit., 94.
[29] Op. cit., 105.

23 April 1993 where the following question was raised. Can human rights be interpreted and justified within religious traditions as the common kernel of a universal morality within these traditions?

Determining Position

To begin with, the problems dealt with in the symposium were set out in a paper reviewing the position. In it, *first of all the relationship between moral codes and religious traditions* was discussed. The religious traditions determine the moral norms and values which their adherents profess. In a society where religions from different traditions coexist, the question arises how their moral norms and values are related to one another. Do they coincide or do they conflict? Is there a common core of moral truth accepted by all of them or are the differences so decisive that we can only speak of a fundamental gulf between them? The religious traditions promote those ideals of human existence which we call the good life. They form an integral part of a religious view of the different dimensions of human existence. The traditions push their way into morality but they are also exposed to criticism by general moral norms. Religious traditions must be judged by norms which are morally acceptable in a pluralistic society. The traditions must be tested according to some kind of universal moral code. It is thus a question of a two-way perspective on religious morality. The problem is how we are to be able to identify a moral norm which is independent of a particular tradition. Such a norm is needed in the interreligious dialogue. Without it, a religious tradition judges another tradition's norms on the basis of its own norms. In this way, one tradition can acquire moral supremacy over another. What is sought, is a morality which is independent of tradition. However this view has been criticised. What is reckoned as morally acceptable in a given society, is largely determined by dominant cultural ideas, whether religious or temporal, including the ideal of the good life. It is therefore difficult if not impossible to defend a moral norm in a way that is independent of a special perspective with regard to these questions.

In reviewing the position, the discussion takes up *secondly human rights between universality and tradition.* The universal declaration of human rights of 1948 offers a universal moral code. The norms and values expressed in this declaration apply to all human beings. At the same time the doctrine of human rights is the product of a special period in the history of Western culture and philosophy. The eighteenth century philosophy of the Enlightenment sought the foundation of moral and religious truth in human nature with the aim of establishing a natural religion and morality. However the conception of human nature with its appeal to reason was embedded in the cultural tradition from which it evolved. The question arises about the universal validity of a doctrine of right which is based upon enlightenment anthropology. The universal declaration of human right must be interpreted from all possible angles and be

342

integrated in all possible frameworks in order to be universally valid. In order to fulfil its demand for universal validity, the doctrine of human rights must allow contextual interpretations. If this is not done, the interpretation of a particular tradition becomes universally dominant. From the viewpoint of all other traditions, the doctrine is a foreign body, something which belongs to another tradition. Human rights are contextually interpreted and it is on the basis of the context that they receive their practical significance and meaning. This presupposes a hermeneutic space without which they cannot be part of the positive morality of particular tradition. At the same time, contextual interpretations endanger the universality of the doctrine. Positive morality is always bound to a tradition and is thus particular and individual, rather than universal.

Thirdly in reviewing the position, *the question of social morality and ideals for human existence* is raised. In the liberal tradition, there are strong feelings about moral and religious pluralism. Individuals with conflicting interests and different ideals about the good life must work together because there is no other general system of belief to guide them. In the liberal society, only issues which are of concern to all people in society can be generally justified. Liberals hold that it is impossible in modern society to have a unifying view of human existence. It is no longer acceptable.

Fourthly, the problem of *a religious dialogue about human rights* is discussed. In nearly every part of our world, whether East, West, North or South, societies lack a unifying moral perspective which contains a defined ideal about the good life as well as rules and principles for general life together. The doctrine of human rights and the norms of religious norms and traditions need the support of one another. The question is raised: can human rights be interpreted and justified within religious traditions so that they are supported and not undermined as the core in a universal morality, common to these traditions? The religious traditions have certain aspects in common especially when it concerns ideals for human existence and true humanity. All religions speak of salvation, the good life and of living well. The interreligious dialogue is the most promising approach to initiating research. All religious traditions share the problem of determining the conditions for establishing peaceful coexistence with one another.

Finally, in reviewing the position, the question of *differences in religious anthropologies* is discussed. The problem is whether the different religious anthropologies pave the way for a common core of universal rights and stimulate their proponents to see them in their cultural context or do they instead prevent them from doing so. The symposium wishes to concentrate upon the implications of religious anthropologies for the possibility of recognizing human rights.[30]

---

[30] A. An-Na'im et al. eds. Human Rights and Religious Values An Uneasy Relationship? 1995 VII–XIV.

Ethical and Philosophical Perspectives

One author in *Human Rights and Religious Values* asks if there are *common moral values which underpin the doctrine of human rights* and to which the interreligious dialogue can have recourse. The question of whether there are such common convictions or not, is a question to be discovered through moral dialogue. No moral system goes beyond the special convictions within the tradition in which it has evolved. It reflects these convictions.[31] All religious traditions treat their view of human nature as true for all human beings. This means that all are driven towards universality. At the same time, they are confronted by differences in the convictions entertained by people from other traditions. Each tradition must therefore account for the relationship between the universal and the particular within its own framework. This is a problem which is common to all.[32]

Another author points out that religious traditions provide a path of life which is intended to help people throughout life. In teaching the right way to live, the various religious traditions make use of stories, in which difficult situations in life are illustrated by the concrete plights of people. The stories deal with the complexities of life, human reflections and the good and bad ideas of people. The religious traditions dispose over tales which exist alongside rules of life and the more dogmatic side of the tradition. Traditional dogma is imparted within the context of life and religious experience. The seeds of a religious view of humanity do not primarily consist in general rules and teachings but in the great paradigmatic stories such as those about Krishna, Buddha, Moses, Jesus and Mohammed. Doctrine is of secondary importance.[33] The ideas about humanity and the moral views in different religious traditions need to be studied. In this way, we can see how far different ideals of humanity coincide. The idea of the truly human as a common basis for a universal ethics acceptable to all religions was discussed, as we have noted earlier in this chapter, by Hans Küng and Karl-Josef Kuschel. The critical question is how broad is a shared concept of the truly human? Every religious tradition has its own idea about what it means to be a good person. The question of how far the concepts of humanity in different religious traditions have something in common, must be discussed and such a study must be supplemented by interreligious dialogue. The strength of religious ideas about humanity lies in the fact that they carefully describe mistaken paths in life and draw upon living experience for their teaching. In contrast to the idea of human rights, they also recommend following a path in life which will bring us to the attainment of a reasonable human existence. We cannot live by human rights alone.[34]

---

[31] Op. cit., 20.
[32] Op. cit., 21.
[33] Op. cit., 27.
[34] Op. cit., 39f.

Cultural and Religious Perspectives

In *Human Rights and Religious Values, a cultural anthropologist raises the problem of the relation between cultural relativism and universal human rights.* If we accept cultural relativism, this entails the rejection of the possibility that human rights can be formulated rationally. When cultural relativism denies the existence of universal rationality, the necessary framework for formulating human rights is lacking. On the other hand, human rights presuppose a shared minimum and a minimal intercultural communication.[35]

A Buddhist writes on *the Buddhist view of human rights from a perspective where it is compared with the Semitic religions*—Judaism, Christianity and Islam. According to the Western view of human rights, these belong only to human beings. Non-human beings are excluded or else are treated as secondary. In Buddhism, human beings are viewed not only from a human standpoint i.e. an anthropocentric basis, but from a cosmic basis. Human beings are a part of all beings.[36] Both Buddhism and the Semitic religions are anthropocentric in the sense that they deal with salvation. The basis of salvation in the Semitic religions is the personal relationship between people and God while in Buddhism the basis is the transpersonal, cosmological dimension which is common to human beings and nature: Dharma, everything which is in the universe.

In Buddhism, human rights are to be understood from this transanthropocentric, universal perspective. The Buddhist view of human rights must be seen in connection with the problem of the I or Self. The Self is not an absolute but a relative entity. When we speak of the Self, this presupposes the existence of the Other. There cannot be some Self independent of the Other and vice versa. The Self and the Other are related to each other. The Self is not an independent entity. Self-preoccupation is the basis of evil and human suffering. The way to salvation goes via the attainment of Non-Self.[37] Our own identity is not absolutely independent. Self identity exists in relative but not in absolute terms. The idea of absolute self identity is a conceptual construction created by human self-consciousness. For Buddhism, it is an illusion. We are relatively different but absolutely alike, fusing with one another while at the same time, retaining our clear identity. The Self and the Divine are relatively speaking different but in absolute terms they are not. They fuse into one another. On this point, Buddhism differs from the monotheistic religions and this has consequences for the issue of religious tolerance. In Judaism, Christianity and Islam, the Divine is the one absolute God.[38]

In the Jewish-Christian tradition, the issue of human rights and human duties with respect to others, must be seen in relation to the exclusive commandment on the Supreme God, while in Buddhism the same problem must be understood in relation to all living creatures in the universe. The first com-

---

[35] Op. cit., 79.
[36] Op. cit., 144.
[37] Op. cit., 145 f.
[38] Op. cit., 146 f.

mandment is not that "You shall have no other Gods but I": it is "do not destroy life". The rights of animals and plants are just as important as human rights. Nature is not only subordinate to human beings; human beings are also subordinate to nature.[39] Buddhism is not based upon a divine relationship but upon self consciousness. [40] Where Christianity speaks of love, Buddhism speaks of compassion. In Christianity, love is accompanied by justice. In Buddhism, compassion is combined with wisdom. Judgement involves a sentence or choice as distinct from wisdom. Buddhist wisdom accepts everything and everything as it is. Justice distinguishes between the just and the unjust, while wisdom creates a feeling of equality and solidarity. Justice often leads to conflict while wisdom leads to harmony. Love and justice go together with difficulty whereas compassion and wisdom complement one another.[41] The emphasis of monotheistic religion on an absolute God, leads to exclusivity.[42]

This analysis of Buddhism in comparison with the Semitic religions— Judaism, Christianity and Islam—shows that it has consequences for the view taken of human rights. Even if human rights are given a basis in Buddhism, they acquire another meaning than when they are based upon monotheistic religion.

In *Human Rights and Religious Values, one author* discusses the theme *divine land and the violation of human rights.* His thesis is that what is treated as the holiest thing in this world can lead to most extreme types of violations of human rights. and even to the removal of rights[43] Since the establishment of the state of Israel, the Jewish people has demanded to live in the Holy land. At the same time, the fulfilment of this demand has meant that many Palestinians have been deprived of land which they consider holy and see as their own. On the one hand, the implementation of sacred demands led to the violation of human rights for one group while on the other hand it led to the right to live in their own land for others. Texts such as Exodus in the Old Testament support the Jewish people's claim to the Holy land. God is understood as his people's King who leads His people to the Holy Land.[44]

In *one essay,* attention is drawn to the contention that *religious sects violate human rights.* Sects are dangerous and undemocratic. They apply brainwashing techniques. Members are exploited and have a very difficult life within the group. Former members are psychologically damaged to such a degree that they can no longer function in society. The sects make absolutist and totalitarian demands; some threaten freedom. In the name of loyalty, they proclaim and insist in practice on absolute submission to the leader who is the centre of such a group. In the name of freedom, he enslaves his followers.

---

[39] Op. cit., 147.
[40] Op. cit., 148.
[41] Op. cit., 149.
[42] Op. cit., 150.
[43] Op. cit., 154.
[44] Op. cit., 155.

346

They claim to develop their consciousness but in fact they suppress their followers´ consciousness, understanding and will.[45] Sects are viewed as pseudoreligious and are suspected of using religion as a cover for illegal or dubious practices.[46]

Denominational and Ecumenical Perspectives

It is natural that *Calvinist thinking and human rights* were an object of particular interest at a symposium held at the Free University of Amsterdam. Calvinism's religious anthropology rejects in principle the idea of human rights. In the Calvinist tradition, human rights as rights which are established and decided by human beings and based upon humanity, are impossible. Human beings are created by God who is sovereign over human beings, even after the Fall. This God is not only the Creator but also the Steersman: He steers the world according to His sovereign will. He appoints governments to serve Him because through them He exercizes His power of foresight. The primary goal for the created beings is know and serve this God i.e. to live in accordance with His commandments. In all human activities, the glory of God is primary. The whole of creation is a theatre for God's glory. The glorification of God through human beings consists in recognizing that human beings do not dispose over themselves but belong to God.[47] God's sovereignty is the central theme in the whole Calvinist tradition. It is a powerfully theocentric tradition. The idea that human beings on the basis of their reason are capable of establishing rights for themselves, of deciding on these by virtue of their own authority and are able to to base these rights upon their own humanity, finds no support. It is impossible to conceive of human beings released from God and His authority. If human beings have rights, they can only be guaranteed by God. The thought that human beings can demand these rights, is absolutely alien to Calvin. God and human beings enter into a covenant with one another but it is a relationship which is founded upon grace, so that it does not provide any grounds for demanding our own rights. If it is possible to speak of human rights through this covenant then they are only guaranteed by this covenant. They are gifts.

Human beings are not only creatures before a sovereign God. They are also sinners before the Holy God. This absolutely rules out any talk of human rights. The sinful being has no rights to assert but is totally dependent on grace. The person who justifies himself and declines God's grace is the prime example of the sinful person. In the Catholic tradition, human nature retains its integrity after the Fall. In Lutheran and Calvinist tradition, on the other hand, human beings are totally depraved. They are completely corrupt. Calvinism also contains a religious anthropology which rules out human rights as an idea

---

[45] Op. cit., 170 f.
[46] Op. cit., 171 f.
[47] Op. cit., 193.

and as an ideology.[48] If humanity possesses rights then according to Calvinist understanding, these are guaranteed by God. They are derived from the sovereignty of God. The humanist idea that they are derived from human beings themselves is rejected.[49]

One paper deals with *the reception of human rights within the ecumenical movement* and points to a division between those who gave individual rights priority and those who gave social rights priority at the St. Pölten consultation of 1974. Both positions have their adherents.[50] At Nairobi 1975, the political dimension of human rights was stressed. They form part of the struggle for the liberation of society.[51] This paper points out that new types of human rights are continually added to the ecumenical movement's agenda: individual rights, social rights, environmental rights and the rights of generations yet unborn.[52]

Local and Universal Perspectives

In a concluding paper, the issue of *local and universal aspects of human rights* is discussed. In it, it is asserted that every conception of human rights is limited with respect to time and place. The exposition of human rights is relative to a particular time and is not eternal: it is local and not universal. All declarations on human rights are historical documents. They mirror the issues of the day. They therefore need to be complemented by new declarations on human rights. The exposition of human rights continues. Closely linked to the issue of the local and universal in human rights, is the problem of the universal and relative. When the USA warns about relativizing human rights, people mainly from Asia and Africa at the Vienna Conference on Human Rights, complain that the West in general and the USA in particular are using their priorities in human rights as a means of imposing their own political ideology and economic policy upon the rest of the world.[53] The idea of human rights has been elastic and has been stretched to encompass new areas of human life. From being concerned with individual civil and political rights the idea has been extended also to cover economic, social, cultural and other group rights as well as environmental rights and the rights of future generations. Different local circumstances influence the content of human rights. During the Cold War, civil and political rights were given priority in the West. In the East, rights pertaining to economic and social welfare were placed first. In the South, group rights or development rights came before individual rights or social rights. Local components determine the hierarchy of human rights.[54]

---

[48] Op. cit., 194 f.
[49] Op. cit., 197.
[50] Op. cit., 209 f.
[51] Op. cit., 210.
[52] Op. cit., 223.
[53] Op. cit., 264.
[54] Op. cit., 265f.

Religion and Human Rights

The symposium in Amsterdam ended with a statement answering the question which had been raised in the beginning. *A religious tradition can defend human rights and contribute to the development of the moral foundations for human rights.* The worldwide reality of religious inspiration which underpins the search for a genuine human way of life, forms a powerful source of support for those whose rights have been forgotten.[55] The symposium calls for a general discussion about the different traditions' ethics and their role in the establishment and maintenance of truly human societies. Religious communities ought to reflect about the idea of human rights and about their opportunities for participating in the promotion of human rights. They ought to take part in the discussion about what they believe establishes true humanity and a genuinely human way of life. The discussion provides support for human rights.[56] The Amsterdam symposium ends with the same conclusions as those of the UNESCO symposium on the ethics of the world's religions and human rights held some years earlier, in which Hans Küng was the driving force, namely: *the truly human and the interpretation of the truly human on the basis of the ethics of the world 's religions and the religious inspiration for a truly human life are the main contribution which the world's religions can make to the global campaign to implement human rights.*

Synthesis

The symposium with the theme of human rights and religious values brought to the fore the issue of universalism and particularism in morals and the question of the instruments to be used in bringing about the strategic goal, namely the good life, in all traditions. Human beings' well-being is the goal of both social and individual existence and the doctrine of human rights must be seen in this light. Is it a suitable means of attaining the good life for people in different cultural and religious contexts? The symposium is concerned with this issue. In order to serve as an adequate tool, human rights must satisfy the demands of both univeralism and particularism. Human rights must be rooted in a core of beliefs which are common for different cultural and religious traditions. At the same time, human rights must be able to be expounded and applied within the framework of particular traditions with their own special character. At the most profound level, the symposium raises the problem of human rights and the good life. *Can cultural and religious traditions function as an instrument for implementing human rights and thereby pave the way for a good life? Or have cultural and religious traditions the opposite effect and raise obstacles for human rights and prevent the establishment of the preconditions for a good human life?* It is these fundamental questions which

---

[55] Op. cit., 268.
[56] Op. cit., 269.

349

the symposium raises although it is far from answering them. For this, an interreligious dialogue and empirical investigations in religious studies are required.

9.5 Religion and Human Rights

The project *Religion and human rights* was inaugurated in 1993. It has the aim of increasing the understanding of the relation between religion and human rights. It consists of four advisory groups specializing in the following problems: *the roots to conflict; religious bellicosity or fundamentalism; universality versus relativism in human rights; religion's positive resources for human rights.* The conflict group is led by David Little, the senior research member in religion, ethics and human rights at the US Peace Institute in Washington. The universalism-relativism group is led by the Moslem, Adullahi An-Nai'm, one of the world's most prolific writers in the field of religion and human rights. The Harvard theologian Harvey Cox is in the group which deals with religion as a positive resource for human rights. Desmond Tutu is one of the honorary chairmen of the project. Among the advisers to the project is the Chicago ecclesiastical historian, Martin E. Marty. He is one of the leaders in the so-called fundamentalist project which covers several religions, not least Christianity and Islam. The project *Religion and Human Rights* issues a publication of the same name. The first issue appeared in 1994. The project aims not only at a deeper understanding of the relation between religion and human rights but wishes also to promote support for human rights. The aim is thus not purely scholarly but is also committed to practical action.

Religion as a Starting Point

Religious traditions provide their adherents with a view of the world and identify the place and role of human and other beings in the world. The religions answer questions about the origin and meaning of existence, the nature of life and death, the meaning of suffering and ways to overcome suffering, the nature of evil and ways to overcome evil, and the ultimate purpose of human life as well as of life in general. Religion exhorts its adherents to live according to these values by means of a prescribed code of practical conduct and relations which can influence many aspects of personal and social life. A religion constitutes a culture which can mould personal and social identity and can influence experience and behaviour in a concrete sense. A religion is thus not simply a question of belief or doctrine. Why does religious belief produce both peacemakers and propagandists of hatred? What is the nature of the tension between universal human rights and the particular value systems of religious traditions? Is democratic liberalism a form of fundamentalism? How can secular human rights experts, the religious leaders of all the different faiths and people with

350

opposed political convictions and divergent social values work more closley together? These questions are dealt with in the project *Religion and human rights*. The participants do not believe that dialogue will soon lead to one single accepted interpretation of a religious tradition but they are involved in the critical process of dialogue. It is high time that the religious dimension in the human rights campaign is examined by people representing different religious beliefs, nationalities and scholarly disciplines. The project *Religion and human rights* seeks to understand more clearly the religious dynamic in conflicts and the reasons why religion can be a beneficent or malign force for human rights and that ways of grappling with this force are beginning to be identified. The project will also mobilize the positive forces in the world's spiritual traditions and in their teaching on compassion, human dignity and the value of life, for the cause of peace and justice.[57]

Religion and the Roots to Conflict

The first chapter in the book deals with religion and conflict and illustrates the problem with the conflict between Jews and Arabs in Palestine-Israel. In the former Yugoslavia, Armenia and Azerbaidzhan, India, Sri Lanka, Egypt and the Sudan, violence occurs in which religion is assumed to be a factor. But in order to understand religion's role in contemporary conflicts, the following questions require particular attention: 1) Can we speak of religion as the root to conflict? Or should we speak of particular religious traditions under special violent circumstances? 2) What is the relation of religion to factors such as ethnicity and race in contemporary conflicts? 3) What is the role of non-religious factors as economic, demographic or political conditions in conflicts? Is religion an independent factor in conflicts or only a function of economic crisis or over-population? 4) What is the relation between the past and present in the phenomenon of religious violence? Religion is able to give persons and groups a feeling of identity, a place in the universe. By means of stories, symbols, rites, articles of belief, sacred texts etc, religious traditions encourage the development of a way of thinking, feeling and acting which serves to arrange human beings' and groups' lives around a view of reality which is considered holy. Described in this way, such a reality serves to get people to carry out a task or to maintain values which are thought of as right, good or true. Conceptions of a holy reality tend to be expressed in a way which assumes their importance in solving existential issues such as the origin of life and death or the meaning of suffering. 1) In order to create a group feeling, religion serves to motivate behaviour which is important for personal and social integration. The group feeling can support behaviour which distinguishes people by drawing up dividing lines between groups. The differences between them are internal and those which are external are a part of religion's differentiating role in human consciousness. This dynamic is at work among Moslems, Croats and

---

[57] J. Kelsay and S. B. Twiss eds. Religion and Human Rights, 1994 IV–VII.

Serbs in the former Yugoslavia. 2) Providing tales, carrying out rites, providing confessions of faith and indulging in other forms of religious behaviour can all serve the purpose of legitimizing an insider group in its struggle with an outsider group. 3) In contemporary religious violence, legitimacy is given to the use of armed force in the fight against an outsider group. 4) The legitimacy of using armed force is usually linked with a insider group's need to dominate a given territory e.g. the Serbian idea of a Greater Serbia.

Serbian identity is bound up with orthodox Christianity, a group feeling and demand for a special place, the province Kosovo. It is difficult to distinguish religion from other factors in the description of group identity. For many people, religion is part of the feeling of ethnic kinship. Some say: those who are not Orthodox, cannot be Serbs. It is undeniable that there is a religious factor in the identity of many ethnic groups. The struggle for power in Yugoslavia began after Tito's death and the end of the Cold War. Slobodan Milosevic and Franjo Tudjman appealed to religious symbols in the ensuing struggle for power. This had an effect because of the economic crisis. Religion is thus not so much a root of the conflict as a tool used by those striving after power and security.

Violence is a means by which ethnic groups seek to create ties between themselves and others, ties meant to protect a common way of life, to promote the cause of truth and justice and to ensure a place in the universe. The potential of religion is a root to conflict which is always present in societies. It is visible in Crusades, pogroms and other events associated with the history of religious traditions. From one point of view, we must look upon religious violence as an expression of tendencies which are always present in the religious life of humanity and which has been expressed in a variety of historical contexts. What makes the difference between groups spill over into violence? Can religious traditions be part of the solution of the problem of religious violence, even if they appear to be part of the problem? Those who have studied the Nazi extermination of the Jews, note that the practice of Jewish faith and the presence of Jews as a distinctive group, challenged Christianity's monopoly position in Europe. The presence of such religious dissent was thought to weaken established structures. Studies of the Holocaust point to a key factor in turning the people's suspicions of a Jewish minority into active violence. This was the growing number of European Jews in positions of influence. When the Jews moved from the Ghettos and were integrated into the urban populations, the fear of this outsider group grew. The encounter between Christians and Jews in Europe along with other factors, can help to explain the Holocaust. The presence of outsider groups is always able to challenge an insider group's religious monopoly. The task has been to determine religion's problematic role in contemporary conflicts. 1) Religious solutions to problems of religious violence must appeal to the same social and psychological needs which contemporary militant forms of religious traditions appeal to. The wish for a secure place in the universe which religious traditions appeal to, in creating a feeling of group identity, cannot be ignored. Every attempt to identify religious resources in order to deal with the roots to conflict must look for ways of turning stories of conflict into stories which promote the kind of mutual respect and tolerance which is to be found in the instrument of human rights. 2) Every attempt to confront religious violence in the longer term must take account of the ways in which current conflicts are probably the seeds to future conflicts.[58]

Fundamentalism

The second chapter of the book deals with the relationship between fundamentalism and human rights. Sometimes religious fanatics use violence to attain their sacred goals. Fundamentalists lay claim to having an unbroken tradition. They oppose patterns of life which are taken as self-evident in contemporary, secular society and culture. They keep their distance and refuse to accept the legitimacy of any culture which is against what they conceive to be the fundamental truths. Secular culture produces a truth which does not respect a holy order. The term *fundamentalism* is problematic. If e.g. fidelity to the text is the criterion of fundamentalist movements within Christianity, Judaism and Islam, it has little relevance in Hinduism. An important aspect of Christian fundamentalism is its apocalyptic outlook, while Moslem and Hindu fundamentalists are involved in a religious transformation of civil society in the contemporary world. Many human beings are apocalyptic without being fundamentalists. Fundamentalism grows from a commitment to normative values when something threatens the essence of the self in the life-death chain of events. Such threats are a necessary prelude to religious or political fundamentalism. Fundamentalism is closely linked to Christianity. In the middle of the present century, a fundamentalist mass movement took shape. Fundamentalism evolved into a group of believing Christians who are born again evangelists, awaiting the imminent return of Jesus Christ. Martin Marty has pointed out that fundamentalists are not only conservative, traditional or orthodox. Fundamentalism is based upon Biblical infallibility and undeviating faithfulness to the letter of scripture. Fundamentalists react negatively to many aspects of modern life such as pluralism, consumerism, materialism and the emphasis on sexual equality. They choose a certain normative basis which defines their beliefs and lives. They are also absolutist. They have no room for ambivalence or relativism which tends to make them authoritarian. They wish to introduce all sorts of prohibitions with respect to sexual matters and woman's role in society. They look upon themselves as agents of the holy. Fundamentalism is perhaps a state of mind, a protest against psychological openmindedness and a sense of ambivalence and ethical relativism.

Democracy is viewed as something steered by the lowest instincts. Democracy lacks fundamental religious values. The fundamentalists stress the need to

---

[58] Op. cit., 1–16.

353

be a part of a community of fellow believers. They emphasize the need for a common i.e. shared system of instruction and upbringing. They experience a solidarity with those who participate in the same struggle against the forces of temporal society. Fundamentalism offers people a sense of identity. It is a movement of the Right and is politically reactionary. The Christian coalition in USA is trying to assume control of the Republican party and create a kind of theocratic state. In many Middle Eastern countries, fundamentalism is political in character. Non-believers are treated as the embodiment of heresy. For fundamentalists, human rights must be based on ideas of divine and common rights. Demands for individual rights are seen as expressions of cultural pluralism and of religious and moral relativism. Those who wish to share in rights, must share also in the duties which God places on human beings. According to fundamentalism, being a human being is not simply being a person but also involves accepting the Divine word and teaching as well as following it in practice. Other people are unbelievers, heretics and enemies. In order to be human, one must believe. Christian fundamentalists in the USA can be deeply committed to goals for the human rights movement which promote justice. But fundamentalists of all kinds tend to be exclusive and authoritarian.

All need instruction in their religious tradition. Only if people are enlightened are they able to fight against oversimplifications and generalizations upon which the fundamentalists build their arguments. Religions are more complex and speak with more voices than the presentations of the fundamentalists would have us believe. Many types of belief are to be found within the great traditions. Only by making sure that people are completely informed about the many faces of religion, can we fight the monolithic perspective of fundamentalism. Defenders of human rights have an interest in supporting religious instruction of the widest and deepest kind. Leaders who aim at encouraging a complete and complex education, need support. Education is too important to be left only in the hands of the fundamentalists. Fundamentalists can involve themselves in social and political areas. What above all feeds fundamentalism in Christianity and perhaps in other religions, is the lack of faith among ordinary people in the future of mankind. With faith, human life will continue. Peace and justice will convince fundamentalists to live peacefully with other human beings created in God's image.[59]

Universalism Contra Relativism in Human Rights

The third chapter of the book analyzes the issue of universalism versus relativism in human rights. Does the idea of universal human rights potentially conflict with cultural traditions or can such universality be adapted to all traditions so that they are able to recognize human rights? The normative idea of universal human rights is uneasily combined with moral and cultural diversity in the

---

[59] Op. cit., 19–28.

world. Human rights ought from a normative point of view to be universal by definition and with respect to area and application. They ought to constitute a globally accepted set of moral and legal demands which all people are obliged to follow without exception, by virtue of their humanity. But the meaning and implications of specific human rights norms are determined by the historical and cultural experiences of human societies and traditions. The application of such norms in concrete situations ought to be specific for a given human society in its own time and place. A moral system applicable to one society is not completely adequate for other societies which need to develop their own systems on the basis of their respective historical and cultural circumstances. This means that it is paradoxical to speak about the universal value of a given set of human rights formulations. This gives rise to the tension. Some hold that this potential conflict limits the universality of human rights. Human rights as a goal are not unattainable. The recognition of a tension between universality and relativism with respect to certain human rights norms does not mean that many other human rights norms are treated as universal by the world's cultural traditions. Many states have ratified legally binding universal human rights instruments. The tension creates a practical problem but it does not mean moral bankruptcy. There is a discrepancy between local culture and religious traditions as well as between human rights and international law. A strategy needs to be worked out as regards human rights which is both sensitive to the aims of universalism and the reality of particular cultural traditions. It is important to have popular support for human rights norms and this means involvement in cultural moral traditions.

Those who are involved in the discussion about universality versus relativism in human rights have different perspectives—that of the powerful or of the powerless; they represent different interested parties on whose behalf they speak; they have different motives—a concern for morality or mere self interest; they speak different languages and behave differently. The representatives of the state speak from a position of political power. They often use the language of cultural and moral relativism to speak against the universalism of rights. The spokesmen for undemocratic governments speak on behalf of the political interests of these regimes. Religious representatives do not act in human rights issues from a position of self interest and power. They try to speak on behalf on the oppressed. They try to translate human rights norms into cultural idioms so that they can be more effectively respected. The oppressed, whose human rights are violated, participate also in the discussion about universalism versus relativism in human rights. This applies not least to women who because of their lack of literacy need help to formulate their demands. The oppressed have no difficulty with the universality of human rights. In non-Western societies, there is often a gap between two different groups and this prevents a better understanding of human rights. One group is secular and universalist in their approach to human rights. It contains intellectuals and people acquainted with international law. The second group consists of priests, ministers and religious leaders familiar with their own cultural traditions but not at home in international law and human rights. The one group relies upon international law and the other upon moral and religious conceptions. Women are discriminated on cultural and religious grounds. It is reckoned that between 90 to 100 million women in Africa and the Middle East are forced to submit to female circumcision. The implementation of this ritual practice upon women raises a string of human rights issues.[60]

Religion's Positive Resources for Human Rights

The fourth chapter of the book is devoted to religion as a positive resource for the development and implementation of human rights. These rights are violated with inspiration from religion. But religious traditions have also inspired prominent defenders of human rights: Gandhi, Dalai Lama, Martin Luther King Jr., Mother Teresa. Religious traditions can inspire and promote human solidarity. But religious traditions are complex. Religions can constitute positive resources for human rights. 1) They can widen the framework of human rights 2) they can throw light upon the relation between different articles in the the universal declaration of human rights 3) they can strengthen the idea of human rights. In the classical formulation of different religious traditions, precursors to human rights can be identified. Human rights can also be traced to reform movements within religious traditions. In the religions, there are passages in their sacred writings which support the claim to human dignity expressed in the universal declaration of human rights. Every religious tradition expresses a conviction in the unity of mankind. The theistic religions formulate this unity in terms of a single Creator. Other traditions articulate the same thing in different ways. The same traditions express the unique value of every person. Human life is seen within a framework of a divine or cosmic order. When God is excluded from the declaration, this is done not only on account of Buddhism but also because moral awareness is more universal than the theistic account.[61]

The Dialogue on Religion and Human Rights

The fifth chapter in the book reflects the dialogue on human rights which resulted from the presentation of the material in the four previous chapters of the same work. The four studies in these chapters were tested and evaluated at a meeting in New York from 22 to 24 May 1994 arranged by the project on *Religion and human rights*. The project wished to stimulate cooperation and dialogue. Abdullahi An-Na'im emphasized that religion is a source of conflict and tension, violence and injustice but also a cause of justice and peace. He thus points to what is usually called religion's Janus social face. What is im-

---

[60] Op. cit., 31–59.
[61] Op. cit., 61–79.

portant, is not the name Christian, Moslem or Jew, but the content and meaning of our beliefs, not simply how we formulate them but also how we live and practise them. It was also the principal thesis of Pedro Arrupe, the General of the Jesuits, that religious faith is not primarily concerned with verbal articulation but with concrete practice in our lives. Only if religion is mobilized for human rights can we achieve globally a human rights culture. If we are unable to give our support to human rights on a religious basis, then human rights will find themselves opposed. If we reject the dialogue between religion and human rights, it is the human rights cause which will be the loser.[62] An-Na'im will thus mobilize religion in support of human rights to strengthen the cause for which human rights stand. Without the support of religion, the work of the human rights movement will be weakened. This leads inevitably to the following reflection. It is not only the cause of human rights which is strengthened by the support of religion; religion too is revitalized through its involvement in human rights.

Concluding Reflections

The book closes with a section entitled *Concluding reflections*. The aim of the Project *Religion and human rights* is to increase knowledge about human rights and to develop those values which maintain them. The dialogue of religions is noted as an important element in this programme. Research and dialogue were the aim of the project. The project wished to encourage by its work the religions to contribute to the reinforcement and extension of human rights. It concentrates on four areas: *religion and violence, religion as a resource for peace and human rights, the status of human rights vis a vis religious traditions and the policy to recognize human rights*. Religion is one of the most constructive and also one of the most destructive forces in human life. The problem is to identify the factors which contribute to constructive development and reduce its destructive potential. This cannot take place if we stick our heads in the sand and pretend that religion is only peaceful and constructive. Religions introduce distinctions between insider and outsider groups but the majority of them also emphasize a universalism which embraces all human beings in one great family. Religion has been an important factor for many who have fought for the implementation of human rights e.g. U Thant, Dag Hammarskjöld, Eleanor Roosevelt, Muhammed Zafrullah Khan, Martin Luther King Jr., Thich Nhat Hanh and the Dalai Lama.[63]

The book presented above, which involves the collective work of the world's foremost specialists on the problem of religion and human rights, offers the most detailed material on the various issues which is available at present. The explanation for this is probably to be found in the fact that the work was carried out,not by individual authors, but on a group basis with the

---

[62] Op. cit., 81–112.
[63] Op. cit., 113–123.

participation of experts with differing cultural, religious and scholarly backgrounds. The project *Religion and human rights*, as exemplified in the book with the same title, illustrates admirably that human rights appear as an intercultural, interdenominational and interreligious issue. It is therefore natural to summarize this investigation by giving the document's central analyses. In it, human rights are not presented primarily as a problem in the history of ideas which is divorced from its social context; rather they are depicted in different settings of conflict or within the framework of what is usually called historical reality. The presentation has a beneficial concreteness to it and is securely based in ordinary life with its host of aspects.

CHAPTER 10

Human Rights and the Churches—Christian Conceptions of Human Rights

10.1 Introduction

Human rights specialists speak of three generations or dimensions of human rights. The first includes the classic individual and political freedoms. The second contains economic, social and cultural rights. The first category has in particular the support of the Western nations while the second has been supported by the Soviet bloc states. The third generation includes the rights to life and survival and is supported particularly by nations in the Third World. To this last group of rights, also belong the claims which nature makes upon human beings.

The tension between capitalism and communism during the Cold War was shown in the fact that the protagonists emphasized different aspects of human rights. Individual rights dominated the picture during the first decades after the Second World War but they were eventually counterbalanced by social rights. This polarization between the two main types of human rights ceased with the collapse of Soviet communism in 1991.

However the conflict between North and South remained and was shown *inter alia* in different aspects of human rights being emphasized. Ecological rights continued to retain a distinguishing effect. Interest in an unpolluted environment was greater in the developed countries of the West than in the former states of the Soviet bloc and in the Third World. In these latter countries, greater priority was given to more immediate and tangible problems than the crude exploitation of nature's limited resources. The shift within the World Council of Churches from the responsible society and the responsible world society both of which were established on the basis of freedom and justice to a just, participatory and sustainable society which had justice as its central principle, corresponded to the shift from individual rights which place the freedom of the individual at the centre to social rights and the right to life, both of which are based upon justice. The slogan of the World Council of Churches—justice, peace and the integrity of creation—completes the picture by not only urging the principle of justice but also the demand for ecological rights.

The churches issued no common declaration of human rights in the years

1945–1995 which is the period analyzed in the present enquiry. On the other hand, they produced important contributions which could be used for constructing such a declaration: the St. Pölten consultation of 1974; the statement of the Pontifical Commission Justitia et Pax *The Church and human rights* of 1975; the statement from the World Alliance of Reformed Churches, *The theological basis of human rights* of 1976; and the statement of the Lutheran World Federation *Theological perspective on human rights* of 1976.

As to the question whether the church bodies which have been studied, responded to new developments in human rights issues or acted as initiators in the implementation of human rights, it must be answered by saying that they fulfilled both functions. They have both more or less passively and actively worked for social change. It is particularly noteworthy that PCR within the World Council of Churches was a driving force in the campaign against apartheid in South Africa.

10.2 The Ideology of Human Rights and the Transformation of Society

The changes in the ideology of human rights within the denominational communities which have been studied during the half-century from 1945 to 1995, were due principally to the repercussions of radical social transformations upon the churches. A paradigm shift took place in the 1960s with the focus moving away from individual rights to social rights and the right to life. This paradigm change in a most profound sense derived from the fact that the ideology of the welfare state had won general support as well as the conviction that the gap between the developed and underdeveloped parts of the world remained to be bridged. The socio-political processes had an effect on the ideology of human rights.

The 1980s witnessed a similar development, when the breakthrough of the ecological movement on a broad front ensured that the ideology of the rights of nature came high on the agenda. The issue was how social justice in the form of social rights could be implemented without crude exploitation of the finite resources of nature.

It is the socio-economic processes in society and the changes within them which decisively determine the content and formulation of the discussion on human rights in the churches.

From what has been said, the general conclusion should not be drawn that religion and theology were used within the churches to legitimize the ideology of human rights in its shifting formulations. Nor can it be asserted generally that religious belief functioned as a cutting edge in bringing about social change within the movement for human rights, in which the churches participated. On the other hand, it is obvious that the churches in their actions on behalf of human rights demonstrated that religion has both these functions.

360

The movement for human rights played a crucial role in the liberation struggle of the American blacks, in the collapse of the Soviet Union and in the dismantling of the South African apartheid system. In the USA, Poland, East Germany and South Africa, the church was to be found taking the lead. The church functioned as one of the initiators of social change. At the same time, the idea of human rights was considered a basis for theological reflection and was given a theological motivation. The historical process of development was a complex one in which religious factors interacted with a host of others. It is tempting when we try to explain the historical transformation to simplify and specially single out particular forces in the historical chain of events. But the historical changes in the USA, Poland, East Germany and South Africa where human rights have been involved, are the result of several factors, one of which is the religiously motivated idea on human rights.

It is an indubitable historical fact that the American civil rights movement through its foremost leader, Martin Luther King Jr., received inspiration from religious belief. It is also clear that in the same way several of those fighting apartheid were religiously motivated. It is obvious that John Paul II's evangelical campaign for human rights in Poland had religious roots. The religiously motivated idea of human rights has thus played a role in the creation of modern history.

Martin Luther King Jr., Beyer's Naudé and John Paul II are examples of the interaction between religious belief and the campaign for the successful implementation of human rights. In all cases, action led to profound social change and the religious factor played together with other factors a decisive role in the social transformation. It would seem, however, to be impossible in particular cases to distinguish between what is primary and what is secondary, what is cause and what is effect: we must content ourselves with pointing out the complexity of the historical process of development, while maintaining that religious conviction was the most important motive force in Martin Luther King's, Beyers Naudé's and John Paul II's actions.

Charles Villa-Vicencio in *The Spirit of Hope Conversations on Politics, Religion and Values* 1994, has interviewed a number of prominent persons who were active in the implementation of human rights in South Africa.

They were inspired by different motives since they had divergent backgrounds with respect to their views of life. Among them were Christians, Moslems, Jews, Hindus, agnostics and atheists. But it is striking that all of those interviewed give more fundamental motives for their actions;in the case of the religious, these are of a religious kind. Nihilism and scepticism show that they are not a fertile foundation for socio-political action and heroic contributions. A belief in the future and in the possibility of change united those actively involved in the campaign against apartheid.

10.3 Problems

Catholics, Orthodox, Lutherans and Calvinists have a shared basis for their theology of human rights in Christian anthropology, namely that human beings are created in the image of God.

The theological arguments which lead to this common thesis, however differ. Catholics prefer to emphasize that the source of human rights is the natural law. Calvinists see God's covenant as the basis of human rights. Lutherans base human rights on the justification of human beings by the grace of God.

A shift in the Catholic standpoint, however, took place due to the influence of the Biblical research movement from the Second Vatican Council so that alongside the natural law foundation of human rights, there was an attempt to anchor them Christologically. This Christological basis unites Catholics with Lutherans and Calvinists who base their theology of human rights upon Christology and upon justification by faith and the new covenant in Christ.

The direction of the development allows one to speak of an ecumenical theology of human rights which has different points of emphasis but also certain common components. The latter include anthropology and the Christological basis. The Catholics find the Christological basis more justified than the natural law one in a religious world which is increasingly pluralistic and in a secularized Europe. Christian anthropology and Christology as the basis of the idea of human rights are designed to present the Christian standpoint in a multireligious and multicultural world. The natural law basis of human rights was motivated in the medieval world with its unitary Christian culture and this basis was developed in the theology of Thomas Aquinas. However this theological standpoint appears increasingly artificial in the modern world and the Second Vatican Council made this entirely clear when it downplayed scholastic theology in favour of a theology based upon contemporary exegetics. The modern Bible movement had already made inroads before the Council took place in the new theology, *la nouvelle theologie,* in France; but during the Second Vatican Council, it also made itself felt in the Council texts which deal with human rights e.g. the Church in the contemporary modern world. In it, reference is made to the Bible. "Man created in the image of God is the source, centre and goal of all economic and social life."

From the 1960s, the denominational traditions converge in the area of human rights so that we can talk of an ecumenical theology.

Christian anthropology is thus the basis of the Christian view of human rights. But the theological paths leading to this shared view are, as we have seen, not the same. One variant is to base human rights upon natural law. Another variant is to take as one's starting point God's covenant with his people and the new covenant in Christ. A third variant is to start with justification by grace in Christ. Catholics prior to the Second Vatican Council have predominantly taken the first path, the Calvinists the second and the Lutherans the third. The traditions meet in ecumenical theology and provide human rights primarily with a Christological basis. The various issues were discussed at a working conference on the theological basis of human rights in 1980.

10.4 The Roman Catholic View

Human rights are based upon some form of natural law theory and the idea of the general good or what is best for all. Human rights founded upon nature's laws and the natural light of reason belong to the natural order. The call of the church belongs to the supernatural order of grace. At the same time, it must speak prophetically as the defender of human rights. Grace extends beyond, heightens and completes the natural human rights.

After the Second Vatican Council, it was emphasized that the church proclaims human rights by virtue of the Gospel. Human rights movements have to be examined in the spirit of the Gospel.

10.5 The Eastern Orthodox View

The Eastern Orthodox scholars have developed a natural law theory as a support for their defence of human rights. Natural law binds the formulation of positive laws in the state and can have a healing effect against the abuse of human rights. Eastern Orthodoxy lays the foundation to a universal view of human rights. The ultimate basis for the restoration of human rights is the Gospel of Jesus Christ.

Within the World Council of Churches, it was above all the Orthodox who from their Trinitarian starting point in understanding the creation, were behind the demand for the integrity of creation. It is a work of God which creates, redeeems and sanctifies. In their ecological theology, they spoke about a cosmic Christ.

10.6 The Lutheran View

Lutheran theology stands for the two kingdoms doctrine with the Kingdom of God and the Kingdom of the World, the sphere of the church and the sphere of the state. Christians live in both kingdoms in dialectical balance and tension. God is Lord over both, ruling in the former through the Gospel and in the latter through the law. Justification by faith is the norm in the first Kingdom and justice in the second. Human rights belong to the Kingdom of the World.

Reason, enlightened by law and the Gospel, is needed so that Christians can deal with human rights and promote their implementation. As regards earthly life, it is a question of a rational approach while Biblical faith is the norm for life in the church. Human rights cannot be derived from particularly Christian principles. They are rights for all mankind even for thoose who do not, or will not, live according to the Gospel. From the perspective of the Gospel, the discovery of human dignity by secular human rights movements and their emphasis upon it, is something to be welcomed. The implementation of human rights is to be understood as a humanization process for everyone.

The Lutheran dichotomy between law and Gospel, reason and belief, the worldly order and the spiritual order, means that there are no clear Biblical principles which motivate Christian involvement in the campaign for human rights. This is true even if human rights contain a transcendental factor so that respect for human beings has a deeper meaning and that God forgives us our sins and receives us through grace into a union with Himself.

The two Kingdoms doctrine is the definitive model. Human rights belong to God's temporal Kingdom. In the church, human beings are brothers and sisters, members of one family. But even in the temporal Kingdom, human beings living according to the law must show that they are called to be the images of God.

The church has a critical and creative task as the defender of justice. The churches must make those in power responsible before the law of God. Their task is to proclaim the hope which God offers to victims of human rights violations. The church must protest where human rights are violated and oppose it. It must not justify the status quo but undertake passive resistance when open opposition is impossible.

10.7 The Reformed View

The theological contribution of Christian faith is to base the fundamental human rights upon Divine Right i.e. God's demands on human beings. Human rights are not based upon human nature. They reflect God's covenant with His people. No earthly authority can lawfully deny or suspend human beings' rights and dignity.

The forces of evil disturbed the covenant and human rights. Against this is set the liberating power of Jesus Christ. Theology contributes to the theory and practice of human rights by serving the Gospel. Obedience to this call means confrontation, struggle and suffering.

The Christian congregation's witness in the world is only credible and effective if it offers a faithful representation of the new creation, in which the image of God is re-established. The church can be a symbol to the world of true human existence under the dominion of Jesus Christ. In relation to society and culture, the church ought to point to the causes of violations of human rights. The Christian congregation has an obligation to counter the forces of oppression.

10.8 The View of the World Council of Churches

There is a parallel between the development in the UN and that in the World Council of Churches. Both have drawn the attention of the world to issues related to human rights.

In Amsterdam in 1948, it had been laid down that a responsible society is one where freedom is the freedom of human beings to feel a responsibility for justice and general order. Those who exercise political and economic power are responsible for their actions before God and the people whose welfare depends upon them.

Human rights implied above all religious liberty. This perspective was broadened at New Delhi in 1961. Human rights is a long series of things and religious freedom is one of that series.

At Uppsala in 1968, human rights were linked to social justice. The rights of the invdividual are linked to the struggle for an improved standard of living for the underprivileged in all nations.

At St. Pölten in 1974, it was laid down that individual rights and collective rights are not in opposition to one another. They are related to one another. The aim of society is to secure the welfare of all while the individual's goal is to serve what is best for all. The fundamental human right is the right to life.

At Nairobi in 1975, human rights were treated from the viewpoint of the struggle for freedom and against injustices. The human right which is mentioned first, is the right to life.

10.9 Towards an Ecumenical Theology of Human Rights

In the denominational bodies, three key terms occur: covenant, natural law and the worldly kingdom. In the Reformed tradition, human rights are linked to the covenant which God has entered into with mankind; in the Catholic tradition, human rights are linked to natural law; and in the Lutheran tradition, they are linked to the worldly kingdom. The Reformed churches base human rights, not only upon the old, but also upon the new covenant in Christ. Lutherans base human rights, not only upon the worldly kingdom, but also upon the spiritual kingdom. Finally Catholic base human rights, not only upon natural law, but also upon Christ. The trend towards an ecumenical theology of human rights is obvious. Human rights can only be fully understood in the light of Christ's life and works.

A shift takes place in all three denominations towards a more Christocentric foundation of human rights. This was part of the original teaching of the Reformed churches but has been reinforced and enters as a new element in the thinking of Lutherans and Catholics. Although human rights are to be found in God's covenant with mankind, in the worldly kingdom and in the natural law, it is God's work of redemption in Jesus Christ which is the real basis of human rights. For Lutherans, human rights grow from justification by faith. For the Reformed churches, God has made a new covenant in Christ from which human rights emerge. In the new man Christ, a new humanity is bestowed upon all who believe. This creates the preconditions for a complete implementation of human rights.

Basing human rights upon what is most holy and sacred, can lead to increased respect for them. What is most sacred varies from religion to religion; at the same time, it is to be found in all religious traditions. It gives a firmer basis for human rights than purely secular grounds in the form of philosophical or ideological traditions. Ultimately human rights are a question of morality. Religions, in contrast to secular ideologies, provide ethics with an absolute basis. Christian faith anchors human rights on God's revelation in Jesus Christ. All religions base ethics and human rights upon the divine. For Christians, the divine means specifically Jesus Christ. The Christian message about Jesus Christ reveals for mankind the deeper meaning of human life and therefore of human rights. It also encourages human and social changes which are necessary if human rights are to be attained.

From the accustomed intellectual standpoint, moral systems are seen as based upon a a particular society's tradition and with its particular history, culture and world view. The perspective of the believer is,however, another— whether Christian, Jew, Moslem, Hindu or Buddhist.

The Reformed churches are the least willing to find a basis for human rights outside the gospel since their perspective is holistic. But Catholics with their natural law and Lutherans with their worldly kingdom are prepared to see human rights outside the action-radius of the Gospel. Such rights are common for all human beings independently of faith. Complete insight into them, however, can only be achieved in the light of the Christian Gospel.

10.10 Concluding Reflections

The issue of human rights is universal. One possibility is to end up in cynical pessimism. Another possibility leads to optimism. According to Reinhold Niebuhr, it is necessary for the Christian to be realistic. The Kingdom of God has not been attained but constitutes our hope for the future.

The churches are agreed that human rights issues are important. This speaks for future unanimity in their pursuit.

In different Christian traditions, the theological accentuation varies in the motivation and formulation of human rights. However, they arrive at similar conclusions.

They diverge in theory but not in practice. This is also true of different Christian traditions in relation to the world religions. The theological arguments concerning human rights are advanced in these religions on the basis of other theoretical presuppositions and other frames of reference than the Christian. At the same time, the representatives of these non-Christian religious traditions demand the implementation of human rights.

The same words in differing religious and cultural traditions have, however, different meanings. In Christian belief, human beings are thought of as ambivalent and the world as dualistic. This view is not shared by all humanists.

In classical Roman Catholic theology this dualistic perspective was expressed in the scholastic view of nature and grace. Grace complements nature. The general sector of life, the state of nature is good but the state of grace is better.

In this Catholic view, human rights belong to the lower order of nature. They belong essentially to natural theology. But since the states of nature and grace are linked to one another, human rights belong also to the church. The church has the task of functioning as the conscience of society. It can therefore speak out about human rights issues.

Eastern Orthodoxy has also a dual perspective on reality. Human rights are a question of obedience to the natural law. There is a lower ethic based upon natural law and a higher ethic of the Gospel.

Within Lutheranism, there is also a dualistic view of reality and it is expressed in the dichotomy between law and the Gospel. There are two kingdoms which cooperate: the Kingdom of God and the Kingdom of the World. God's rule is present in both. In the former, He rules through the Gospel and in the latter through the law. In the church, human beings live according to the Gospel of justification by faith alone while social life is ruled according to the law of justice. Christians, as believers, live according to the Gospel of love and, as citizens, according to the law of justice.

Human rights belong to the Kingdom of the World and it is the duty of the state to secure them. But the implementation of human rights is also a matter for the church. There are links between the church and the world. The life of the Christian congregation must be reflected in society.

In the Roman Catholic, Eastern Orthodox and Lutheran traditions, there is a dualism in ethics. One norm applies to life within the church, Christian congregation and the Kingdom of God. Another norm is valid for the world, civil society, the Kingdom of the World.

The dualistic perspective is lacking in the Calvinist tradition's approach to human rights as it is expressed in the World Alliance of Reformed Churches. The Calvinist world view is holistic in its approach to issues of justice and human rights. It reckons with threee basic relations for human beings—to God, our neighbour and to the environment. Human rights relate to human beings in all their relations in life, to human beings in communion with others and to human beings in their communion with the non-human part of creation.

The World Council of Churches advocated in the beginning a liberal emphasis on human beings' supreme value as individuals. This later switched to a more collectivist view of human rights. Human rights are dependent upon so-

367

cial structures. The World Council of Churches acquired a more holistic approach to human rights when these were not simply defined as religious freedom. Human rights cannot be dealt with independently of questions about social structures and social justice. The World Council of Churches deal with human rights in the tension which exists between individual and society. Christian congregations must work to bring about the type of society which bears traces of the Kingdom of God and in which human beings, individually and collectively, can attain their full human potential.

The traditional denominationally determined theologies of human rights fade steadily into the background, giving way to an ecumenically oriented human rights theology which has taken its starting point in the perspective of God´s Kingdom and in the work of redemption of Jesus Christ. Among the signs of the arrival of the Kingdom of God was the reduction in human rights violations and Christ decisively paved the way for the Kingdom of God through His life and work. This ecumenical human rights theology which was accepted not only by the denominational traditions represented in the World Council of Churches but also by the Roman Catholic Church, was clearly Christological. Its most important precondition was historical-critical Biblical research and modern exegetics which extended over all traditional denominational boundaries. When it grew in strength in the Roma Catholic church, it influenced in a decisive way the outcome of the Second Vatican Council and paved the way for a new ecumenical theology which also included human rights.

Two parallel historical processes took place within Catholic and Lutheran theology. The former, after the Second Vatican Council, freed itself from a human rights theology which was exclusively based upon natural law and became receptive, due to the influence of modern exegetics, to a theology which was based upon Christology. The latter freed itself from a human rights theology which totally took its starting point in the Lutheran doctrine of the two kingdoms and switched more to basing its theology also upon the the idea of the Kingdom of God as it is presented in the New Testament, which modern Biblical research considered of central importance.

In both Catholic and Lutheran human rights theology there was a shift in emphasis and a new orientation due to the influence of modern exegetics. It has had a visible effect in human rights theology and makes it ecumenical. Modern Biblical research frees both Catholic and Lutheran human rights theology from a one-sided, rigid adherence to old theological categories such as the scholastic doctrine of natural law and the Lutheran doctrine of two kingdoms. These theological traditions come nearer to one another and are able to bridge old theological differences. Human rights theology is a watershed for this movement towards ecumenical agreement, mainly inspired by the modern Bible movement.

Sources and Bibliography

Abraham, G., 1989. The Catholic Church and Apartheid The Response of the Catholic Church in South Africa to the First Decade of National Party Rule, 1948–1957.

Adler, E., 1974. A Small Beginning An Assesement of the First Five Years of the PCR.

Al-Azmek, A., 1993. Islam and Modernities.

Alberts, L. and Chikane, F. (eds.), 1991. The Road to Rustenburg The Church Looking Forward to A New South Africa.

Alexeyeva, L., 1987. Contemporary Movements for National Religious and Human Rights.

Alfaro, J., 1973. Theology of Justice in the World Pontifical Commission Justice and Peace 3.

Alston, P. (ed.), 1992. The United Nations and Human Rights A Critical Appraisal.

ANC, 1971. African National Congress (South Africa) PCR.

Andelson, R. V., 1971. Imputed Rights An Essay in Christian Social Theory.

André-Vincent P, J. 1983. Les droits de l'homme dans l'enseignement de Jean Paul II (Paris Librairie Générale de Droit et de Jurisprudence, 1983).

Anglican Consultative Council Report of the 4th Meeting 1979, 8th May–18th May 1979. A Theological Basis of Human Rights, 1979.

An-Na'im A. A., 1992. Human Rights in Cross-Cultural Pespectives A Quest for Concensus.

An-Na'im A. A., 1990. Toward an Islamic Reformation Civil Liberties Human Rights and International Law.

An-Na'im A. A. and Deng F. M. (eds.), 1991. Human Rights in Africa Cross-Cultural Perspectives.

An-Na'im A. A., Gort J. D., Jansen. H. and Vroom, H. M., 1995. Human Rights and Religious Values An Uneasy Relationship?

Ansbro, J. J., 1982. Martin Luther King Jr., The Making of a Mind.

Armstrong, R. and Shenk, J. 1982. El Salvador The Face of Revolution.

Arrupe, P., 1980. Justice with Faith Today Selected Letters and Addresses.

Arrupe, P., 1972. Witnessing to Justice Pontifical Commission Justice and Peace (Justice in the World, No. 2).

Aubert, J. M., 1987. Droits de l'homme et libération évangélique.

Aubert, J. M., 1986. Human Rights Challenge to the Churches Theology Digest 1986, 33 (1).

Austad, T., 1978. The Theological Foundation of Human Rights i Lissner, J. and Sovik, A. (eds.). A Lutheran Reader on Human Rights LWF Report.

Avineri, S. and de-Shalit, A., 1992. Communitarianism and Individualism.

Bailey, D. (ed.), 1988. Human Rights and Responsibilities in Britain and Ireland A Christian Perspective.

Baker, E. (ed.), 1971. Social Contract Locke Hume Rousseau.

Baldwin, L. W., 1991. There is a Balm in Gilead The Cultural Roots of Martin Luther King Jr.

Baldwin, L. W., 1992. To Make the Wounded Whole The Cultural Legacy of Martin Luther King Jr.

The Barbados Discussion International Review of Mission, Vol. LXII, No. 247, 1973.

Barreiro, J. 1975. In Defence of Human Rights ER 27:2 (1975).

Barth, K., 1960. The Christian Community and the Civil Community in W. Herberg ed Community State and Church Three Essays.

Bartolomei, M. L., 1994. Gross and Massive Violations of Human Rights in Argentina: 1976–1983. An Analysis of the Procedure under ECOSOC Resolution 1503.

Bassarak, G. and Wirth, G., 1977. Herausforderung des Gewissens Über den ökumenischen Beitrag zum Kampf gegen den Rassismus.

Baum, G. and Coleman, J. (eds.), 1982. The Church and Racism Concilium.

Baur, J. (hrsg), 1977. Zum Thema Menschenrechte Theologische Versuche und Entwürfe.

Beck, L. and Keddie, N., 1978. Women in the Muslim World.

Beckmann, K. M., 1971. Anti-Rassismus Programme der Ökumene Dokumentation einer Auseinandersetzung zusammangestellt und kommentiert.

Beddard, R., 1980. Human Rights and Europe A Study of the Machinery of Human Rights Protection of the Council of Europe.

Bent, A. van der (ed.), 1986. Breaking Down the Walls WCC's Statements and Actions on Racism 1948–1979.

Bent ,A. van der, 1986. Christian Response in a World of Crisis A Brief History of the WCC's CCIA.

Bent, A. van der, 1995. Commitment to God's World A Concise Critical Survey of the Ecumenical Social Thought.

Bent, A. van der, 1985. Incarnation and New Creation The Ecumenical Movement at the Crossroads.

Bent, A. van der, 1978. Index to the WCC's Official Statements and Reports 1948–1978.

Bent, A. van der, 1981. Major Studies and Themes in the Ecumenical Movement.

Bent, A. van der, 1983. Six Hundred Ecumenical Consultations 1948–1982.

Bent, A. van der, 1986. Vital Ecumenical Concerns Sixteen Documentary Surveys.

Berbe, D., 1987. Grace and Power Base Communities and Nonviolence in Brazil.

Berting, J. et al. (eds.), 1990. Human Rights in a Pluralist World Individuals and Collectivities.

Best, T. F. (ed.), 1990. Vancouver to Canberra 1983–1990 Report of the Central Committee to the Seventh Assembly of the WCC.

Between Honesty and Hope Documents from and about the Church in Latin America where the Crisis Deepens and Violence Threatens, 1970.

Biardeau, M., 1992. Hinduism The Anthropology of a Civilisation.

Bindman, G. (ed.), 1988. South Africa Human Rights and the Rule of Law 1988. International Commission of Jurists.

Birch, C. and Cobb, J. B., 1981. The Liberation of Life.

Bischofssynode 1974, 1974. Botschaft über Menschenrechte und Versöhnung Herder Korrespondenz Monatshefte für Gesellschaft und Religion, Heft 12, 28 Jahrgang, Dezember 1974.

Blanchard, P. and Landstreet, P. (eds.), 1989. Human Rights in Latin America and the Caribbean.

Blaustein, A. P., Clark, R. S and Siegler, J. A. (eds.), 1987. Human Rights Sourcebook.

Bloed, A. (ed.), 1990. From Helsinki to Vienna Basic Documents of the Helsinki Process.

Bloed, A. and Dijk, P. van (eds.), 1991. The Human Dimension of the Helsinki Process The Vienna Follow-up Meeting and its Aftermath.

Board of Church and Society of the Methodist Church ed The Quest for Human Rights in Engage/Social Action March, 1978.

Boesak, A., 1984. Black and Reformed Apartheid Liberation and the Calvinist Tradition.

Boesak, A., 1977. Farewell to Innocence A Socio-Ethical Study on Black Theology and Black Power.

Boesak, A., 1982. The Finger of God Sermons and Faith and Socio-Political Responsibility.

Boesak, A., 1987. If This is Treason I am Guilty.

Boesak, A., 1984. Walking on Thorns The Call to Christian Obedience.

Boesak, A. and Villa-Vicencio, C. (eds.), 1986. When Prayer Makes News.

Boff, C., 1987. Feet-on-the Ground-Theology A Brazilian Journey.

Boff, L., 1981. Church Charism and Power Liberation Theology and the Institutional Church.

Bolté, P. E., 1975. Les droits de l'homme et la papauté contemporaine synthese et textes.

Bonino, J. M., 1977. Whose Human Rights A Historico-Theological Meditation International Review of Mission, 1977.

Bourdeax, M., Hebly, H and Voss, E. (eds.), 1976. Religious Liberty in the Soviet Union WCC and USSR A Post-Nairobi Documentation.

Brackney, H. (ed.), 1990. Faith Life and Witness The Papers of the Study and Research Division of the Baptist World Alliance 1986–1990.

Branch, T., 1988. Parting the Waters America in the King Years 1954–63.

Brazilian National Bishops Conference A Universal Declaration of Human Rights, LADOC 4 (October 1973): 1–7.

Breslin, J. B., 1981. A Voice for the Voiceless America 1981, 144 (24).

Brezjnev, L. I., 1980. Socialism Democracy and Human Rights.

Brockmann, J. R., 1982. The Word Remains A Life of Oscar Romero.

Broderick, J. W., 1975. Camillo Torres A Biography of the Priest-Guerrillero.

Brugger, H., 1986. Les droits de l'homme dans la pensée de Jaques Maritain Theses ad doctorum in S theologia Pontifical Universit Roma.

Brugger, W., 1980. Menschenrechtsethos und Verantwortungspolitik Max Webers Beitrag zur Analyse und Begründung der Menschenrechte.

Burke, E. III and Lapidus, I. M., 1988. Islam Politics and Social Movements.

Böckenförde, E. W. and Spaemann, R. (hrsg), 1987. Menschenrechte und Menschenwürde Historische Voraussetzungen-Säkulare Gestalt- christliches Verständnis.

Calvez, J. Y., 1985. Droits de l'homme justice evangile conférences de Careme 1985 a Notre Dame de Paris texte intégral et compléments.

Calvez, J. Y., 1985. Foi et justice La dimension sociale de l'évangélisation.

Calvez, J. Y., 1966. Johannes XXIII und die Menschenrechte (Freiheit und Ordnung Soziale Fragen der Gegenwart 46).

Calvez, J. Y., 1965. The Social Thought of John XXIII.

Camara, H., 1970. Kapplöpning med tiden.

Camara, H., 1970. Spiral of Violence.

Camara, H., 1971. Våldets spiral.

Campbell ,T., 1983. The Left and Rights A Conceptual Analysis of the Idea of Socialist Rights.

Camps, A., 1983. Partners in Dialogue Christianity and Other World Religions.

Carr, B., 1975. Biblical and Theological Basis for the Struggle for Human Rights, ER 27:2, 1975.

Carter, J., 1984. Human Rights Dilemmas and Directions Transformation 1984, 1 (4).

Casalis, G., 1977. Torture and Prayer International Review of Mission 1977.

Catholic Church National Conference of Catholic Bishops Brothers and Sisters to us US Bishops' Pastoral Letter on Racism in Our Day November 14, 1979. Washington DC United States Catholic Conference 1979.

Central Committee of WCC Minutes and Reports of the Twenty-Fourth Meeting at Addis Ababa Ethiopia January 10–21, 1971, of the Twenty-Fifth Meeting at Utrecht The Netherlands August 13–23, 1972, of the Twenty-Sixth Meeting at Geneva Switzerland August 22–29, 1973, of the Twenty-Ninth Meeting Geneva Switzerland 10–18, August 1976, of the Thirtieth Meeting Geneva Switzerland 28 July–6 August 1977, 1971–1977.

Central Committee of WCC Kingston Jamaica January 1–11 1979, Document No. 13, 1979.

Chalidge, V., 1975. To Defend These Rights Human Rights and the Soviet Union.

Chamarik, S., 1981. Buddhism and Human Rights Human Rights Teaching, UNESCO 2:1, 1981.

Chandran, U. M., 1975. Is Christ no Male or Female, ER 27:2, 1975.

Chapelle, P. de la, 1967. La déclaration universelle des droits de l'homme et le catholicisme Lettre liminaire de René Cassin; préface de Jean-Yves Calvez.

Chernenko, K. U., 1981. Human Rights in Soviet Society.

Childs, J. M., 1980. The Church and Human Rights Reflections on Morality and Mission Currents in Theology and Mission 1980, 7 (1).

Chileote, R. H. (ed.), 1970. Revolution and Structural Change in Latin America 1–2.

Chouriri, Y. M., 1990. Islamic Fundamentalism.

Christian Existence in Dialogue Doing Theology in all Seasons In Memory and Appreciation of Josef L Hromadka, 1990.

Christian and Race Relations in Southern Africa Report on Ecumenical Consultation, 1964.

The Church and Human Rights Pontifical Commission Justitia et Pax Working Paper No. 1, 1975.

Church and Nation Theological Conference Papers (Grand Rapids:Reformed Ecumenical Synod 1981), 1981.

The Church and Racism Towards a more Fraternal Society Pontifical Commission Iustitia et Pax, 1988.

The Churches in International Affairs CCIA Background Information

1975/2 The Churches and Human Rights in Africa.

1975/3 M Ndoh Violation of Human Rights in Africa.

1975/5 Conference on Security and Cooperation in Europe The Helsinki Declaration A First Summary and First Appraisal.

1975/8 Human Rights and Christian Responsibility.

1978/8 H Thoolen The Need for an International Convention against Torture.

1979/1 Human Rights in the Republic of Korea.

1981/1 El Salvador One year of Repression.

1981/3 J. Zalaquette The Human Rights Issue and the Human Rights Movement.

1982/3 Militarism and Human Rights.

1983/1 Human Rights Violations in the West Bank.

1983/3 E Weingärtner Human Rights on the Ecumenical Agenda.

The Churches in International Affairs CCIA/WCC Reports 1970–1973, 1974–1978, 1979–1982, 1983–1986, 1987–1990, 1974–1991.

Churches Responding to Racism in the 1980s The Report of the World Consultation on Racism called by the WCC held in Noordwijkerhout Netherlands 16–21 June 1980, 1983.

Claude, R. P. and Weston, B. H. (eds.), 1992. Human Rights in the World Community Issues and Action.

Cleary, E. (ed.), 1989. Path from Puebla Significant Documents of the Latin American Bishops since 1979.

Clemens, J., 1984. Menschenwürde und Recht Die Menschenrechte in der neueren theologischen Diskussion.

Cohn, H. H., 1984. Human Rights in Jewish Law.

Coleman, J. A. (ed.), 1991. One Hundred Years of Catholic Social Thought Celebration and Challenge.

Coleman, J. and Baum, G. (eds.), 1991. One Hundred Years of Catholic Social Teaching Concilium.

Collange, J. F., 1983. The Churches and Human Rights in Europe, RW 1983, Volym 37 (8).

Collange, J. F., 1989. Théologie des droits de l'homme.

Colonnese, L. M. (ed.), 1970. Human Rights and the Liberation of Man in the Americas.

Comblin, J., 1992. The Church and Defense of Human Rights i E Dussel ed The Church in Latin America 1492–1992.

Comblin, J., 1979. The Church and the National Security State.

Cone, J. H., 1969. Black Theology and Black Power.

Cone, J. H., 1970. A Black Theology of Liberation.

Cone, J. H., 1984. For my People Black Theology and the Black Church.

Cone, J. H., 1993. Martin and Malcolm and America A Dream or a Nightmare.

Conyers, A. J., 1988. God Hope and History Jürgen Moltmann and the Christian Concept of History.

Cooper, J. W., 1985. The Theology of Freedom The Legacy of Jaques Maritain and Reinhold Niebuhr.

Coste, R.,1988. L'Église et les droits de l'homme.

Crahan, M. E. (ed.), 1982. Human Rights and Basic Needs in the Americas.

Crawford, S C. (ed.), 1989. World Religions and Global Ethics.

Cronin, K., 1992. Rights and Christian Ethics.

Da Fonseca, G., 1975. How to file Complaints of Human Rights Violation A Practical Intergovernmental Procedures.

The Dalai Lama, 1984. A Human Approach to World Peace.

Danelius, H., 1984. Mänskliga rättigheter.

From Dar es Salam to Budapest 1977–1984, Reports on the Work of the, LWF 1984.

Dassin, J. (ed.), 1986. Torture in Brazil A Report by the Archdiocese of Sao Paulo.

de Broucker, J., 1969. Dom Helder Camara The Violence of A Peacemaker.

Debt, D. H. P., 1989. Development and Democracy Recent trends in Latin America in P. Blanchard and and P. Landstreet eds Human Rights in Latin America and the Caribbean.

de Gruchy, J. W., 1979. The Church Struggle in South Africa.

de Gruchy, J. W., and Villa-Vicencio, C. (eds.), 1983. Apartheid is a Heresy.

de Santa Ana, J., 1979. New Frontiers of Christian Mission in Areas of Political Tension International Review of Mission 1979, 68 (272).

Dobel ,J. P., 1977. Bearing Witness and Human Rights Christian Century 1977, 94 (27).

Dodson, M., 1979. The Christian Left in Latin American Politics Journal of Inter-American Studies and World Affairs, Febr. 1979.

Dokumente der Moskauer Helsinki-Gruppe Texte der Förderungsgruppe zur Erfüllung der Beschlüsse von Helsinki in der UDSSR 1977.

Donelly, J., 1991. Human Rights and World Politics.

Donelly, J., 1989. Universal Human Rights in Theory and Practice.

Downing, T. E. and Kushner, G. (eds.), 1988. Human Rights and Anthropology.

Drinan, R. F., 1987. Cry of the Oppressed The History and Hope of the Human Rights Revolution.

Drinan, R. F., 1981. Human Rights in Argentina America 1981, 145 (10).

Drinan, R. F., 1982. Human Rights in El Salvador America 1982, 146 (7).

Les droits de l'homme et l'église Réflexions historiques et théologiques Conseil Pontifical Justice et Paix Relations présentées a un Colloque international organisé a Rome du 14 au 16 november 1988 par la Conseil Pontifical Justice et Paix 1990.

Duchrow, U., 1994. Alternativen zur kapitalistischen Weltwirtschaft Biblische Erinnerung und politische Ansätze zur Überwindung einer lebensbedrohenden Ökonomie.

Duchrow, U. hrsg, 1976. Die Ambivalenz der Zweireichlehre in lutherischen Kirchen des 20. Jahrhunderts.

Duchrow, U., 1969. Christenheit und Veltverantwortung Traditionsgeschichte und systematische Struktur der Zweireichlehre.

Duchrow, U., 1977. Lutheran Churches—Salt or Mirror of Society Case Studies on the Theory and Practice of the Two Kingdoms Doctrine.

Duchrow, U., 1977. Two Kingdoms—The Use and Misuse of A Lutheran Theological Concept.

Dunér, B., 1992. Fria och lika i värde Mänskliga rättigheter i ett samhällsvetenskapligt perspektiv.

Dussel, E. (ed.), 1992. The Church in Latin America 1492–1992.

Dwyer, K., 1991. Arab Voices The Human Rights Debate in the Middle East.

Dyck, A. J. (ed.), 1985. Human Rights and the Global Mission of the Church Boston Theological Institute Annual Series, Vol. 1.

Dähn, H., 1982. Konfrontation oder Kooperation Das Verhältnis von Staat und Kirche in der SBZ/DDR 1945–1980.

Eagleson, J. and Scharper, P. (eds.), 1979. Puebla and Beyond Documentation and Commentary.

Economic Justice for All Pastoral Letter on Catholic Social Teaching and the US Economy National Conference of Catholic Bishops NCCB Washington DC 1986.

The Ecumenical Review WCC A Special Issue on Human Rights Vol. XXVII, No. 2, April 1975.

Ecumenical Statements in Race Relations Development of Ecumenical Thought on Race Relations 1937–1964, 1965.

Edwards, R., Henkin, L. and Nathan, A. (eds.), 1986. Human Rights in Contemporary China.

Eide, A. and Helgesen, J. (eds.), 1991. The Future of Human Rights Protection in A Changing World Fifty Years since the Four Freedoms Address Essays in Honour of Torkel Opsahl.

Eide, A., Krause, C. and Rosas, H. (eds.), 1995. Economic Social and Cultural Rights A Textbook.

El Salvador's Decade of Terror Human Rights since the Assassination of Archbishop Romero 1991.

The Encounter of the Church with Movements of Social Change in Various cultural contexts 1977.

Erdozain, P., 1981. Archbishop Romero Martyr of Salvador.

Evangelical Witness in South Africa a Critique of Evangelical Theology and Practice by South African Evangelicals 1986.

Evans, A., 1981. Worker's Rights are Human Rights IDOC International Rome.

Evans, R. A. and A. F., 1983. Human Rights A Dialogue Between the First and Third Worlds.

Evans, S. H., 1972. Christianity and Human Rights i An Introduction to the Study of Human Rights Introduction by Sir F. Vallat.

Evanston to New Delhi WCC 1961.

Falconer, A. D. (ed.), 1980. Understanding Human Rights An Interdisciplinary and Interfaith Study The Proceedings of the International Consultation held in Dublin 1978.

Falk, R. A., Kim, S. S., Mendlovitz, S. H. (eds.), 1991. The United Nations and A Just World Order.

Farer, T. J., 1988. The Grand Strategy of The United States in Latin America.

Fein, H., 1979. Accounting for Genocide National Responses and Jewish Victimization during the Holocost.

Fenton, T. P. and Heffron, M. J. (eds.), 1989. Human Rights A Directory of Resources.

Filibeck, G., 1994. Human Rights in the Teaching of the Church: from John XXIII to John Paul II Collection of Texts of the Magisterium of the Catholic Church from Mater et Magistra to Centesimus Annus 1961–1991.

Finnis, J., 1980. Natural Law and Natural Rights.

The First Six Years 1948–1954, WCC 1954.

Forbes, R., 1968. Humanism and Human Rights A Christian View.

Formicula, J. R., 1988. The Catholic Church and Human Rights Its Role in the Formulation of US Policy 1945–1980.

Forms of Solidarity Human Rights 14–25 August 1987, Centre International Réformé John Knox 1988.

Forrester, D. B., 1985. Christianity and the Future of Welfare.

Franck, T. M., 1982. Human Rights in Third World Perspective, 3 Vols.

Frank, A. G., 1969. Latin America Underdevelopment or Revolution.

Freeman, M. and Veerman, P. (eds.), 1992. The Ideologies of Children's Rights.

Freire, P., 1972. Pedagogik för förtryckta.

Friedman, J. R. and Sherman, M. I. (eds.), 1985. Human Rights An International and Comparative Law Bibliography.

Fruhling, H., 1987. Political Repression and the Defense of Human Rights.

Fuchs et Stucki ,P. A., 1985. Au Nom de l'autre Essai sur le fondement des droits de l'homme.

Galtung, J., 1977. Human Needs as the Focus of the Social Sciences.

Gandhi, M.,1961. None High None Low.

Gandhi, M. K., 1983. Autobiography The Story of My Experiments with Truth.

Garreton, M., 1979. On the Problem of Human Rights Today Human Rights and the Social Crisis in Human Rights Concerns LWF.

Garton, A. T., 1983. The Polish Revolution Solidarity 1980–82.

Gauding, A. K., 1991. Hellre tända ett ljus än förbanna mörkret Om Diakonias arbete för mänskliga rättigheter i Latinamerika.

Gau-Jeng, J., 1990. Kants Lehre vom Menschenrecht und von den staatsbürgerlichen Grundrechten.

George, R. P. (ed.), 1992. Natural Law Theory Contemporary Essays.

Gerassi , J. (ed.), 1971. Revolutionary Priest The Complete Writings and Messages of Camillo Torres.

Gibellini, R. (ed.), 1983. Frontiers of Theology in Latin America.

Gill, D. (ed.), 1983. Gathered for Life Official Report of the VI Assembly of the WCC Vancouver, Canada, 24 July–10 August 1983.

Gilsenan, M., 1990. Recognizing Islam Religion and Society in the Modern Middle East.

Goodall, N., 1968. The Uppsla Report 1968 Official Report of the Forth Assembly of the WCC Uppsla, July 4–20 1968.

Green, R. M., 1988. Religion and Moral Reason A New Method for Comparative Study.

Greidanus, S., 1984. Human Rights in Biblical Perspectives Calvin Theological Journal 1984, 19 (1).

Gremillon, J., 1977. World Faiths and the New World Order A Muslim-Jewish-Christian Search Begins.

Gutiérrez, G., 1983. The Power of the Poor in History.

Gutiérrez, G., 1973. A Theology of Liberation History Politics and Salvation.

Guzman, G., 1969. Camillo Torres.

Hafner, F.,1992. Kirchen im Kontext der Grund- und Menschenrechte.

Hagon, W., 1990. The Social and Legal Status of Women A Global Perspective.

Haider, S. M. (ed.), 1978. Islamic Concept of Human Rights.

Hampton, J., 1986. Hobbes and the Social Contract Tradition.

Hanson, E. O., 1987. The Catholic Church in World Politics.

Harakas, S. S., 1982. Human Rights An Eastern Ortodox Perspective Journal of Ecumenical Studies 1982 19 (3).

Harrelson, W., 1980. The Ten Commandments and Human Rights.

Harris, I., 1994. The Mind of John Locke A Study of Political Theory in its Intellectual Setting.

Hassan, R., 1982. On Human Rights and the Quaranic Perspective Journal of Ecumenical Studies 19:3 1982.

Hebbletwaite, P., 1982. Human Rights in the Church Journal of Ecumenical Studies 1982, 19 (2).

Hebbletwaite, P., 1984. John XXIII Pope of the Council.

Hebbletwaite, P., 1993. Paul VI The First Modern Pope.

Heckel , R., 1979. The Struggle Against Racism Some Contributions of the Church Pontifical Commission Iustitia et Pax 4 The Decade of Action to Combat Racism 1973–1983.

Hedin, C., 1988. Alla är födda muslimer Islam som den naturliga religionen enligt fundamentalistisk apologetik.

Heinz, S. H., 1980. Menschenrechte und Dritte Welt Zur Frage nach den Ursachen von Menschenrechtsverletzungen.

Heller, A., 1987. Beyond Justice.

Heller, A. and Fehér, F., 1991. From Yalta to Glasnost The Dismantling of Stalins Empire.

Henkin, L., 1990. The Age of Rights.

Hennelly, A. and Langan, J. (eds.), 1982. Human Rights in the Americas The Struggle for Consensus.

Herr, T., 1982. Johannes Paul II und die Menschenrechte Neue Wege der katholischen Soziallehre? (Kirche und Gesellschaft 90).

Hertz, K., 1987. Tutu and Boesak Liberation Theology as Praxis Mid-Stream 1987, 26 (1).

Heuvel, A. van den, 1979. Shalom and Combat A Personal Struggle Against Racism.

Hewitt, W. E., 1991. Base Christian Communities and Social Change in Brazil.

Hewitt, W. E., 1989. Strategies for Social Change employed by Communidades Eclesiais de Base (CEBs) in the Archdiocese of Sao Paolo i P Blanchard and P Landstrect eds Human Rights in Latin America and the Caribbean.

Hick, J., 1989. An Interpretation of Religions.

Hobbes, J., 1969. Leviathan.

Hoffman, J. hrsg, 1991. Begründung von Menschenrechte aus der Sicht Unterschieldlicher Kulturen Das eine Menschenrecht für alle und die vielen Lebensformen.

Holleman, W. L., 1987. The Human Rights Movement Western Values and Theological Perspectives.

Hollenbach, D., 1979. Claims in Conflict Retrieving and Renewing the Catholic Human Rights Tradition.

Hollenbach, D., 1982. Human Rights and Religious Faith in the Middle East Reflections of a Christian Theologian i Human Rights Quarterly, Vol. 4, No. 1, 1982.

376

Hollenbach, D., 1988. Justice Peace and Human Rights American Catholic Social Ethics in a Pluralistic Context.

Honecker, M., 1978. Das Recht des Menschen Einführung in die evangelische Sozialethik.

Hopkins, D. N., 1989. Black Theology USA and South Africa Politics Culture and Liberation.

Hsiung, J., 1985. Human Rights in East Asia A Cultural Perspective.

Huber, W., 1989. Menschenrechte- Christenrechte i Rechte nach Gottes Wort Menschenrechte und Grundrechte in Gesellschaft und Kirche.

Huber, W. und Tödt, H. E., 1977. Menschenrechte Perspektiven einer Menschlichen Welt.

Hufton, O. (ed.), 1995. Historical Change and Human Rights The Oxford Amnesty Lectures 1994.

Hug, J. E., 1980. Moral Judgment the Theory and Practice in the Thought of Jaques Maritain.

Human Rights and Christian Responsibility (Preparatory Documents for the St. Pölten Conference) WCC Mimeographed, 1974.

Human Rights and Christian Responsibility (2nd Series of Preparatory Documents for the St. Pölten Conference) WCC Mimeographed, 1974.

Human Rights and Christian Responsibility (Report from the Working Groups St. Pölten 1974) WCC 1974.

Human Rights and Christian Responsibility Report of the Consultation St Pölten Austria 21–26 October 1974, WCC CCIA 1974.

Human Rights and Christian Responsibility St. Pölten The statement of Paul VI and the Synod of Bishops etc. RW Vol. 33, No. 4, Dec. 1974

Human Rights and the Church Historical and Theological Reflections Conferences presented at an International Colloquium organized by the Pontifical Council for Justice and Peace Rome 14–16 November 1988, 1990.

Human Rights—Helsinki Belgrade and Beyond RW Vol. 35, No. 1, March 1978.

Human Rights Christianity and Other Religions Studia Missionalia 1990.

Human Rights Comments and Interpretations A Symposium ed by UNESCO with an Introduction by J. Maritain 1950.

Human Rights in Latin America 1964–1980. A Selective Annotated Bibliography Compiled and edited by the Hispanic Division 1983.

Human Rights Teaching Biannual Bulletin, Vol. II, No. 1, 1981 UNESCO, Place of Human Rights in Different Religious Pespectives 1981 .

Human Rights Teaching Biannual Bulletin, Vol. IV, 1985, UNESCO Enseignement des droits de l'homme 1985.

The Human Rights Watch Global Report on Women's Human Rights Human Rights Watch Women's Rights Project 1995.

Human Rights WCC Documentation 1979.

Humphreys, C. (ed.), 1979. The Wisdom of Buddhism.

Höffe, O. et al., 1980. Jean Paul II et les droits de l'homme.

Höffe, O., Macheret, A., de Oliveira, C. J. P and de Habich, C., 1981. Johannes Paul II und die Menschenrechte Ein Jahr Pontifikat.

IDOC International ,The Church at the Crossroads Christians in Latin America from Medellin to Puebla 1968–1978, 1978.

Inada, K. K., 1982. The Buddhist Perspective on Human Rights Journal of Ecumenical Studies 19:3, 1982.

Institutet för mänskliga rättigheter Åbo Akademi Hur tackla rasismen Föreläsningar om mänskliga rättigheter och rasism 1989.

International Dimensions of Humanitarian Law UNESCO 1988.

International Institute of Philosophy UNESCO hg Philosophical Foundations of Human Rights 1986.

International Review of Mission A Special Issue on Human Rights with Biblical and Theological Insights, Vol. LXVI, No. 263, July 1977, 1977.

Iwe, N. S. S., 1986. The History and Contents of Human Rights A Study of the History and Interpretation of Human Rights.

Jackson, W. A., 1990. Gunnar Myrdal and America's Conscience Social Engineering and Racial Liberalism 1938–1987.

Jacobs, F. G., 1975. The European Convention on Human Rights.

Jean Paul II, 1980. Les droits de l'homme Textes de Jean Paul II (Octobre 1978–Décembre 1979).

Jean Paul II, 1980. En France mai–juin 1980.

Jenkins, D. E., 1974. Human Rights in Christian Perspective in Study Encounter, No. 2, 1974.

Jenkins, D., 1975. A Theological Inquiry Concerning Human Rights Some Questions Hypotheses and Answers, ER 27:2, 1975.

The Jesuit Assassinations The Writings of Ellacuria, Martin Baro and Segundo Montes with a Chronology of the Investigation (November 11 1989–October 22 1990) 1990.

Johannes XXIII, 1963. PT Rundskrivelse om freden på jorden i sannning rättfärdighet kärlek och frihet. Särtryck ur Credo katolsk tidskrift 1963:4.

Johannes Paulus II, 1982. Päpstliche Kommission Iustitia et Pax Die Menschenrechte Texte von Johannes Paulus II.

Johannes Paulus II, 1989. Sollicitudo Rei Socialis Kyrkans omsorg om utveckling och fred.

Johannes Paulus II, 1979. Die Würde des Menschen in Christus Die Antrittsenzyklika RH Papst Johannes Paulus II Mit einem Kommentar von Bernhard Häring.

John Paul II, 1979. In Mexico His Collected Speeches.

John Paul II, 1988. Mulieris Dignitatem On the Dignity and Vocation of Women Apostolic Letter August 15.

John Paul II, Pilgrim of Peace The Homilies and Adresses of His Holiness Pope John II on the Occasion of His Visit to the United States of America. October 1979.

John Paul II, The Pope Speaks to the American Church John Paul II's Homilies Speeches and Letters to Catholics in the United States.

John Paul II, 1979. Return to Poland The Collected Speeches of John Paul II.

John Paul II, 1980. The Social Teaching of John Paul II Pontifical Commission Iustitia et Pax 1979–1982, Volym 3. Religious Freedom (October 1978–November 1979) Presented by R. Heckel.

John Paul II, 1981. The Social Teaching of John Paul II Pontifical Commission Iustitia et Pax 1979–1982, Volym 7. Human Rights Texts of John Paul II (October 1978–December 1979) Presented by G. Filibeck.

Johnson, D. (ed.), 1975. Uppsala to Nairobi Report of the Central Committee to the Fifth Assembly of the WCC.

Jong-Sun, N., 188/89. Human Ecology in a Divided Land Toward A Theology of Silver Fishes in the Imjeen River RW 1988/89.

Journal of Ecumenical Studies A Special Issue on Human Rights 1982, 19:3, 1982.

Joyce, J. A., 1978. The New Politics of Human Rights.

Joyce, J. A., 1980. World Labour Rights and Their Protection.

Kalivoda, 1968. Freedom and Equality The Origin of The Ideals and the Problem of their Realization LW 1968.

Kanger, H., 1984. Human Rights in the UN Declaration.

Karpat, K. H. (ed.), 1982. Political and Social Thought in the Contemporary Middle East.

Kaufmann, H. N., 1981. The Dynamics of Human Rights in US Foreign Policy.

Kelsay, J. and Twiss, S. B. (eds.), 1994. Religion and Human Rights Religion and the

Roots of Conflict Religious Militancy or Fundamentalism Universality vs Relativism in Human Rights Positive Resources of Religion for Human Rights The Project on Religion and Human Rights.

Kerber, W. hrsg, 1991. Menschenrechte und kulturelle Identität O. Hoffe, W. Pannenberg, H. Scholler, W. Schild, Ein Symposion.

Khan, M. Z., 1970. Islam and Human Rights.

Die Kirche und die Menschenrechte Ein Arbeitspapier der Päpstlichen Kommission Justitia et Pax 1976.

Klaiber, J., 1992. The Catholic Church in Peru 1821–1985. A Social History.

Konvitz, M. R. (ed.), 1972. Judaism and Human Rights.

Koshy, N., 1994. Churches in the World of Nations International Politics and the Mission and Ministry of the Church.

Kotb, S., 1953. Social Justice in Islam.

Kowalczyk, S., 1984. The Possibilities of Christian-Marxist Dialogue on Human Rights Soundings 1984, 67 (2).

Kramer, D. C., 1982. Comparative Civil Rights and Liberties.

Krogh, D. (ed.), 1985. Central America Human Rights and US Foreign Policy.

Krogh, D. (ed.), 1990. Church and Politics in Latin America.

Krogh, D. (ed.), 1981. Romero El Salvador's Martyr A Study of the Tragedy of El Salvador.

Krusche, G., 1977. Human Rights in a Theological Perspective A Contribution from the GDR, LW 1977, 24 (1).

Kubik, J., 1994. The Power of Symbols against the Symbols of Power The Rise of Solidarity and the Fall of State Socialism in Poland.

Kühnhardt, L., 1987. Die Universalität der Menschenrechte Studie zur ideengeschichtlichen Bestimmung eines politischen Schlüsselbegriffs (Studien zur Geschichte und Politik 256).

Küng, H., 1997. A Global Ethic for Global Politics and Economics

Küng, H., 1991. Global Responsibility In Search of a New World Ethic.

Küng, H., 1988. Theology for Third Millenium An Ecumenical View.

Küng, H. et al., 1986. Christianity and the World Religions Paths to Dialogue with Islam Hinduism and Buddhism.

Küng, H. and Ching, J., 1994. Christianity and Chinese Religions.

Küng, H. and Kuschel, K. J. (eds.), 1993. A Global Ethic The Declaration of the Parliament of the World's Religions.

Küng, H. and Moltmann, J. (eds.), 1986. Christianity among World Religions Concilium.

Küng, H. and Moltmann, J. (eds.), 1990 The Ethics of World Religions and Human Rights Concilium.

Laccy, M. J. and Haakonssen, K. (ed.), 1991. A Culture of Rights The Bill of Rights in Philosophy Politics and Law—1791 and 1991.

Land, P., 1972. An Overview Pontifical Commission Justice and Peace 1.

Land, P., 1972. Vue d'ensemble La justice dans le monde Synode des eveques Commission Pontificale Justice et Paix.

Lang, J., 1988. Inside Development in Latin America A Report from the Dominican Republic Colombia and Brazil.

Langan, J., 1982. Human Rights in Roman Catholicism Journal of Ecumenical Studies 19:3 1982.

Lange, M. and Iblackes, R. (eds.), 1980. Witnesses of Hope The Persecution of Christians in Latin America.

Lapeyre, A., de Tingny, F. and Vasak, K., 1990. Les dimensions universelles des droits de l'homme I–III.

Larsen, E., 1980. Amnesty international im Namen der Menschenrechte.

Larsen, E., 1978. A Flame In Barbed Wire The Story of Amnesty International.

Latin American Bishops Discuss Human Rights Papers collected and reprinted from LADOC No. 15, 1977. Admist Persecutions and Consolations 1977.

Lederer, K. (ed.), 1980. Human Needs A Contribution to the Current Debate.

Lefebvre, L., 1989. Economic Human Rights Satisfaction of Basic Needs i P Blanchard and P Landstreet eds Human Rights in Latin America and the Carribean.

Lehmann, D., 1990. Democracy and Development in Latin America Economics Politics and Religion in the postwar Period.

Lendvai, P., 1983. Religionsfreiheit und Menschenrechte.

Lernoux, P., 1982. Cry of the People The Struggle for Human Rights in Latin America the Catholic Church in Conflict with US Policy.

Lernoux, P., 1978. Notes on a Revolutionary Church Human Rights in Latin America.

Levine, D. H. (ed.), 1979 Churches and Politics in Latin America.

Levine, D. H. (ed.), 1986. Religion and Political Conflict in Latin America.

Lewis, B., 1993. Islam and the West.

Lienemann-Perrin, C. and Lienemann, W. (eds.), 1988. Political Legitimacy in South Africa.

Lienhard, M., 1978. Luther and Human Rights i J. Lissner and A. Sovik (eds.). A Lutheran Reader on Human Rights, LWF Report.

Lienhard, M.,1982. Luther Witness to Jesus Christ.

Lienhard, M., 1981. Protestantism and Human Rights Human Rights Teaching UNESCO 2:1, 1981.

Lindgens, G., 1978. Katholische Kirche und moderner Pluralismus Der neue Zugang zur Politik bei den Päpsten Johannes XXIII und Paul VI und dem Zweiten Vatikanischen Konzil.

Lindholm, M., 1992. Moderna martyrer Om Ignacio Ellacuria och andra jesuiters kamp för fred och rättvisa i El Salvador.

Lindholm, T., 1990. The Cross-Cultural Legitimacy of Human Rights Prospects for Research Publication, No. 3, Norwegian Institute of Human Rights.

Lindholm, T. and Vogt, K. (eds.), 1993. Islamic Law Reform and Human Rights Challenges and Rejoinders Nordic Human Rights Publications.

Linscott, M., 1972. Education and Justice.

Lissner, J. and Sovik, A. (ed.), 1978. A Lutheran Reader on Human Rights LWF Report.

Lissner, J., 1977. The Politics of Altruism A Study of the Political Behaviour of Voluntary Development Agencies.

Little, D. et al., 1988. Human Rights and the Conflict of Cultures Western and Islamic Perspectives on Religious Liberty.

Lochman, J. M., 1980. Reconciliation and Liberation Challenging a One-Dimensional View of Salvation.

Lochman, J. M. and Moltmann, J. (eds.), 1976. Gottes Recht und Menschenrechte Studien und Empfehlungen des Reformierten Weltbundes.

Locke, J., 1976. The Second Treatise of Civil Government.

Locke, J., 1988. Two Treatises of Government Cambridge Texts in the History of Political Thought.

Logan, W. H. (ed.), 1988. The Cairos Covenant Standing with South African Christians.

Lorenz, E. (ed.), 1983. The Debate on Status Confessionis Studies in Christian Political Theology LWF Studies.

Lorenz, E. (ed.), 1981. How Christian are Human Rights An Interconfessional Study on the Theological Bases of Human Rights Report on an Interconfessional Consultation. Geneva April 30–May 3, 1980 LWF.

Lorenz, E. (ed.), 1984. To Speak or not to Speak Proposed Criteria for Public Statements on Violations of Human Rights.

Lorenz, E. hrsg, 1984. Widerstand Recht und Frieden Kriterien legitimen Gewaltgebrauchs Studien aus dem Lutherischen Weltbund.

Luker, R. E., 1991. The Social Gospel in Black and White American Racial Reform 1885–1912.

Lutheran World Human Rights 1948–1968 LW, No. 3, 1968.

The Lutheran World Federation Reports 1963–1969, 1970.

The Lutheran World Federation Reports on the Work of Its Branches and Related Agencies 1970–1977, 1977.

Macfarlane, L. J., 1985. The Theory and Practice of Human Rights.

Mac Pherson, S., 1987. Five Hundred Million Children Poverty and Child Welfare in the Third World.

Mainwaring, S., 1986. The Catholic Church and Politics in Brazil 1916–1985.

Malik, M. I., 1981. The Concept of Human Rights in Islamic Jurisprudence in Human Rights Quarterly, Vol. 3, No. 3, 1981.

Man's Disorder and God's Design Reports of the Assembly, 1948.

Maritain, J., 1975. Les droits de l'homme et la loi naturelle.

Maritain, J., 1968. Integral Humanism Temporal and Spriritual Problems of a New Christendom.

Maritain, J., 1951. Man and the State.

Maritain, J., 1949. On the Philosophy of Human Rights In Human Rights Comments and Interpretations.

Maritain, J., 1972. The Person and the Common Good.

Maritain, J., 1971. The Rights of Man and Natural Law.

Marshall, P., 1983. Human Rights Theories in Christian Perspective.

Marshall, P. and Vanderkloet, E., 1981. Foundations of Human Rights.

Martin, J. P. (ed.), 1983. Human Rights A Topical Bibliography.

Martin, R., 1985. Rawls and Rights.

Marty, M. E. and Appleby, R. Scott (eds.), 1991. Fundamentalisms Observed.

Mawdudi, A. A., 1978. The Economic Problem of Man and Its Islamic Solution.

Mawdudi, A. A., 1983. First Principles of the Islamic State.

Mawdudi, A. A., 1976. Human Rights in Islam.

Mawdudi, A. A., 1979. Islamic Way of Life.

Mawdudi, A. A., 1982. Rights of Non-Muslim in the Islamic State.

Mawdudi, A. A., 1980. Towards Understanding Islam.

Mawdudi, A. A., 1982. Unity of the Muslim World.

Mayer, A. E., 1991. Islam and Human Rights Tradition and Politics.

Mbali, Z., 1987. The Churches and Racism A Black South African Perspective.

Mc Afee Brown, R., 1978. Theology in A New Key Responding to Liberation Themes.

Mc Donald, H. D., 1981. The Christian View of Man.

Mc Dougal, M. et al., 1980. Human Rights and World Public Order The Basic Policies of an International Law of Human Dignity.

The Meaning of Human Rights and the Problem They Pose ER 1975, April 27:2.

Melander, G. (ed.), 1990. Konventionssamling i mänskliga rättigheter.

Mendiola, M. R., 1977. Human Rights—Content or Context of Mission Evangelisation and the Phlippines Situation International Review ofMission 1977.

Menneskerettigheder - en tekstsamling 1–2 Det danske Center for Menneskerettigheder, 1988.

Die Menschenrechte im ökumenishen Gespräch Beiträge der Kammer der Evangelischen Kirche in Deutschland für öffentliche Verantwortung 1979.

Menschenrechte und Menschenbild in der dritten Welt Arbeitskreis dritte Welt und Studium Generale Der Johannes Gutenberg Universität Mainz 1982.

Mignone, E., 1990. The Catholic Church Human Rights and the Dirty War in Argentina in D. Keogh (ed.) Church and Politics in Latin America.

Mignone, E. F., 1986. Witness to the Truth The Complicity of Church and Dictatorship in Argentina 1976–1983.

Militz, E., 1985. Bank Loans to South Africa Mid–1982 to End 1984.

Mill, J. S., 1975. On Liberty.

Miller, A. O. (ed.), 1977. A Christian Declaration on Human Rights Theological Studies of the WARC.

Miller, W., 1976. International Human Rights A Bibliography.

Mission in South Africa Cattesloe Consultation Report, 1960.

Mitra, K., 1982. Human Rights in Hinduism Journal of Ecumenical Studies 19:3, 1982.

Moltmann, J., 1976. A Christian Declaration on Human Rights, RW Volyme 34, No. 2, June 1976.

Moltmann, J., 1977. A Definitive Study Paper in A Christian Declaration on Human Rights, ed. A. O. Miller.

Moltmann, J., 1984. On Human Dignity Political Theology and Ethics.

Moltmann, J., 1977. The Image of God and Human Rights i Centro Pro Unione 1977.

Moltmann, J., 1979. Menschenwürde Recht und Freiheit.

Moltmann, J.,1977. Original Study Paper A Theological Basis of Human Rights and of the Liberation of Human Beings i A Christian Declaration on Human Rights, ed. A. O. Miller.

Moltmann, J., 1971. Theological Basis of Human Rights and the Liberation of Man, RW 1971, 31 (8).

Moltmann-Wendel, E. (ed.), 1974. Menschenrechte für die Frau Christliche Initiativen zur Frauenbefreiung.

Moltmann-Wendel, E., 1975. The Womens Movement in Germany, LW 1975, 22(2).

Montgomery, J. W., 1986. Human Rights and Human Dignity.

Montgomery, J. W., 1983/84. The Marxist Approach to Human Rights Analysis and Critique Simon Greenleaf Law Review 1983/84 3.

Morris, A. D., 1984. The Origins of the Civil Rights Movement Black Communities Organizing for Change.

Mortimer, E., 1982. Faith and Power The Politics of Islam.

Mott, S. C., 1993. A Christian Perspective on Political Thought.

Mowen, A. G., 1991. Regional Human Rights.

Mscamble Wilson, D., 1979. American Catholics and Foreign Policy Past Limitations Present Obligations America 1979, 141(18).

Mulligan, J. E., 1991. The Nicaraguan Church and the Revolution.

Muravchik, J., 1986. The Uncertain Crusade Jimmy Carter and the Dilemmas of Human Rights Policy.

Mutambirwa, J., 1989. South Africa the Sanctions Mission Report of the Eminent Church Persons Group.

Müller, A. and Greinacher, N eds, 1979. The Church and the Rights of Man Concilium.

Müller, J. and Kerber, W. hrsg, 1991. Soziales Denken in einer zerissenen Welt Anstösse der Katholischen Soziallehre.

Myrdal, G., 1944. An American Dilemma.

Nairobi to Vancouver 1975–1983 Report of the Central Committee to the Sixth Assembly of the WCC 1983.

Nash, R. F., 1989. The Rights of Nature The History of Environmental Ethics.

Nasir, J. J., 1990. The Status of Women Under Islamic Law and Under Modern Islamic Legislation.

Neumann, J., 1976. Menschenrechte auch in der Kirche?

New Delhi to Uppsala 1961–1968 Report of the Central Committee to the Fourth Assembly of the WCC 1968.

Nherere, P. and d'Engelbronner-Kolff, M., 1993. The Institutionalisation of Human Rights in Southern Africa.

Nicgorski, W., 1982. Democracy and Moral-Religious Neutrality American and Catholic Perspectives Communio International Catholic Review 1982, 9 (4).

Niebuhr, R.,1959. The Structure of Nations and Empires A Study of the Recurring Patterns and Problems of the Political Order in Relation to the Unique Problems of the Nuclear Age.

Nielsen Jr., N. C., 1978. The Crisis of Human Rights An American Christian Perspective.

Nielsen, N., 1991. Revolutions in Eastern Europe The Religious Roots.

Nilsson, K. O. (ed.), 1971. Evian – före och efter 1971.

Nino, C. S., 1991. The Ethics of Human Rights.

Nolde, O. F., 1970. The Churches and the Nations.

Nolde, O. F., 1968. Free and Equal Human Rights in Ecumenical Perspective With Reflections on the Origin of the Universal Declaration of Human Rights by C. H. Malik.

Nolde, O. F. (ed.), 1946. Towards World-Wide Christianity.

Nordholt, H. H. hrsg, 1983. Apartheid und Reformierte Kirche Dokumente eines Konflikts Im Auftrag des Reformierten Bundes zusammengestellt.

Novak, M., 1993. The Catholic Ethic and The Spirit of Capitalism.

Novak, M., 1989. Free Persons and the Common Good.

Novak, M., 1990. This Hemisphere of Liberty A Philosophy of the Americas.

Novak, M. (ed.), 1987. Liberation Theology and the Liberal Society.

Novak, M., 1986. Will it Liberate Questions about Liberation Theology.

Novak, M. and Schifter, R. (eds.), 1981. Rethinking Human Rights Speeches by the United States Delegation to the 37th Session of the United Nations Commission on Human Rights Geneva Switzerland Februari 2–March 14 1981. The Foundation for Democratic Education.

Nute, B. R., 1974. Hélder Camara's Latin America Friends Peace and International Relations Committee.

Oates, S. B., 1985. Martin Luther King 1929–1968.

O'Brien, D. J. and Shannon, T. A. (eds.), 1992. Catholic Social Thought The Documentary Heritage.

O'Donnell. G., Schmitter, P. C. and Whitehead, L., 1987. Transitions from Authoritarian Rule.

O'Donell, G., Scmitter, P. C. and Whitehead ,L., 1988. Transitions from Authoritarian Rule Comparative Perspectives.

O'Grady, R., 1979. Bread and Freedom Understanding and Acting on Human Rights.

Oldham, J. H., 1924. Christianity and the Race Problem.

Ordnung, C. hrsg, 1975. Menschenrechte sind Mitmenschenrechte zur ökumenischen Diskussion.

Palumbo, M., 1982. Human Rights Meaning and History.

Pannenberg, 1985. Anthropology in Theological Perspective.

Paths to Peace A Contribution Documents of the Holy See to the International Community Permanent Observer Mission of the Holy See to the United Nations 1987

Paton, D. M. (ed.), 1976. Breaking Barriers—The Official Report of the Fifth Assembly of the WCC Nairobi 1975.

Paul VI, 1971. Apostolisches Schreiben OA Lateinisch-deutsch Eingeleitet von Oswald von Nell-Breuning SJ Nachkonziliare Dokumentation 35.

Paul VI, 1974. Botschaft über Menschenrechte und Versöhnung in Herder- Korrespondenz 28 1974.

PCR Information Reports and Background Papers WCC, 1979/3. Bank Loans and Investments in South Africa A Survey of Actions taken by Churches and Groups in relation to WCC Policies Grants from the Special Fund 1979 1980/5–9 Churches Responding to Racism in the 1980s.

Preparatory Documents and Reports of the National and Regional Consultation leading to the World Consultation on Racism which took place in Noordwükerhout the Netherlands 16–21 June 1980 A Special Edition of PCR

1982/14 The Churches' Involvement in Southern Africa.

1983/16 Land Rights for Indigenous People.

1983/17 South Africa in Crisis.

1984/19 Women under Racism.

1985/20 Southern Africa The Continuing Crisis.

1985 Challenge to the Church A Theological Comment on the Political Crisis in South Africa The Kairos Document and Commentaries.

1986/22 Racism in Asia Race and Minority Issues.

1986/23 Southern Africa—The Harare and Ai-Gaims Declarations A Call for Freedom and Independence for South Africa and Namibia.

1987/24 The Economic Basis of Racism.

1991/30 From Cottesloe to Cape Town Challenges for the Church in a Post-Apartheid South Africa.

Peace—The Desparate Imperative The Consultation on Christian Concern for Peace Baden Austria April 3–9 1970, 1970.

Perkins, J., 1977. What it means to be the Church Reflections on Mission and Human Rights International Review of Mission 1977.

Petras, J., 1970. Politics and Social Structure in Latin America.

Pfürtner, S. H., 1976. Die Menschenrechte in der römisch-katholischen Kirche in Zeitschrift für evangelische Ethik 1/1976.

Phan, P. (ed.), 1990. Christianity and the Wider Ecumenism.

Pilters, M. und Walf, K. hrsg, 1980. Menschenrechrte in der Kirche.

Piscatori, J., 1991. Islamic Fundamentalisms and the Gulf Crisis.

Pohier, J. and Mieth, D. (eds.), 1982. Unemployment and the Right to Work Concilium.

Polish, F., 1982. Judaism and Human Rights Journal of Ecumenical Studies 19:3, 1982.

Pollis, A., 1993. Eastern Ortodoxy and Human Rights i Human Rights Quarterly, Vol .15, No. 2, May 1993.

Pollis, A., 1981. The Philosophy of Human Rights by A S Rosenbaum ed Rec in Human Rights Quarterly, Vol. 4, No. 4, 1981.

Pollis, A. and Schwab, P. (eds.), 1979. Human Rights Cultural and Ideological Perspectives.

Pollis, A. and Scwab, P. (eds.), 1981. Toward a Human Rights Framework.

Pope, C., 1985. Human Rights and the Catholic Church in Brazil 1970–1983 The Pontifical Justice and Peace Commission of S'o Paulo Archdiocese Journal of Church and State 1985 27 (3).

Preston, R. H., 1987. The Future of Christian Ethics.

Prior, A. (ed.), 1982. Catholics in Apartheid Society.

Programme to Combat Racism 1970–1973, ER Vol. XXV, No. 4, 1973.

Public Statements and Letters in the Area of International Affairs and Human Rights issued by the Lutheran World Federation 1984–1990, April 1990–May 1991 (WCC/LWF).

Punt, J., 1987. Die Idee der Menschenrechte Ihre geschichtliche Entwicklung und ihre Rezeption durch die moderne katholische Sozialverkündigung.

Putz, G., 1991. Christentum und Menschenrechte.

Racism and South Africa I–II Resolution of WARC in Ottowa 1982 Canada 26 August 1982 PCR Information 1982/15, 1982.

Racism in Theology Theology against Racism Report of A Consultation organized by The Commission on Faith and Order and the PCR 1975.

Radhakrishnan, S. P., 1961. The Hindu View of Life.

Rahula, W., 1974. What the Buddha Taught.

Ramet, S. P. (ed.), 1992. Protestantism and Politics in Eastern Europe and Russia The Communist and Postcommunist Eras.

Randall, P. (ed.), 1971. Directions of Change in South African Politics The Study Project of Christianity in Apartheid Society.

Raiser, L., 1975. Menschenrechte in einer gespaltenen Welt Erwägungen zum Stand der ökumenischen Diskussion in Evangelische Kommentare, No. 4, 1975.

Raiser, L., 1982. Vom rechten Gebrauch der Freiheit Aufsätze zu Politik Recht Wissenschaftspolitik und Kirche.

Randall, P. (ed.), 1971. Directions of Change in South African Politics The Study Project on Christianity in Apartheid Society.

Rawls, J., 1971. A Theory of Justice.

Recht nach Gottes Wort Menschenrechte und Grundrechte in Gesellschaft und Kirche Im Auftrag der Synode der Evangelisch-reformierten Kirchen in Nordwestdeutschland herausgegeben von Landeskirchenvorstand, 1989.

Reichley, A. J., 1985. Religion in American Public Life.

Rendtorff, T. et al., 1968. Human Rights 1948–1968, LW15 (3).

Rendtorff, T., 1968. Freedom and Human Rights, LW 1968.

Renteln, A. D., 1990. International Human Rights Universalism Versus Relativism.

Report of Conference on Women Human Rights and Mission WCC Sub-unit on Women in Church and Society 1979.

Report on the Human Rights Programme 1980 HRAG.

Report on Human Rights in El Salvador compiled by Americas Watch Committee and the American Civil Liberties Union, 1982.

Report of a Limited Research Project on the Theological Basis of Human Rights, RW 36:8, 1981.

Res Testimony on Human Rights The Reformed Ecumenical Synod, 1983.

Reuver, M. (ed.), 1983. Human Rights A Challenge to Theology CCIA IDOC International.

Rice, P., 1990. The Disappeard A New Challenge to Christian Faith in Latin America i D Keogh ed Church and Politics in Latin America.

Richard, P., 1987. Death of Christendom Birth of the Church Historical Analysis and Theological Interpretation of the Church in Latin America.

Richardson, N., 1977. The WCC and Race Relations 1960–1969.

Riga, P. J., 1982. Human Rights as Human and Christian Realities.

Riga, P., 1964. Peace on Earth A Commentary on Pope John's Encyclical.

Riley, P., 1982. Will and Political Legitmacy A Critical Exposition of Social Contract Theory in Hobbes Locke Rousseau Kant and Hegel.

Rogers, B., 1980. Race No Peace without Justice Churches Confront the Mounting Racism in the 1980s.

Rogers, E., 1975. The Right to Live, ER 27:2, 1975.

Rogers, E., 1978. Thinking about Human Rights.

Romero, O., 1982. Romero Martyr for Liberation.

Romero, O., 1985. Voice of the Voiceless—the Four Pastoral Letters of Oscar Romero and Other Statements.

Rosenbaum, A. S. (ed.), 1980. The Philosophy of Human Rights International Perspectives.

Rothe, S., 1989. Der Südafrikanische Kirchenrat 1968–1988. Aus liberaler Opposition zum radikalen Widerstand.

Rouner, L. S. (ed.), 1986. Civil Religion and Political Theology.

Rouner, L. S. (ed.), 1988. Human Rights and the World's Religions.

Rousseau, J. J., 1949. A Discourse Upon the Origin and Foundation of the Inequality of Mankind.

Rousseau, J. J., 1978. On the Social Contract.

Rubin, B. M. and Spiro, E. P. (eds.), 1979. Human Rights and US Foreign Policy.

Ryan, C., 1990. Beyers Naudé Pilgrimage of Faith.

Said, A. A., 1978. Human Rights and World Order.

Said, A. A., 1979. Precept and Practice of Human Rights in Islam i Human Rights Quarterly, Vol. 1, No. 1, jan–march 1979.

Sakharov, A., 1978. Alarm and Hope.

Sakharov, A., 1990. Memoirs.

Sakharov, A. D., 1968. Progress Coexistence and Intellectual Freedom.

Schall, J. V., 1981. Human Rights The So-Called Judaeo-christian Tradition Communio International Catholic Review 1981, 8 (1).

Scharf, K., 1977. Human Rights of the Malefactor On Visiting the Baader-Meinhof Group International Review of Mission 1977.

Scheuner, U., 1975. Die Menschenrechte in der ökumenischen Diskussion in Ökumenische Rundschau, No. 2, 1975.

Schillebeeckx, E., 1983. God is New Each Moment In Conversation with Hunt Oosterhuis and P. Hoogeveen.

Schooyans, M., 1980. The Place of Human Rights in Catholicism Lumen Vitae 1980, 35 (2).

Schoultz, L., 1981. Human Rights and United States Policy Toward Latin America.

Schuck, M. J., 1991. That They Be One The Social Teaching of the Papal Encyclicals 1740–1989.

Schwartländer, J., 1978. Menschenrechte Aspekte ihrer Begründung und Vervirklichung.

Schwartländer, J. hrsg, 1979. Menschenrechte - eine Herausforderung der Kirche.

Schwelb, E., 1964. The Roots and Growth of the Universal Declaration of Human Rights 1948–1963.

Segundo, J. L., 1975. The Liberation of Theology.

Sell, A. P., 1991. A Reformed Evangelical Catholic Theology The Contribution of the WARC 1875–1982.

Serfontein, J. H. P., 1982. Apartheid Change and the NG Kerk.

Sexism in the 1970s Discrimination Against Women A Report of a WCC Consultation West Berlin 1974, 1975.

Shute, S. and Hurley, S. (eds.), 1973. On Human Rights The Oxford Amnesty Lectures 1993.

Sidorsky, D. (ed.), 1979. Essays on Human Rights Contemporary Issues and Jewish Perspectives.

Sieghart, P., 1983. The International Law of Human Rights.

Sieghart, P., 1985. The Lawful Rights of Mankind An Introduction to the International Legal Code of Human Rights.

Simmons, J., 1992. The Lockean Theory of Rights.

The Situation of the Indian in South America Contribution to the Study of Inter-Ethnic Conflict with regard to the non-Andean Indians 1972.

Sjollema, B., 1982. Isolating Apartheid Western Collaboration with South Africa Policy Decision by the WCC and Church Responses.

Skilling, H. G., 1981. Charter 77 and Human Rights in Czechoslovakia.

Smith, B. H., 1979. Churches and Human Rights in Latin America Recent Trends in the Subcontinent Journal of Inter-American Studies and World Affairs Febr 1979.

Smith, C., 1991. The Emergence of Liberation Theology Radical Religion and Social Movement Theory.

Smith, R., 1973. The Theological Work of the WARC and the Ecumenical Context, RW 1973, 32 (7).

Sobrino, J., 1990. Archbishop Romero Memories and Reflections.

Southern Africa Confessional Integrity Preparatory Material for the LWF Executive Committee Meeting July 31–August 9 1989, 1989.

386

Spykman, G., 1984. Human Rights A Selected Bibliography Transformation 1: 3 July–Sept 1984.

Spykman, G., 1979. Toward an Biblical View of Human Rights Res Theological Forum 7:1 December 1979.

Stackhouse, M. L., 1984. Creeds Society and Human Rights A Study in the Cultures.

Stackhouse, M. L., 1981. Some Intellectual and Social Roots of Modern Human Rights Ideas Journal for the Scientific Study of Religion 1981, 20 (4).

Stackhouse, M. L., 1984. Theology History and Human Rights Soundings 1984, 67 (2).

Stern, C., 1980. Strategien für die Menschenrechte.

Stokes, G. (ed.), 1991. From Stalinism to Pluralism A Documentary History of Eastern Europe Since 1945.

Strain, C. R. (ed.), 1989. Prophetic Versions and Economic Realities Protestans Jews and Catholics Confront The Bishop's Letter on the Economy.

Studia Missionalia, Vol. 39, 1990. Human Rights and Religions.

Studia Missionalia, Vol. 37, 1988. Teachers of Religion.

Swidler, A. (ed.), 1982. Human Rights in Religious Traditions.

Swidler, A. (ed.), 1982. Human Rights in Religious Traditions i Journal of Ecumenical Studies Vol. XIX, No. 3, 1982.

Swidler, L. m.fl. (eds.), 1990. Death or Dialogue From the Age of Monologue to the Age of Dialogue.

Swidler, L. (ed.), 1986. Religious Liberty and Human Rights in Nations and in Religions.

Swidler, L. (ed.), 1987. Toward a Universal Theology of Religion.

Swidler, L. and O'Brien, H. (ed.), 1988. A Catholic Bill of Rights.

Synod of Bishops 1974 Statement on Human Rights and Reconciliation Origins 4, November 7 1974.

Suggate, A. M., 1987. William Temple and Christian Social Ethics Today.

Sundman, P., 1996. Human Rights Justification and Christian Ethics.

The Ten Formative Years 1938–1948 WCC 1948.

Tergel, A., 1995. Church and Society in the Modern Age Acta Universitatis Upsaliensis Uppsala Studies in Social Ethics 17.

The Theology of Human Rights and the Theology of Liberation Document RW Vol. 33, No. 6, June 1975.

The Theological Basis of Human Rights Document WARC in RW Vol. 34, No. 2, June 1976.

Theological Perspectives on Human Rights Report on an LWF Consultation on Human Rights Geneva June 29–July 3 1976, 1977.

Thomas, M. M. and Abrecht, P. (eds.), 1967. Christians in the Technical and Social Revolutions of Our Time World Conference on Church and Society Geneva July 12–26 1966 The Official Report WCC.

Thompson, K. W., 1968. Christian Ethics and Human Rights, LW 1968.

Thompson, L., 1985. The Political Mythology of Apartheid.

Thunberg, A. M. (ed.), 1971. Rättvisa och fred En ekumenisk rapport.

Tibi, B., 1988. The Crisis of Modern Islam A Preindustrial Culture In the Scientific-Technological Age.

Tibi, B., 1990. Islam and the Cultural Accomodation of Social Change.

Tibi, B., 1994. Islamic Law/Shari'a Human Rights Universal Morality and International Relations Human Rights Quarterly, Vol. 16, No. 2, May 1994.

Tjönneland, E. N., 1992. South Africa after Apartheid The End of Apartheid Future Regional Cooperation and Foreign Aid.

Tomasevski , K. (ed.), 1987. The Right to Food Guide Through Applicable International Law.

Tomasevski, K., 1993. Women and Human Rights.

Torres, S. and Eagleson, J. (eds.), 1981. The Challenge of Basic Christian Communities.

Traer, R., 1991. Faith in Human Rights Support in Religious Tradition for a Global Struggle.

Troeltsch, E., 1986. Protestantism and Progress The Significance of Protestantism for the Rise of the Modern World.

Tschuy, T., 1985. An Ecumenical Experiment in Human Rights The Churches' Human Rights Programme.

Tuck, R., 1979. Natural Rights Theories Their Original and Development.

Tyson, B., 1975. The Mission of the Church in Contemporary Brazil The Case of a Church in a Land of Poverty and Repression Missiology 1975, 3 (3).

Tödt, H. E., 1977. Theological Reflections on the Foundations of Human Rights, LW 24 (1), 1977.

Törnquist, P. B., 1992. The Wheel of Polish Fortune Myths in Polish Collective Consciousness during the First Years of Solidarity.

Ulin, R. C., 1988. Understanding Cultures Perspectives in Anthropology and Social Theory.

van Dyke, V., 1985. Human Rights Etnicity and Discrimination.

Vasak, K., 1982. The International Dimensions of Human Rights 1–2 UNESCO.

Veatch, H. B., 1985. Human Rights Fact or Fancy.

Villa-Vicencio, C., 1986. Between Christ and Caesar Classic and Contemporary Texts on Church and State.

Villa-Vicencio, C., 1994. The Spirit of Hope Conversations on Politics Religion and Values.

Villa-Vicencio, C., 1982. The Theology of Apartheid.

Villa-Vicencio, C., 1992. The Theology of Reconstruction Nation-Building and Human Rights.

Villa-Vicencio, C., 1988. Trapped in Apartheid A Socio-Theological History of the English-Speaking Churches.

Villa-Vicencio, C. and de Gruchy, J. W. (eds.), 1985. Resistance and Hope South African Essays in Honour of Beyers Naudé.

Vincent, J., 1970. The Race Race.

Vincent, R. J., 1986. Human Rights and International Relations.

Viola, F., 1982. Les droits de l'homme Point de rencontre entre la nouvelle chretiente et l'humanisme contemporaine Nova et Vetera 1982, 57 (1).

Violence Nonviolence and the Struggle for Social Justice ER Vol. XXV, No. 4, 1973.

Vischer, L. (ed.), 1990. Rights of Future Generations Rights of Nature Proposal for enlarging the Universal Declaration of Human Rights Studies from the WARC.

Visser't Hooft, W. A. (ed.), 1955. The Evanston Report The Second Assembly of the WCC 1954.

Visser't Hooft, W. A. (ed.), 1948. The First Assembly of the WCC held at Amsterdam August 22 to September 4 1948.

Visser't Hooft, W. A. (ed.), 1962. The New Delhi Report The Third Assembly of the WCC 1961.

Wallis, J. and Hollyday, J. (eds.), 1989. Crucible of Fire The Church Confronts Apartheid.

Walsh, M., 1994. John Paul II A Biography.

Walsh, M. and Davies, B. (eds.), 1991. Proclaiming Justice and Peace One Hundred Years of Catholic Social Teaching Documents from Johannes XXIII to John Paul II.

Walsh, M. and Davies, B. (eds.), 1991. Proclaiming Justice and Peace Papal Documents from Rerum Novarum through Centesimus Annus Revised and Expanded.

Walshe, P., 1983. Church versus State in South Africa The Case of the Christian Institute.

Warc North American Area ed, 1975. The Theology of Human Rights and the Theology of Liberation Document in RW, Vol. 33, No. 6, June 1975.

Ward, B., 1973. A New Creation Reflections on the Environmental Issue.

Washington, J. M. (ed.), 1986. A Testament of Hope The Essential Writings and Speeches of Martin Luther King Jr.

Webb, P. (ed.), 1994. A Long Struggle The Involvement of the WCC in South Africa.

Weigel, G., 1992. The Final Revolution The Resistance Church and the Collapse of Communism.

Weigel, G. and Royal, R. (eds.), 1993. Building the Free Society Democracy Capitalism and Catholic Social Teaching.

Weingärtner, E., 1988. Behind the Mask Human Rights in Asia and Latin America An Inter-Regional Encounter.

Weingärtner, E. and M. (eds.), 1977. Human Rights is More than Human Rights A Primer for Churches on Security and Cooperation in Europe IDOC.

Weingärtner, E., 1983. Human Rights on the Ecumenical Agenda Report and Assessment CCIA Background Information 1983, No. 3.

Weinreb, L. L., 1987. Natural Law and Justice.

Weiss, N. J., 1989. Whitney M. Young Jr. and the Struggle for Civil Rights.

Weisse, W., 1975. Südafrika und das Anti-Rassismus-Programm Kirchen im Spannungsfeld einer Rassengesellschaft.

Welch, C. E. Jr. and Meltzer, R. I., 1984. Human Rights and Development in Africa.

Werkane, P. H., Gini, A. R. and Ozar, D. T., 1986. Philosophical Issues in Human Rights Theories and Applications.

Wheaton, B. and Zdenek, K., 1991. The Velvet Revolution Czechoslovakia 1988–1990.

Wiarda, H. J., 1987. Finding Our Way Toward Maturity in US-Latin American Relations.

Wiarda, H. J. (ed.), 1982. Human Rights and US Human Rights Policy Theoretical Approaches and Some Perspectives on Latin America.

Wiesemann, U., 1979. Mission und Menschenrechte.

Will, J. E., 1981. Claims in Conflict by David Hollenbach S J Rec i Human Rights Quarterly, Vol. 3, No. 1, Febr 1981.

Williams, G., 1981. The Mind of John Paul II Origins of His Thought and Action.

Wilmore, G. S. and Cone, J. H., 1979. Black Theology—A Documentary History 1966–1979.

Wilmore, G. S., 1993. Black Religion and Black Radicalism An Interpretation of the Religious History of Afro-American People.

Wimer, A., 1975. On Step on a Journey ER 27:2 1975.

Wingren, G., 1975. Human Rights A Theological Analysis ER 27:2 1975.

Wojtyla, K., 1979. The Acting Person.

Women in the Lutheran Tradition Proceedings of the International Consultation of Lutheran Women Theologians Karjaa Finland 18–23 August 1991, LWF 1992.

Women's Human Rights LWF Studies A Joint Project by the Desk for Social Issues and the Desk for Women in Church and Society 1984.

Workshop for Theology and Human Rights RW Vol. 34, No. 7–8, Sept.–Dec. 1977.

The World Council of Churches and Bank Loans to Apartheid, 1977.

World Directory of Human Rights Research and Training Institutions UNESCO, 1992.

Wronka, J., 1992. Human Rights and Social Policy in the 21 st Century A History of the Idea of Human Rights and Comparison of the United Nations Universal Declaration of Human Rights with United States Federal and State Constitutions.

Yannoulatos, A., 1984. Eastern Ortodoxy and Human Rights International Review of Mission 1984, 73 (292).

The YMCA and Human Rights A Study on the Christian Basis of Human Rights, 1980.

Yotopoulos and Marangopoulos, A. (ed.), 1994. Women's Rights Human Rights.

Zaehner, R. C., 1962. Hinduism.

Zalaquett, J., 1981. The Human Right Issue and the Human Rights Movement.
Characterization Evaluation Propositions CCIA Background Information 1981, No. 3.

Zamoshkin, Y., 1984. Individualism and the American Dream Personality and Society
in America from a Soviet Perspective Soundings 1984 67 (2).

Zuijdwijk, T. J. M., 1982. Petitioning The United Nations A Study in Human Rights.

Zwiwerblosky, R. J., 1981. Judaism and Human Rights Human Rights Teaching
UNESCO 2:1 (1981):8.

Abbreviations

AAS	Acta Apostolicae Sedis
ANC	African National Congress
CA	Centesimus annus Johannes Pulus II 1991
CCIA	The Churches in International Affairs
EN	Evangelii nuntiandi Paul VI 1975
ER	The Ecumenical Review
GS	Gaudium et spes Second Vatican Council 1965
HRAG	Advisory Group on Human Rights
HRROLA	The Human Rights Resources Office for Latin America
IDOC	International Documentation Center Rom
JM	De justitia in mundo Synod of Bishops 1971
LADOC	Latin America Documentation Center
LE	Laborem exercens Johannes Paulus II 1981
LW	Lutheran World
LWF	Lutheran World Federation
MM	Mater et magistra Johannes XXIII 1961
NCCB	National Conference of Catholic Bishops Washington DC
OA	Octogesima adveniens Paulus VI 1971
PCR	Programme to Combat Racism
PP	Populorum progressio Paulus VI 1967
PT	Pacem in terris Johannes XXIII 1963
RH	Redemptor hominis Johannes Paulus II 1979
RN	Rerum novarum Leo XIII 1891
RW	The Reformed World
Sodepax	Committee for Society Development and Peace
SRS	Sollicitudo rei socialis Johannes Paulus II 1987
UNESCO	United Nations Educational Scientific and Cultural Organization
WARC	World Alliance of Reformed Churches
WCC	World Council of Churches

Index of personal names

Abe, Masao 196
Alfaro, Juan 155, 156
Allende, Salvador 115, 240, 260
Almeida, Dimas 229, 230
Alston, Philip 80
Amin, Idi 76
Angelli, Eurique 136
An-Na'im, Addullahi Ahmed 79, 80, 82-84, 94, 95, 111, 341, 350, 356, 357
Arendt, Hanna 78
Arkoun, Muhammed 196
Arns, Paulo Everisto 115, 116, 119, 140, 242
Arrupe, Pedro 153, 155-159, 357
Assman, Hugo 125
Augustine 87, 265
Austad, Torleiv 272-274
Barreiro, Julio 229
Barth, Karl 56, 265, 282, 305, 323
Bent, Ans van der 194, 212
Bentham, Jeremy 61
Berger, Peter 42
Bergson, Henri 157
Berting, J. 334
Biko, Steve Bantu 182, 301, 316
Bindman, G. 328
Blake, Eugen Carson 253, 298
Boesak, Allan 180, 254, 314, 322
Boff, Clodvis 119, 129
Boff, Leonardo 119, 124, 125, 129, 130
Bonhoeffer, Dietrich 254
Bonino, José Miguez 242, 243, 307
Bonner, Jelena 70, 71
Bora, Katarina von 291

Bormann, Maurice 197
Borowitz, Eugene 196

Braaten, Carl E. 245, 246
Branch, Taylor 213
Brezhnev, Leonid 70
Brosseder, Johannes 193, 194
Brown, Robert Mc Affee 298
Brugger, Hans 141
Bukovsky, Vladimir 71
Burke, Edmund 61
Butelezi, P. F. J. 182

Calvez, Jean Yves 156
Calvin, Jean 254, 322
Camara, Helder 116, 119, 123-127, 139, 140
Camps, A. 335
Carr, Burgess 229
Carter, Jimmy 72, 73, 114, 115, 134, 198, 297, 306, 336
Casal, José 230
Cassin, René 16, 81, 209
Chandran, Victoria M. 229
Chernenko, Konstantin U. 72, 73
Cleary, E. 119
Columbus, Christofer 47
Comte, Auguste 87
Cone, James H. 298, 300, 305, 306
Cooper, John W. 141
Crahan, M. E. 58
Crawford, S. Cromwell 50, 336
Cromwell, Oliver 55
Dahlén, Olle 228
The Dalai Lama 341, 356, 357
Dassin, J. 239
Dhavawony, Mariasusai 197
Dibelius, Otto 260
Djilas, Milovan 70
Dobel, J. Patrick 115
Dubcek, Alexander 69